A linguist by profession, Avis Pightling lived in Italy for some years and now resides in the Chilterns. Her previous book on Italy dealt with its earlier history and struggle for independence. She has also written a book on the European Union. Her interests include history, dance, music, gardening and the countryside.

Dedicated to Agli Italiani

Avis Pightling

THE ENIGMA OF MODERN ITALY

AUSTIN MACAULEY PUBLISHERS™

LONDON • CAMBRIDGE • NEW YORK • SHARJAH

A CIP catalogue record for this title is available from the British Library.

ISBN 9781528996396 (Paperback)
ISBN 9781528996402 (Hardback)
ISBN 9781528996419 (ePub e-book)

www.austinmacauley.com

First Published 2022
Austin Macauley Publishers Ltd®
1 Canada Square
Canary Wharf
London
E14 5AA

LIECHTENSTEIN · VADUZ

BERNA

SVIZZERA

AUSTRIA

Confine di Stato
Confine di regione
Limite della piattaforma continentale definito dai trattati internazionali
Limite della piattaforma continentale non definito dai trattati internazionali
ROMA   Capitale di Stato
Bari   Capoluogo di regione
Pavia   Capoluogo di provincia

Bolzano/Bozen
Trentino-Alto Adige/Südtirol
Trento
Friuli-Venezia Giulia
Belluno · Udine
Pordenone · Gorizia
Trieste

Valle d'Aosta/Vallée d'Aoste
Aosta/Aoste
Varese
Como · Bergamo
Sondrio
Veneto
Vicenza
Treviso
Novara
Lombardia
Vercelli · Milano · Brescia
Verona · Padova
Venezia
Torino
Pavia · Cremona
Mantova
Piemonte
Asti
Alessandria · Piacenza
Rovigo
Cuneo
Parma
Reggio nell'Emilia · Ferrara
Modena
Savona
Liguria
Genova · Emilia-Romagna
Ravenna
Bologna
MONACO
Imperia
Forlì
La Spezia · Massa
SAN MARINO
Pistoia
Pisa · Lucca · Firenze
Pesaro
Ancona
MAR LIGURE
Livorno
Toscana
Marche
Macerata
Siena · Arezzo
Perugia
Ascoli Piceno
FRANCIA

IUGOSLAVIA

ELBA · Grosseto
Umbria
Terni
Teramo
MARE ADRIATICO
Viterbo
Rieti
Pescara
Chieti
TREMITI
CORSICA
L'Aquila
Lazio
Abruzzo
CITTÀ DEL VATICANO
ROMA
Molise
Campobasso
Bocche di Bonifacio
Frosinone
Iserfia
Foggia
ASINARA
MADDALENA · CAPRERA
Latina
Benevento
Bari
Caserta
Campania
Puglia
Sassari
Napoli · Avellino
Matera
Brindisi
ISCHIA · Salerno
Potenza
Taranto
Nuoro
CAPRI
Lecce
Basilicata
Golfo di Taranto
Sardegna
Oristano
MAR TIRRENO
S.PIETRO
Cagliari
S.ANTIOCO
Cosenza
MAR IONIO
Calabria
Catanzaro
ISOLE EOLIE (ISOLE LIPARI)
USTICA
Palermo
Messina
Reggio di Calabria
ISOLE EGADI
Trapani
Sicilia
Stretto di Messina
Caltanissetta · Enna
Catania
Agrigento
Siracusa
Canale di Sicilia
PANTELLERIA
MARE DI SICILIA
Ragusa
TUNISI
ALGERIA
TUNISIA
0   100   200 km
VALLETTA
MALTA
ISOLE PELAGIE

Canale d'Otranto

Introduction

We begin our story in 1945, with Italy at rock bottom, racked by war and defeat. The monarch is banished and replaced by a republic, together with the establishment of a constitution and parliamentary democracy. The economy gradually recovers, culminating in the 'economic miracle' of the '60s; together with EEC membership welcoming Italy back into the European fold after the Fascist years of Mussolini. Yet beneath this positive scenario of materialist satisfaction there lurk dark forces that have not yet been played out, displayed in the 'hot autumn' crisis of 1969, with widespread protests from workers and students who oppose a system that does not satisfy their aspirations of reasonable pay and working conditions, nor a decent education and living conditions.

A series of right-wing plots emerges in the 1970s, involving the older generation intent on undermining a fragile democracy, harking back to the conflict of Fascism pitted against Communism; and continued by the younger generation of right-wingers, peaking in the Bologna bombing in 1980. The counter attack is led by a youthful band of left-wing terrorists, hitting at the heart of the Italian state and culminating in the abduction and murder of Aldo Moro, arch politician of the Establishment who sought a consensus between left and right. Italy reached its nadir in 1992 with the assassination of the prosecuting magistrates Falcone and Borsellino; coupled with the massive corruption scandal of Tangentopoli, after which confrontation ebbed away, with precious little achieved and leaving an aura of disillusion.

How did such a state of affairs come to pass, given the glories of the Roman Empire and Italy as the cradle of the European Renaissance? Following the fall of Rome, the Peninsula suffered waves of invasions such as from the Arabs and Normans. Italy sank into retreat with the development of local communes followed by the rise of the city states; and with people's first loyalty being towards their family and local town or village, reinforced by the use of dialects. Such a scenario promoted staunch regionalism and individualism, the Italians playing a cloak and dagger game of factional rivalry, as well as pitting their wits against foreign interlopers to survive, until unity was finally achieved in 1861, albeit in name only. Major left-wing terrorists such as Curcio and Feltrinelli hailed from the unstable Trentino region long seeking independence, whilst Simioni came from separatist Veneto: the city of Venice had remained aloof from the mainstream of Italian politics, cloaked in its glorious past. The North-South fault-line split the Peninsula in half, with the north looking towards Europe, whilst the Mafia criminal organisation filled the power vacuum in the South with its own harsh code of law and order, looting and killing to terrify citizens into submission.

The Italians' love of intrigue and partisanship was expressed in the *chiaroscuro* of politics, reinforced by the concept of clientelism: the art of patronage politics extant since Roman times when a citizen was loyal to his lord and master in exchange for favours. The trend of shifting alliances *trasformismo* resurfaced in the 19th century with the establishment of parliamentary politics. The young and fragile state lacked respect, inveigling Italians into plundering the national wealth of power and money.

Religion has played a crucial role in Italian lives. The Catholic Church offered succour to the people and a defence against waves of invaders. Catholic reasoning pervades Italian life, with its incessant search for the absolute truth, its ritual of confession of a sin, absolved by a pardon to remove the burden; yet all too often entwined into political manipulation to escape civil punishment. To sum up, an intricate web of factors has fashioned the Italian psyche and its approach to dealing with events and situations.

I have been fortunate in having an excellent range of authors to draw upon for their invaluable contribution to understanding Italian history and politics. In particular I would like to extend my sincere thanks to Paul Ginsborg for his authoritative account of post-war Italy; David Lane for his incisive analysis of Berlusconi and the Mafia; Messrs. P.Sidoni and P.Zanetov for their sterling work on criminal organisations; and lastly, but by no means least, Judge Falcone on his remarkable account of the Mafia.

Every effort has been made to trace and acknowledge ownership of copyright. The author and publisher will be glad to make arrangements with any copyright holders with whom it has not been possible to contact.

Although every precaution has been taken in the preparation of this book, the author and publisher assume no responsibility for errors or omissions. Neither is any liability assumed for damages resulting from the use of this information contained herein.

I am happy for material to be used from my book, provided that the source is quoted.

I have appreciated the challenging task of writing this work, and hope that you will enjoy reading it.

Avis Pightling

Chapter One
Renewal from the Ashes

In 1945 Italy was devastated. Twenty years of Fascism had undermined a fragile democracy. Morale was at rock bottom, Mussolini had seized power in 1922, with the March on Rome. His principal achievements were the creation of state corporations to drive the economy, and effecting a reconciliation with the estranged Vatican by the signing of the Lateran Accords in 1929, with Pope Paul VI (1925-33) thereby ending sixty years of schism between Church and State. On the debit side, he suppressed all opposition: political parties, the media and trade unions. Mussolini created the grandiose EUR *Esposizione Universale di Roma* southwest of Rome as his monument to the ancient capital: the 1930 World Fair was held here. The two key pillars of Fascism resided in colonial expansion, which appealed to the patriotic middle classes and recalled the glory of imperial Rome; together with economic expansion and self-sufficiency, which attracted the business and industrial sectors. Support for the dictator and his Fascist PNF party also came from civil servants, the church, the army, the king and landowners.

Mussolini's major achievement was the settling of the Roman Question: The Schism with the Pope, who since 1870 had shut himself away in the Vatican, excommunicated the King and refused to recognise the new Italian state. His issue of the *non expedit* forbade Catholics either to hold secular office or vote. Mussolini felt it would be useful to have the Pope's support and so crafted the Lateran Accords. Composed of three treaties, the Accords designated the Vatican City an independent state of 108 acres, in return for which the Pope recognised the new state of Italy. The Vatican was assigned authority over its own bank, police, postal system and radio transmitter. Crimes perpetrated on Vatican soil would be tried in Italian courts. The Pope renounced former papal territory in return for financial compensation, but retained several Roman churches, catacombs and basilicas. He was assigned a summer residence at Castel Gandolfo, near to Rome. Religious institutions could own property and were exempt from taxation. The loss of papal property was compensated by granting a generous indemnity to the Vatican, which would be managed by the Vatican Bank. Catholicism was confirmed as the sole state religion, to be universally taught in schools, with the Church having authority in civil matters such as marriage and its annulment. Priests were prohibited from engaging in political activity; whilst the appointment of bishops was subject to approval by the state. Mussolini insisted on no dialects in school to encourage a standardised Italian for national cohesion. The poet Dante reckoned there were some thousand dialects during his day, of which many still survive.

In 1940 Mussolini allied with Hitler and brought Italy into the Second World War; albeit reluctantly, since he knew that the economy was insufficiently geared to wartime production. Italy suffered military defeat in Greece and lost her East African colonies to the British: Eritrea, Somalia and Abyssinia (Ethiopia). Intense Allied bombing targeted the Northern cities and their factories, especially Turin with a population of 600,000; also Milan, from where half a million civilians had fled by 1942. Hundreds of thousands were left homeless. *Il Duce* leader, as Mussolini was known, was facing mounting opposition to his increasingly harsh and corrupt dictatorship. Subsequent to a decisive vote by the Fascist Grand Council led by Dino Grandi, the King Vittorio Emmanuele III, fearing civil war, exercised his constitutional rights by dismissing Mussolini and had him placed under arrest. The Council accorded full constitutional powers and control of the armed forces to the King, who had supported Fascism but disapproved of Mussolini. Many Italian generals were Monarchist.

Victor Emmanuel requested Marshal Badoglio of the Grand Council to set up a new government. Previously Commander-in-Chief of the Italian army until 1941, Badoglio dismantled the Fascist apparatus but continued the ban on all opposition parties for the sake of a united front. There ensued a tense hiatus during the summer of 1943, whilst the King and Badoglio decided on a course of action. On 3rd September, they signed an Armistice with the Anglo-American Allies, with unconditional surrender and Italy classified as neutral. Defeat destroyed Mussolini's aspirations of Italian military prowess. The King and Badoglio left Rome and ostensibly set up a government in Brindisi on the Adriatic coast, but were in fact ruled by the Allies. This unsettled period, known as the Forty-Five Days, was marked by mass industrial strikes and demonstrations. The first since Mussolini seized power, they involved over 100,000 workers, centred on Milan and Turin, protesting against the protracted war and rejoicing in the end of Fascism. Mussolini had failed to win them over with his political indoctrination which embraced every aspect of Italian life, including their *dopolavoro* leisure time, and which in no way appealed to their individualistic nature.

Il Duce's exhortation to obedience, patriotism and self-sacrifice had come at too high a price for most workers, who had suffered a drastic fall in wages and living conditions during his dictatorship. In 1943, 4,000 Fiat workers in Turin marched for an end to the war, and fulminated against bread rationing, mounting inflation, the bombing and the military defeats. By 1943, over 200,000 Italian soldiers had perished (many died in Hitler's abortive Russian campaign), whilst over half a million had been taken prisoner. In response to the grave unrest the government and employers wisely granted concessions. The Germans turned on their former ally, wreaking havoc in the north and taking Rome, where the film director Luchino Visconti suffered at their hands. They rescued Mussolini from his prison, high up in the mountains of Gran Sasso in the central Apennines, whence he proceeded to establish his puppet Italian Social Republic RSI in Salò by Lake Garda, located in German occupied territory. Many Italians joined RSI simply to be fed.

The Communists formed more than half of the Italian Resistance, which grew out of the anti-Fascist movement and lasted eighteen months. Many came from Emilia-Romagna, historically anti-Catholic, owing to centuries of harsh treatment by the Vatican. During 1943, its numbers swelled from 9,000 to over 200,000 by April 1945. The partisans consisted of 40% factory workers and urban artisans, 20% rural workers and 25% middle class intellectuals. Many disaffected Fascists joined their ranks, together with young men, who had become disillusioned with the radical direction and corruption of totalitarianism. Many Italians were now tired of almost constant belligerence since 1935, having been dragged into the Spanish Civil War, as well as the conquest of Abyssinia in 1935 and Albania in 1939. The Catholic tradition of a strong family bond enabled many Italians to resist Fascism's invasion of their privacy, quietly paying lip service to its creed in order to keep their jobs and lead an undisturbed life. Giuseppe Volpi, president of the huge insurance empire *Assicurazione Generali* (which also had interests in chemicals and electricity) prudently blew with the

Fascist wind whilst it suited him, subsequently changing tack to generously finance the Resistance fighters.

A few days after the Armistice, the banned political parties created the *Comitato della Liberazione Nazionale* CLN (National Liberation Committee), a nationwide organisation set up to spearhead the Resistance and work with the Allies. The CLN comprised the Communists PCI, the Christian Democrats DC, the PLI Liberal businessmen, the Socialists PSIUP *Unità proletaria* and the Resistance *Partito d'Azione* Action Party, formed in 1942 and named after Mazzini's radical party of the *Risorgimento*. Composed mainly of young professional men and women who advocated a fairer version of capitalism, the Action Party was led by Ferruccio Parri, who became deputy commander of the CLN Resistance forces. Grouped into Garibaldi Brigades, the partisans drew inspiration from the *Risorgimento* of the 19th century when Italians fought to rid their country of the Austrian invader, and at last achieving unification in 1860 thanks to Garibaldi's clinching victory at Volturno. The Italians were now fighting on two fronts: a second *Risorgimento* to banish the Hun and restore national unity; and a civil war with Fascists pitted against partisans.

In July 1943, following upon their victory over the Germans in North Africa, the Allies landed in Sicily whence they proceeded to mainland Salerno (in the region of Calabria) and on to Rome which suffered dreadful bombardment, in which 600 soldiers and civilians perished. Up against a challenging terrain of mountains rising to 2,000 metres, deep ravines and fast flowing rivers, the Allied Fifth Army was welcomed by the local population. The Germans occupied Rome from September 1943 until June 1944. At Anzio the Americans suffered severe casualties in one of the fiercest battles of the war on Italian soil. To his credit Pope Pius XII (1939-58), who was an able diplomat and much respected by the people, remained steadfastly in the Vatican. On a number of occasions, he nobly appealed to the Germans to exercise moderation, but with scant success. South of Rome, Montecassino, founded in 529, was the site of a tortuous battle, with its monastery and precious library left in ruins. Fortuitously two German officers managed to persuade their commanding officers and Church authorities to remove to Rome for safe keeping over 80,000 books and manuscripts, together with old master paintings and 100,000 prints; and accompanied by all the monks.

Locals assisted in the operation, being paid in extra food rations and cigarettes.[1] Some years ago, I visited Anzio: its quiet seaside charm belies its turbulent past.

By mid-September Italy was riven in half, with the Milan branch of CLN undertaking the government of the North. That month the Allies entered Naples, where they stayed until December 1944 and, together with the Italian government, established the Kingdom of the South, which precluded any Resistance movement. Naples, with a population of over one million souls and a thriving black market, suffered terribly from the bombing, especially the port. Harold Macmillan, Resident Minister in the Mediterranean at that time and reporting directly to Churchill, records the dire situation in Naples in January 1944: 'There is only a minimum subsistence ration of food (125 grams a day of bread)…The Germans destroyed or carried off 92% of the whole stock of sheep and cattle and 86% of the poultry. There is a flourishing black market… There is a very bad clothing situation: no boots or shoes or underwear. There is very little soap. With all this, typhus is naturally beginning.'[2] The Allies were dependent on the Sicilian Mafia and Neapolitan Camorra for vital supplies. In return they turned a blind eye to their post-war control of these areas which, together with the landowners' domination, assured a return to the *status quo ante*. Badoglio conscripted Southerners into fighting alongside the Allies but many were reluctant to take part in a war which politically was alien to them, viewing it as a Northern affair. Even in wartime, North and South were polarised. On 30th October, the King declared war on Germany.

In the spring of 1944, widespread industrial action flared up again, spreading to cities such as Florence and Venice. Verona suffered severe bombing. The Germans blew up all ten bridges spanning the river Po to sever communications, whilst all the villages between Florence and Rome were razed to the ground, though mercifully these two historic cities escaped severe damage, as did Siena and Orvieto. In October the Allies communicated to the CLN Resistance that further advance upon the enemy was now impossible until the spring, and advised the partisans to lie low. The Protocols of Rome accorded them a financial subsidy. The winter of 1944-45 was dreadfully severe, with sub-zero temperatures. There was no fuel, whilst food was critically scarce, largely

---

[1] 'Lady Catherine & the real Downton Abbey' by the Countess of Carnarvon. The author offers an excellent account of the war.

[2] Alastair Horne: Macmillan Vol.1 1894-1956 p.201. See also Sophia Loren: 'Yesterday, Today and Tomorrow' for a moving account of wartorn Naples.

controlled by rural peasants on the black market. Many partisans managed to slip through enemy lines to the relative safety of the low hills and plains near the large cities or in the Po valley, but many did not survive. In 1944 German reprisals were of an unspeakable savagery. The Emilian landless labourers refused to hand over their grain to the Fascist landlords: 2,390 men, women and children from two settlements were annihilated. A garrison of nearly 10,000 Italian troops on the Greek island of Cefalonia was slaughtered. 335 innocent Italians were massacred in the Ardeatine caves near Rome as a punishment for killing 32 German military police. On the eve of Rome's liberation its citizens dared not rise up on account of this appalling carnage. Richard Lamb, who served with the Royal Italian Army at the time, condemns the Germans' vengeance on their former allies as 'cold-blooded slaughter'[3].

Some years ago, an elderly villager from a remote village in the Abruzzo Mountains recounted to me the harrowing tale of a young man who had returned there to recuperate from his war wounds. A German patrol came upon him, ordered him to dig a pit and shot him. Such an occurrence was not uncommon. The Roman Imperial Army had particularly feared engagement with the Hun. Eric Newby vividly describes his experiences as an escaped prisoner of war in 'Love and War in the Apennines'; whilst 'War in Val d'Orcia' by Iris Origo depicts the moving account of hiding a group of children in Tuscany.

In the spring of 1945, in anticipation of a clinching offensive, the Allies advised partisans, now numbering over 100,000 and including women, to save electrical and industrial plant from bombing destruction, much of which the Germans had dismantled and shipped to Germany, together with 350,000 Italian workers, which included soldiers, as forced labour by 1942. Machinery was hidden away in mountain valleys, ready for use after the war. The Cinecittà film studios hid valuable cinema equipment. Many Italians, including industrialists who disliked the economic disruption caused by the war, adopted a cautious 'wait and see' attitude *attendismo,* dreading fearful reprisals from the Germans. Fiat managed to pass details of German production requests to the Allies. Their patriotic honour demanding that their success be independent of Allied support, the Italians now mobilised to lead the final push against the enemy. Urban GAP saboteurs *Gruppi di Azione Patriottica* sprang up, assisted by SAP groups *Squadre di Azione Patriottica* who harried the Germans and destroyed their

---

[3] R.Lamb: War in Italy Ch.4

equipment. Female partisans played a vital role, able to weave unobtrusively amongst the local population to garner information and supplies.

During the spring of 1945, while the Allies were moving north from Emilia, a huge wave of strikes and revolts broke out, fuelled by mass unemployment, extensive damage to factories and a lack of raw materials, some of which had previously been imported from Britain. In 1944 the British Field Marshal Alexander launched a spring offensive, crossing the river Arno at Florence and pushing towards the northern cities of Turin, Milan and Trieste. The Resistance had taken control of Florence in August 1944, assisted by a British captain. Mercifully, tacit agreement by the co-belligerents avoided major destruction to this historic city. The Italians rejoiced at the arrival of the Allies. Macmillan and his escort arrived in Modena ahead of the Americans: 'Our arrival at the Town Hall caused some excitement. There was a lot of shouting and embracing. The leader of the partisans kissed me on both cheeks on being told that I was the famous Haroldo Macmillano, said by the BBC to be the ruler and father of the Italian people'[4].

Workers armed themselves to defend their factories in the major industrial strongholds of Turin, Genoa and Milan against a widespread attack from the Germans. In Milan the Third Garibaldi Brigade managed to secure all the main factories, such as Pirelli, from damage. On 25th April Italy was at last declared to be liberated, and that day became a national holiday. Milan followed the day after and by 1st May all of northern Italy was free. Garibaldi would have been proud of his eponymous descendants. Not surprisingly old scores were settled. Official figures from the Ministry of the Interior state that over 9,000 Fascists were killed by partisans or sentenced to death by the CLNAI, or disappeared; whilst other sources suggest over 15,000 deaths, which is probably more realistic. By the spring of 1945, out of a total of over 200,000 Resistance fighters, some 40,000 had lost their lives and 21,000 were injured. 10,000 civilians were shot by Nazi-Fascist squads; whilst 10,000 soldiers died fighting with the Allies, plus 30,000 abroad in liberation movements. Some 8,000 Jews died in concentration camps (the writer Carlo Levi, one of the few survivors, wrote of his experiences at Auschwitz). 800,000 troops were interned in Germany and kept in appallingly substandard conditions, despite Mussolini's protests to Hitler, and of whom 33,000 perished. It is difficult to be precise over figures but they do give some idea of the dreadful carnage wreaked.

---

[4] H. Macmillan op.cit.p248

The 52nd Garibaldi Brigade arrested Mussolini at Lake Como, executed him and strung him up with his mistress, Clara Petacci, in Piazzale Loreto in Milan; and where in the previous year the Germans had shot 15 political prisoners in retaliation for a GAP attack. Badoglio was replaced by Ivanoe Bonomi, an anti-Fascist Liberal, who in June 1945 was succeeded briefly by Parri until December 1945. The Paris peace treaty of 1947 obliged Italy to relinquish all her colonies; accept a vast bill for war reparations to Greece, Russia, Albania, Ethiopia and Yugoslavia; and hand over Dalmatia, Istria and Fiume to the latter, ruled by the Communist Marshall Tito at that time. He also had his sights on Gorizia, Trieste and Venezia Giulia. However, Trieste was placed under international governance as a free territory. President de Gaulle coveted neighbouring Aosta for its hydroelectric power, but President Truman scotched that idea. This snapping at Italian territory by foreign powers recalls earlier tussles over the centuries.

The provisional post-war coalition government of national unity, involving the DC, PCI, PSI and minor parties, was formed in December 1945, led by the centre/right-wing Christian Democrat Alcide De Gasperi, who replaced Parri as prime minister. The Socialist leader, Pietro Nenni, was deputy leader. It also included the Communist leader, Palmiro Togliatti, a Sardinian who had returned to Italy after 18 years of exile in Moscow to escape Fascism, where he served under Stalin as Vice Secretary of Comintern (Third International), and whom he much admired. Togliatti was a founder member of the PCI in 1921, together with Antonio Gramsci (who died in 1936, having spent many years in prison writing his *Taccuini* notebooks on political theory). Nevertheless, in a spirit of national consensus and as a supporter of parliamentary democracy, Togliatti agreed to join the new government. De Gasperi and his colleagues objected to the presence of the King owing to his collaboration with Mussolini since 1922, further compounded by his cowardly escape from Rome in 1943. Victor Emmanuel decided to abdicate in favour of his son Umberto, and took himself off into exile in Portugal.

On 2nd June 1946, a Referendum was held to decide upon a new political order. The result was finely balanced. 12.7 million Italians (54%) mainly in the Centre/North (especially Emilia-Romagna 77% and Trentino 85%) decided in favour of a Republic. Sicily too voted overwhelmingly for the Republic since both the landowners and the peasantry considered such an option would afford them greater autonomy from the Piedmontese mainland. Governed by their own parliament in medieval times, the Sicilians had fought for independence during the war, organising an army to attack the police and national army. 10.7 million people (46%), predominantly in Rome and the South, voted for the monarchy (such as anti-Fascist landowners), having fared reasonably well under Bourbon rule since the 18th century, especially in Naples where the Bourbon court offered work and subsidies. The more conservative Southerners felt that the concept of a centralised Republic was alien and fabricated by the remote North. The results of the referendum highlighted the stark fault-line between the North and South, which had persisted for centuries. Umberto, the short lived 'May king', followed his father into exile in Portugal.

On the same day as the referendum, the first post-war elections, being the first after the Fascist twenty-year *ventennio*, were held by De Gasperi's government for the Constituent Assembly. Shortly before polling day *Confindustria*, the employers' confederation, awarded generous pay increases to deter Communist sympathizers. The Christian Democrats DC won 207 (37%) of the 556 seats, faring particularly well in rural areas and winning over Southern monarchists. The Socialists took 115 seats (20%) polling well in Turin and Milan. The Communists, dominant in the central 'red belt' of Emilia Romagna with half a million members by 1947, being 19% of the adult population, returned 104 deputies. Jointly they gained a slightly higher share, reinforced by their renewal of the 1944 Unity of Action pact; and bolstered by their virtual control of the General Confederation of Labour CGL, which included the smaller Catholic unions. The Pope, anxious to keep the Communists at bay (Catholics were ill-treated in Russia) intoned that it was a mortal sin not to vote. Minor parties such as the Action party and Republicans made up the balance. The new right-wing *Fronte dell'Uomo Qualunque* (Common Man's Front party), established by a Neapolitan playwright, G. Giannini, polled over a million votes, especially in the South, and returned thirty deputies. Thus, De Gasperi's 1946 second administration formed a cross party coalition of the *Democrazia Cristiana* DC, *Partito Socialista Italiano* PSI and the *Partito Comunista Italiano* PCI.

Origins of the Christian Democrat Party

The Christian Democrat DC party grew out of the PPI *Partito Popolari Italiano* party founded in 1919 by the Sicilian priest Don Luigi Sturzo. Benefiting from the strong Catholic orientated popular culture, the *Popolari*, as the PPI members were known, attracted a strong following amongst the small-scale conservative peasant farmers (for whom Don Sturzo had set up co-operatives in Sicily), together with the trade unions and young leaders of Catholic orientated organisations. The PPI became strong in Lombardy, Piedmont and Veneto, also south of Rome. With the relaxation of the *non expedit* veto in 1904 and 1909, the Papacy's secular influence was partly restored since a few Catholic deputies now sat in the Chamber of Deputies, especially from the 'white' (Catholic) Veneto area. In the past the Catholic Church had defended the peasants here against their harsh treatment under Austro-Hapsburg rule, which secured their eternal gratitude. In the 1919 elections, partly thanks to Giolitti's introduction of universal suffrage in 1918 and proportional representation, the PPI gained 1.2 million votes which assured them 100 seats; and increasing to 107 seats in the 1921 polls.

By 1926 the PPI had disintegrated thanks to internal divisions, Mussolini's hostility and the Pope's indulgence towards the dictator since he sanctioned Catholic education in schools. In fact, few priests had supported fascism and suffered accordingly, which created a division between them and the Pope. Furthermore, many in the PPI had objected to the Fascist Acerbo bill of 1923, which proposed that the party winning a minimum of 25% of the overall votes would automatically be awarded 66% of the parliamentary seats. In the 1924 elections, the PNF gained 66% of the vote anyway, so just over half of the deputies were Fascists. The PPI division over the Bill split the party and Don Sturzo resigned. Once Rome was liberated in 1944, the Pope gravitated towards the DC but, mindful of Don Sturzo's fate, the party remained wary of his motives.

In 1942 a group of PPI veterans and some Catholic anti Fascists set up the Christian Democrat party, which advocated the Christian values of tolerance, fraternity and individual responsibility. Similar in outlook to the PPI, the DC's values appealed to small business proprietors, together with conservative rural and industrial workers. The middle class viewed the DC as the party of law and order. The party also included FUCI the Catholic Graduate Association, which counted Giulio Andreotti and Aldo Moro, future prime ministers, amongst their members; as well as key ministers Leone and Colombo. Pope Paul VI was their religious adviser.

Alcide De Gasperi had served as the last General Secretary of the PPI, which accorded him greater influence over the party than the post of Prime Minister. He came from the Trentino, which during his youth was ruled by Austria as Sud

Tirol, and served as a Catholic deputy during 1911-18 in the Austro-Hungarian parliament housed in Vienna. For a time, he worked in the Vatican library, where he met Andreotti. Keenly supportive of parliamentary democracy, he was kidnapped by the Fascists and spent 16 months in prison. An upholder of traditional family values, his political approach was a *via media* of moderate conservatism, combined with his skilful embrace of left-and right-wing parties throughout his eight post-war administrations.

De Gasperi realised that the party needed to create a broader electoral base by reaching out to all classes of society through its existing organisations, and so reduced its dependence on *Azione Cattolica* (Catholic Action AC) which was the secular arm of the Church. Formed at the turn of the century, in the 1950s AC was run by Luigi Gedda. Many prominent politicians were members, such as Andreotti, Moro and Fanfani. By 1954 AC had grown to over 2.5 million members and held particular sway in Lombardy, Piedmont and the Veneto. Organised in civic committees, AC directed a range of socio-religious activities with separate groups for young and adult men and women, such that it pervaded all aspects of everyday life, reminiscent of Mussolini's all-embracing approach. AC provided *doposcuola* after school care, nurseries, and old people's homes; sports, prayer meetings and summer camps; together with the new phenomenon of the cinema, which proved highly popular. There existed a strong synergy twixt Pope Pius and the DC to promote their religious and political objectives: Catholicism gave the DC credibility, whilst the Pope enjoyed secular influence.

Another Catholic-orientated organisation was *Coldiretti,* which represented the peasant farmers. It was set up by Paolo Bonomi in 1944, to manage the needs of the smallholder farmer proprietors, providing health insurance, old age and disability benefits through its *Casse Mutue*; also the sale of farming equipment and fertilisers through its *Federconsorzi*. By 1956 over 1.6 million families enjoyed *Coldiretti's* social activities which were provided for all ages, including females; and being similar to the PCI's *Case del Popolo* which traced their origins back to 19th century mutual aid societies. Urban factory workers were represented by ACLI Association of Christian Workers set up in 1944 and which had organised working men's clubs, membership of which rose to over a million by 1960. Originally conceived as a trade union to protect Catholic workers, and the oldest of the Church's lay movements, the ACLI clubs subsequently offered a social meeting point for all ages for the promotion of Catholic family values; as well as cinema: in short mirroring the Catholic Action programme. Over time

ACLI was supplanted by the CISL trade union, which supported moderate Catholic workers who sought redress through negotiation with their employers rather than resort to militancy.

The CCI *Confederazione delle Cooperative Italiane* built up a strong nationwide network of Catholic co-operatives, which were principally involved in farming but also some construction. With over two million members by 1962 and larger than the PCI League of Cooperatives, the CCI was particularly strong in Lombardy and Veneto; also in Emilia-Romagna, Sicily and Sardinia. There were also many small Catholic farmers in the remote Apennine Mountains. Together these organisations gradually exerted greater control over much of the electorate, welding the disparate elements into a cohesive political force. Yet beneath the benevolent veneer of social assistance and *bonhomie* the underlying aim was the winning of votes to stem Communist and far right influence.

The cross-party Assembly, which included the Communists but not the Fascists, was charged with the drawing up of a new Constitution which, following 18 months of deliberation came into force on 1ˢᵗ January 1948 and replaced the 1848 Piedmont Statute extant since unification in 1860. Article 1 of the Constitution declares that sovereignty belongs to the people, which finally realised the aspirations of the 19ᵗʰ century revolutionary, Mazzini. The document affirms that the State is based on a 'democratic republic founded on labour', with the workers' right to strike and form trade unions, both of which had been banned by Mussolini. Article 46 confirms the right of workers to participate in the management of their workplace, but this was not put into practice at the time.

The Constitutional text was somewhat vague, wary of according too much power to any one institution after the Mussolini *ventennio*; perhaps also in an effort to please everyone. As a result, the Constitutional Court was set up in 1956, charged with its interpretation. Consisting of fifteen members who hold office for nine years, they are chosen equally by Parliament, the President and the Judiciary. Over the years, the Court came to be widely respected for its politically independent approach, standing firm against the DC's meddling power politics. It eventually annulled the Fascist penal and civil codes which Parliament refused to effect, thereby safeguarding civil liberties and according the judiciary greater autonomy. The Court revised the 1929 Lateran Accords for inclusion in the Constitution, since Parliament and the Vatican dithered, and to which the Communists acquiesced for the sake of national consensus. To date the Court has dealt with just one case of impeachment: that of the defence ministers Gui and Tanassi in 1975, for accepting bribes from the US Lockheed aircraft company. Furthermore, the Constitution provided for the use of Referenda, with a minimum of 500,000 signatures, which provide national debate on key issues such as divorce and abortion, both supported by the Court. It upheld workers' rights and promised equality for females, but this had to wait until the 1970s. The Court welcomed the regulations of the EEC European Economic Community as an external lever on political interference.

Article 104 of the Constitution ordained that the Judiciary (consisting of judges, public prosecutors and magistrates) would be independent of government, which upset the politicians, to be overseen by the Superior Judicial Council, set up in 1958 and chaired by the President of the Republic. The Council is composed of twenty judges chosen by the judiciary, together with twelve legal experts selected by Parliament. Italian civil and penal law is based on the Napoleonic Code and has no history of precedent as with English common case law; nor the right to *habeus corpus*. In 1945 the death penalty was abolished. Many of the senior judges had Fascist leanings, which skewed judgements in the early days, until they retired and were replaced by younger more liberal men. The Constitution forbade the return of any member of the royal family; though in 1996 Umberto II, grandson of King Vittorio Emmanuele 3rd, was allowed a brief visit. Umberto, son of Victor Emmanuel 3rd, died in 1983 and was buried in French Savoy, being the place of his family origins.

In a spirit of balancing unity with liberty, and to counter any reversion to authoritarian power, the Constitution made provision for the establishment of twenty autonomous regions, immediately setting up those for Sicily, Sardinia, Francophone Val d'Aosta and Teutonic Trentino-Alto Adige (formerly South Tyrol). Each had their own statutes and elected parliaments. Total regionalism did not come about until the 1970s, partly because the DC feared the loss of centralized power, particularly in Communist dominated Emilia-Romagna, Tuscany and Umbria. The Constitution retained the original 94 provinces, divided into communes, which were created by Napoleon and are represented by prefects.

The Constitution specified a Parliament with two legislative Chambers: an upper Senate (minimum age 40) and a lower Deputies (minimum age 25) the latter holding 574 deputies in 1948, currently 630 members equally split; both elected every five years (originally seven for the Senate) by universal suffrage, and in 1912 granted to all males and later extended to women. There are 32 electoral colleges. The Senate comprises six representatives from the regions, plus life senators (similar to the House of Lords) and including former presidents. The President of the Senate is second only to the President of Italy, and deputises for the latter should he be incapacitated. The Chamber of Deputies is housed in *Palazzo Montecitorio* (built by Bernini as a private palace and later the Papal Hall of Justice) and the Senate in *Palazzo Madama*; whilst the President of the Council of Ministers (Prime Minister) resides at *Palazzo Chigi*; all situated in Rome. Voting for the Deputies and Senate is through proportional representation, reflecting the individualism of the Italians. Final votes are always secret, so the prime minister is unsure of whom has betrayed him. All parliamentarians must declare their personal income. Parliamentary immunity from prosecution covers the Prime Minister, the Speakers of the Deputies and Senate (the latter is unofficially a vice president); as well as the President of Italy and the President of the Constitutional Court.

Both the Senate and Chamber of Deputies share the same functions but this arrangement duplicates workload and causes delays in the legislative process. To counter this inefficiency committees are used: fourteen for the Chamber of Deputies and twelve for the Senate. This system speeds up the passage of bills, achieving much needed social reform over the years; but it does not allow for parliamentary debate on those matters. Deputies are left to squabble over *leggine* minor laws, and are permitted to speak for up to 45 minutes: a feat easily achieved by the loquacious Italians!

Parliament has the dual role of passing legislation and overseeing the executive. The latter relationship is often strained, with Parliament often obstructing the PM's office, hence his resort to decrees out of pure frustration. Parliament has carried out several closed sessions on major issues, for instance the Mafia and the murder of Aldo Moro; yet with inconclusive results, given the wrestling of conscience required by the Catholic concept of forgiveness. Parliament was also consulted on the reorganisation of the secret services following years of scandal and deceit.

The President of the Republic is Head of State and is elected every seven years by the electoral college of Chamber of Deputies and the Senate; together with delegates from the twenty Italian regions. His election is usually a protracted affair due to factional haggling. The first interim president of the new Republic was the Neapolitan lawyer, Enrico De Nicola, until the Constitution came into effect in 1948. For many years the Presidency was dominated by the

Christian Democrats. The President is Commander-in-Chief of the Armed Forces, presides over the Supreme Council of Defence, and is Chairman of the Superior Judicial Council. The presidential role is not precisely defined in writing, and in some respects resembles that of the British monarchy. As prescribed by Walter Bagehot, the 19th century constitutionalist, the monarch has 'the right to be consulted, to encourage and to warn.' Essentially apolitical, he (so far) provides continuity and may intervene in moments of crisis. Indeed the President, somewhat akin to the Pope's pastoral role, is deemed to be above politics but can intervene if necessary. He exercises a stabilising influence over the fraught melée of party politics, for which he is respected by the Italian people, especially in critical moments.

The President has the right to dissolve or refuse to dissolve Parliament. He can call an election, take soundings on the choice of the President of the Council of Ministers[5] (Prime Minister PM) and indeed appoint a candidate in the event of a stalemate. Furthermore, he can nominate one third of the members of the Constitutional Court; summon extraordinary parliamentary sessions; sign or refuse new laws and decrees. He ratifies international treaties, has the power of amnesty, as well as the final vote on legislation. He can declare war. Technically the President's acts must be approved by an appropriate minister, but this is a grey area: in practice the President usually treads cautiously. He is liable to impeachment and trial by Parliament: fortunately this has not yet occurred. He resides in the Quirinale Palace in Rome, named after one of the seven hills of the city, and previously the residence of the Pope and the monarchy. He enjoys a summer residence at Castel Porziano near Ostia on the coast.

The role of President of the Council of Ministers is another ill-defined area of the Constitution, mindful of the perilous years of authoritarian Fascism. Head of the executive, the Prime Minister is essentially weak. Although appointed by the President of the Republic, he is a puppet of the party/faction leaders, and is thus obliged to preside over a large cabinet of unwieldy super egos, whose sole aim is political power regardless of the common good. The cabinet consists of some twenty ministries plus about six without portfolio; all scrupulously allocated amongst the *correnti* factions according to the Cencelli manual, in the Catholic spirit of a 'fair' government which, including under-secretaries, involves about a hundred people to placate. It takes up to six weeks to complete

---

[5] Equivalent of British Cabinet: the terms Cabinet & Prime Minister are used in this text for brevity.

the intricate wheeling and dealing, resulting in a highly unstable grouping. Few ministers are technically qualified in their allotted field, most being political appointees, and aggravated by the short tenure of an administration which hinders long term planning.

Resembling a feudal power struggle, the government is subject to interminable squabbles over policy, which culminate in a series of crises and its eventual collapse; only to start the entire process all over again. Since the 1970s, the PM has resorted in desperation to the use of smaller interministerial committees which usually expedite matters more efficiently. The most drastic measure is use of the decree, which enforces laws within 60 days, though subject to ratification by Parliament. It was much used by Craxi and latterly by Renzi. Since 1948, there have been over fifty governments (inclusive of reshuffles) with an average survival rate of ten months. Attempts at reform are soon grounded. The Prime Minister and his Cabinet depend upon the legislative support of the Chamber of Deputies and Senate, since laws have to be passed by both Houses.

Palmiro Togliatti, appointed as Minister of Justice, was keen to establish harmony and co-operate with the Christian Democrats, drawing up an agreement to a general amnesty in 1946 towards Fascist sympathizers. Yet his approach played into the hands of the centre/right-wing DC and disappointed many of the more radical Communists hoping for a brave new world. Britain and America favoured the retention of a Fascist administration to deter Communism. Despite his close involvement with Mussolini's administration, Marshal Badoglio had sensibly introduced a limited democracy, reinstating workers' commissions, lightening censorship and increasing political freedom. His successor, the Liberal Ivanoe Bonomi, perhaps wishing to avoid a flare-up of the 1943-5 civil war, refused to recognise CLNAI as the northern government; and over-rode the CLN partisans' demands for a thorough purge of the army, civil service, police (most chiefs and their deputies were Fascists) judiciary and the prefecture. All but one of the prefects were Fascist, who represented central government in the provinces. However, these bodies remained discredited in the eyes of the people, since they were prejudiced against former Resistance and Communist supporters.

The right-wing judiciary courts were indulgent towards Fascists, since many judges were appointed by Mussolini. They carried out a far more extensive purge and harsher treatment of partisans, thereby portraying a biased interpretation of the Catholic concept of forgiveness. The Italian law courts did sentence many

Fascists guilty of heinous crimes, such as murder committed by members of the Black Brigades and the RSI; only to see their rulings overturned by the supreme Court of Cassation. Fascist culprits benefited from friends in high places and got off scot free, or received only minimal punishment; others fled to the South. Some 10,000 names were submitted to the purge commissions, of which one third related to serious offences. Of these 587 cases were dismissed, 1,461 were subject to minor sanctions and 1,530 acquitted. Many Fascists remained in education and industry, retorting that a severe purge would only encourage the spread of Communism. In fact, a comprehensive overhaul would have denuded the state organisations, for instance IRI (set up by Mussolini to manage major industries) of an effective management; nevertheless, it angered the partisans. Many civil servants had paid lip service to Fascism simply to retain their posts and livelihood, drawing a fine line on collaboration. Indeed, many preferred to forget the *ventennio* and concentrate on performing their public duty. To quote Queen Elizabeth 1st, there was little desire to 'make windows into men's souls'. Yet wartime Fascism would later spill over into peacetime unrest.

The Fascist civil and penal codes (the latter known as the *Codice Rocco*[6]), retained in the Constitution to deter Communism, were slowly revised over the years by the Constitutional Court. The 1938 race laws were rescinded and Jews' civil and political rights were reinstated, but this was scant retribution for their dreadful sufferings. The Scelba law banning the PNF Fascist National Party was never enforced. In 1946 its replacement, the MSI *Movimento Socialista Italiano*, was allowed to appear, for whom 1.5 million Italians voted in the 1953 elections. Support was particularly strong in Rome, Naples and Sicily amongst the lower middle classes and former monarchists who favoured traditional values. Indeed, the DC availed themselves of Fascist support to stay in power, keep the PCI at bay and to secure their choice of president of the republic, for instance Segni in 1962 and Leone in 1971. When the DC shifted closer to the Socialists the MSI was put out into the cold. The failure to root out deep-seated Fascism perpetuated nationalist ideas which remained latent until the 1950s, when neo-Fascist groups appeared carrying out attacks to avenge the deaths of their former comrades, possibly some 20,000, by partisans: for instance the Italian Army of Liberation, the *Fasci* of Revolutionary Action and the Italian Anti-Bolshevik Front. Their existence later led to right-wing plots and terrorism in the 1970s.

---

[6] After the justice minister responsible for its drawing up. Italian laws usually take the name of their creator.

In January 1947 De Gasperi reshuffled his Council of Ministers (which equates to a new and so third administration in Italian politics). Cognizant of the need for American and Catholic support, in May De Gasperi ousted both the Communist and Socialist parties from his government, further encouraged both by France's rejection of Communism that year and America's proclamation of its anti-Communist Truman Doctrine. The DC now held exclusively the reins of power. The PCI had served their purpose in a brief moment of reconciliation and national solidarity; whilst that same year the PSI split into a far-left pro-Moscow party under Pietro Nenni (who remained at the helm until his demise in 1984) and falling within the PCI shadow. The more moderate smaller group PSDI (initially PSLI) Social Democratic party under Giuseppe Saragat edged away from the Soviets, taking 52 of the 115 PSI deputies.

On 18th April 1948, the first parliamentary elections under the new Constitution were held. The new element of female suffrage boosted the Catholic-orientated DC since women were regular Church-goers. Pope Pius, keen to regain political influence through *Azione Cattolica*, declared that it was a mortal sin not to vote: thus Catholics voted for the DC. Prudently the Americans increased their financial support under the Marshall Plan at this time to nudge voters right: they granted Italy a $100 million export-import loan. They also sent food and medicines; as well as a roving ambassador who hinted that further aid would not be forthcoming should the Communists be returned to power. Indeed, the United States was prepared to intervene militarily if need be. Italo-Americans, numbering some 600,000, urged their relations back home to keep out the Communists. The prefecture and police clamped down on left-wing demonstrations.

The Pope encouraged the DC to embrace the far right. Yet De Gasperi disagreed since, as a devout Catholic, he was trying to steer a consensual middle course, and sought to distance his party from the Vatican in order to have a freer hand in political affairs. In 1949 the Pope excommunicated all Communists. However, the local parish priest, central to the community, remained crucial to Communists seeking work since he had to supply them with a character reference. Consequently, many attended Mass out of sheer necessity to earn a living. It was said that twenty priests or two million lire sufficed to become a parliamentary deputy.

The DC's outright victory was further facilitated by the Communist *coup d'etat* in Prague in February 1948, which proved unpopular with Italian

Communists; together with the prospect of regaining Trieste (promised by the Allies but lost in the 1947 Peace Treaty, and eventually reacquired in 1954). Once more the DC gained votes from the far right: the Southern Monarchists, the MSI and the CMF. The DC won 48.5% of the total votes, claiming 305 of the 574 seats in the Chamber of Deputies, having regained lost ground in the 1946 elections: the first instance of a single party gaining an overall majority. A further reason for the DC's victory was the success of Einaudi's 1947 budget backed up by their promise to rebuild the post war economy and improve the lamentable living conditions of the people: their nutritional levels were even worse than in the 1930s under Fascism. By 1948 there were over two million unemployed. The Communists and Socialists, combined into the Popular Front, secured 31% with respectively 140 and 41 seats: less than in 1946 due to the recent PSI split, with the balance taken up by the lesser parties. With the Popular Front marginalized the scene was set for a virtual one-party state which would dominate the Italian political scene for half a century until the DC's dramatic downfall in 1992.

In 1948 the Chamber of Deputies was highly fluid, there being no dominant left or right-wing grouping, so De Gasperi again decided on an all-inclusive administration. This political approach of shifting alliances was not new: Cavour had arranged a *connubio* centre left coalition to form a viable government. Having completed the process of unification the moderate right-wing government *Destra Storica* lost its momentum and fell into disarray. The old guard of the *Risorgimento* was gone; whilst the Liberal left *Sinistra Storica* was merely an amorphous grouping, too fragmented and ill-disciplined to form a strong counter party. Following unification, the Chamber of Deputies came to be dominated by the new intake (up to 40%) of individualistic and ill-disciplined Southerners, principally landowners and lawyers: a forceful clique who lacked any sense of national consciousness, and who were highly susceptible to corruption, unlike the morally upright Piedmontese who had dominated the earlier years.

The left-wing Agostino Depretis, a Piedmontese, was Prime Minister during 1876-87 and had served with Garibaldi in Sicily. He decided that the only way to provide a semblance of decent government would be to unite the various factions in temporary alliances: *trasformismo* to establish a policy and pass a law, facilitated by the use of bribery: a government post or honorary title, a financial tip-off or an amenity for the deputy's constituency to keep his supporters happy. Herein lie the beginnings of *clientelismo* patronage. This Catholic inspired consensual approach enabled the passing of legislation through cross-party support, which would dissolve to realign for the next political manoeuvre; and quite unlike the British bipolar system, given Italy's creation of fragile and short-lived administrations. The Southern deputies allowed their Northern counterparts to govern and drive the industrial economy, in return for which they continued to rule the South, which only reinforced the North-South divide. The Chamber of Deputies came to be described as an amalgam of private interests.

Crispi, an impetuous Sicilian who was close to Garibaldi, succeeded Depretis in 1887, opposed *trasformismo* and tried to create clear-cut party lines, but failed. At times ruling by decree, Crispi opined that Italians had no sense of loyalty towards the State and its institutions. Giolitti, from Piedmont and prime minister during 1892-3 and 1901-14, adopted *clientelismo* since he needed the support of the Southern landowners. The new Constitution and post-war elections had heralded a spirit of change and renewal, yet the powerful blend of *trasformismo* with *clientelismo* merely imitated the *status quo ante*, bypassing the voice of the people through an ineffective democratic parliament to control the political factions, which engendered distrust and scorn amongst the electorate who viewed the deputies as self-serving manipulators; and with dire results later on.

Chapter Two

Economic Take-Off

At the time of unification in 1861, industry was minimal compared to Germany and Britain, with barely 1% annual growth and with very few factories. For centuries the Peninsula had essentially been an agriculturally based economy, centred on Tuscany and the Lombardy Plain/Po valley, with pockets of commercial interest in the main cities: Milan, Florence, Venice and Bologna, in particular textiles (woollen cloth, cotton and silk), based on family-owned artisanal workshop trades since medieval times. The Bourbon government established an iron foundry and a factory producing heavy machinery near Naples. Industry in this area, mainly engineering and textiles (partly set up by Swiss and English businessmen) had benefited from the protective tariffs imposed by the Bourbon rulers. Sulphur was mined in Sicily. The national population, totalling 32 million in the 1860s, was predominantly rural and so possessed very little purchasing power. Many Liberal Right politicians such as Cavour believed that a bottom-up approach driven by agriculture and business, created along the Franco-British lines of free trade, would energise the Italian economy. To this end, tariff free commercial treaties were arranged with neighbouring countries: England, Belgium, and especially France in 1863. Public works were organised to provide employment and stimulate trade both internally and abroad.

Progress proved to be slow, partly because the north European markets lay stagnant during the 1870s, intensified by the agricultural depression throughout the continent, including England. It was gradually realised that the Italian economy could not lead with agriculture, and so politicians and entrepreneurs became attracted towards the German top-down capitalist development of industry, underpinned by state protection, which was transforming Germany into an economic powerhouse. However, many feared that industrialisation would provide a breeding ground for socialist ideas.

Another contributory factor was the state of the Italian state finances, which had got off to a bad start in 1860, weighed down by the immense cost of the struggle for independence. Half of the 60% budget deficit was due to military expenditure and interest on the national debt. Following unification in 1860, the Liberal right-wing government, based in Turin until 1864 and dominated by the Piedmontese, sold off Church and communal lands at lucrative prices to the rising affluent middle classes in order to pay for the wars. Furthermore, they imposed punitive taxation throughout the Peninsula, which eventually balanced the books by 1876, but came at great political cost. Italian taxation was the highest in Europe at that time, which included the hated grist (grain milling) tax and fell heavily on the poor, encouraged massive tax evasion and created a lack of purchasing power, which in turn depressed the fledgling industrial base.

Unification had provided the spurt to develop the railways (Cavour much admired the English network) which were financed by state taxation imposed by Giolitti, unlike in Britain where private joint stock companies were formed. In 1839 Naples built the first railway, five miles in length. Rail construction companies channelled their surplus cash into the expanding electricity sector, including hydroelectric power HEP projects. The Livorno banker, Pietro Bastogi, set up a company for rail construction, and invested heavily in electricity.

The 1880s saw the first take-off of the Italian economy, especially in the north-west regions of Piedmont, Lombardy and Liguria, which possessed abundant supplies of HEP and good communications with the north European markets. Textiles in the Veneto and central Italy had a close link with manufacturing through their cottage industry of weavers, as in Britain at that time. The tariff free regime had encouraged cheaper imports, such as iron, steel and foodstuffs, but it also led to the undercutting of Italian production. Consequently, the Liberal Left government, which succeeded the Liberal Right in 1876, decided to impose a protective customs tariff in order to guarantee high prices against cheaper imports. In 1878 the first to benefit were machinery and textiles (such as the prized woollen cloth of Biella and Prato, as well as Lombard cotton, extant since medieval times) followed by shipbuilding, iron and steel. These sectors were bolstered by state support in the form of subsidies, which guaranteed high prices against cheaper imports. Unfortunately, this policy led to a tariff war with France which undermined Italian exports.

Italian Banking has its origins in the medieval banking families of Venice, Florence, Siena and Genoa, which financed the business activities of manufacturers and merchants who shipped goods to France, Spain, Antwerp and London, especially textiles; also further afield to North Africa, Russia, the Levant (Middle East) and China. Florence boasted some forty banks which traded throughout Europe and the Middle East, and whose profits were channelled into banking loans extended to popes and kings, such as Edward III of England.[7] Lombard banks were eventually ruined by English kings defaulting on their huge debts. *Monte dei Paschi di Siena* is reputed to be the oldest bank in the world, founded in 1493. Italian bankers invented double entry book-keeping, the bill of exchange and the letter of credit (from the Italian *credere* to trust). A staunchly independent republic, the Genoese Bank of Saint George became an international banking hub, financing the Spanish kings Charles V and Phillip II. The bank's presence in Milan established an important money market there. By the 16th century, these city states had suffered a decline in their trade, due to strong competition in the shipping of mass consumer products by the Dutch, French and English. As a result, Italian financial expertise dwindled over time, exacerbated by Spain's domination of the Peninsular for two hundred years and the Spaniards' antipathy towards business. People now looked to the public administration and the law for employment.

Prior to unification Italian banking was hindered in its development by the lack of industry and the fragmented nature of regional states. In the early 19th century, the *casse di risparmio* savings banks appeared, mainly in the north. Derived from charitable institutions, such as church or communal organisations, together with the old *Monti di Pieta*[8] pawn institutes, they extended credit against security. By the 1850s, these non-profit making savings banks had become widespread in most cities and towns, as well as in Sicily and Naples in the south. A notable example is the Lombard *Cassa di Risparmio*, founded in 1823, now known as Cariplo[9], which mainly extended credit for building.

---

[7] See author's book 'From Subjugation to Independence'.

[8] The term 'monte' derives from the state bond issued by the Papacy during the 16th century.

[9] Cariplo recently revived its philanthropic origins and remains a major mortgage lender.

These institutions placed their assets principally in *titoli di stato* state bonds, in particular for the acquisition of land and property, a popular investment since medieval times, rather than favour economic enterprise. They were largely responsible for the financing of SMES small and medium sized enterprises, descendants of the medieval artisans. In the Kingdom of Naples, there existed a number of private pawn institutes, which merged into the Bank of Two Sicilies, part of which became the Bank of Naples entrusted with the region's state treasury. In 1860 the Bank of Sicily replaced the older municipal banks on that island. In 1875 postal savings banks began to appear and expanded steadily. The Milan *Borsa* Stock Exchange was founded in 1808 and continued to be governed by its original laws until the mid 1970s.

In 1844 the Bank of Genoa was set up by traders, that independent-minded city being the most dynamic in the Peninsular at that time, and building upon her medieval prosperity. It was one of the earliest types of modern bank, offering both deposit and current accounts. The Genoese presence in Milan encouraged the establishment there of an important money market. In 1849 the Bank of Genoa absorbed the short-lived Bank of Turin (of which Cavour was a director) and later became the National Bank of Italy, founded and managed by the Genoese industrialist Carlo Bombrini, the first of many banking specialists. He introduced modern banking to Italy and established a monetary policy, extending generous loans to industry, in particular Ansaldo Engineering of Genoa, the largest company at that time, to assist them in competing with foreign rivals.

In 1853 Cavour commanded Parliament to assign the state Treasury to the Bank of Italy. The bank proceeded to take control of the banks within the Emilian duchies, Florence, the Vatican state, the two Tuscan banks set up by the Livorno banker, P. Bastogi; and later the Venetian Bank. An Austrian bank continued to manage Lombard finances. State finances were insufficiently covered by taxation so the government resorted to the banks for funds, as well as to the expanding middle class, through the issuance of *Buoni di Tesoro* state treasury bonds by Cariplo and other savings banks, together with the smaller *banche popolari* co-operatives and savings banks. The bonds were guaranteed and offered a good rate of interest. These banks were mainly responsible for the financing of SMEs in central and northern Italy. The South remained largely agrarian, funded by smaller banks in which prudent farmers placed their hard-earnt savings.

Rising economic prosperity prompted the money markets to avail themselves of the new credit institutes created by the French banker Pereire, which fuelled the property building boom following unification, a service which was also offered by the new banks such as *Credito Mobiliare*. The Paris branch of the Rothschild banking group acted as adviser to the Italian government. However, the banking sector over-reached itself through excessive lending, leading to a property bust in the 1870s and a bank crisis. As a result, in 1874 the six main issuing banks were grouped into a consortium to minimise risk: National, Naples, Sicily, Romana and the two Tuscan banks.

The injection of fresh capital boosted production throughout the 1880s: imports of raw cotton almost trebled the output of chemicals and minerals rose steadily, whilst the nascent metallurgy sector forged ahead. During this period industry achieved an overall increase of 37% with an annual growth rate of 4.6%. In 1884 the first Italian steelworks started up at Terni, an old Roman town in central Umbria, as a trust (which guaranteed a business venture) using iron ore from the island of Elba, and backed by a state subsidy guaranteeing high steel prices. Terni supplied mainly the navy, as well as armaments owing to the rise in international rivalry. Shipping lines were also subsidised, whilst the growing machinery sector relied on state orders for railways. The strengthening of the industrial base allowed the government in 1887 to extend the customs tariff to agriculture which was in deep recession, especially cotton and sugar.

The small *Banco di Roma* appeared in 1880, founded by a clerical aristocrat and with links to the monarchy and the Vatican, later extending its client base to families and Catholic co-operatives. In 1914 the pope set up the Italian Banking Federation which included the larger *Credito Nazionale* CrNaz, and which aspired to providing finance for a Catholic-based political party. The smaller banks formed a joint stock company to distance themselves from CrNaz. Blocked from expansion at home by CrNaz, Banco di Roma developed a base in Libya, at that time under Turkish sovereignty, forging links with local trade and shipping. In 1911 Banco di Roma became the largest bank but suffered a low liquidity ratio which, combined with poor management and competition from CrNaz and BCI (see below) sent it into decline.

During the 1880s, there occurred a series of banking scandals, caused by the building boom and overlending by the six major issuing banks. In 1892 Prime Minister Giolitti was obliged to hold a parliamentary enquiry into various banking irregularities, such as the circulation of duplicate banknotes, centred on the *Banca Romana*. Established in 1833, the bank had previously failed twice, due to corrupt administration and financing the Vatican. Furthermore, it had unwisely made unsecured loans to politicians to fund elections, including the ministers Giolitti and Crispi, in return for turning a blind eye to banking malpractice. Even Bombrini at the Bank of Italy was accused of accepting bribes. Giolitti's administration fell as a consequence, only to be replaced by Crispi (who had acted as Garibaldi's political adviser). The national finances were placed on a firmer footing by the 1893 Bank Act which limited banknote issuance to just the three banks of Naples, Sicily and Italy.

Following the banking crisis, a new banking phase emerged during the Giolittian era 1900-13, with the formation of commercial mixed or universal banks in Italy based on the German model, to finance promising private industrial companies. In exchange they received shares and direct control on the Board of Directors. The German model combined the functions of deposit taking and medium to long term credit facilities with industrial investment, as well as discounting exchange bills. The vast sector of Austro-German banks, and to a lesser extent the Franco-Belgian banks, was well experienced in financing private industry, boasting a strong interbank network which helped to minimise risk.

The German concept was favoured by Bonaldo Stringher, director of the private Bank of Italy during 1900-28. Previously the general manager of the Treasury (where he was involved in resolving the 1892 crisis) Stringher was the bank's driving force, transforming it into a central (bankers') bank. He established a policy of monetary stability, with control of the money supply to restrain inflation; and maintain both sufficient reserves together with a steady exchange rate. In order to have greater liquidity, banks were willing to discount their clients' bills of exchange for cash at the Bank of Italy, thereby oiling the wheels of commerce, and which enabled Stringher to have his pulse on the economy. In Stringher's words the bank became 'the natural guardian of the country's economic interests.'

In 1894 the *Banco Credito Mobiliare,* dating from 1862 and a casualty of the banking crisis, was reinvented as the *Banca Commerciale Italiana* BCI. Constituted in Milan as Italy's first private mixed bank, mostly with German-Swiss financial backing, it was managed by a German, Otto Joel, until 1914. BCI was the first Italian bank to appear as a private mixed bank, issuing short-and long-term loans, especially to the steel industry. The other new bank was *Credito*

Italiano, backed by Austro-German money, which appeared at about the same time as BCI, through the merger of the Bank of Genoa and a group of smaller Milanese banks who wished to avoid being excluded by the Germans. Both BCI and *Credito* maintained close links with the German banks until the outbreak of war in 1914; as well as with French and Belgian banks. Stringher persuaded BCI and *Credito* to open branches in Morocco and Abyssinia (Ethiopia) which were undergoing Italian colonisation. Furthermore, both banks financed Cariplo savings bank, which in turn financed SMEs, thereby affording a useful link with industry.

Thanks to a prudent selection of clientele, within a decade BCI and *Credito* had increased their control of industrial credit from 20% to 42%. A synergy existed twixt banker and industrialist, in that they respectively held seats on the boards of both the banks and companies, usually just with one bank per company, thereby establishing a close relationship and providing the bankers with an invaluable insight into the running of the business. The banks underpinned companies' solvency by guaranteeing their shares, underwriting them to place with the general public; and when banks had surplus cash, they bought more shares. Giovanbattista Pirelli, founder of the eponymous rubber tyre industry and a director at *Credito*, supported companies in difficulty. Enrico Rava, manager of *Credito*, was appointed president of Ferriere, the Tuscan iron and steel company, the bank's main interest. Ferriere was later taken over by the Terni steel company, which in turn absorbed Elba steel. *Credito* became heavily involved in financing Ansaldo engineering, established in 1853 as a trust in Genova, later owned by the Perrone family after 1902, and which became the largest company for the manufacture of armaments. Another key client was Edison electrical energy based in Milan, Italy's growing financial centre. *Credito*'s other main interests were sugar, textiles and the nascent chemical sector; whilst BCI concentrated on cotton and public works.

By the late 19th century, the European economy began to recover, which facilitated Italy's economic growth: it nearly doubled industrial output at 7.5% during 1897-1907 from a 1% base rate in the 1800s. Between 1896 and 1913 Italy's average annual growth of Gross Domestic Product GDP was 2.8%, compared with Britain's at 1.7%, 1.9% for France, and second only to Germany's at 3.2%; with the US leading at 4.3%. Italy's first economic boom was helped by the end of the tariff war with France, the increased use of technology and the boost in electrical energy. By the early 1900s, the new core sectors of heavy industry: chemicals, rubber, metallurgy and engineering, were growing strongly, from 11% to 26% of valued added manufacture during 1896-1916. They were centred on the north-west triangle of Milan, Turin and Genoa (respectively in the regions of Lombardy, Piedmont and Liguria). Steel production soared from some 140,000 tons in 1900 to 930,000 tons by 1913.

Italy was transforming itself from a predominantly rural economy into an industrial nation: split at 43% agriculture and 26% industry in 1908, as opposed to 51% and 20% in 1900. Textiles flourished, especially silk (still a niche product in the Biella-Como area) which adopted new techniques of dyeing and weaving; and accounted for one third of the world market by 1914, as well as a quarter of all textile jobs, often taken by females and children. Wool suffered from frequent strikes and out-dated equipment. During the first decade of the 20th century industrial workers increased from 2.5 million to 4.5 million, with exports rising at 4.5% per annum.

By the 1890s, engineering and textiles were well established to the north-west of Milan, with chemicals in the Rho area, whilst steel and heavy engineering based itself to the north-east at Sesto San Giovanni (which became a staunch Communist stronghold) flanking the roads and railways. In 1911 the northwest accounted for 55% of industrial revenue, and the north-east/centre for 29%. The latter was made up essentially of small artisanal family concerns, for instance Beretta armaments in Brescia, and to a lesser extent in the north-west. These small firms were unable to benefit from the protection tariffs since they did not possess the greater economies of scale enjoyed by heavy industry. Yet they did provide a vital backup to the larger companies, and would later form the backbone of commercial enterprise in the north-east as SMEs. The South accounted for just 16% of industry.

Turin and Milan became flourishing cities of enterprising middle-class businessmen and large-scale industrialists. Milan's population doubled between 1880 and 1914 to 580,000 inhabitants, rising to over a million by the 1930s (against Rome's half a million inhabitants in 1911) with a growing middle class and increased purchasing power. Indeed *Mediolanum,* as the city was originally known, had prospered since its mercantile days as a medieval commune. Finance now became a vital arm of Milan's economy, previously controlled by the city states of Florence, Siena and Genoa. The opening of the Saint Gotthard Pass in 1882 facilitated the import of raw materials and, together with the harnessing of

HEP, attracted industry to its hinterland. Einstein's father, an engineer by profession, installed the first electrical power plants on the Paduan Plains.

Private companies were established, which came to dominate not only Italy but later the European stage. Many of the new entrepreneurs were republicans who had actively supported and fought alongside Mazzini and Garibaldi in fighting for the cause of Italian independence. Soldiers of the *Mille* had now become captains of industry: for instance Erasmo Piaggio, manufacturer of arms and machinery; Raffaele Rubattino, Genoese arms manufacturer who provided the two steamers in which Garibaldi and his men sailed to Sicily in 1860; and Luigi Orlando, shipping magnate. In 1872 Giovanni Pirelli, who had fought alongside Garibaldi, started making rubber in Milan for tyres and cables, such as for submarine telegraph communications. The economic boom favoured urbanisation with much speculative building, which ruined parts of Rome and Florence but improved sanitation in Naples. These pioneers of Italian industry formed the small group of Liberals, descendants of Cavour.

By 1880 Ansaldo Engineering had become highly dependent on state orders for railway stock, along with shipping. Montecatini set up his eponymous chemicals company which became a leader between the two world wars. Chemicals assisted the improvement of agriculture with its development of fertilisers; whilst engineering supplied machinery to both farming and industry. In 1883 Edison established Milan's central generating plant, the first in Europe, based on HEP drawn from the swift-flowing Alpine rivers, such as the river Adda whose plant is still in use, and which reduced costly coal imports. The electricity illuminated *La Scala* theatre and the *Galleria Vittorio Emmanuele* (begun in 1861). Electrical power grew substantially, especially in the north: from 100 million kilowatts in 1898 to 950 mkw by 1907 and 2575 mkw on the eve of World War One. By 1913 Italy rivalled Britain's output and overtook French capacity; the South had to wait until later. Edison later diversified into chemicals and became second only to Montecatini; with which it merged in 1966.

Industrial buoyancy boosted agriculture, especially in the north, to feed the fast-growing population. The rise in family incomes allowed more Italians to eat a decent diet and buy some consumer goods. Yet economic growth was still insufficient to offer full employment, particularly in the South. Between 1900 and 1910 some six million Italians emigrated to the New World; as against 1.5 m during 1881–1900. Their remittances home helped their relatives to finance new machinery and factories. In 1911 Libya was conquered with a view to imperial ambitions and absorbing surplus population, yet the venture proved a disillusion.

Centred on Turin, with a population of some 430,000 by 1911, automobiles were a spectacular growth sector, assisted by duty free imports of iron and steel from 1903. Fiat *Fabbrica Italiana Automobili di Torino* was founded in Turin in 1899 by Giovanni Agnelli, a former Piedmontese cavalry officer, who set up his first factory at Lingotto, and was soon exporting cars to the Balkans. In 1911 Fiat produced its first people's car, the *Barilla*. Lancia fired up in 1906. By 1911 there were six major car manufacturing companies in Turin, employing over 6,000 workers. Fiat was the leader, accounting for half the production by 1914. The racing driver Enzo Ferrari (1898-1988) opened his factory in Modena in 1929, mainly racing cars for Grand Prix, as did Lamborghini and other firms in Emilia-Romagna. In 1910 the Alfa Company in Milan *Anonima Lombarda Fabbrica Automobili* teamed up with the French firm Darracq and was financed by the *Banca Agricola Milanese*. By 1914 Alfa employed 250 people and was selling 300 cars per annum. It became a major player in car racing, and was later bought by Nicola Romeo.

Olivetti established itself in 1908, at Ivrea (Piedmont) making office equipment, firstly typewriters, later diversifying into electric calculators and electronic computers. Further south in Rome, from 1922, Snia Viscosa became a major employer for textiles, mainly silk and cotton; later moving into the new synthetic yarns of rayon and viscose. In 1927, Snia was taken over by Courtaulds US and VGF Germany, but later reverted to independence. Foreign trade leapt from £124 million in 1901 to £213 million in 1910 and helped to balance the national accounts. In an effort to inject industry into the impoverished South, in 1904 a steel plant was established by the Ilva company at Bagnoli near Naples; together with a HEP plant on the river Volturno (site of Garibaldi's decisive victory in 1860). In addition to state protection in the forms of financial subsidy and high tariffs, nascent Italian industry profited from cheap labour and long working days, including the employment of women and children, the latter limited to age twelve by a law in 1902, but which was frequently ignored.

In 1907 there occurred a spate of crises in the core sectors of steel and textiles, together with another banking crisis due to excessive speculation on the *Borsa,* such that the Italian banks were unable to settle their interbank debts, and so sold their shares and declined credit to business. Stringher, director of the Bank of Italy, intervened by expanding the money supply to avoid a repetition of the 1892 crisis. *Società Bancaria Italiana* SBI, set up in 1898 and a rival to Credito and BCI, was particularly hit by the crisis. Having over-reached itself, the bank collapsed, which particularly affected Fiat, a major client and itself on the verge of collapse due to a debt crisis; compounded by Agnelli being accused of false accounting practices. Fiat was saved by a group of Torinese bankers and finance companies. In 1902 Ansaldo engineering, now Italy's largest company and owned by the Perrone family since 1902, took over SBI to create the new *Banca Italiano di Sconto* BIS as a rival to BCI and Credito. A banking consortium bailed out the iron and steel sector (with major sites at Ilva and Terni, and lesser ones at Piombino and Bagnoli) where fierce competition had led to overcapacity and huge debts.

Italian industry did well out of the Great War hostilities: armaments, vehicles, military clothing, steel and electrical energy; as did profiteers. Ansaldo thrived on the production of armaments; along with the steel and electricity sectors, together with Fiat. The banks continued to control much of industry. Ever ambitious, Perrone (who illegally traded in German bonds) tried to take over BCI, whilst Agnelli and Snia-Viscosa coveted Credito. The government preferred to raise finance through the banks rather than increase taxation; yet the banks' high rates of interest fuelled inflation and augmented the national debt. In 1915 Stringher established CSVI *Consorzio per Sovvenzioni sui Valori Industriali* under the aegis of the Bank of Italy, to protect industry during the Great War by guaranteeing their bonds. With himself as president, the consortium included savings banks and the two banks of *Istituto San Paolo di Torino* and *Monte dei Paschi di Siena*, which acted as a safety net to guarantee company shares. Planned as a temporary measure, in fact CSVI laid the foundations of state intervention and was the forerunner of IRI.

The 1920s proved to be a bumpy ride for the economy, entailing a post-war slump which brought about rampant inflation and much speculation, for instance one Marinelli who bought and sold banks in an ever-increasing spiral to stay afloat. Italian industry, especially the iron and steel sector, was badly affected by American competition, leading to excess capacity, deflated prices and a consequent liquidity crisis. The banking sector remained highly vulnerable, with several mergers to stay afloat. BIS and BCI fought over control of the electricity sector, whilst ILVA coveted Edison in order to dominate the electric arc furnaces needed for making steel. The *Credito* bank, a major creditor at Ilva, replaced the company management with their own men; whilst BCI was now run by another

German, G.Toeplitz. In 1921, BIS collapsed due to the critical state of its main client Ansaldo, and came under CSVI. (The engineer Guglielmo Marconi had served as the bank's president). The bank's foreign creditors pulled out and thousands of small savers lost their deposits.

In 1913 Nitti, head of the Treasury, favoured state intervention and was keen to supervise the banks more closely, but Parliament objected to their interference in private entities. New state initiatives were put in place to revive the frail economy. Crediop, managed by Alberto Beneduce, a protégé of Stringher, was set up to organise public works such as land drainage, financed through state bonds. ICIPU, similar to Crediop, concentrated on the telephone and electricity sectors. INA *Istituto Nazionale Assicurazione* National Insurance Institute was set up.

Throughout the 1870s/80s, as elsewhere in Europe, the growing middle class realised the value of a decent secondary and tertiary education to gain employment in the fast-expanding civil service following unification, together with the growing professions: not only in the traditional paths of medicine, education, and the law, but also in the new sectors of the media and commerce. The new world of journalism was a strong career attraction, with increased newspaper circulation building upon the influential periodicals of the *Risorgimento*. A census for 1881 indicates that these categories, which included shopkeepers and industrialists, numbered only about one million (6.7% of the total population), as against 14% in France, where the private sector was more developed. During the 1860s, 78% of Italians were illiterate. Since the Fascist period the secondary *ginnasio-liceo* education had offered a curriculum heavily weighted towards the classics: philosophy, history, languages and literature. The technical institutes were looked down upon, in fact they taught little science and economics. The restricted economic base obliged students to settle for a career in public administration or politics, especially in the South. The parliamentary intake moved away from the original landowner base, typified by Cavour, towards Southern deputies with a legal background (about half of the 1913 complement) which made consensus even more tortuous.

The years 1901-1914 are known as the Giolittian period, after the incumbent Liberal Prime Minister Giovanni Giolitti from Piedmont, who was previously Secretary of the General Court of Accounts. Resembling the French *Belle Epoque* and the English Edwardian era, society in northern Italy seemed held in a hiatus of unending delight, political stability and economic prosperity, against a background of French culture, until torn asunder by the Great War. The increasing affluence of a growing middle class helped to drive the economy forward. New leisure activities appeared: the cinema, football and train outings. The tourist industry began to take off.

Sympathetic towards the plight of the working man, and so akin to Britain's Liberal prime minister Lloyd George with his 1909 People's Budget, Giolitti's main pre-war achievement was the foundation of the welfare state: a 'shorter' eleven hour working day for women plus paid maternity leave; the prohibition of employing children aged under twelve; a weekly day of rest, sickness and old age benefits, previously provided by mutual aid societies. A voluntary pension fund was set up, also voluntary accident insurance for farmers. In 1912 Giolitti built on the 1882 electoral reform by extending male suffrage from two to eight million, which accorded the vote to nearly all adult males and substantially increased the conservative rural vote. Giolitti organised a programme of public works in the South.

Giolitti's benevolence towards the workers and his reluctance to intervene in labour disputes, let alone call in the police and army, encouraged the expansion of Socialist trade unionism, such that by 1902 there were almost 250,000 members, mainly in Turin. Many had worked in Socialist Germany where they had absorbed such ideas. These unions were essentially national federations of local artisanal groups. Chambers of Labour also increased: run by local skilled workers they acted as job centres, as well as providing leisure and education amenities; whilst some offered shops and housing organisations. In 1906 the Chambers combined with the federations to create the General Confederation of Labour CGL.

Strikes organised by the unions had the desired effect of securing wage increases in real terms of 2.2% per annum, together with a 3% rise in per capita productivity from 1897 until 1907, when growth was severely checked by a global crisis, which particularly hit steel and textiles. Subsequently there occurred a surge in industrial and agricultural unrest, from an average of nearly 1,000 a year, involving 250,000 workers in the early 1900s, to over 1,500 strikes and 350,000 protesters by 1910. Most industrialists were irritated by Giolitti's indulgent attitude, except those who had travelled abroad and were more enlightened. Bosses such as Agnelli, Olivetti and Pirelli recognised the importance of treating their employees with consideration.

The Rise of Socialism

Anarchism took root in Italy during the 1860s through the arrival of Michael Bakunin, a Russian anarchist. His anti-state and communal ideas appealed especially to Neapolitans, given their sufferance of high taxation and conscription over the centuries. Anarchism was also fuelled by a lack of education and jobs. Many Italian workers supported the anarchists (some of whose members assassinated King Umberto 1st in 1900) since their individualistic approach to life objected to the regimented centralisation of Marxism, which appealed more to university intellectuals. Andrea Costa formed an anarchist group in his native Romagna, then proceeded to set up a less extreme Revolutionary Socialist party in 1881, becoming a parliamentary deputy the following year. In 1885 the Italian Workers' Party was established by Filippo Turati, a Lombard lawyer, but it only lasted a year. In 1895 the Italian Socialist Party PSI was formed, the first Italian political party since 1861, and backed by trade unions and intellectuals such as the Abruzzese poet Gabriele d'Annunzio. Socialism also drew on Mazzini's mutual aid societies of the 1840s.

By the early 20th century, the PSI had become a powerful force to be reckoned with, especially through its agricultural *Federterra* organisation. It had a strong following with the Po valley *braccianti* landless labourers during the prolonged agricultural crisis of the 1880s/90s, as well as in Puglia and Sicily; also the *mezzadri* sharecroppers of central Tuscany and Umbria. *Federterra* increased its membership from half a million in 1919 to 900,000 members just a year later. PSI issued its own newspaper *Avanti!* In 1900 the PSI returned 32 deputies to Parliament with 216,000 votes; increasing in 1913 to 79 deputies and claiming almost 25% of the votes. In 1919, assisted by Giolitti's introduction of universal suffrage and proportional representation, the Socialists took 30% of the vote, securing 156 seats.

By 1919 the PSI had become increasingly radical, but then the momentum for revolution fizzled out for lack of decisive leadership, together with an identity crisis. In 1921 a small group of radicals, led by the Sardinian Antonio Gramsci, a political philosopher, defected to form the Italian Communist Party PCI, which went on to take fifteen seats in the elections. The PCI reduced PSI's appeal since it undermined the latter's twin pillars of trade unionism and agricultural co-operatives. Shortly afterwards, Gramsci was imprisoned by Mussolini, during which time he wrote his *Taccuini* notebooks on political theory. He died in 1936.

The end of the war brought tremendous social upheaval: a scaling back of wartime production led to an economic recession, with another crisis in steel and textiles, together with two million unemployed, swollen by demobilisation. In 1921 protectionist measures were introduced to cushion industry from the drop in exports. There followed rampant inflation, due to the devaluation of the lira. War expenditure had accounted for one third of Italy's GNP, for which Italy borrowed heavily from Britain and America (also importing raw materials from the latter) in order to avoid a rise in taxation, but which pushed her budget deficit to 108% of GNP.

Given this scenario, tension ran high, resulting in the general strike during 1919/20 and known as the *Biennio Rosso* Two Red Years. In the North over one million workers downed tools, involving public workers such as railway and clerical workers, and even middle-class employees such as magistrates. Factories were occupied together with riots in the north and centre over food shortages. Their militancy was all the more intense given the repression of industrial action during the war. Trade union membership once more soared dramatically, as it had before the war: The Communist CGL rose from 250,000 members in 1918 to two million by 1920; whilst the Catholic CIL, established in 1919, claimed more than a million members within a year, made up principally of farmers, sharecroppers and textile workers from Liguria, Lombardy and Veneto.

Their militancy was all the more intense given the repression of industrial action during the war. Their action did not go unrewarded, thanks to the employers' weak bargaining power due to a lack of organisation, coupled with the government's desire for a consensual approach to meeting the workers' demands. In 1919 a raft of concessions were secured, building upon Giolitti's pre-war reforms: a minimum living wage, at long last an eight-hour day, the establishment of factory commissions to settle grievances, and standards for factory hygiene. Compulsory state pensions were introduced, as well as benefits for unemployment and disability; together with a nationwide network of job centres and better job opportunities for women. Some good had come out of the war.

The 1929 Wall Street crash and the ensuing world depression hit the Italian economy badly, especially the core sectors of steel, cars and cotton. Many Italian firms and banks became insolvent, such as *Banco di Roma, Credito* and yet again BCI. The situation became untenable, even the Bank of Italy wobbled. In 1936 Beneduce created the *Legge Bancaria* banking law which split the hold between industry and banks by having the latter deal solely with retail (private) clients. In 1928 Mussolini signed treaties with Germany, giving Italy access to Europe's largest market; also with Soviet Russia, whose government he agreed to recognise. Mindful of previous banking crises, and keen to establish economic self-sufficiency, in 1933 the Mussolini government set up IRI *Istituto Ricostruzione Italiana*, inspired by General Franco's similar model in Spain, and replacing CSVI. IRI was a mix of public/private initiative which undertook to administer industrial and financial holdings, providing a low interest credit facility and tax breaks in return for owning shares in these organisations, thereby imitating the earlier German mixed banks.

IRI was managed during 1933-39 by Alberto Beneduce, a technocrat who dominated the post-war Italian economy. IRI took over Alfa Romeo, Banco di Roma, Credito and BCI, together with the Comit Bank and the old *Banco di Santo Spirito* in Genova. IRI's other role was to liquidate bankrupt industries or sell them off to the private sector: many in fact continued to be run as private enterprises. By 1937 IRI was authorised to buy new companies, thereby increasing significantly Fascism's state control of the economy. Two new public banks appeared in the 1940s: *Mediocrediti* and *Mediobanca.* Under the aegis of Enrico Cuccia (son-in-law of Alberto Beneduce), who had begun his career at Comit in 1938, *Mediobanca* lay at the heart of Italian industry and finance for half a century. During the 1950s, public banking accounted for 80% of the total sector. Beneduce also ran IMI *Istituto Immobiliare Italiano*, set up as a state bank in 1931, until 1936. In 1933 IMI was allowed to issue corporate bonds.

By 1938 IRI was the largest industrial group, second only to Soviet Russia in terms of nationalisation. It was also the largest state-controlled agency *ente pubblico,* eventually managing some 600 subsidiaries. Managed by technical professionals, by 1948 IRI employed 216,000 people, of whom some 160,000 were involved in manufacturing. Overall IRI controlled 45% of steel, including ILVA in Genoa, and 77% of cast iron production through Italsider (incorporated into Finsider in 1937). 90% of shipbuilding was managed through Fincantieri; plus 82% of shipping and 12% of electricity generation; also textiles. After 1945 IRI moved into other areas: aircraft and airport construction together with the Alitalia airline; the three state television channels RAI 1/2/3 combined with advertising; post-war city planning and motorway construction, for instance the Italian half of the Mont Blanc tunnel and the *Autostrada del Sole* begun in 1956, to link the north with the south, and completed in 1963; Italcimenti; SME foodstuffs conglomerate; hotels and catering; Italcable; STET telecommunications and its subsidiaries SIP telephones, SIRTI telecom construction and Finsiel electronics. In 1948 IRI acquired Finmeccanica Engineering which embraced the Ansaldo engineering company. By the 1930s, Ansaldo employed over 30,000 workers in steel, engineering and shipping, placing Genoa on a par with Turin. Its port, Italy's largest, was a hive of activity, with 23,000 sailors and 8,000 dockers. Furthermore IRI arranged commercial agreements with foreign state enterprise.

Mussolini's drive for imperialism, such as the invasion of Abyssinia in 1935, brought lucrative orders for military equipment, notably for Ilva, Ansaldo and Fiat. During this period overall industrial production increased by 7.5%. After the war many Liberal economists and businessmen advocated the dismantling of IRI and placing the companies in the private sector. However, the policy of the Christian Democrat DC party prevailed by grouping engineering and shipbuilding under the new Finmeccanica holding, which later acquired Agusta helicopters. Over time IRI turned increasingly to the private joint stock market for finance rather than rely heavily on Treasury funding.

ENI *Ente Idrocarburi Italiano* was the other massive state corporation, which provided national energy. Established in Rome in 1953 as a private/public entity like IRI, ENI eventually controlled over 300 subsidiaries, foremost among them being the huge AGIP oil company *Azienda Generale Italiana Petroli* founded in 1926, and which later moved into nuclear energy. With its vast plant at Ravenna, AGIP rose to become the world's sixth largest petrochemicals company. *Snamprogetti* headed up ENI's engineering and construction division. Composed of five major divisions, ENI further diversified into hotels and motorways, synthetic rubber, steel piping and textiles. The DC politicians sensibly retained the professional and technical managers appointed by the Fascist government, who were often Republicans or Liberals. They were usually long serving which provided continuity of policy.

Chief amongst them was ENI's first boss Enrico Mattei, a former partisan, who successfully established advantageous contracts with the Middle East for the supply of vital oil supplies, to the exclusion of American and British middlemen. His international contacts and commercial power made him Italy's unofficial foreign ambassador. He founded the newspaper *Il Giorno*, which lauded the virtues of his exploits. ENI's ability to supply cheap energy was a decisive factor in Italy's rapidly growing economy. In 1962 Mattei died in a suspicious air crash. Italy has no significant indigenous reserves of raw materials such as coal, iron or oil. In 1949 natural gas (methane) was found in the Po valley, but was exhausted by 2000, by which time Italy had become dependent on supplies from Russia and Algeria. In 1992 ENI became a private joint stock company.

The Dictator's thrust towards economic self-sufficiency encouraged research into new synthetic products, given Italy's limited supply of raw materials. An important chemicals and electrometallurgical sector developed, centred on Porto Marghera, Venice. By 1933 the value added in industry had at last overtaken agriculture. Building on earlier development in the 19th century, the centre/north-east area became increasingly important, especially Emilia, Marche, Tuscany and Veneto. Firms, often employing up to just twenty employees or sometimes up to 250, used up-to-date technologies built on their vibrant artisanal tradition formed during medieval times and the Renaissance, to expand into the sectors of clothes, leather goods, ceramics and furniture; and which would form the basis of the post-war SMEs small and medium enterprises. Southern industry was not neglected, with IRI investing in the steel works at Bagnoli, as well as shipbuilding and aeronautics at Taranto and Bari. Yet the input was insufficient to place the area on a par with the North: the South accounted for only 18% of industry nationwide, with small factories and limited mechanisation.

By 1938 industrial production nationwide had regained 1929 levels but it came at a price: a vast budget deficit, together with greater personal taxation which depressed wages and upset the prudent middle class. Mussolini attempted to bring galloping inflation under control by implementing Quota 90: an exchange rate of 90 lira to the Pound Sterling. The absence of large financially stable companies, due partly to undercapitalised banks, together with the perennial dearth of raw materials, were to hamper Italy's military performance during World War Two. Mussolini knew this, hence his reluctance to rush into a military alliance with Hitler.

In 1956 the new Ministry of Holdings was created to assume responsibility for all the public sector agencies. In 1962 EFIM—*Ente Partecipazione e Finanziamento Industria*—was set up to take charge of mechanical engineering and, together with IRI, ENI and IMI, set up GEPI *Societa per la Gestione di Partecipazioni Industriali*, a new state holding in 1971, in order to limit state liability and control by selling off failed companies. In 1962 EFIM nationalized electricity by setting up ENEL. These four state holdings controlled over a thousand subsidiaries, accounted for one third of Italian sales and half of its fixed investment in the early years.

These massive holdings lay at the heart of *Sottogoverno* since they fell under the aegis of the government which effectively controlled the pursestrings and management of the country's essential industries. The Italian state's partnership with the private economy was governed by a paternalistic partnership of politicians, bankers and technocrats, and resembled the Fascist model of a planned economy. In effect the ruling politicians appointed pliable directors, which gave rise to *partitocrazia:* the parcelling out of posts to coalition parties, with the bosses wielding immense power over the allocation of contracts. For instance, many regional banks were allocated to the various factions, as well as the new credit institutions. However, stronger managers began to challenge the DC's monopoly of state corporations, for example Eugenio Cefis, head of ENI. The Italian state was now set to participate in the Economic Miracle.

Chapter Three
The Southern Question

In 1860 the Italian population stood at some 32 million, on a par with England and compared with 36 million in France. At this time, the Peninsula was essentially a rural society, with some 60% engaged in agriculture. Payment was predominantly in kind since disposable cash was scarce, and was spent on food, clothing and shelter. Commerce was further hindered by poor roads, especially in winter. Italy was second to France in wheat production, yet its fast-growing population required imports from that country, also from England and Germany. Consumption of maize (corn) was so high that many suffered from pellagra, a skin disease leading to dementia. Sugar, hemp, flax (linen) and rice were grown in the north; whilst silk production was an important industrial export. During the 1890s sugar beet was introduced to boost sugar supplies.

The most prosperous and efficient farming areas were Lombardy and Piedmont in the north, employing the most advanced techniques. Central regions also fared well: Tuscany and the fertile Lombardy Plain/Po valley, together with the Emilia-Romagna region, thanks to enlightened and progressive owners and agronomists during the 18th century.[10] The principal crops were grain, olive oil and wine. In Tuscany the Grand Duke Leopold sold off many of his vast estates to tenant farmers to boost grain production, creating the equitable *mezzadria* sharecropping system (also practised in Emilia-Romagna, Umbria, Marche and parts of the Veneto) whereby tenant farmers leased the land in return for a share of the profits, and which deterred emigration. The *mezzadro* landlord exerted considerable influence over his men: for instance his consent was required to work elsewhere or for marriage. Security of tenure could be hazardous, whilst crippling taxation often led to serious indebtedness. During the 19th century the

---

[10] See author's book: *From Subjugation to Independence*

rice-growing areas of the Po delta and Piedmont invested in machinery, fertilisers, pesticides, land reclamation, training and technical back-up. Here farms were worked on a commercial basis whereby agreements were established with value added food processing firms.

The South constitutes 40% of the Italian Peninsula and covers the regions of Campania, Basilicata, Calabria, Puglia, Abruzzo, Molise, together with the islands of Sicily and Sardinia. The most productive regions in the South were Bari, together with the coastal tracts of the Terre d'Otranto in the Gulf of Taranto in southern Puglia; and the rich volcanic soils of Mount Etna in eastern Sicily. These zones, covering 10% of the South but containing half of its population, produced olive oil, wine, olives and citrus fruits; with a mix of mainly large farms and some small peasant holdings. In the 19th century, most of this produce was exported to France and Russia. Livestock were raised in Lazio; whilst Sardinia's main activity was sheep farming.

The poor mountainous areas were dotted with small peasant holdings, whence many emigrated during the 1880s-1930s. During 1860-1914, some 2.5 million people left the South, being about half its total population. Elsewhere the hills, extensive plains and plateaux of the interior were the domain of the large-scale landowners, together with some tenant farmers, both of whom employed the *braccianti* landless labourers. Their *latifondi* large estates accounted for 80% of the land in Sicily, and were put over to wheat cultivation and winter pasture. They were extensive, ostensibly to ensure a decent income from unenriched soil. The South had suffered widespread deforestation by the Romans seeking timber for their vast fleets, leading to critical erosion. The Greeks settled in the area during the 7th-8th centuries; followed in the 9th century by the Arabs, who cared for the land and introduced new crops. As elsewhere in the Peninsula, the South possesses no indigenous supplies of either coal or iron ore, whilst the shallow erratic rivers do not favour HEP.

The Normans arrived in the early 11th century, and proceeded to ruin the Arabs' achievements by imposing their hierarchical feudal system, suppressing the civic independence of the free cities and maritime republics such as Amalfi, Naples and Palermo. They inflicted heavy taxation on the merchants and wheat-growing landowners, which hindered agricultural improvement, to the detriment of the export trade through the ports. Monoculture of wheat exhausted the minimal topsoil, with no sheep or cattle to fertilise it; further ruined by summer drought and landslides, hailstorms and autumn winds. The South was and is a country of desolate beauty, but presents a challenging environment for human existence: *Chi ara diritto muore disperato*: 'He who ploughs straight dies desperate.'

Malaria was endemic on the plains which, together with tuberculosis and other respiratory illnesses, engendered a feeling of apathy and resignation. During the late 19th century, the disease killed about 15,000 souls a year. The rural worker was reduced to eking out an existence, and nothing more, by renting at high cost small widely dispersed feudal strips of land from the landowner, performing seasonal work on the great man's estate, and tending his own meagre plot for subsistence crops. In their profound despair, they sought refuge in a pagan religiosity, together with their family and village ties. Women were treated little better than beasts of burden. Naples and Palermo had experienced medieval parliaments but they were controlled by the factional nobility.

During the two hundred years of domination by the Spaniards in the 16th and 17th centuries, the South suffered punitive taxation and military conscription to fight the Spanish wars abroad. They introduced their Mesta system for sheep rearing, centred on Puglia, collecting exorbitant rents from grazing rights. The Southern economy could not withstand such a load. Indolent Spanish grandees neglected their estates, which deteriorated over time in the production of just wheat and olives. The Church also possessed vast estates in the region. The absentee landlords inherited the legacy of Spanish arrogance and disdain of work, neglecting their serfs, and viewing the quantity of land and labourers as a status symbol. They frittered away their vast unearnt incomes on the pleasures of the few towns, notably Naples, the largest city in the Peninsula at that time with over 450,000 inhabitants by 1871; and with Italy's oldest university dating back to 1224. At least the Spanish court sustained a flourishing silk industry, together with other luxury goods produced in Palermo. Naples and Palermo had experienced medieval governments but they were controlled by the factional nobility. Given this parlous state of affairs it is hardly surprising that brigandage was rife in the South.

Joseph Bonaparte, Napoleon's brother and king of Naples 1806-08, carried out some drainage and irrigation schemes. He ordained that 25% of demesne common lands, used for pasturage and gleaning, and purloined during the 18th century by the landowners, should be returned to the peasants which were theirs by historic legal right: predictably they refused. During the 1820s/30s, the government of the day had attempted to hold down the price of wheat, lessen taxation and redistribute estate land to the poor, but the landowners blocked that scheme too.

In the South, the feudal landowner barons treated their peasant serfs harshly, exacting high rents on short term tenancies, which led to constant indebtedness and instability. *Braccianti* were hired on a daily or weekly basis. According to Judith Chubb,[11] with the disintegration of feudalism families grouped together for loyalty and defence; although brothers fought bitterly over the division of their meagre portion of land inheritance. Rival family units offered protection against the unruly barons and landlords in the absence of any other legitimate authority, which engendered mistrust and suspicion of the city states in the distant north, which for centuries were often in alliance with or controlled by foreign powers. Anyone from north of Rome was looked upon with suspicion and hostility; likewise the northern perception of the south.

The North presented quite a different picture. Following the wave of invasions after the fall of the Roman Empire, autonomous communes grew up during the 11th-12th centuries. The Lombards from central Asia crucially retained the Roman administrative system, absent in the South and built upon the old Roman *municipiae*, the strongest of which developed into powerful city states such as Venice, Milan and Genoa. Those working as artisans in the towns and later cities developed a strong worker base which would later develop into mass political movements. Northern farmers boosted their input and reaped fat profits which were recycled into agricultural improvements, but which resulted in a reduction of manual labour, so farmers used *braccianti* only when needed, such as for sowing and the harvest. Artificially high prices led to overproduction in sugar: an early type of Common Market surplus. In the 1880s, the national government adopted a policy of colonial expansion to relieve population pressure and economic penury, begun in Eritrea and Abyssinia, but the venture proved disastrous.

With unification in 1861, the northern government endeavoured to impose its power on the South, but to little avail, since by now banditry had become too well entrenched, exacerbated by the Spanish custom of vendetta. Few Southerners were allocated government posts since they were considered untrustworthy. Origins of the Mafia possibly date back to the arrival of the Arabs, which caused the indigenous population to seek refuge on higher ground from the invader. In the absence of any other authority, over time the Mafia came to

---

[11] J.Dunnage: *20th Century History*

dominate southern Calabria and western Sicily (the eastern part being dominated by Mount Etna and so devoid of large estates). They crafted a tight social web of interfamilial ties and rivalry for survival through *comparaggio*: a close friend or village leader acting as godfather to the children of friends. Over time, the Mafia came to replicate the Norman feudal system in its pyramidal organisation. Organised in small armies, they defended the peasants against the *gabelloto*: originally tenant farmers but who often managed the *latifondo* in the landlords' long absences. The Mafia's more illegal activities concerned cattle rustling, smuggling and control of water supplies. Violence and extortion, such as exaction of the *pizzo* protection payment, were practised if need be to ensure obedience and inculcate a sense of fear. The Mafia code of *omertā* silence derives from the Normans: '*Chi parla more, chi tace campa*': 'He who speaks dies, he who remains silent lives'.

The first official mention of the Mafia occurs in northern documents dating from 1865. Martial law was frequently imposed to deal with the many insurrections by the peasants. By the mid 1860s, up to 100,000 troops were deployed in the war against brigandage. One of the worst uprisings occurred in 1866, involving 40,000 rioters in Palermo, Sicily where military conscription was bitterly resented. The city was bombarded, and many rioters, including women, were arrested or executed. Garibaldi harangued the deputies in Turin for creating 'a fratricidal war' through their dreadful treatment of the Southerners, many of whom had nobly fought with him in 1860 to banish the foreign interloper. The Mafia took advantage of the fluid northern politics of *trasformismo* shifting alliances to extract an understanding that they continue to manage the South, in return for which they would guarantee electoral support, acting as intermediary between the state and local society. They took control of elections through the landowner and his *gabelloto* foreman who acted as go-between, harrowing people to vote as directed by his boss and the Mafia. The local prefect, who represented the national government, also took care to ensure politically correct voting. Thus began the spread of *clientelismo* to the South. Over time the Mafia became involved in legal affairs, protection rackets, prostitution, transport and local produce markets, price fixing and post-war construction. During World War Two the Americans availed themselves of assistance from the Mafia, thereby unwittingly strengthening their power in the absence of any other legitimate force.

In the 1870s, Liberal free trade ministers allowed in cheap imports of American and Russian wheat to feed the burgeoning population. This policy depressed Italian agriculture nationwide; although vine exports held up well owing to the spread of the phylloxera disease in France. In 1887 northern industrialists, in a spirit of equality, felt that they should support the farming community by extending the 1876 customs tariff barrier to wheat; also sugar, hemp and rice. However, this policy sparked off a tariff war with the French which particularly affected Southern exports of oil, wine and citrus fruits; also with Russia. Wheat imports duly fell, but in the South the guaranteed high prices discouraged even further any incentive by the idle *galantuomini* landowners to modernize their estates and increase productivity, let alone improve the dreadful semi-feudal living conditions of the starving peasantry, in particular the *braccianti* who were the most oppressed of the workforce.

The cheap grain imports and tariff war with France contributed to the agricultural slump of the late 1870s/80s, also prevalent throughout Europe, and led to widespread unemployment, especially in the Po valley where in 1884 a wave of often violent strikes broke out, led by the *braccianti*. They protested against the high grain milling tax, demanding better pay and working/living conditions. In 1869 there were riots in Emilia-Romagna against the milling tax. Their agitation was ruthlessly put down by the police and army, who also suppressed the recently-formed Socialist co-operatives and peasant leagues, modelled upon Mazzinian mutual aid societies from the 1840s. 1892 saw the beginnings of the *fasci* organisations in Sicily to improve the peasants' lot. Violence broke out and was crushed by 40,000 soldiers, sent by Prime Minister Crispi. Further uprisings broke out in Apulia and the Tavoliere tablelands of Foggia near Bari. Nationally over a quarter of the peasantry was disenfranchised as a result of the insurrections.

The electoral reform of 1882 was decisive in the future destiny of the South. Politicians generally agreed that universal suffrage would be imprudent, given the high level of illiteracy (78%) amongst the urban and rural workers, which made them ill-prepared to have a say in how they were governed. Universal suffrage was increased from 2% to 7% of the electorate, viz. from under half a million to over two million voters. It worked in favour of the lower classes in the more populated northern towns, and to the disadvantage of the more backward rural South where there existed greater illiteracy, and where the few voters were mainly lawyers, journalists and mature students. The Southern landowners, who

55

formed a block vote of up to 40% in the Chamber of Deputies, reinforced this scenario by opposing the reform for fear of encouraging Socialism, by means of exacting a literacy qualification which excluded two-thirds of their peasantry. For this same reason they also opposed industry in the South, allowing the Northern politicians and industrialists to take the lead in government and the economy; in return for non-interference in the South, where the economic base was restricted to local government and the law, with occasional public works projects to keep the locals content. Thus thanks to this incongruous pact nothing changed. In the 1890s, Crispi planned to divide up the larger Sicilian estates and lease the land to the peasants, but predictably his scheme was also thwarted by the landowners.

On a more positive note, the electoral reform did encourage extremists to divert their enthusiasm into the quieter parliamentary channels of Socialism. In 1881 the anarchist Andrea Costa founded the Revolutionary Socialist Party in the Po valley, and a year later became the first Socialist parliamentary deputy. Socialism was strong in Tuscany, Umbria, Puglia and Sicily, but especially in the Po valley with its large group of landless labourers. Socialist ideas were later encouraged by the eventual granting of the vote in 1912.

The Giolittian period at last brought improvement to the South, thanks to Francesco Nitti, a Liberal economist. In 1904 a special law was passed to set up the Bagnoli steel works near Naples, and a hydroelectric plant on the river Volturno (site of Garibaldi's decisive victory in 1860), and which supplied electricity to Naples and the Campania region. A public works programme was set up for the poorest regions of Basilicata and Calabria (previously directed only in the North): aqueducts, drainage and reclamation, reafforestation, drinking water, farm buildings, together with much needed tax incentives and loans to individual farmers; plus relief for the Messina earthquake in 1908.

Prior to the 1880s, many Italians from the north of the Peninsula undertook seasonal work in France, Austria, Belgium and Switzerland, and especially Germany. However, they were not always welcome since they accepted lower wages. Here they became acquainted with Socialist ideas and trade unionism which they eventually took back to their homeland, together with new working methods. The northern government's failure to address the Southern Question led to a mass exodus to the Americas: between 1881 and 1900 some 4.7 million Italians left their homeland, of which about half returned; followed by six million during 1900-1915, of which about 80% came back. They sailed on a cheap passage to the New World to work on the building sites and in factories; domestic service was another important job sector for women. To sum up, it is estimated (historical figures are somewhat unreliable) that, out of a total population of 34 million, during 1871-1920 some 13 million souls emigrated to the Americas, mostly to the United States but also to Brazil and Argentina. Indeed many political exiles had fled to the New World in the 19th century, Garibaldi being one.

Recent research[12] suggests that many migrant Italians returned, of which half were day labourers from the South, usually going abroad to lighten the family burden. Many brought back not only funds but also new methods and political ideas. After 1921, the United States introduced an immigrant quota, thereby closing a vital safety valve for the South. Many who returned were bitterly disappointed by the impossibility of making a smallholding a viable concern, mainly because the plot was too small and infertile: the prime reason for their initial emigration.

The post-war wave of industrial unrest, known as the *Biennio Rosso* of 1919-20, also involved widespread mass agitation by the farming industry. By 1920 over a million rural workers had gone on strike. *Federterra*, the Communist Federation of Agricultural Workers, had amassed 900,000 supporters, particularly the *braccianti* on the large estates of the Po valley and the *mezzadri* sharecroppers in Puglia and Sicily. Encouraged by wartime solidarity against the enemy, their combined front won them some important concessions. Henceforth the farmers would use only *Federterra*'s employment exchanges for hiring labour, with a fixed number of workers per hectare of land *imponibile*, higher wages for the *braccianti* and an improved sharecropping agreement. In Tuscany and Umbria half a million Socialist sharecroppers downed tools in 1920, having previously struck in 1902 and 1906. They secured over half of the harvest, with the greater onus of the production costs being passed to the landlord. They also gained security of tenure, annual settling of accounts to avoid long term indebtedness, and involvement in farm management. Post-war inflation had eroded land rent values, which allowed the more prosperous sharecroppers and tenant farmers to buy up land and enlarge their smallholdings. In the South, it was usually the Catholic peasant leagues and war veterans who took over land to sow it and then demanded payment from the landowner.

---

[12] *20th Century Italy*, p14

Mussolini's regime waxed lyrical over the joys of rural life, but the reality was somewhat different. The 'battle for grain' policy aimed at self-sufficiency and guaranteed an attractive price, so that farmers could afford to invest in new techniques and replace labourers with machinery. However, wheat monoculture impoverished the soil and reduced the cultivation of other crops, as well as holding back the beef and dairy sectors for lack of pasture. Nationally some eight million peasants continued to survive in semi-feudal conditions and in a state of perennial debt, caused by high taxation and a decline in agricultural prices for the produce consigned to the *ammassi* public granaries. Mussolini held back from dealing with the Southern Question, since he needed the support of the landowners who constituted a formidable group in the Chamber of Deputies, and who indeed controlled the PNF Fascist party in the South; and against whom the peasants had no alternative for political representation. For instance, *Il Duce* annulled decrees sanctioning the seizure of land by the peasants after the war. Furthermore, he only half-heartedly tried to clamp down on the Mafia in the 1920s, since his henchmen were hugger mugger with the *capi*.

Il Duce's agricultural adviser, Arrigo Serpieri, was keen to introduce a land reclamation scheme, to which the *latifondisti* landowners would have to contribute financially or be expropriated. They succeeded in cancelling the latter condition, which simply left the project in tatters. The sole achievement under the Fascists was the control of malaria by draining the Tuscan Maremma, where corn once grew, and the 60,000 hectares of the Pontine Marshes south of Rome; followed by the establishment of farms and settlements. The South was airbrushed out by the Fascist regime, since public discussions on crime and poverty were forbidden. The global crisis after 1929 exacerbated the Southern economy, since it damaged Southern exports of citrus fruits, which forced thousands of peasants to move north or emigrate. Now excluded from entry to the United States, during 1926-30 over one million Italians emigrated elsewhere in Europe and South America; also to the Italian colonies of Abyssinia, conquered in 1935, and Libya in 1911. Many moved north to Rome, where the service and public sectors were expanding. Most of these migrants were ill paid and resented by northern workers.

In 1940 one million Southerners were conscripted into the army, which at least alleviated population pressure in the region. The arrival of the Allies was a mixed blessing. Naples, now with a population of more than one million, was badly bombed and over 200,000 were left homeless. Inflation soared, fuelled by the Allied Amlire notes. Grain and other foodstuffs became critically scarce and dependent on a huge black market. The Allies were reliant on the Mafia for supplies, which were under their control. The Mafia engaged the services of the Italo-American bandit Salvatore 'Lucky' Giuliano, who had helped to prepare the Allied landings. On May Day in 1947, during the regional elections, he fired on a crowd of 1,500 people in Portella delle Ginestre to remind them of who ruled the city. Eleven perished and many were injured. On a more positive note, the Allies sprayed the South with DDT to eradicate malaria.

After 1945, many Italians moved to Australia and Canada, as well as to the USA; whilst some found employment in the Bedfordshire brickworks in England because they could withstand the heat of the furnaces. Once industry took off in the north-west of the Peninsula, during 1945-70 some four million southern Italians moved north, leaving behind the sick and the elderly, which only exacerbated the parlous condition of the Southern economy. They worked their way north in stages, via the main cities of Palermo, Naples and Rome, to join their relations in the factories of Fiat and a myriad other companies, working 10-12-hour shifts. The North profited immensely from this pool of cheap labour: Turin, a rapidly growing industrial city, rivalled Palermo and Naples for the number of its Southern immigrants. Between 1953 and 1973, there were some nine million internal migrants, peaking in the early years.

Reform

In 1944-46 Fausto Gullo, a Communist lawyer from Calabria, was Minister of Agriculture. He proposed far-reaching reforms relating to agrarian contracts, uncultivated land and bonuses to encourage the consignment of crops to the state granaries. Spurred on by Gullo's decrees and Communist support, during 1944-47 a quarter of a million starving peasants took it upon themselves to occupy 165,000 hectares of the vast estates with the intention of sowing, centred on Sicily, Calabria and Lazio, that had either been left barren by the landowners, or which they considered public property since they had previously been common demesne land. With the assistance of the Communist trade union CGIL, between 1944 and 1949 the rural workers set up 1,187 co-operatives numbering about 250,000 members; also Chambers of Labour, in order to assume collective responsibility and create nationwide solidarity.

Inevitably, given past history, this ground-breaking initiative was doomed to failure thanks to the wall of opposition presented by the landowners, the sixty-two nationwide prefects responsible for local government, the Mafia, the Liberal businessmen and the Christian Democrat DC political party, the latter as ever dependent on the crucial landowner vote. They demanded that the land allocation should be decided by local commissions consisting of the local magistrate, a landowner and a peasant, and so were automatically prejudiced against the latter. The upshot was that insufficient land was distributed. In Sicily only 987 demands for uncultivated land were granted, totalling 86,000 hectares, and poor-quality land at that; as against a rejection of 3,822 demands for 820,000h. Allocated to some 85,000 people, the average holding of only one hectare made the plot unviable. Gullo was unable to guarantee financial assistance to the co-operatives, so their members slid into disunity, their hopes bitterly dashed. The only scant consolation was the arrival of fifteen tractors from Russia.

In 1946 Gullo's scheme to offer bonuses and rent reductions to encourage the delivery of harvest produce to the state granaries was kicked into the long grass by Fascist magistrates and the Court of Cassation. Furthermore, Gullo failed to dislodge the farm estate foreman *gabelloto*, who operated as an aggressive intermediary between the landowner and the peasant. Togliatti, the PCI leader, was sympathetic towards Gullo's programme but remained neutral so as not to be excluded from the ruling coalition.

As in 1920, *Federterra* had greater success in lending support to the sharecroppers of central Italy. They demanded 60% of the harvest instead of 50%, security of tenure, equal management status and an end to the supply of free services and gifts (chickens, eggs, rabbits and wine). Eventually, it was Gullo's successor, the Christian Democrat Antonio Segni, a rich landowner from Sardinia, who awarded the sharecroppers 53% of the produce, with the landowners putting aside 4% for farm improvements. During 1947-49, 600,000 destitute landless labourers of the Po delta went on strike and managed to extract some essential concessions in their work and wage conditions. Segni then proceeded to undermine Gullo's efforts by allowing landowners to reclaim land if peasants had infringed certain conditions. As a result, in 1948 they swiftly seized back much of the land taken by the peasants during 1946-47.

In 1949 a second wave of widespread unrest broke out, which lasted for over a year. In Calabria 14,000 rural-folk set out on a march and occupied the great estates, distributing the land for sowing. At Melissa, in the Crotone *latifondo* area, they clashed with the police and three peasants were killed. Amazingly, given the gulf between North and South, the event caught the interest of the far northern newspapers such as *La Stampa* of Turin, whose historical source confirmed that half a million hectares of demesne land belonged to the peasants by right. The protests spread to Basilicata involving 20,000 peasants (one village was led by two women). In the Abruzzi the peasants organised a work-in, supported by a general strike in the area, to reclaim 2,500 hectares of Lake Fucino which had been drained in 1878 by Prince Torlonia, depriving the peasants of their fishing rights.

In Sicily the Bourbons had presented Admiral Nelson with a large estate (partly demesne land) in recognition of his assistance in the Neapolitan counter revolution of 1799. The peasants later killed the local citizens who had held on to the demesne land, but the land was not returned to the peasants. The widespread protests did have the desired effect of convincing the DC to again attempt reform in 1950 with two major schemes: the Sila law for Calabria and the Sicilian law. The programme would involve some 650,000ha over eight areas spread over 36 provinces, and to be expropriated from the large estates (as with Gullo's plan), and of which 70% lay in the South.

The Sila Law (named after the desolate Calabrian plateaux used mainly for sheep pasture) envisaged the expropriation of 573,000 hectares, with reform boards to distribute the land either as a *podere* small farm for those without land, or as a *quota* for those who already held smallholdings and who were expected to join a co-operative. Landowners were obliged to offer 'unimproved' land (used for pasture and without irrigation) so many craftily erected a shack to avoid confiscation. In Calabria only 15% of the total plan was allocated to peasants, representing 75% of the families. 60% of this land lay in the inhospitable hills and mountains, and previously was the domain of the *latifondisti;* 30% in the desolate Crotone area; and only 10% on the fertile coastal plain where olives, oranges and lemons were grown. The figures were in fact inflated since they included Gullo's original distribution to rural co-operatives.

At first, reasonable credit facilities were made available to the new landowners, but were later tightened up in 1957-58 in favour of the more profitable farms who were able to repay the loans, unlike the small and infertile holdings. A few prospered, whilst the rest held on until the Economic Miracle called them north. In the far south, some 14,000 farmsteads were built, of which 800 were sited in hamlets on the Sila plateaux, offering animal husbandry and later tourism. Three lakes were impounded for HEP. Co-operatives provided for wheat threshing; whilst irrigation facilities supported deciduous trees and vine planting, tobacco and sugar beet, together with fruit and vegetable production, such as tomatoes for canning, oranges, peaches apricots and peas. Training was offered to the new inexperienced farmholders.

In Sicily the reform board was rife with corruption and overflowing with surplus clerks, many of whom voted DC in return for job security. By 1954 only 4,300 families had received 19,000 hectares in tiny plots out of the total 74,000ha made available. Other areas fared better, for instance the Tuscan Maremma where the reform board acquired 182,000ha along the Tyrrhenian coast between Pisa and Rome, where larger *poderi* with 16-hectare plots were sensibly offered. To sum up, the 1950 reforms proved woefully inadequate in land redistribution, failing in the reform of agrarian contracts, land reclamation and wages of the *braccianti*. The boards failed to assist with housing, irrigation, credit and technical advice. Segni's farming contract was approved by the Chamber of Deputies and the Senate, only to be quietly shelved thanks to pressure from the landowners. Steps towards trade union control over the *collocamento* employment were reversed back in favour of the landowners. The *imponibile* suffered a similar fate, being declared illegal by the Constitutional Court in 1958. For their part, the landowners felt betrayed by the DC who had dented their centuries-old power over the South, and many moved to the far right. The DC had eventually heeded the desperate pleas and demonstrations of the poor peasants, but had failed to secure adequate reform, leaving them bitterly disappointed.

Despite the many tortuous setbacks and lacklustre progress, the DC embarked on a third phase of Southern reform. In an effort to promote support amongst small conservative farmers to combat Communist influence, the government offered long term mortgages on generous terms. This enabled peasants to buy up 667,000 hectares by 1956. *Coldiretti*, the DC's Catholic association of peasant proprietors founded by Paolo Bonomi in 1944, who ran the Ministry of Agriculture, became increasingly involved in the management of state funds for rural areas. It took over the state organisation of *Federconsorzi*, which distributed farming machinery and fertilisers; credit facilities; and offered agricultural training. With a membership of 1.6 million families by 1956, *Coldiretti* held big rallies extolling the virtues of the rural family, and promoted the continuance of local dialects and folk traditions. Bonomi stole a march on the Communists by offering the Catholic version of paternalist welfare for the needy. He persuaded Deputies, of whom he held fifty in his pocket, to sanction the creation of *Casse Mutue* which offered pensions for old age and invalidity (the latter awarded subjectively with the connivance of the local doctor employed by the *Cassa*) together with health insurance to peasant farmers. These measures at last put rural workers on an equal footing with their urban counterparts.

In 1950, and after almost a century since unification, the Christian Democrats were still determined to improve the plight of the Southerners, and keen to promote small conservative farmers to combat Communism. They set up the *Cassa per il Mezzogiorno* Southern Fund, which would prove to be definitive in the long-term development of the South. The Fund covered the regions south of Rome (Campania, Basilicata and Apulia), the central regions of Molise and Abruzzi, together with the islands of Sicily and Sardinia. Both the Fund and the agrarian reform boards received finance from Marshall Aid, for which Bonomi was responsible. It was yet again planned to redistribute the land more equably by breaking up the *latifondi* into five-hectare farms; but the project proved defective, with the perennial reason that it left many with too small a plot of infertile soil. Some unscrupulous landowners had earlier parcelled up their estates to avoid division, or used outright bribery. The *Cassa* encouraged co-operative societies to sell their produce to the North, facilitated by the construction of the *Autostrada del Sole*; introduced mechanisation; the building of dams for water and HEP; and improved irrigation, for instance the Apulian aqueduct. Yet these reforms benefited just a meagre 5% of the rural population.

Billions of lire were poured into the Fund, which was managed by party officials who were often the local landowner acting as party deputy for the ruling DC, and who came to be used as a vehicle for political patronage: *clientelismo*. Often it was the *gabelloto* estate foreman who liaised between his absentee boss/party deputy and his labourers, cajoling and threatening them to support their employer; and calling upon the services of the Mafia to assist him should the need arise. The ruling DC's supporters, be they friends, family or the Mafia, were favoured with public works contracts, subsidies and employment, in return for their vote. The civil service, centred on burgeoning Naples, provided abundant jobs for the rising middle class, now wedged between the landowners and peasantry. Hunger was a more powerful weapon than ideology: the alternative to no job was a life of crime, probably with the Mafia, otherwise emigration or heading north to the factories in search of a better life. Dominant on the *latifondi* of western Sicily, rival Mafia 'family' groups offered protection of the land, providing a type of security absent from the official state organisms.

In 1954 the DC Prime Minister Amintore Fanfani persuaded his Finance Minister, Ezio Vanoni, to draw up a Plan aimed at creating four million new jobs in the non-agricultural sector of the South. By 1958 the Vanoni Plan (plans and laws are usually named after their initiator) had created 2.6 million jobs, but without narrowing the economic-cultural gap with the North. Italian farmers hoped to benefit from the 1958 EEC Mansholt Plan, part of the Common Agricultural Policy CAP, together with the Italian Green Plans of 1961 and 1966. Mansholt guaranteed minimum prices to farmers; an intervention price to buy surplus produce; plus an import duty on non EEC foodstuffs. The grants targeted electrification and irrigation which favoured the already profitable larger scale capitalist farmers in the centre and north, with their foodstuffs destined for the north European markets; yet at the expense of the smaller and uneconomic Mediterranean cultivators and their more modest produce. The Plans also took arable land out of cultivation (set aside). By 1963 Italy was sufficient only in rice, fruit, vegetables and wine, producing less than France or Germany; also less meat, milk and sugar. In 1950, 38% of the workforce toiled on the land, reduced to 12% by 1983, mainly in the South where large families were needed to make ends meet, if they were lucky. In the 1950s, per capita income in the South was 40% of that in the North, rising to 48% by 1967.

In the end many Southern landowners retained most of their estates and the poor were left with even less productive holdings; thus yet again a return to the *status quo ante*. Little had changed in the South. The Southern system replicated the feudal bond between landowner and peasant; the 19th century arrangement between Northern and Southern deputies; and the Fascist approach of offering job and pay security in return for electoral support, by obliging the peasant to vote for his master. Such a long-standing arrangement suited the DC in order to increase their share of the vote, which compensated for the strong left-wing presence in the Centre/North; and lessened their reliance on the Church to influence peasant voters.

The Mafia took advantage of the fluid northern politics of *trasformismo* shifting alliances, by which they extracted an understanding from the DC that they would continue to manage the South, in return for which they would guarantee electoral support, acting as intermediary between the state and local society. They controlled elections through the landowner and his *gabelloto* foreman who acted as go-between, harrowing people to vote as directed by his boss and the Mafia. The local prefect, who represented the government in the far north, also took care to ensure politically correct voting. The Mafia became involved in legal affairs, protection rackets, transport and local produce markets. Over time, the DC was locked in ever closer to the forces of the Mafia, which bode ill for the future.

Industry in the South

In the 1950s, De Gasperi was instrumental in setting up the *Cassa* Fund to finance badly needed infrastructure and agriculture in the South. However, realising that this policy had failed to sufficiently develop the Southern economy or combat the high rate of unemployment, the DC decided to reverse the post-war trend of attracting southern labour to the northern factories, by prodding major industries to move south, thereby narrowing the economic gap with the North and encourage national unity. Northern industrialists were highly reluctant to relocate since they foresaw the pitfalls of being caught in the vice of political *clientelismo* and organised crime which demanded their cut.

In response to pressure from Southern politicians such as Emilio Colombo, Prime Minister 1970-72, and Giulio Pastore, Minister for the South, in 1957 the government passed a law allocating 40% of IRI's total investment capability and 60% of its industrial plant investment to the South; plus 12% of the *Cassa* budget viz.30 billion lire rising to L230bn by 1973: a total of over L8,000 billion during 1957-75. The major development areas *poli di sviluppo* centred on Lazio south of Rome, Naples-Caserta-Salerno, Bari-Brindisi-Taranto in Puglia; and Catania-Augusta-Siracusa along the coast of eastern Sicily; together with smaller industrial nuclei. The poorest areas of Calabria, Basilicata and Molise were largely ignored, creating a two-tier South. Environmental matters were also tackled, for instance a project aimed at cleaning the heavily polluted Gulf of Naples, but to little effect and at great cost.

During the 1960s, Finsider, part of the giant IRI state holding, established a huge steel making complex at Taranto (a naval base since the 1940s) on the southern coast of Puglia, involving five blast furnaces, which became the largest in Europe and rivalled Germany's output. 50,000 workers applied for the 5,000 jobs. Taranto specialised in steel pipes for the Saharan oilfields; also cement, refractories, and metal manufacture. Bari became a centre for oil refining and mechanical engineering. ANIC, a subsidiary of ENI, developed a petrochemicals plant at Gela in southern Sicily, employing over 2,500 workers by 1967. Colombo and Pastore cajoled major captains of northern industry into making their contribution to the South, through financial enticements of a non-repayable grant of 20% of the initial investment, combined with a 70% loan repayable over 15 years at 4% interest; and supplemented by tax relief. SIR set up two petrochemical plants at Porto Torres and Cagliari in Sardinia; Olivetti established its presence at Pozzuoli near Naples; Fiat built a factory at Poggioreale in Sicily; whilst Montecatini erected a vast petrochemical/plastics works at Brindisi. Top jobs tended to be taken by Northern specialists.

In 1968 Alfa Romeo set up its Alfasud car plant at Pomigliano d'Arco near Naples, thanks to pressure from Silvio Gava, the local DC leader. However, it suffered from a combination of low production levels, inefficient management and the 1973 oil crisis. Costs ballooned sky high thanks to Mafia meddling and rife corruption at all levels: it cost a million lire to produce one sole car, resulting in a huge company loss which eventually brought down the company nationally: it was sold off by IRI in 1986.

A fifth steel complex, part of the Colombo Package, was planned for Finsider at Gioia Tauro near the sleepy Calabrian town of Reggio Calabria, partly to compensate for the town's rejection in 1970 as the regional capital in favour of Catanzaro, and which had provoked a year's protest. The town's main activity was based on a myriad of small retail shops which made it impossible to earn a decent per capita income. Only 5,000 people in the whole of Calabria worked in large stable firms. In 1969 riots in Battiopaglia had broken out when local factories were threatened with closure. Finsider was reluctant to proceed since there was no ready-made industrial hinterland. Furthermore, the area dwells in a high-risk seismic zone: in 1908 Reggio had suffered from a serious earthquake, with many still living in the 'temporary' huts in the '70s. Fertile groves of citrus fruits and olives were grubbed up and a huge port erected. The plan envisaged 7,500 jobs and the production of 4.5million tons of flat laminates for cars and electro-domestic goods. Predictably the Mafia and the Calabrian 'Ndrangheta cashed in on the lucrative infrastructure contracts.

Finsider's worst fears were realised. The initiatives in steel and cars came at the time of the steel recession due to saturation in the global construction sector, exacerbated by the oil crisis in 1973 and the consequent spike in prices, which badly hit these so-called 'cathedrals in the desert', now drifting against the global trend with their huge fixed costs. Taranto, with a planned doubling of capacity from 2m to 4m tons by 1972, came on stream just as the crisis broke. Chemical plants constructed in Sardinia, Sicily and Calabria never came into operation for the same reason.

Local politicians and trade unions urged Finsider to press on with the plans for the cold rolling mill to produce 200,000 tons per annum. Production was scaled down by the mid 70s and the project was kept alive to entice EEC funding; but it remained unviable and was finally scrapped in 1978. Insurmountable debts at Gioia Tauro and Taranto, combined with political and criminal meddling, eventually brought down Finsider's operations in the north. Gianni Agnelli, boss of Fiat, spoke of the 'Italian risk: terrorism, the dark interstices of public life, the kidnappings, the Mafia, the Camorra, the payoff'. Furthermore, he spoke of the 'southern Italian risk', referring to worker absenteeism, low productivity, labour unrest and low mobility.[13] Not all was lost. During the 1990s, an enterprising shipowner envisaged the potential of transforming the unfinished port of Gioia Tauro into a transhipment terminal for container ships, the new age of transport. Well placed on Mediterranean sea routes, especially for Asian trade, by 2013 Gioia Tauro had become the largest container port in Europe; and has even managed to resist extortion by the 'Ndrangheta.

Mindful of past militancy in Turin and Genoa, judicious siting of the plants had carefully dispersed pools of labour in order to minimise trade union/worker disruption, especially by metalworkers. Fazed by the overnight transformation from a backward rural economy into an industrial base, high levels of absenteeism occurred since the men were unused to the regimented monotony of assembly work. Strikes occurred, sometimes provoked by the Mafia. Those who failed to find industrial work poured into the major cities of Naples, Palermo, Bari and Catania, hoping for a job in the burgeoning civil service, which was also infested by the Camorra and 'Ndrangheta. In Naples some 800,000 out of the total population of 1.2 million had no fixed income, whilst some 280,000 destitute souls survived on hawking contraband goods in the meanest of living conditions, their sole comfort being the now ubiquitous television set. The rural poor became the urban poor, sliding into drugs and crime. Both Palermo and Naples sprawled outwards in haphazard fashion, with barely a thought for sensible planning and ruining the environment in the process.

Towards the end of the 1970s, some success was achieved in establishing small private businesses SMEs, such as clothing and furniture in Abruzzo, electronics and textiles in Caserta; and tourism, for instance along the Amalfi

---

[13] Spotts & Wieser page236

coast. Many of these artisanal firms were started up by the fresh input of the younger generation; however, they suffered from being undercut by cheaper mass-produced goods from the North, and were held back by the lack of disposable cash to encourage a strong consumer base. Agricultural workers had little time for running an ancillary business, except for tomato canning and fruit packing. Over time, people turned to the new trades such as electrician and car mechanic, or joined the swelling pool of public employees. Between 1951 and 1976 Southern GDP doubled but was still far below that of the North. The *Cassa* increased investment from 28% of the national total in 1969 to 34% by 1973, but failed to significantly boost employment: it was abolished in 1984 by referendum. During 1945-70, some four million southerners went north or to Switzerland and the EU. Henceforth the South came to depend on government transfer (welfare) payments and structural funds from the EU (the Italian South was its greatest beneficiary) but with predictable inefficiency and corruption. The South was ruled jointly by the unholy alliance of the DC and criminal gangs, the latter guaranteeing votes in return for its stranglehold on the local economy.

By the early 1980s, the South was much improved but still lagged behind the North with per capita incomes 40% below the national average, 29% below in Sicily and 42% below in Calabria. Illiteracy rates in the South were 6% compared to 0.6% in the north; with 24% of national GDP and unemployment double that in the North. Some 200 firms invested three billion dollars in the South: most left. Overall development of Southern industry was motivated by altruistic political motives rather than sound commercial criteria: for instance, sites were dictated by local pressures in the form of jobs for DC votes. These huge complexes were predominantly capital intensive that required a low level of labour, with minimal skills development due to widescale automation. The Southern pipedream was destined to remain as such *sine diem.*

Chapter Four

The Christian Democrats and the Art of Patronage Politics

Since its outright victory in the 1948 elections, Alcide De Gasperi's government had failed to deliver on its promised reforms, such as fiscal revision and a new penal code, which he felt would alienate a large spectrum of moderate Christian Democrat DC support. Instead he concentrated his energies on maintaining power in order to combat Communism and the onset of the Cold War. Mindful of the DC's decline in popularity, and in preparation for the 1953 national elections, De Gasperi engineered a law whereby any alliance of parties with more than 50% would receive two thirds of the seats in the Chamber of Deputies. He also hoped that the law would marginalise the far left and right so that the DC could hold the centre ground. His opponents labelled the law as the *legge truffa* swindle law, which resembled Mussolini's Acerbo law. De Gasperi favoured coalition government since it expanded the DC electoral base, and chimed with the Catholic teaching of pacifism. He proceeded to ally with the Liberals, Social Democrats and Republicans, all of whom received the body of their support from the middle classes; but a small group of minor parties refused to cooperate. The upshot was that the DC alliance just failed at 49.85% to secure an outright victory in the '53 elections, the DC party having lost electoral ground by 8% since 1948, and which led to the end of De Gasperi's career. He died the following year.

The neo-Fascist MSI profited from De Gasperi's manoeuvring. Managed by former leaders of the Salò Republic, a sinister link with the past, its electoral success with 5% of the votes demonstrated that Fascism's authoritarian and nationalist approach continued to appeal to a significant block on the far right. The MSI was particularly strong in southern cities, also Rome where many government clerks owed their jobs to Fascist support. The MSI also gained votes from the embittered Southern landowners who had been forced to cede land in the DC's agricultural reforms. The Monarchists fared well, increasing their share of the vote to 7%. The PCI took 23% whilst the Socialists only obtained 13% due to their recent split (see below).

Fundamentally, the DC presented itself as the moderate party of law and order to the *ceti medi* middle classes: the lower middle class of artisans and shopkeepers (whom the DC favoured with shop licences instead of supermarkets and chain stores); the growing class of white-collar workers, especially the civil service throughout the Peninsula; and the professional classes: doctors, lawyers, architects and accountants. In order to win over the private business sector, De Gasperi favoured the conservative-minded Confindustria (equivalent to the Confederation of British Industry) by sanctioning a low tax rate on their large membership of small firms; and by supporting larger companies who resisted trade union demands for higher wages and better working conditions. The organisation had previously supported the Liberals but their influence had waned, and was now dominated by the electricity trusts who resented the power of the state corporations and feared being nationalized. They were also sceptical about the EEC since tariff removal would expose them to tough competition. The trusts hobnobbed with the bosses of high finance and the press barons whose influential mass readership was strongly provincial middle class.

The ultra-conservative Pope Pius XII had helped the DC win the 1948 election through the Vatican's secular arm, *Azione Cattolica* Catholic Action. By 1954 membership had risen to 2.6 million, being strongest in the 'white' (Catholic) Veneto and Trentino; also in Piedmont and Lombardy; and so replicating the DC geographical coverage. Pope Pius, keen to regain political influence, encouraged the DC to embrace the far right. However, De Gasperi disagreed since, as a devout Catholic, he was trying to steer a consensual middle course, and sought to distance his party from the Vatican in order to have a freer hand in political affairs. In 1949 the Pope had excommunicated all Communists. Yet the local parish priest, central to the community, remained crucial to Communists seeking work, since he had to supply them with a character reference; so many attended Mass out of sheer necessity to earn a living. It was said that twenty priests or two million lire sufficed to become a parliamentary deputy.

1956 marked a crucial turning point in Italian Communism. Following the demise of Stalin in 1953, Khruschev denounced the dreadful brutality of the dictator's regime, with his awful purges of the Russian people during the 1930s and the denial of democracy. Publicly Togliatti showed himself to be severely disillusioned by these revelations and proceeded to distance himself from Moscow. Yet as he had served under Stalin in Moscow as Vice Secretary of Comintern (International Communism) during the 1930s, he must have been aware of Stalin's atrocious behaviour. Krushchev's revelation came as a great shock to the Italian communists, who had venerated Stalin as a god. Following upon the Soviet crushing of the Prague Spring in 1948, the suppression of the Hungarian and Polish uprisings in 1956 by the Soviet army was the last straw: up to 400,000 deserted the party for the PSI, thereby restoring the Socialists' credibility after its poor showing in the 1953 elections. Togliatti now favoured a policy of greater independence of national parties from Moscow. During the 1950s, new younger blood joined the PCI, offering a more open approach compared to the hardline Resistance partisans. The Socialist leader Nenni drew away from the PCI to attempt a reconciliation with Saragat's more moderate PSDI but failed, and so proceeded to establish his party on a more independent footing.

In an attempt to minimise the Communist threat, the DC frowned upon trade unionism and endeavoured to suppress such activity, made easier by the split of the CGIL umbrella in 1948. Employers viewed increased wages and better working conditions as a brake on economic growth and profit. They preferred non-union labour such as Southerners who were more compliant. Left-wing organisations were pestered by tax inspectors, government commissions and withdrawal of licences or simply closed down. Workers responded with strikes and demonstrations. The Fascist penal and criminal codes had remained in force, tightened further in 1948 to deal with the outbreak of serious disturbances which resulted in several deaths. Farmworkers still ran the risk of being killed by their unreasonable masters at the hands of the estate foreman. Most *questori* and prefects had served under Fascism.[14] During 1946-58, the prefects suspended 81 left-wing mayors and abolished 38 left-wing councils. They also engineered election results. The more militant workers took factory jobs in the North.

It was under the leadership of Amintore Fanfani (1958-63) that the DC forged ahead to set up a power base to wield political, financial and economic power through the control of the state agencies: in fact a policy initiated by Mussolini. Born in Tuscany in 1908, he was briefly a Fascist, and was professor

---

[14] The Questore is a public official responsible for the police in a provincial capital, and who reports to the Prefect in overall charge of the province.

of economics at the Cattolica University in Milan for 20 years; then at Rome University throughout his political career from 1954 to 1983. He served under De Gasperi as minister of agriculture, responsible for the redistribution of two million acres of farmland to 150,000 peasant families, mainly in the South. Subsequently as minister for labour he worked on establishing non-Marxist trade unions to reduce Communist influence.

During Fanfani's political career, the DC became highly factional, reminiscent of the shifting alliances of 19th century *trasformismo*, with between seven and ten ruling oligarchies at any one time, which engendered frequent discord. Fanfani belonged to the faction *Iniziativa Democratica* formed before World War Two. Like De Gasperi, Fanfani's paramount aims were opposition to Communism and the Cold War, independence from the Vatican yet the promotion of Catholic family values, tempered with individual liberalism and economic growth. His approach to foreign policy was like a breath of fresh air after the disastrous international forays by Mussolini. He supported NATO such that Italy looked west not east. After his resignation in 1959, Fanfani endeavoured to improve relations with the Soviets by having talks with Krushchev in Moscow in 1961; and favoured Mao Tse-Tung's request for China's membership of the United Nations. He also took it upon himself to meet a delegation from Hanoi in search of a peace solution for Vietnam. Later in 1987, he arranged a meeting between Mikhail Gorbachev and Pope John Paul II. Fanfani's calm and measured approach was welcomed with relief by Italians, and which brought back respect for Italy on the international stage.

At the time of unification during 1861-1870, the Piedmontese government established a highly centralized and hierarchical administration with a strong legalistic base, instituted by Napoleon's tenure, in order to counter the historically regional character of the Peninsula by moulding regions into national unity. Some 50,000 bureaucrats issued a hive of over 100,000 laws, statutes and directives, ostensibly for the benefit of the citizen. At first the Piedmontese dominated the state bureaucracy, but an increasing number of Southerners entered, many of them lawyers and with no prospect of any other tangible employment in the economically depressed South. By 1954, 56% of the civil service hailed from the South which accounted for just 37% of the Peninsula's population. By contrast Northerners were finding an increasing number of jobs in the private sector of the expanding economy.

All ministries were based in Rome, where all decisions were taken, the most influential being Internal Affairs and Justice; and all dominated by Finance. Civil service chiefs, sympathetic towards the DC, were directly appointed by the government who thereby controlled the state departments, giving rise to malpractice, dishonesty and corruption. In fact many civil servants resented political interference in the performance of their duties and retaliated with technical delaying tactics. The eventual dominance of the system by so many legalistic clerks only exacerbated the gross inefficiency and interminable delays. The excessive degree of control from the upper echelons of government stifled any initiative in the civil service, most functionaries being unwilling or unable to take any decisions, leading to stalemate, obfuscation and a conflict of overlapping interests within departments and ministries. It is hardly surprising that the civil service from its very inception in the 1860s became a breeding ground for corruption, especially in the South, whereby irritated citizens bribed government officials to expedite matters, satisfy requests for jobs and favours, in return for electoral support; and quite unlike the largely apolitical British civil service.

In 1910 the first special agencies appeared: *aziende autonome* autonomous state agencies which set up the railways, post office and telephone, and included the existing state salt and tobacco monopolies. These agencies functioned alongside the traditional government ministries and civil service, giving rise to the description of *sottogoverno* parallel or sub-government. They became power enclaves within the state, run by particular factions and reminiscent of the individualistic politics of the medieval commune and city state. The civil service soared to 377,000 employees, creating a new white-collar class, all closely linked to central ministries which were beholden to no-one, least of all the hapless citizen. During the Fascist *ventennio* 1922-40, 260 *enti pubblici* state agencies appeared, employing over a million functionaries, partly due to the surge in primary school teachers. Mussolini mused that it was prudent to keep Southern intellectuals employed rather than have them create mischief. By 1947 the number had risen to 841 agencies. Towering over these special agencies were ENI, the oil and petrochemicals giant; and IRI, the largest state organisation with 216,000 employees by 1948, of which 160,000 were located in manufacturing and of those just 27,000 workers in the South.

Mussolini also created the smaller *parastato* insurance agencies. INPS National Health Insurance Institution boasted the largest budget and fund allocation, managing old age and disability pensions; also family and maternity benefits and minor unemployment subsidies. INAM concerned itself with health insurance whilst the smaller INAIL insured against accidents at work. All three bodies were independent financially and administratively, but proved to be chaotically run as private fiefdoms, rife with conflicting interests, with constant arguing over documents and endless queuing for the long-suffering citizen. Lastly there existed minor *parastato* welfare institutions for sport, culture and recreation. Formally known as *enti utili* useful bodies, they came to be known as *enti inutili* useless bodies, since there was much duplication of responsibility and tremendous dissipation of funds in salaries and administrative costs. Ironically, in 1950 the Office for the Reform of Bureaucracy was set up which proposed and mooted improvements throughout the civil service: all were rejected.

In regard to local administration, regional government was not fully implemented until the 1970s since it went against the quest for national unity. Another reason was the DC's fear of Communism, which remained strong in Emilia-Romagna and Tuscany, two former strongholds of wartime partisanship. The smaller provinces within the regions were restricted in power and funds; whilst the local communes took responsibility for public health, transport, policing and some welfare services; and with limited power to raise taxes. In 1947 there were 7,680 communes, of which 90% numbered fewer than 10,000 inhabitants. The provinces and communes within a region were subservient to centralized power which was overseen at their level by the prefects, who had wielded considerable influence since their introduction by Napoleon.

By the 1950s, the DC controlled virtually all city councils through a network of coalitions, a notable exception being the regional capital of Bologna held by the Communists, who dominated the central region of Emilia-Romagna. Furthermore, local governments were overshadowed by the dominant agencies such as the *Cassa* Fund in the South. Such a *sistemazione* arrangement weakened Parliament, the executive source of power, which was reduced to rubber stamping minor laws *leggine* passed by parliamentary committees. The Council of Ministers (Cabinet) was equally emasculated, frittering its time away in party squabbling and political machination.

DC politicians exploited these state agencies as a means to distribute division of the spoils within the party's own factions (endemic since medieval times amongst rival noble families) known as *lottizzazione;* and to coalition parties, known as *partitocrazia.* Allocation of spoils was based on the Cencelli Manual, with the complex allocation of points for each ministry. The Southern *Cassa* Fund and the agrarian reform boards were managed by Ivanoe Bonomi who held the support of five deputies in his pocket. Over the course of a decade, he disbursed over 1,200 billion lire, as directed by Fanfani. Giulio Andreotti, a future prime minister, remained at the helm of the Ministry of Defence for seven years. The Social Democrats controlled the state insurance agency INPS during 1949-65; whilst the DC Mariano Rumor led the dominant Dorotei faction with a strong power base in Veneto and Trentino. Named after a monastery in Rome where the first meeting was held, the Dorotei began to hold sway in 1959, and controlling the DC for 20 years, and included top politicians such as Fanfani. In 1956 the Ministry of State Holdings was created to facilitate government control of all state agencies and exclude the Communists from the corridors of power. Over time, they became breeding grounds for the phenomenon of *clientelismo:* the art of patronage politics, whereby politicians and public officials promised jobs, pensions, contracts and licences to friends, family and businessmen, in return for their personal and electoral loyalty.

Government nominees ran the banks and savings institutions, many of which were regional, controlled by DC factions and coalition partners for the disbursement of vital funds; as well as new credit institutions such as IRFIS and CIS. ENI became notorious for its clientelistic practices under Mattei. Amazingly the Bank of Italy remained staunchly independent, governed by Guido Carli during 1960-75 (and later president of Confindustria). Fanfani accepted the inherited system of state machinery and politicized it for the DC's own ends: what Duggan describes as the DC's 'colonisation of the state'.[15] The DC became a powerful political machine bent on power for power's sake, rather than service towards the citizen democracy, and which eventually alienated much of their grassroots support, ending in their downfall over *Tangentopoli*.

Officially, entry into the Civil Service is by public examination *concorso* but many secure a post through a personal *raccomandazione*, which skews the job market. There are even official forms available for the application. Entry spans four levels: executive, administrative, clerical and custodial. Promotion is slow and pay is mediocre, but the job is virtually guaranteed for life except for gross dereliction of duty, and with early retirement. Some 40% of the intake are lawyers, especially in the South where there is limited choice of employment; and who offer a theoretical rather than a practical approach to problem solving.

---

[15] C.Duggan: 'The Force of Destiny' page 563

Ministries such as the Interior, Justice, Foreign and Treasury, are run quite efficiently; others such as Education less so. Short-lived governments lead to brief stays in ministerial posts, which hampers long term planning. More dynamic individuals choose the paths of business, banking and industry, particularly in the North. Ministries close at 2pm so many go off to a second job to boost their mediocre pay; absenteeism is common. Long-suffering citizens view state officials as self-serving and incompetent: as a consequence, they are reluctant to pay their taxes. Processing matters is snail-like: for instance, it takes about three years to obtain a building permit; whilst war claims were still outstanding in the 1980s. The Ministry for Administrative Reform was set up in the 1950s but achieved little.

Clientelismo in the South

During the 1960s, patronage politics became highly developed in the South. The aim was to create a mass client voter base by locking in political support through the concession of public works contracts and personal favours. Such a system acted as a counterweight to the more left-wing and democratically minded North by securing a strong electoral base in the South in order to boost the overall vote, where DC membership crept up to 1.3 million. Philip II of Spain had awarded public posts and favours to Southern Italians in return for loyalty; whilst the Southern landlord expected his peasant workers to vote for him in return for tenure of the land.

The process had got under way after unification in 1861, as a quid pro quo arrangement between the nascent northern government and the entrenched interests of the landowners and Mafia in the South, who wheedled their way into the control of strategic government posts, in return for securing the DC vote. Under Fanfani the DC proceeded to politicize key areas of the Southern economy: construction, industry and local government, by placing DC friendly officials in key posts: in a word *clientelismo*. The relationship between the patron/state and the client/voter was based on an elaborate pyramid of interconnections, highly fluid for wheeling and dealing, yet with defined layers. At the top presided the *capi correnti*: factional leaders, former ministers and prime ministers. Over the years these people came to exert a tremendous hold over the maze of *enti pubblici* municipal bodies, such as social welfare, transport, public housing, utilities and credit institutions. Over time clientelism drifted all too easily into bribery and corruption of government officials to secure contracts and favours.

In the South reigned Giulio Andreotti (close to the Mafia), Giovanni Leone, also Emilio Colombo and Aldo Moro, the latter two with local power bases respectively in Basilicata and Puglia. Not only did they control key ministries but they also established regional enclaves through their *protégés* at the next level: deputies, junior ministers, chiefs of special state agencies and local party officials. Giovanni Gioia, Fanfani's deputy, became provincial secretary of Palermo in 1953; Nino Gullotti, Rumor's puppet, ran Messina's building sector. Silvio Antonino Drago, protégé of Emilio Colombo, ruled Catania in Sicily, where by the mid '70s there were 34 local bodies: 18 for social welfare comprising health, pensions, sickness benefit and social security, 11 for utilities, and five for housing: all ripe for the plucking. By the mid '60s the DC controlled 79 directors and 22 presidents in Catania. Salvo Lima, another disciple of Fanfani, governed Naples as mayor, and which was later ruled by Silvio Gava.

These DC men controlled all disbursement of government funds and all regional, provincial and local government posts, from the highest ranks down to the most menial. Many municipal key posts were handed out to friends and cronies who were unqualified or inexperienced. Ironically many enthusiastic novices criticised the lack of political morality but accepted the status quo once ensnared within the system. The city party secretaries relied on the goodwill of the local bigwigs for support: mayors and councillors, landowners, together with the professional businessmen, doctors, lawyers and even the clergy, all of whom received their percentage in return for turning a blind eye to rife malpractice such as misappropriation of public funds to cover inflated prices of raw materials, the costs of bad management, or for personal property speculation. Such people could offer the DC a block vote from their colleagues and extensive families.

Given the national government's policy of developing the South, the most important post in local administration was that of Assessor of Public Works concerning urban planning. Planners, architects and builders were beholden to him for *appalti* tenders for public works contracts: the securing of land concessions and the award of highly lucrative tenders whose values were wildly inflated, in tacit collusion between tenderer and government officer, the latter receiving a generous percentage: *tangente*. These building tenderers would be obliged to use the financial resources of an appropriate DC vetted credit institution, including savings banks; in return for which the contractor would offer a *bustarella* cash donation in an envelope to the local administrator as acknowledgement of the favour granted, and the promise of a vote for the DC, not only from himself but also from his web of family and business connections. Over time businessmen reaped enormous profits from the system, such as Francesco Vassallo responsible for construction works in Palermo during the '50s and '60s: he was close to Gioia and Lima, who in turn were hand in glove with the Mafia. Building works not only gave a boost to engineers and surveyors but also benefitted small manufacturing firms who produced home furnishings and equipment; as well as skilled and unskilled workers. In short, a vast quantity of public money slid into private hands rather than the state coffers.

Businessmen, together with the predatory criminal organisations of the Mafia in Sicily and the Camorra in Naples, were quick to cash in on the highly lucrative public contracts managed by the DC. In Palermo, under the control of Fanfani's faction, the bulk of public works projects were awarded to businessmen by the Assessors Salvo Lima (1956-58) and Vito Ciancimino (1959-64) at a time of huge expansion in the city, especially to the north-west where cheap agricultural land was bought up for housing and infrastructure. In 1964 Ciancimino was found guilty of collusion with the local Mafia and forced to resign. In 1984 he was arrested, having again been accused of collusion by Tommaso Buscetta, the turncoat Mafia boss. Lima was murdered in 1992. The Mafia also had their hands deep in the *Cassa* till, which disbursed over a thousand billion lire on infrastructure during its early years; as did many officials and contractors who held key positions both in the DC party and public offices.

In the absence of any effective trade unionism, the Mafia controlled the supply of labour; as later did the Camorra of Naples who profited from the 50,000 billion lire rebuilding programme after the earthquake in Irpinia, Campania in 1980, where temporary prefabs remained for years on end. Another earthquake in 1968 in north-west Sicily killed over 500 people and left 90,000 homeless, of which two-thirds were still sheltering in Nissen huts a decade later.[16] Not surprisingly many projects were never started or completed; at times building work carried out was, and is, shoddy: collapsed flats, bridges and

---

[16] The Apulian/African tectonic plate is pushing north, moving under the Iberian plate shifting east. The two plates sometimes clash in the Apennines with disastrous results e.g. L'Aquila in 2009.

motorways.[17] In 1966 new high-rise buildings collapsed in Agrigento, Sicily, built without planning permission and overlooking ancient Greek temples. In 1998-99 apartment blocks collapsed in Foggia and Rome. Such malpractice also occurred in the North but to a lesser extent.

The other major form of securing support involved the electoral engineering of ordinary citizens requiring medical care and pensions, collectively known as *assistenzialismo*. Welfare transfer payments were massive to help minimise the gap with the North. The pension payout for the South was hugely inflated, with up to 80% of final salary for civil servants; and far exceeding the actual working population owing to the inclusion of so-called disability pensions; also minimum social pensions awarded to retirees with insufficient regular contributions. Other areas concerned job-seeking, either for the applicant or a relative, a licence for a shop or business, or the expediting of documentation. Citizens needed a municipal contact to act on their behalf and so turned to a patron 'saint in heaven': *capi elettori* grass roots activists, usually from the lower middle-class ranks, who either concentrated on a particular geographical area or a sector such as construction. Local bodies responsible for these public services, and run by DC supporters, would deal with the citizens' requests, in return for cash or a modest gift in kind plus the promise of a DC vote. In 1963, one unscrupulous DC politician had patients wheeled to a politically correct hospital in Catania in order to secure their vote.

The system covered all forms of jobs, from the highest post down to the most menial, for instance from teacher to cleaner. In an effort to absorb unemployment, during 1953-68 Naples witnessed an explosion of 15,000 in the number of municipal employees; whilst Palermo enjoyed the services of some 2,500 dustmen and street cleaners; but the two cities remained unclean. Jobs were and remain, including the North, highly dependent on the *raccomandazione*: a personal recommendation to a third party. The system was exclusively geared to keeping the DC in power at the top, binding in the electorate, and financed appropriately by the recipients of favourable treatment for contracts and personal favours.

In 2016, one Giovanni Cafaro set up a firm to offer the novel service of *codista* queuer so that companies need not waste the time of their own staff. Signor Cafaro offers a proper contract with a minimum wage of ten Euros. He

---

[17] The collapse of the road bridge in Genoa in 2018 may have been due to defective aggregate, caused by an excess of sodium which corrodes the concrete.

provides his staff with a five-hour training course on Skype to learn the ropes of haggling with the state departments in order to obtain documents, signatures and charges. In fact wealthy Italians have long used people to queue up to pay bills and the like in the course of everyday bureaucracy. The consumer group Codacons reckons that Italians spend some 400 hours a year waiting in line. As from 2016, Italians can access public services online with an identification number, but many still prefer to stand in long queues to pay in cash over the counter. When I arrived in northern Italy in 1989 with my family, we required a *nulla osta* authorisation for the release of our lorryload of goods and chattels, but which first required the obtaining of our *permesso di soggiorno* residency permit which would take some time. Miraculously our possessions turned up out of the blue without the permit, which we managed to acquire later.

Voting was further complicated by the use of a preference vote for a particular candidate on the electoral list representing a certain faction within the party, highlighting the fragmented nature of the Italian political system. Political tentacles spread deeply and widely. In essence the DC party had succeeded in displacing the centuries-old power of the Southern landowners through its control of the local state bureaucracy. By the '50s the DC wielded power in virtually most major cities with the exception of Bologna, which was in the hands of the more moral Communists, now ironically perceived as the party of decency, law and order. Over time *clientelismo* shifted north: the rot had set in long before 1992. The increasingly bloated public sector demanded ever higher public borrowing, inevitably leading to a massive budget deficit and national debt. Raising income tax was and is considered political suicide; hence the indirect VAT tax is more effective. Duggan states that 'the state bureaucracy came to resemble a medieval kingdom: a patchwork of feudal lordships, each semi-autonomous, and quite ready if the occasion suited to rebel against the centre.'[18]

The leaders of the *Risorgimento* had called for a strong state united both politically and morally. Yet the 19th century Prime Minister Crispi, himself a Sicilian, had remarked that Italians lacked a sense of loyalty to the state and its institutions. Mussolini's idea of national unity through war and conquest had tarnished the concept of patriotism, which was now displayed principally through sporting events such as cycling, motor racing and football. A certain degree of unity was perceived in post-war modernisation and economic prosperity. Regionalism remained deeply entrenched, reinforced by the

---

[18] C.Duggan: A Concise History of Italy page 268

continued use of dialects (many of which are still spoken) and blocking a sense of national history and patriotic sentiment as exists in Britain, embodied in the largely apolitical English monarchy. The Peninsula was further riven by the centuries-old north-south gulf, and latterly by the Catholic-Communist divide.

The forces of law and order leaned towards the reactionary right, partly because of latent post Fascist sympathies ostensibly acting as a bulwark against Communist penetration. Judges and magistrates who dared to protest were silenced or removed, making for a pliant judiciary. Parliament was riven by faction, which precluded efficient government. Hence, given the weakness of the state elements, the DC saw fit to take control of the ministries, civil service, state agencies and local government, leaving the Church to offer moral guidance. Eventually the DC's politicisation of the state cynically exploited its resources for its own ends, through corruption, personal enrichment and clientelism, and at the expense of financial prudence and technical feasibility.

The phenomenon of political corruption was not peculiar to Italy: it was the sheer scale. The Liberal Prime Minister Lloyd George sold peerages and knighthoods for cash. One chap refused a minor title, remarking that 'when I want a peerage, I will buy one, like an honest man'. [19] Lloyd George was also implicated in irregular share dealing in the Marconi Company. The former Prime Minister Tony Blair was involved in an investigation concerning cash loans for peerages. Post-war citizens, now better educated and more politically aware, came to view the Christian Democrats as self-serving and with a scant sense of democracy, social justice or morality. Over time they refused to display loyalty, patriotic pride or civic duty towards the Italian state, expressed in massive tax evasion and membership of secret societies, such as P2 and the Mafia, as alternative power enclaves. Intellectuals bypassed national sovereignty in favour of supranational organisations such as the EEC, which brought economic wealth and peace.

---

[19] A.Marr: The Making of Modern Britain.

Chapter Five
Politics, Religion and Conspiracy

The general election of 1958 proved to be a quiet affair. The Christian Democrats maintained their lead with a small increase from 40 to 42%, likewise the PSI from 13 to 14%. Both the MSI and Monarchists dipped in popularity, whilst the Communists barely gained. Fanfani, in power since 1954, became increasingly autocratic, arrogating to himself the key posts of President of the Council of Ministers (Prime Minister of the Cabinet) and Minister for Foreign Affairs, whilst remaining party secretary. In fact, the latter post wielded greater influence within the party as a whole since, not being a member of the Council of Ministers, he could manoeuvre behind the scenes. Fanfani was keen to ally with the PSI to press ahead with social reforms and deepen state intervention in the economy, whilst continuing to isolate the Communists. The local elections in 1960 saw the Socialists take control of key cities such as Milan, Florence, Genoa and Florence, which reinforced the logic of the so-called 'opening to the left'. Such a strategy would give the DC a strong majority in the Chamber of Deputies, and at the same time weaken the PCI.

However, strong opposition from his own party, including his own pre-war faction '*Iniziativa Democratica*', and the newer Dorotei faction, led to the fall of Fanfani's government in March 1959 and his resignation. DC deputies found themselves in difficulties over choosing a new leader, so it fell to President Gronchi to appoint Tambroni, a right-wing lawyer, to form a new government. His tenure proved to be short-lived since, being dependent on the MSI vote, he permitted the party to hold its congress in Genoa, a Communist stronghold and a key centre of the wartime Resistance. Tambroni allowed Basile, a former RSI prefect of Genoa, to attend: he had been responsible for the deportation of many workers and Republicans to Nazi Germany. Violence broke out and Tambroni ordered the police to shoot on the demonstrators. Several died and the CGIL called for a national strike. Tambroni was persuaded to stand down and allow Fanfani to be reappointed as caretaker leader.

The American Democrat president John F. Kennedy was encouraged by his special adviser, Arthur Schlesinger, to support Fanfani's overtures to the PSI. However, the US Secretary of State for Defence, Dean Rusk, remained cool towards the initiative, as did the military chiefs and the CIA office in Rome. Led by Nenni's moderate 'Autonomous' faction, the majority of the PSI favoured an alliance with the DC, and now supported NATO. In January 1962, Aldo Moro, now DC party secretary, gave a rather lengthy and opaque speech (typical of Italians) supporting alliance with the left; reinforced by Andreotti's approval and 80% of the conference delegates. Private industry, led by the dynamic trio of Fiat, Pirelli and Olivetti, also gave their backing to the policy since they hoped state planning would boost the economy and lessen worker tension. Public sector industry was more cautious, whilst Confindustria opposed the project, especially the dominant electricity trusts who feared nationalisation under a centre left government.

In March 1962, Fanfani set up an interim administration with the Social Democrats and the Republicans, but excluding the Socialists since he now felt the moment was not yet ripe. Nenni, PSI leader, was willing to support the government provided three essential reforms were executed: regionalism, schools and the nationalisation of the five electricity trusts (which included Edison). The first subject was shelved since it would extend the Communist power base, particularly in central Italy. Secondly, the school leaving age was raised from 11 to 14 to create a single comprehensive middle school, abolishing the higher-level schools, and which increased the number of girl pupils.

Nationalisation of the electricity trusts appealed to the Socialists, since it would weaken the conservative element of Confindustria. The reform made sound economic sense: pricing tariffs and power resources would be planned nationally, with suitable investment especially in the South. The sticking point was compensation, since the trusts would remain as finance companies, as advised by Guido Carli, Governor of the Bank of Italy, so that the money could be reinvested in the industry, as had happened earlier with the advent of the national railways. However, others felt that the trusts should be abolished and the cash paid to the former share-holders. It was this argument that won the day, leading to the creation of ENEL, with a large investment plan using the compensation funds paid by the State. Yet only about half of the 1500 billion lire made available was received, the rest being frittered away without trace, without reducing costs to consumers, and with the electricity bosses still exerting political control.

Since the war housing had become a top priority and, as a consequence, the Peninsula suffered a spate of uncontrolled building, especially during 1958-63, which devastated thousands of kilometres of coastline, wooded areas, mountains, historic towns and cities. The government had adopted a *laissez faire* attitude which gave free rein to unscrupulous property speculators, who bribed local officials to throw up shoddy *palazzi* flats built haphazardly. Fiorentino Sullo, the DC Minister of Public Works, was keen to minimise land speculation and environmental damage. He referred back to the 1942 law which allowed the local communes to control local development but which in fact had never been implemented. The law had also favoured landowners' rights and allowed builders to retain their profits untaxed. Sullo proposed that municipal bodies should issue compulsory purchase orders on all undeveloped land within a city's *piano regolatore* town planning scheme; provide the necessary infrastructure; then sell the land back to private buyers at a higher price to cut out land speculation. Secondly, new owners would own only the building whilst the local council would retain control of the land and planning. Public money was available for such a scheme thanks to the economic boom at the time. Sadly Sullo's proposals were met with an avalanche of opposition by entrenched interests, accusing him of Communist nationalisation of the land. In the end, under pressure from Moro, Sullo reluctantly had to back down and the project withered away, much to the detriment of urban planning and further obliteration of the environment for decades.

Public (council) housing construction was limited, unlike in post-war Britain and Germany, accounting for only 16% during 1948-63. For instance by 1971 Milan's housing was 43% private, 34% of residents lived with relatives and friends, and only 6.4% public. In 1949 Fanfani created INA-Casa with a 1,000 billion lira fund which made some headway in providing a modest number of dwellings. In 1963 INA-Casa was replaced by GESCAL which achieved precious little due to corruption and clientelism; and was wound up in the early '70s. The third public organisation, IACP, suffered from a lack of funds. Property developers such as the huge *Società Generale Immobiliari*, in which the Vatican was the main shareholder, set about the so-called 'sack of Rome'[20]

---

[20] The first was perpetrated in 1527 by the Emperor Charles V.

where, both in the centre of the Eternal City and its outskirts, they threw up shoddily built and ugly blocks of flats lacking any amenities. Rome's housing department in the 1950s was portrayed as devoid of clerical assistance, with planning applications left to gather dust, such that out of pure frustration many poor souls took it upon themselves to build their own homes; and so some 400,000 people came to live in *case abusive* illegal habitations.

In the general election of April 1963, the fourth since 1948, the DC vote slipped to 38% compared to 42% in 1958. The Liberals did well who, having opposed the so-called 'opening to the left', saw their share of the poll rise from 3.5% to 7%; whilst the MSI rose slightly to 5%. The Monarchists dwindled to less than 2%. The pro Fanfani Socialist PSDI increased a little to 6%, whilst the far-left PSI dipped to 14%. The Communist vote rose from 23% to 25% nationwide, especially in northern immigrant areas and with emigrant workers abroad. President Segni, who had replaced Gronchi, asked Aldo Moro to form his first government. A university professor from Bari (Puglia) in the South, Moro had served as under-secretary at the Ministry of Foreign Affairs, then as president of the DC centrist Dorotei group in the Chamber of Deputies. The members included Giulio Andreotti, Mariano Rumor and Emilio Colombo. Yet after the Tambroni débâcle the DC could not risk moving right and so Moro and the Dorotei leader, Mariano Rumor, decided to make an approach to the left.

After months of bickering, in December 1963 the PSI joined the DC government, with Nenni as deputy PM. The Socialist Antonio Giolitti, grandson of the turn of the century prime minister, became Minister of the Budget. The far left of the PSI refused to serve under Moro, and in January 1964, 38 deputies and senators, being 30% of the PSI and which included top CGIL officials, broke away to form the PSIUP *Partito Socialista di Unità Proletaria* (a name used previously in the 1940s), leaving a weakened rump under Nenni. The PSI had split twice in a matter of two decades, previously to the right in 1947 with Saragat and now to the left in 1964, which revealed the party's fragility.

Moro presented an ambitious reform programme: taxation and social insurance, bureaucracy, agriculture, Southern investment and town planning, but achieved virtually nothing due to his inherent procrastination and factional bickering. He insisted on waiting for an upturn in the economy before embarking upon reform, which unsettled the Socialists. Since 1962 there had been an increase in strikes, with alarming riots in Piazza Statuto in Genoa. In the north the labour market was tightening up for the first time since the start of the economic miracle, allowing wages to rise significantly above nationally agreed contracts. Large companies with fat profits could absorb these high increases but not the smaller firms SMEs who put a brake on investment. Bosses passed the wage increases on in prices which, together with the shortage of manufactured goods due to lack of materials, led to a return to inflation not experienced since the end of the war. Investors moved capital abroad to avoid the newly imposed withholding tax on stock dividends, designed to reduce tax evasion through the creation of a public register. The former electricity trusts continued to influence the financial markets by creating a climate of unease, so that share prices and business confidence dwindled. Small and medium savers, part of the bedrock of the DC electorate, were badly affected. Given this parlous state of affairs, and with an election looming in 1963, the DC called a halt to reform, nervous about upsetting anyone.

In 1963 Guido Carli, Governor of the Bank of Italy during 1960-73, imposed a credit squeeze, reinforced the following year by widescale deflationary measures (previously imposed by Einaudi in 1945). As a result, unemployment rose, many small firms failed or were taken over; and consumption dropped. Reform of the *Federconsorzi* (bulk purchase of farming supplies) was blocked by Bonomi's Southern faction. In June 1964, Moro, fearful of alienating the powerful lobbies of construction, business, agriculture and the former electricity trusts, gave up the fight and resigned after barely six months in office.

In July 1964, President Segni invited Moro to form a new administration, but the usual dithering continued. No enthusiast of the centre left government, Segni entered into discussions with General Giovanni De Lorenzo concerning the possible replacement of such an arrangement with an 'apolitical' administration, perhaps with enhanced presidential powers akin to those of de Gaulle in France, and backed up with military support through the implementation of De Lorenzo's 'Solo' plan. The plot, ostensibly of a defensive nature in the event of political destabilisation by the left, intended that the *Carabinieri* (part of the Army) of whom De Lorenzo was appointed Commander-in-Chief in 1962, would take control, equipped with his own state-of-the-art mechanized brigade, and arrest the perpetrators: Communists, Socialists and trade unionists.

A Sicilian by birth, De Lorenzo had enjoyed a brilliant career, serving on the Russian front in World War Two, then as vice-commander of the CLN Resistance intelligence. Whilst head of SIFAR *Servizio Informazioni Forze Armate* since 1955, the Italian military secret service, De Lorenzo had collated over 100,000 personal files, including tapes, on a number of suspects, such as socialists, trade unionists and communists. However, the *Carabinieri* in Rome and Milan remained sceptical about the venture, viewing it effectively as a military coup d'etat. Miraculously the Socialist leader Nenni sensed a potential crisis and guaranteed his party's support to Moro, allowing him to at last form a government in August 1964. The crisis had subtly been averted. A military coup would have undermined parliamentary democracy, ushering in the return of the far right which would have been anathema to most of the Italian people.

In 1965 De Lorenzo was appointed Chief of Staff of the Army and so was in line for the top job of Defence Chief of Staff of the armed services. But in 1966, his SIFAR dossiers were revealed and he was dismissed. In 1969 the Solo plan came to light and a parliamentary commission strongly criticised his manoeuvring, but declined to take further action. They concluded that De Lorenzo had breached the Constitution but had not planned an actual coup. Meanwhile he had become a Monarchist deputy, later switching to the MSI. He died in 1973.

The De Lorenzo affair was only one of many conspiracy theories, the behind-the-scenes *dietrologia* so beloved by Italians, that would come to permeate post-war Italy, recalling the medieval politics of Cesare Borgia together with so many other plotters and schemers over the centuries. The recent incidents showed that Fascism, a relic of the past, continued to lurk just beneath the surface of Italian life and would not go away easily; yet a post war government could not rule with their support. The De Lorenzo affair cast a shadow over Moro's second administration, now tacitly supported by Confindustria, and which merely replicated the inertia of his first. The bag of reforms remained on the shelf, Moro hiding behind the need for economic stability. The DC was perceived as strong on traditional Catholic values but hypocritically weak on implementing social reform. On a more positive note, Saragat was elected the first Socialist President of the Republic 1964-71, and with Communist backing.

Moro's second government fell in February 1966, but was immediately followed by his third and final administration, now in coalition with the Socialists, Social Democrats and Republicans. In that year the PSI and PSDI united into the PSU *Partito Socialista Unificato*. Yet again Moro's administration was practically ineffectual, despite an uplift in the economy with a surplus balance of payments, stable wages and muted militancy. In July '66 a complex of high-rise buildings collapsed in Agrigento, Sicily; followed in the autumn by devastating floods in Florence and Venice, due respectively to lack of proper town planning and inadequate flood defences. Mancini's *legge ponte* bridging law managed to apportion responsibility to the landowners of primary urban costs such as roads and utilities, and part of the secondary costs of infrastructure, such as schools and parks. In 1968 two ministerial decrees established building density along roadsides plus a balance between built up areas and open spaces. There was a scramble to obtain construction permits in the year before the decrees became law, wreaking yet more ugly destruction of the landscape. Lastly, further secondary school and university reform was proposed, but languished due to student protests.

Throughout his three administrations, Moro had lived up to his adherence to minimalist intervention, avoiding root and branch reform. In his defence lack of reform was also due to the failure of the DC, PSI and PCI to sink their ideological differences at a time of economic prosperity, further exacerbated by the vested interests of the financial and industrial lobbies. Moro's incessant bargaining worked on the premise that the issue would either dissipate or resolve itself. A golden opportunity was missed, for which the state and its citizens would later pay dearly; and Moro with his life. As part of Moro's administration even the Socialists had begun to realise the tortuous difficulties of governing, let alone tackling root and branch reform of the state institutions, and so tagged behind Moro with his *piedi di piombo* leaden feet. More worryingly they latched on to the personal and political benefits of DC *clientelismo* and corruption. By the end of the 60s, the finger was being pointed at Socialist abuse of power, in particular Giacomo Mancini, Minister of Public Works and later Socialist party secretary. So much for a new relationship between citizen and state. Atrophy reigned.

Affairs at the Vatican

The succession of Pope John XXIII in 1958, following the demise of the ultra-conservative Pius XII, Pope since 1939, opened up a refreshing new era in papal politics, welcoming a *rapprochement* with the left to heal political divisions. Born in Bergamo of humble peasant stock, Pope John had previously served as a foreign diplomat in Bulgaria and Paris, then became Patriarch of Venice in 1953. His low-key humility and simplicity of language made a welcome change to his predecessor's controversial approach and, during his brief tenure as Pope until his death in 1963, his 'common touch' and sympathy were warmly embraced by the Italian people. Pope John welcomed some change, such as the advent of television and the 'opening to the left': a discreet nod to the DC.

Pope John exercised a modernising influence, *aggiornamento,* to address the needs of the modern world rather than dwell on the past. He encouraged greater tolerance towards non-Catholics. His encyclical *Pacem in Terris* Peace on Earth, addressed towards 'all men of good will', appealed for international peace, an end to the Cold War and third world colonialism, a better life for the working classes and a greater public role for women. His 1961 encyclical *Mater et Magistra* laid emphasis on the Church's social teachings. Italian replaced Latin in Church liturgy.

In 1962 Pope John inaugurated the Second Vatican Council, closed in 1965 (the first was in 1870) in order to redefine the role of the Catholic Church on the international stage. He wished to accord the papacy greater independence, renouncing papal involvement in secular affairs, so that the incumbent could devote his energies to pastoral and spiritual duties. Pope John's reforms separated the responsibilities of the Vatican and the Italian Church, hitherto entwined historically. The territory of the Vatican has existed as an independent state since the Lateran Accords of 1929, and by which the Pope is not only Bishop of Rome but also head of the Italian Church and the international group of over one hundred Catholic Churches. Pope John increased the College of Cardinals from 80 to 120 members, but with just 28 Italians by 1971, thereby diluting the influence of the Italian Church. The Vatican's affairs were administered by twelve cardinals of the Curia.

Pope John was keen to accord greater prominence to the bishops, considered the natural successors of the original apostles, and whose Synod (Council) govern the Italian Church, encouraging them to devote more time to pastoral duties. He reduced the number of Council bishops to sixteen by consolidating their dioceses into that number of clerical districts. He also decreased the number of elected bishops from 315 to 270. Another 13 elected bishops would attend various commissions dealing with doctrine and faith, clergy and liturgy, family and society, education and work. In 1966, the CEI collegial body inaugurated its bishops' conference.

His successor Paul VI 1963-78 followed through Pope John's modernising approach, combined with a more spiritual approach, and generally refraining from public political debate. He retained close links with the DC, having known Andreotti and Moro in the FUCI Catholic graduates association, when as

Cardinal Montini he served as their chaplain. He was profoundly concerned about the rise in terrorism, and appealed to the Red Brigades to release Moro. He travelled widely abroad, regardless of religious domination: India, the Middle East; also the United Nations. He saw his prime responsibility as Bishop of Rome, encouraging the pastoral nature of episcopal work at grass-roots level, and appointing more modern-minded men, for instance Cardinal Carlo Maria Martini as Archbishop of Milan, Italy's largest diocese with a population of five million.

Martini devoted considerable time and energy to charitable works in the absence of adequate state welfare, yet assisted by a host of volunteers in supporting the down and outs: the unemployed, homeless, aged, homosexuals, prostitutes, immigrants. In 1990 there were some 2,000 homeless in Milan. The Franciscan friars were also proactive in this regard, whose down to earth sympathy with modern life issues made them highly popular, projecting a pacifist image in an increasingly violent world. Indeed, during the 1980s priests armed themselves against attack and burglary. An extension of the bishops' pastoral role was seen in the number of active lay movements, such as *Azione Cattolica*, the oldest since the 1900s; the right-wing *Communione e Liberazione* C&L begun in 1956, similar to Opus Dei and popular amongst university students; along with its offshoot *Movimento Popolare* set up in 1976, whose volunteers sold cheap food to the poor and needy.

Pope John Paul Wojtyla 1978-2005 was the first foreign pope to be elected since 1522, the cardinals being unable to agree on an Italian candidate. His experiences as archbishop of Cracow in Communist Poland moved him to speak out in a militant fashion to defend the Church against Communism, and welcoming the fall of the Berlin Wall in 1981. As Bishop of Rome, he too upheld the spirit of the Second Vatican Council, supporting the enhanced pastoral role of bishops. Affectionately known as Papa Wojtyla (popes are usually known by their surnames by the Italians) he proved to be an international roving pope, viewing Italian affairs more objectively through foreign eyes and although possessed of diplomatic skills, did not hesitate to comment strongly on political matters. He displayed the Vatican in an international light, previously dimmed by involvement in national politics. He spoke out at Iraq's invasion of Kuwait in 1990, and addressed a hundred ambassadors over America's subsequent invasion of Iraq. In a spirit of ecumenical harmony, in 1986 he conducted a prayer meeting for international peace at Assisi; also at the Wailing Wall of Jerusalem for the

2000 Jubilee. He visited non-Catholic countries such as Britain. On the home front, in Sicily 1993 Wojtyla denounced the Mafia following the murder of the judges Falcone and Borsellino, echoing the revulsion felt by Catholics. Cardinal Pappalardo also railed against the Mafia and political corruption.

Very much a traditionalist on social matters, Wojtyla thundered against excessive materialism. His encyclical *Familiaris Consortio* stressed the importance of family values, exhorting women to have children: '*Fatevi i figli!*' In 1981 he waged a crusade against the abortion referendum campaign, defending the sanctity of life, even opposing therapeutic abortion. He lambasted the biotechnology industry for playing at God in their use of fertility treatments. Four days before the referendum an attempt was made on his life, allegedly by Bulgarian intelligence at the instigation of the Soviets. He did support sexual equality, albeit with the stress on the role of the female as mother and home-maker.

The referenda on divorce and abortion marked a definitive watershed in relations between the Church and Italians. They increasingly resented Church interference in issues now viewed as personal. Religion had become largely irrelevant to their modern lives which had become ever more materialistic and less spiritual. During the 1980s, ostensibly 85% of Italians were Catholic but only 30% were practising, and with only some 10% regularly attending Church. By 1991 over a quarter of marriages were celebrated in a registry office (the 1865 civil code had allowed civil marriage but not divorce). Prudently, the Church accepted the shift in values, and tacitly shifted its stance away from moral-religious issues to concentrate on socio-economic concerns.

The Vatican Bank affair: A Murky Tale

The Vatican bank, known as IOR Institute for Religious Works, was reorganised in 1942, its early investors consisting of ecclesiastics, Vatican residents and a few Italian citizens. During the 1960s/70s, IOR received control of the funds allocated to the Vatican as a result of the 1929 Concordat with Mussolini. The bank channelled these funds into investment in Italian industry and property, centred on Rome. Its assets were probably worth at least about a million dollars at the time. Since the Vatican was decreed an independent state by the Concordat, it was exempt from Italian tax, nor subject to banking regulations; nor did it issue public accounts until 2013.

In 1968 IOR became liable for tax on stock dividends, so its director, Archbishop Marcinkus, an American of Latvian descent and with no financial expertise, approached Michele Sindona, a Sicilian banker, for assistance in transferring the IOR's funds abroad into foreign companies. As an independent state the Vatican did not require permission to export currency. Sindona had amassed a fortune from illegal trading in grain under the wartime allied government, when he possibly became entwined with criminal organisations. He invested IOR funds heavily in American industry, finance and property, such as the Watergate complex in Washington.

Following the spate of bankruptcies during the 1930s, banks were banned from buying non-banking interests. To circumvent this inconvenience, Sindona set up two small banks, the *Banca Unione* and *Banca Privata* (in which IOR held shares) using his clients' deposits for the speculative buying and selling of companies at a great profit, further enhancing their value by buying up shares on the Milan stock exchange. His wheeling and dealing rewarded his banking clients, which included Catholic co-operative banks, with a generous remuneration. He financed politicians, especially the DC party, which provided him with political cover for his covert operations. Creative accounting hid any losses on the banks' balance sheets.

The scheme demanded constant trading expansion to maintain the heady gains. Sindona bought heavily into a major cement company, Pesenti, to the extent that it was obliged to buy back the shares at an exorbitant price. Sometimes his manoeuvring met with resistance. He tried to buy the National Agricultural Bank in Milan but the Bank of Italy blocked him. He then proceeded to engineer an attack on Bastogi, the oldest quoted industrial company. He planned to take over Centrale, the former electricity holding that held shares in various companies, and launched an IPO initial public offering, the first ever in Italy. However, the manoeuvre was opposed by the business world and Guido Carli, governor of the Bank of Italy. Sindona then proceeded to merge his two banks into the *Banca Privata Italiana* BPI. He concluded a deal with the prestigious English banking house of Hambro, by which he intended to increase the capital base of his new financial house Finambro, tying it in with the Franklin National bank in Manhattan that he had recently acquired.

Sindona planned to use the Franklin bank as a vehicle by which he could speculate heavily on currency dealing, in order to accumulate massive gains. However, he launched his scheme in 1974, when there occurred a hike in oil prices (Italy is a high importer of oil) which triggered wild fluctuations in currency movements. 1970 saw the end of the Bretton Woods system of fixed interest rates established in 1944, to be replaced by floating rates. He gambled badly this time, betting on a rise in the dollar, which in fact plummeted in value, bringing about huge losses at the Franklin, which duly crashed. Ugo La Malfa, Republican Treasury Minister, refused to authorise Sindona an injection of new capital for his BPI bank (though Carli was favourable) and so this too collapsed. A banking consortium, backed by the Bank of Italy, was set up to reimburse the creditors of BPI, the bulk of the losses falling on the Bank of Rome which had heavily financed BPI. IOR lost tens of millions of dollars in the Franklin crash. The Bank of Italy was also involved in reimbursing clients of a Swiss bank, the so-called '500 list' of depositors which probably included Sindona's companies, IOR and other outfits involved in the illegal export of capital.

In 1974 Sindona's empire disintegrated and he fled to America, where he was arrested to face trial at a New York court for bankruptcy at the Franklin bank. He was sentenced to 25 years for illegal currency dealing and grand larceny. Yet he was not imprisoned, apparently because the Americans had persuaded him to broker a deal with the Mafia to set up a Cruise missile base in Comiso, Sicily. In Italy, magistrates charged IOR's second highest official, together with his predecessor and the bank's chief accountant, for complicity with Sindona. The latter avoided prosecution for illegal currency dealing by citing his 500 list from the Swiss bank, with a view to blackmail since the list named prominent Italians who were also guilty of that offence. Sindona was extradited to Italy and imprisoned, where apparently he died of suicide or was possibly poisoned, much to the relief of all concerned.

Roberto Calvi was Chairman and Managing Director of the Banco Ambrosiano, founded by a priest in 1896. His career at the bank spanning 35 years, Calvi's ambition was to take financial control by acquiring a majority shareholding. An associate of Sindona, Calvi acquired the liquidated deposit funds from the latter's failed banks, and took over the transaction of business for IOR, which had substantial shareholdings in the Ambrosiano. The latter was controlled by companies in which it possessed a financial interest, such as Toro Insurance. Another major function of the Ambrosiano was as financial arm to Licio Gelli's P2 masonic lodge. [21]

---

[21] See Chapter Eight

Known as God's banker, Calvi adopted Sindona's expansion strategy of profiting from the use of other people's money by using the Ambrosiano bank as a central hub, around which he spun his intricate web of speculation and financial trafficking. The ruse consisted of creating foreign 'shell' companies based in Latin America and Panama, which acted as a conduit for the receipt and re-routing of monies. Calvi bought up Italian companies on behalf of these shell companies controlled by the Ambrosiano, and selling them back to the latter at a higher price, the difference in capital being re-exported to Calvi's overseas holdings. From here he used the money to purchase shares or place it in the San Gottardo bank in Switzerland, owned by the Ambrosiano, whence he directed the monies to political parties, groups and individuals, thereby locking them all into his control and eventual blackmail. IOR owned ten of Calvi's shell companies, with Archbishop Marcinkus sitting on their boards; as well as being a director of the Ambrosiano operation in the Bahamas. It may have been that Marcinkus was under pressure to produce high yield returns to cover the Vatican's burgeoning budget deficits of some $20-30 million per annum. He remarked: 'We place our money where it earns the most'.

Calvi pursued his expansion in other quarters, such as buying up solid local banks, for instance *Credito Varesino,* in order to milk their funds; yet he was not always successful. As with Sindona, he moved to acquire control of the Centrale electricity company, but Ciampi, Governor of the Bank of Italy, intervened to stop its sale. Calvi inveigled Carlo De Benedetti, head of Olivetti, onto the board of the Ambrosiano. However, when De Benedetti realised that something was amiss, Calvi dismissed him with a golden handshake. De Benedetti received a six-year sentence against which he appealed. Sindona was miffed that Calvi had not come to his rescue, so he had one of his own colleagues inform the Bank of Italy of Calvi's murky dealings. The bank had harboured suspicions about the Ambrosiano, and in 1977 twelve inspectors carried out an investigation, which revealed Calvi's deception. Ciampi had the bank's internal regulations changed, and called in loans. Analysis of the Ambrosiano's foreign interests centred on the export of capital, the key to all the financial movements, which proved so entangled that it was impossible to give a precise valuation. The revelations led to the collapse of Calvi's financial empire in 1981. Faced with 16 charges for fraudulent currency transactions, he was sentenced to four years' imprisonment and a fine of $16 billion, and forced to reveal the names of his fellow directors at the Ambrosiano.

In 1979 Paolo Baffi, governor of the Bank of Italy, together with Mario Sarcinelli, deputy director, began their investigations into the Ambrosiano bank. Their enquiry was suddenly halted by Antonio Alibrandi, a right-wing magistrate in Rome, who had Sarcinelli imprisoned for almost a fortnight. He was released for lack of legal evidence. Baffi had his passport taken, and retired shortly afterwards in protest. It was widely rumoured that Alibrandi had acted for political motives in an effort to bury the case. Released on bail, in 1982 Calvi fled to London where, four days before his trial in Milan, he was found early one morning hanging from Blackfriars Bridge. The first English inquest returned a verdict of suicide, but the Italians were not convinced. His wife thought suicide impossible since the insurance would not pay out for such an act; though apparently Calvi had been depressed shortly before his death. The day before he died his secretary had jumped out of her office window to her death, leaving a note in which she denounced her boss. A second inquest returned an open verdict.

The Ambrosiano bank was wound up, with debts amounting to over a billion dollars, probably the largest loss in Europe since 1945. It seems that Calvi had financed some $1400 million to unknown people and groups; and possibly donating some $50 million to the democratic Solidarity movement in Poland. The Vatican denied any legal responsibility regarding violation of currency regulations and tax evasion. However, in recognition of its moral involvement, it paid off $244 million to its creditors and agreed to submit the disputes to the Italian courts for arbitration, thereby accepting liability under Italian law. To the discomfiture of major international banks, Ciampi refused to recognise Calvi's enormous debts to them. The Ambrosiano was re-invented as the *Nuovo Banco Ambrosiano*, having briefly involved the *Istituto San Paolo di Torino* and *Banca Nazionale del Lavoro* BNL; and later merging with *Banca Cattolica del Veneto* to become *Amroveneto*, the largest private bank at that time.

Chapter Six

Economic Miracle

In 1945 the Italian economy was moribund, with massive unemployment and highly disruptive strikes centred on Turin in 1947, which the government wisely dealt with in moderation. Miraculously, much of Italian industry had survived unscathed, with 85% of its plant intact, thanks to prudent protection during the war; but roads and railways were severely damaged. Heavy bombing by the Germans and the Allies had devastated housing everywhere, such that in Milan and other cities many lived in hovels and on the streets. Wartime rationing of food and fuel was lifted and no price controls were imposed, which unleashed galloping inflation. Food and other essential items, even indigenous products such as flour and olive oil, became extremely scarce and outrageously expensive, dominated by a thriving black market. Women were reduced to selling themselves to feed their children.

In order to promote exports vital to the economic recovery, especially textiles, no foreign exchange controls were put in place, which allowed exporters to hold foreign currency used to invest in new machinery. They also preferred to trade in dollars rather than lira, as did the government, which encouraged speculation. The banks offered unlimited credit facilities which, together with the circulation of the Allies' Amlire currency, further exacerbated inflation. In 1947 Prime Minster De Gasperi appointed the Liberal Luigi Einaudi[22] as Budget Minister. Formerly Professor of Economics & Finance at Turin University, he was appointed governor of the Central Bank of Italy from 1945 to 1948. He immediately imposed a tough deflationary budget to rein in inflation. He

---

[22] Einaudi was President of Italy 1948-55. He wrote for the Economist newspaper until 1946 whilst Governor of the Bank of Italy. His grandson Ludovico is the pianist and composer.

restricted credit to business, froze 25% of bank deposits and made drastic cuts to government expenditure. By 1949 he had managed to stabilize the Lira at 625 to the dollar by imposing exchange rate controls, which settled the economy and restored international confidence in Italy after the debacle of the Mussolini years.

Einaudi's stability budget proved popular with the cautious middle classes and conservative rural workers, which enabled the Christian Democrat party to secure victory in the 1948 elections. Left-wingers also approved of his budget since they viewed the fixed exchange rate as a wealth tax on the Liberals, who in turn naturally considered the policy an erosion of their hard-earnt income. Einaudi's credit squeeze restricted trade unions' demands for higher wages, which were simply impractical at that time, since keenly priced goods were vital for healthy receipts from higher value exports. By the 1950s private companies were able to build up sufficient profits to reinvest the proceeds in their businesses, rather than having to resort to expensive bank loans. Bosses usually voted for the smaller Liberal and Republican parties who promoted free trade and opposed state intervention.

Thanks to Einaudi's prudent management of the economy, in 1947 Italy became a member of the International Monetary Fund IMF. Prodded by De Gasperi's trips to the United States, between 1943 and 1948 the Americans supplied over two billion dollars to Italy under its Lend Lease scheme; supplemented by $1.5 billion under the Marshall Plan during 1948-52 (also known as the European Recovery Programme), the latter sum constituting 2% of Italy's GNP and 11% of the total funds disbursed for Europe. 80% of the $1.5bn was allocated firstly to grain, coal and steel; later the emphasis shifted to purchasing machinery for state and private industry, especially to Fiat, Finsider, Edison and the thermoelectric companies. The remaining 20% came in the form of soft loans, targeted on textiles. A counterpart fund *fondolire* was put in place for various projects, equal to income received in dollars; and which increased the Bank of Italy's severely depleted currency reserve to ensure stability. Funds were also allocated to the South to the *Cassa per il Mezzogiorno* Southern Fund and the agricultural reform boards.

The inflow of American cash was vital to Italy's economic recovery; helping to place her in the vanguard of Europe's advancing economy. American supplies of desperately needed food and fuel helped stave off hunger and social unrest, which dampened enthusiasm for Communism. The United States was now the world's foremost economy and was keen to access new export markets, hence its interest in Italy. The tens of thousands of Italians who had emigrated to the US since the 1880s, made excellent ambassadors for their host country, seen as the land of hope and opportunity, sending remittances to their families back home: all of which encouraged Italy's appreciation of their benefactor. The American company Aramco assisted Finsider in the design of new steel mills. Smaller firms, especially in engineering, also benefited from applying American technology, thereby boosting their exports. American marketing techniques, promoted by the advent of television advertising, were adopted in order to create a mass consumer base to boost sales and employment, and which in turn raised the standard of living.

In 1946 CGIL *Confederazione Generale dei Lavoratori Italiani* General Confederation of Italian Workers, re-formed in 1944 by the Pact of Rome and encompassing all political persuasions, agreed to mass lay-offs demanded by *Confindustria,* the employers' organisation, in order to cut costs and become more competitive for export markets. Even state companies within the IRI fold laid off 75,000 workers. Out of a total population of some 45 million, unemployment stood at 1.6 million in 1947 and reached over two million by 1951, with four million on short time working, which particularly hit women involved in domestic piece-work such as toys, clothing and lace-making. On a more positive note, the unions managed to secure nationally a guaranteed minimum national wage, together with an annual Christmas bonus *il tredicesimo* and more holidays; and setting a minimum wage difference of 14% between North and South. Employers were becoming increasingly anxious over the rising tension of the Cold War with Communist Russia; as well as the nuclear menace from Korea. As a result, both state and private employers preferred to hire rural youngsters who had no link with trade union militancy.

Blue collar workers, led by union leaders, many of whom had fought in the Resistance, protested at the job cuts by occupying factories: bosses counter-attacked by organising lock-outs. At the Ansaldo steelworks in Genoa workers occupied the factory for two months, only to end in voluntary redundancy and sackings. Private companies such as Fiat, Olivetti and Pirelli made strenuous efforts to marginalise CGIL workers, yet at the same time increasing their workforce. The Americans were concerned about Communist infiltration at Fiat, in response to which its president, Vittorio Valletta, mollified them by stating that militants were dismissed, and that many new workers were trained at Fiat's own technical school. The police suppressed any whiff of subversion, such as factory trespass, even charging those who put up Communist posters or sold its newspaper *L'Unita*. Such was the price to be paid for American aid.

The Communists had remained strong in the 'red belt' of central Italy which was historically anti-clerical, especially in Emilia-Romagna, due to repressive rule by the Papacy over the centuries. Many had belonged to the Garibaldi Resistance brigades and had fought heroically alongside the Russians against Hitler. By 1947 the PCI Communist Party claimed half a million members through its farming co-operatives in this region, rising to over two million by 1954. That year some 600,000 *braccianti* landless labourers went on strike in the Po valley. They comprised the largest sector of workers, along with *mezzadri* sharecroppers, and small artisanal firms. The PCI managed to exercise a restraining influence on the restless labourers to avoid a repetition of the extremism of the 1920s *Biennio rosso*. The PCI also had a strong base in the industrial zone of Porto Marghera by Venice, a 'red' oasis within the 'white' Catholic zone. The city of Bologna, historically a vibrant commune, later became a showcase of Communist respectability, a beacon of virtue outside the clientelistic jungle of their DC rivals, not least for its government's moral probity and model of efficiency, with balanced books and generous social welfare.

In 1947 the Communists took control of the League of Cooperatives dominant in Emilia-Romagna. They were responsible for wine and dairy production in the provinces of Reggio Emilia and Modena; whilst those in Ravenna owned or rented large farms. The League also managed building co-operatives in the cities, together with housing associations and retail shops. Many young people and former partisans ran the co-ops, attracted by the ethic of democratic fraternity which also involved a fair number of middle-class Italians. The smaller Republic and Social Democrat parties also formed their own co-operatives.

Under Togliatti the Communists endeavoured to spread their net wide to embrace many sections of society, adopting a similar catch-all approach to that of the DC. Their *Case del Popolo* 'Houses of the People' harked back to the earlier mutual aid societies of the 19th century, organising a social mix of discussions, films, sports and children's activities; some provided public baths and medical centres. The Communist *Feste dell'Unitā* were the annual highlight, especially those in Rome, with their programme of open-air song and dance. Begun by Italian exiles in Paris in the 1930s, this socio-political event also attracted non-Communists.

The PCI teamed up with the PSI Socialist party, who were weaker in central Italy, to jointly promote ANPI National Association of ex-Partisans; also with the UDI Union of Italian Women, an offshoot of the women's Resistance group. By 1954 UDI claimed over a million members, with their own journal *Noi Donne*. Outwardly concerned with the care of children, the sick and the elderly, crucially the association brought women into the political world and helped to present women with a wider social framework. In fact, the process that had begun during the war when many acted as partisans. Soviet attitudes towards family life were similar to the Italian model, although many Italian wives resented the amount of time their husbands spent away from home at political meetings. But politically the Communist party was out in the cold, upstaged by CGIL, having failed to secure better pay and working conditions, and prioritising ideological rhetoric which did not put food into workers' stomachs.

In 1948 an attempt was made on Togliatti's life. The attack unleashed an outburst of strikes, demonstrations and factory occupations. Prisons were besieged. Vittorio Valletta at Fiat was taken hostage but was released unharmed. The revolt spread to Genoa where a curfew was imposed; also to militant miners in Tuscany. The rioters tried to take over Palazzo Chigi, the PM's residence in Rome. In the South there were street battles in Naples and Taranto. Civil war threatened. Thankfully the PCI called off the strikes and after three days the dangerous moment passed. The police and army arrested or charged some 7,000 rioters; 15 lost their lives. Togliatti died in 1964, having led the PCI for twenty years and latterly disillusioned by Stalin's increasing autocracy and brutality. His funeral was attended by over a million people.

In 1952 the *Scala Mobile* Wage Index was introduced, which at last lifted workers' wages (previously suppressed by Mussolini and the trade unions) from well below the European average by linking pay to inflation and revised every two months. Yet the Index eventually created a wage dualism since it gave preference to public employees in local government and state industry. Smaller firms had no trade unions, 90% having five or fewer workers, which allowed them to pay lower wages and no insurance. Despite these improvements in working conditions, hard times persisted. In addition to widespread unemployment there existed a dire housing shortage, such that thousands still lived in woeful circumstances. Outside Rome people camped in former barracks, made shift in shacks and caves, or inhabited the *borgate* shanty districts which the Fascists had thrown together as temporary accommodation. CGIL did put forward a sensible plan *Piano del Lavoro* to combat mass unemployment and poverty by proposing a vast public spending programme on new housing, schools and hospitals; together with agricultural improvements in the South and nationalisation of electricity. Yet De Gasperi's government and Confindustria resented CGIL's initiative and rejected the plan as being politically motivated, declaring that all available money was already being spent on other projects.

Following the attempt on Togliatti's life and subsequent strikes, in 1950 the CGIL split into three unions: its eponymous Communist/Socialist core strong in central Italy; the Catholic/DC CISL *Confederazione Italiana Sindacati Liberi* and the smaller Social Democrat/Republican UIL *Unione Italiana Lavoratori*; with an overall total of some 5.5 million members. As a consequence, the DC ACLI Association of Italian Christian Workers (technically not a trade union), with one million members by 1960, gravitated towards more social activities, centred on its *circoli* clubs; whilst CISL adopted a more political stance, attracting the more moderate and younger workers, especially from the Catholic Veneto. Given that Catholic leaders such as Fanfani frowned upon their right to strike, CISL targeted bargaining at company level and better pay linked to productivity, and developed a more amenable relationship with employers. CISL grew in membership, firstly in the textile strongholds of the Catholic Veneto and state industry, and later appealing to the young.

In the early 1950s, Oscar Sinigaglia, an experienced steel magnate, who was involved in the ECSC[23] negotiations, and the first president of Finsider, put forward his Plan for the modernisation of iron and steel to transform it into a powerhouse for Italy's industrial take-off; as previously with Britain, France and Germany; and more recently China. Steel also came to be viewed as a symbol of national unity: production rose from 1.6 million tons in 1937, 2.3mT 1950, 10.2mT 1963, 29mT 1974, and reaching 41m tons by 1981, when Italy became second only to Japan. As a comparison China's output in 2015 was 1.2 billion tons. The Sinigaglia Plan provided for the renovation of the older Ilva works at Bagnoli near Naples, also at Piombino, with both sites producing heavy custom materials. The modernized Cornigliano plant near Genoa began to produce steel from its blast furnace (forging steel out of iron ore) concentrating on plate and sheet laminates for cars, production of which tripled during 1958-63; also for electrical goods and domestic appliances. The Plan also supported private companies, such as Fiat and paper mills, since politicians felt that the state should

---

[23] European Coal & Steel Community

assist the private sector both with regard to output and employment, in order to achieve a balanced mixed economy and defuse social tension.

The economy at last began to pick up, with improving exports and per capita income returning to pre-war levels. Between 1958 and 1963, Italy's industrial production doubled, and its GNP grew by 6.3% per annum, replicating her first boom at the turn of the century; as against Europe's rate of 4.5%, though Italy had started from a lower base. Investment in factories and machinery rose by an average of 14% per annum; whilst industrial output rose at 8% p.a, led by engineering and chemicals, being second only to Japan's and rivalling West Germany's, and thus ranking Italy as the world's seventh industrial nation. Electrical energy trebled, whilst the newly discovered gas in the Po valley rose sevenfold. Montecatini propelled the petrochemicals sector, focusing particularly on synthetic rubber and fertilisers. The company later merged with its arch rival Edison to form Montedison. A myriad of smaller companies underpinned the larger companies in pyramid fashion, interdependent for ensuring a smooth supply chain.

The creation of the EEC in 1956 put an end to national protectionism, but the Italians rose to the challenge with a diverse product range and the use of advanced technology. The percentage of Italian exports to the EEC, Italy's new trading partner, rose in leaps and bounds from 23% in 1955 to 30% in 1960 reaching 40% by 1965. Early exports concentrated on the traditional labour intensive/low productivity sectors of food, furniture, textiles, clothing and footwear; to be superseded by higher value high tech manufactures: cars, chemicals, oil products, plastics, artificial fibres, electronics and precision tooling. Consumer durable white goods (refrigerators and washing machines), considered luxuries at that time for the domestic market, provided another significant export sector. By 1962 Olivetti was producing 652,000 typewriters; whilst plastics increased fifteen-fold between 1951 and 1961, with soaring exports. Imports usually exceeded exports but the balance of payments was rectified by remittances home from workers abroad.

These years of immense economic expansion came to be known as the Economic Miracle. As elsewhere in Europe, the core industries of iron and steel, chemicals, metallurgy, energy (especially HEP), engineering and textiles spearheaded the post-war boom. The figures speak for themselves. During the period 1951-64, steel production rose from three million to nearly ten million tons; chemical fibre more than doubled to 320,000 tons, petrol soared from

1.3mT to 8.5mT, and electricity rose from 29.2mKw to 76.3mKw. The automobile industry manufactured 118,000 cars in 1950, rising to over a million annually by 1963, and dominated by FIAT. The company was founded in 1899 by Giovanni Agnelli, engineer and later a senator. Mussolini looked favourably on the development of Fiat which prospered throughout the 1930s-40s. Agnelli's older grandson Giovanni, also known as Gianni and born in 1921, was the older son of Edoardo Agnelli (who died in an air crash in 1934) and Princess Virginia Bourbon del Monte di San Faustino. Gianni's maternal grandmother was American and a successful hostess in Rome. Gianni studied at Ford in Detroit (Henry Ford was a friend of his father), then returned to Italy to join the army and serve on the Russian front, followed by North Africa where he served with distinction. After the war he studied law and was always known as *Avvocato* lawyer, although he never practised. Italians are fond of such appellations, for instance *Cavaliere* for a businessman, *Ingegnere* for engineer and *Onorevole* for parliamentary deputies.

With the death of Giovanni Agnelli Senior in 1945, Vittorio Valletta took over Fiat. Impressed by American production methods, in 1953 he installed a vast assembly line at Mirafiori for the production of the 600cc 4 and 6-seater models. Nearly four million were sold during 1957-75, replacing the popular 500cc Topolino which had gone into production in 1937 (now being restored), and which started the Italians' love affair with the car. By 1965 there were 5.5 million cars on the road, providing Italians with undreamt mobility. Previously the bicycle had been the sole means of transport, followed by the Vespa and Lambretta scooters. The Vespa scooter was introduced in 1946 by Piaggio, established in 1884 at Pontevedra near Pisa, and which became Europe's biggest scooter maker.[24] Piaggio also owns MotoGuzzi motorbikes, based near Como.

Thanks to Valletta's skilful management, by the mid-60s sales were approaching $1.5 billion and with production of a million vehicles per annum, later diversifying into trucks, tractors and aeroplanes. In 1966 Fiat opened a factory at Togliattigrad in Russia, and secured exports to Turkey and Argentina. The Fiat 124, introduced in 1966, became a best seller, and in 1969 the company overtook Volkswagen as the largest car manufacturer, controlling 90% of Italian car sales, as well as 20% of trucks and cars. Fiat restricted the importation of Japanese cars until the 1980s. ENI kept the price of petrol artificially low to assist

---

[24] Piaggio went public in 2006. It entered into a joint venture with a Chinese company, developing the hybrid 'green' scooter; also the 'Ape' bee three wheeler popular in India.

Fiat, whose profits leapt by 45%, second only to 54% in chemicals. Fiat drove the economy, resembling Ford in its economic hegemony through its underpinning of an army of small firms supplying a myriad of products. It was quipped that, if Ford sneezed, the rest of the US economy caught a cold: Fiat was the Italian equivalent. Fiat thrived by keeping wages low, trade unions weak, and using American style production assembly lines to produce small affordable cars.

A serious road accident in 1952 prompted Gianni Agnelli to abandon his hedonistic lifestyle and join the Fiat business, becoming MD under Valletta. His grandfather had taken him under his wing, appointing Gianni chairman of IFI *Istituto Finanziario Industriale,* a holding company he had created to manage an umbrella of interests: oil, shipping, arms, banking, insurance, retailing and manufacture. The group also owned *La Stampa* and *Corriere della Sera* newspapers; Turin's football team, Juventus; and a private ski resort. In 1953 Gianni married Princess Marella Caracciolo di Castagneto from an old Neapolitan family: she was formerly a Vogue fashion model and photographer. They had a son and daughter. Sadly their son, Edoardo, became a drug addict and apparently took his own life. Gianni's nephew, Giovanni, died of cancer aged 33, and his father Umberto, heir to Fiat, died 16 months later. In 1966 Gianni Agnelli took over at the helm, installing state of the art assembly lines and employing forward-thinking managers trained in American business methods. He died in 2003, to be succeeded by the Italo-Canadian Sergio Marchionne.

Following in the footsteps of their Roman forebears for excellent road-building, the explosion in car ownership in the Peninsula led to the construction of motorways, the first being the A8 motorway north to the lakes and northern Europe and the first in Europe; whilst the *Autostrada del Sole* was begun in 1956 and finished in 1963, running the length of the western Peninsula and symbolizing national unity. Yet the boom in motor cars deterred investment in public transport. Vehicles also demanded huge inputs of oil, steel, rubber, plastics, glass and textiles. It is estimated that Fiat's production plan determined about one fifth of national economic investment. Key to the success of the Economic Miracle was the availability of cheap labour, cheap energy, cheap steel, modern production techniques, a free market and entrepreneurial initiative, all bolstered by the IRI state umbrella providing subsidy, tax credits and low interest rates. Both large public and private companies, such as ENI, Olivetti and Fiat, employed businessmen trained at Harvard or MIT in the States, offering linguistic skills and applying the American methods of up-to-date marketing, advertising and production.

Post-war emigration continued on a large scale, of which 74% came from the South. In 1963 there were 300,000 Italians in West Germany, accounting for 86% of the total emigrants there: 37% of the Italian intake worked on building sites and 25% in metalworking factories. France, Belgium and Switzerland (in the Italian speaking canton of Ticino, part of the Swiss Republic since 1803) remained favourite destinations, such as for fruit picking, with respectively 380,000, 160,000 and 200,000 workers. By 1971, 100,000 Italians had arrived in Britain, following upon their 19th century forebears. Some worked in the Bedfordshire brickworks because they could withstand the heat; whilst others toiled in the Libyan oil-fields. Migrants were usually single men working long hours, staying for about a year and returning nostalgically to their villages. During 1946-57, emigration overseas continued on a large scale, as ever to the Americas: USA 166,000, Argentina 380,000 and Venezuela 128,000; also Canada 165,000. Australia 138,000 became a popular destination.

Northern industry acted like a magnet to the economically depressed and overpopulated rural South: three million Southerners moved north to work in the factories. Many others moved from the north-eastern regions: Trento-Alto Adige and Friuli-Venezia Giulia. Veneto shed the highest percentage of its population: some 237,000, mostly to Piedmont and Lombardy. Internal migration throughout the 1950s and 60s totalled over nine million, with a surplus pool of unemployed workers standing at 8% (despite two million emigrants by 1956) against 2% in the rest of Europe. During 1951-64, the number of agricultural workers plummeted, including women, especially in the north east, from 48% to 26%. Most settled in Milan and Turin, but lesser cities exerted their economic pull, for instance Bergamo, Brescia, Padua, Varese and Verona. Milan absorbed 70% of its immigrants from Lombardy and Veneto, and 30% from the south. Its population jumped from 1.3 million in 1951 to 1.7m by 1967. The Milanese hinterland expanded rapidly in towns such as Monza and Rho. The number of metalworkers in Lombardy, the largest industrial sector, shot up by 200,000. Pirelli alone already employed 140,000 by the 1940s. Turin was by far the greatest host to immigrants, particularly from the Calabrian provinces of Bari and Foggia. The city grew from 720,000 in 1951 to over a million by 1967; whilst its hinterland of 23 communes expanded by over 80%. Turin was described as the third Southern city after Naples and Palermo, due to its huge intake of migrants.

In central Italy, Marche and Umbria lost a total of 100,000 inhabitants; Emilia-Romagna's stayed unchanged; whilst the Rome-Florence axis within the red belt of Tuscany absorbed 47,000. The area experienced a rural decline from 44% to 23%, especially amongst sharecroppers, from two million to under half a million by 1971. The South witnessed a drop from 57% to 37%, concentrated on Basilicata, Campania and Puglia. Many of them moved to Rome, as did those from Abruzzi: the capital's population rose from under two million in 1951 to 2.6 million by 1967. By 1961, 38% of the Italian population was involved in industry, with 32% in the fast expanding service sector; and with a drop to 30% in agriculture.

Initially the Northern migrants took the low paid unskilled jobs. They worked on building sites, for instance the centenary exhibition *Italia 61* in Milan and the construction of the city's underground railway. They worked long hours on short term three to six month contracts, often in dangerous conditions. They later moved on to more highly skilled work, for instance car assembly at Fiat, or at one of the myriad of its support firms. Urban youth often gained experience in the black economy then switched to the open market where acquired skills were essential. Migration proved to be a challenging venture. Uprooted from a backward slow-moving rural society to one of hectic urban living, many suffered a culture shock, wonderfully described in Italo Calvino's novel *Marcovaldo*. Many viewed factory life as a prison compared to their former working life out of doors. Illiterate migrant schoolchildren, speaking only their local dialect, were bewildered by the experience of being placed in northern schools.

The luckier ones stayed with relatives, who had already made the move. Otherwise, the single men shared rooms, built a rudimentary home, or simply slept rough. Washing and toilet facilities were virtually non-existent. Many found work through co-operatives, of which there existed some 300 in Turin, organising some 30,000 men, until 1960 when they were declared illegal. Southerners suffered discrimination on two counts: from their northern counterparts and employers since they were prepared to accept lower pay rates and perform the worst tasks; and from older urban southerners who now considered themselves superior to their country yokel cousins. Yet most men were only too relieved to at last be earning a regular wage with defined hours, unlike the precarious rural existence they had previously endured. Most returned home for a few days, to see their loved ones and donate part of their income. Southern women began to work in the northern factories but with lower pay than their menfolk; yet many revelled in their new freedom and economic independence (reminiscent of Englishwomen during the war). Married women did piece work at home or dressmaking. Many migrants worked in bars, shops and restaurants: signs of increasing prosperity in the services sector.

A significant sector concerned smaller and medium sized family enterprises SMEs that stretched from the north-west regions of Lombardy and Piedmont further south along the line of Roman *municipiae* market towns on the Via Emilia, passing between the northern plain and the Apennines to the south, through Piacenza, Parma, Reggio, Modena, Bologna (regional capital of Emilia Romagna) into the Veneto on the Adriatic; and into Marche and Abruzzo. Firms in these areas constituted Third Italy, a term coined by an Italian sociologist to describe businesses offering a different approach from the traditional large state and private companies which had evolved under Fascism. Employing up to fifty workers but often fewer than twenty (just five workers was not uncommon) who were mostly self-employed, SMEs worked in artisanal goods, important since the days of the medieval communes and the beginnings of mercantilist expansion. They now diversified into modern sectors, such as precision tooling and parts for larger metalworking companies.

Highly dependent on the larger companies for work, these firms thrived in a close-knit Catholic community which engendered a sense of mutual trust between boss and workers, and ensured decent wages and benefits which helped to defuse socio-political tension. Apart from the state owned Mediobanca, Italian banks were no longer geared up for large scale investment in big companies and so confined themselves to local lending to SMEs whose requirements were more modest than their grander cousins. The State was indulgent towards them in matters of taxation and bureaucratic supervision.

Paul Ginsborg[25] offers a comprehensive survey of employment amongst SMEs. Light manufacturing, known as *industrializzazione diffusa*, spread out into the countryside. Industrial districts tended to specialize, for instance hosiery at Carpi, ceramics at Sassuolo (both near Modena), and textiles as ever at Prato and Biella in Piedmont. Como (Lombardy) switched from traditional silk factories to high tech home-based weaving, whilst Vigevano south-west of Milan produced a quarter of Italy's shoe exports; also at Ascoli Piceno (Abruzzo). An

---

[25] Op.cit.page 234

interesting development was the number of young *mezzadri* sharecroppers who abandoned farming to their parents and set up in business in the towns, often pulling together as a family to drive the business forward. *Braccianti* landless agricultural labourers, who had suffered centuries of ill-treatment, drifted into workshops. In the 1960s, the discovery of methane reserves in the Po valley attracted oil refineries and petrochemicals along the north Adriatic coast, together with associated sectors.

Vera Zamagni[26] describes SMEs as 'large scale niche capitalism', offering a more viable model better suited to the Italian artisanal workshop tradition, backed up by good technical schools; as opposed to the monopoly capitalism of state-run organisations, or the large American style company run on assembly lines and mass production. Forming the backbone of the Italian economy, SMEs would often be run as a group of small companies, with employees being allowed to set up their own units. Parallel to the new dynamism of high powered executives in the large company sector, export industries often involved small family firms who, untrammelled by trade unionism and possessed of creative design, took on a new breed of technically competent *liberi professionisti* self-employed white-collar professionals, who could adapt production swiftly to changing market conditions. Healthy profits made these businesses self-financing, boosted by remittances received from relatives overseas to pay for raw materials, new machinery and state of the art production methods. At this time some 90% of factories employed just twenty people or fewer. As a comparison, in 2015 British firms employing up to 250 workers constituted 60% of the private sector.

The white goods sector provides an interesting example of the development of some SMEs into large multinational companies. In their early days Candy produced one washing machine a day, its rival Ignis near Varese employed just a few dozen workers, whilst Zanussi at Pordenone (Friuli) had 250 workers. By 1967, Zanussi had produced 3.2 million refrigerators and dishwashers, ranked third after the US and Japan, and was the largest European manufacturer. The company brought much prosperity to its local town. Candy and Ignis were also strong in refrigerators.

The Economic Miracle gave rise to a changed employment mix, particularly in the white-collar sector (including office staff and white coat technicians) from just under 2 million in 1951 to 2.6m by 1961 and 3.3m by 1971 i.e. from 10% to

---

[26] P.MacCarthy: Italy since 1945 page 55

17% of the total workforce. Comparison figures were 19% in France for 1968 and 23% in Britain for 1966. Petrochemicals, cars and typewriters were vast growth sectors; whilst newer avenues such as public relations, advertising and journalism, grew apace. Again, Italy's rise was all the more remarkable since it started from a lower base rate. With regard to the public-sector white-collar workers constituted 4.5% of the active workforce in 1951, 6% in 1961 and 9% in 1971; as against 7% in France in 1968 and 11% in Britain in 1966. The building and transport sectors saw significant expansion, together accounting for 23% of the total workforce in 1951, 29% in 1961 and 33% by 1971. Lower middle-class artisans remained stable during 1951-71, now attracting electricians and car mechanics; as did shopkeepers, bastion of the Christian Democrats.

Gradually, the workers and their families began to be better off, such that by the late '50s/early '60s Italians themselves could at last begin to afford the luxury of domestic appliances such as the refrigerator and the washing machine: no more handwashing at the communal laundry or fountain, though they did provide a social focus. Mass produced clothing banished homespuns, whilst a decent pair of shoes was no longer a dream. Many could now afford to eat hitherto luxuries of meat, milk and sugar. Standards of hygiene improved, with running water, inside toilets and drains. People were now better fed and housed, with increased life expectancy. Infant mortality declined, as did major diseases such as malaria in the South; also illiteracy as more children attended school. A rise in post-war marriages led to a baby boom in the '60s, after which urban living ushered in the nuclear family, with fertility dropping to two or three children per family. The smaller family offered greater privacy, yet maintaining family solidarity. Maternity pay (at 80% of final salary) was one of the most generous in Europe at that time, although the civil service encouraged married women to give up work, as in Britain. From a base rate of 100 in 1950, per capita income rose to 234 by 1970 against 132 in Britain, 136 in France; and by 1976 had risen to 60% of that in France and 82% of that in Britain. Tired of Fascist indoctrination and war, people simply wanted to rebuild their lives with a decent job and acceptable standard of living.

In 1954 the advent of television, RAI *Radio Audizioni Italia* helped to standardise the Italian language throughout the Peninsula and offered a sense of national unity. The Peninsula boasted hundreds of dialects: until recently villagers in neighbouring mountain valleys could not comprehend each other. The new medium revealed an utterly new world to parochial Italian viewers, which was reinforced by the growth of tourism displaying different lifestyles. Previously radio, established in 1924, had been the sole source of information for the illiterate. Television now became the essential news source in the absence of a tradition of reading books and newspapers accessible only to the well-educated and which, together with the theatre and cinema, were still subject to Fascist censorship laws until 1962 and closely monitored by the Church. The small screen offered a cheering mix of light entertainment, comedies, romantic films and quiz shows with pretty girls. For instance, the quiz *'Lascia o raddoppia'* 'Double or Quits' was immensely popular, whilst the ten minute *Carosello* programme catered for children but cunningly interspersed with seductive advertising. Television sets proliferated throughout the '60s, becoming a focal social point in the village bar, helping to while away the long winter evenings. National sports were popular viewing: cycling, motor racing and football. On the debit side television was politically biased, with just one nationwide programme *RAI Uno* controlled by the DC.

Picture-based glossy magazines, such as *Oggi, Gente* and *Epoca,* depicted glamorous American film stars, lighting up people's humdrum lives and at the same time improved their Italian. The news magazine *L'Espresso* started up in 1955. In 1965 Mondadori produced its first mass paperback Oscar series. The age of mass consumerism had arrived. Newspapers such as *Corriere della Sera* remained a select sector, its heavy reading making it accessible only to the well-educated, until the advent of *La Repubblica* which presented news in a clearer language and better format. They were mainly regional and often controlled by business empires with a political bias, for instance *La Stampa* of Turin was owned by Fiat.

Cinema became enormously popular, having appeared during the Fascist years, albeit subject to censorship by Mussolini and the Church. In its early days cinema was dominated by Hollywood imports depicting glamorous lifestyles totally extraneous to Italian viewers; yet brilliantly contested by Fellini's *La Dolce Vita,* with Monica Vitti splashing about in the Trevi Fountain in Rome. Gradually the Italian film industry developed during the 1950s, centred on the sunny Cinecittà studios outside Rome. Influenced by Francois Truffaut's *Nouvelle Vague*, Neorealist drama dealt with social problems ignored by escapist television, employing a simple direct style and in total contrast to the wave of American films. They were shot in the open air, with directors improvising as they went along, for instance Bertolucci's *Proibito Rubare* 1948 and

L'Imperatore di Capri 1949. His 1953 film *Pane, Amore e Fantasia*, a light romantic comedy, proved to be a great success, and introduced Gina Lollobrigida from Abruzzi.

Rossellini's first production *Roma città aperta* Rome open city drew on the wartime Resistance experiences of partisans working together for a common cause. Vittorio De Sica's *Ladri di Bicicletta* Bicycle Thieves underlined the importance of that sole means of transport for many during war time. Film producers portrayed the brutal reality of life which often shocked audiences: for example Pier Paolo Pasolini's *Mamma Roma* 1962, with Anna Magnani portaying a prostitute mother. Luchino Visconti's *Rocco & his Brothers* 1960 depicted the tale of young Sicilians who move to Milan in search of a better life. Vibrant *diva* actresses symbolised the new image of post-war Italy, such as Sofia Loren who came from a humble Neapolitan background and who showed that one could rise from rags to riches. The film director Luigi Comencini often worked with children, such as *Le Avventure di Pinocchio*, which starred Gina Lollobrigida. Comedies *cinema rosa* were also popular, for instance the comedian Totò from Naples.

In 1942 Luchino Visconti directed his first film *Ossessione*. Later he created *Il Gattopardo* The Leopard, beautifully written by Tommaso di Lampedusa in 1958. One of Italy's first best sellers, the book was rejected by Einaudi but snapped up by Feltrinelli who appreciated the magical quality of the book. The story recounts the tale of a Sicilian noble family who learn to change just a little in order to remain the same at the time of the Risorgimento. In 1971 Visconti created Death in Venice, set to the haunting *adagietto* of Mahler's Fifth Symphony. The director Francesco Rosi from Naples sometimes worked with Visconti on socio-political themes, such as corruption in the South. Antonioni's Blow-Up, produced by Carlo Ponti, Sofia Loren's husband, was a revelation in technique and style, dazzling cinema goers with its portrayal of London in the Swinging Sixties, along with its enigmatic play on empty spaces and a silent tennis match. The theatre gradually relaxed the Fascist censorship to allow for the portrayal of sex and homosexuality.

Post-war Italy produced a feast of excellent writers, to name just a few: Calvino, Levi, Moravia, Ginsborg, Pasolino and Sciascia. Giorgio Bassani's novel *Il Giardino dei Finzi Contini* dealt with the plight of a Jewish family in wartime Italy (he was one of the few to survive Auschwitz). De Sica crafted a sensitive film of the book. Later Umberto Eco achieved fame with his mystery

Il Nome della Rosa. A rich selection of female writers came to the fore, for instance Natalia Ginsborg and Oriana Fallaci.

In 1952 Italy was invited to participate in the European Coal & Steel Community ECSC, which gave the state holding Finsider a foothold in the European steel market: it eventually rivalled Germany in output. In 1958 Italy became a founder member of the European Economic Community EEC, which abolished all protective tariffs so as to boost trade amongst the six founder nations in order to regenerate the European economy. De Gasperi was much involved in the negotiations. Alfiero Spinelli, leader of the European Federalist Movement, favoured such an approach to promote political union; together with the free movement of people to resolve Italy's huge unemployment problem. However, economic issues prevailed such that the EEC evolved into essentially a trading pact for the time being. Psychologically the EEC restored Italian self-confidence and offered a way forward from its Fascist experience. A further boost to Italy's self-esteem was her membership in 1949 of the European Defence Community EDC, which automatically included her in NATO, boosted by the transfer of its headquarters to Naples in 1951. The pull of the US and NATO, combined with that of the EEC, encouraged Italy to look West rather than to the Soviet/Communist East, as well as North not South to the Mediterranean. Italy had re-established herself on the international stage.

Chapter Seven

Hot Autumn: From Economic Miracle to Crisis

By 1963 the labour market in the North was beginning to tighten as the supply of workers dried up from the South, resulting in full employment. The economic miracle had started from a low base rate and had now peaked, with apparently no more room for manoeuvre to sustain the miracle. Factory workers had become dissatisfied with the monotony of long hours of repetitive assembly work and resented the regimented approach of their bosses. Many nostalgically remembered the more relaxed and individualistic rhythm of working on the land in the open air. Bosses, more powerful than the fragmented trade unions at this time, invested in new technology which would reduce manning, given that rising labour costs were affecting productivity and exports, which in turn fuelled inflation and upset the national balance of payments. A labour-intensive economy no longer seemed viable.

People had been obliged to adapt to radical changes during a brief timespan, and consequently social frustrations had built up to a dangerous level. Outside work people were exasperated by the dearth of essential infrastructure: crammed into grim high-rise flats in the middle of nowhere, devoid of amenities with no decent roads or public transport (the latter neglected partly due to pressure from Agnelli at Fiat); and deprived of local shops, schools and hospitals. Socially Southerners felt discriminated against in the North, being referred to scornfully as *terroni* and echoing the centuries-long regionalism of the Italians. Many had left the South in sheer desperation, expecting to find a better life in the north. Yet they had simply exchanged one form of enslavement for another and were bitterly angry. Discontent was further fuelled by the stark contrast of tantalising films and advertising shown on television, which preyed upon people's latent desires.

Younger workers were now better educated, including Southern migrants who had grown up in the north. Politically aware, they were now equipped to present their demands and lead their comrades, coupled with their knowledge of superior conditions abroad (in the previous century many Italian workers in Germany had been inspired by Socialism). Workers came to despise their bosses and the politicians for their failure to provide a better standard of living and a more congenial workplace. They now wanted a greater slice of the cake. In addition to improvements in pay and working conditions, employees demanded health and safety procedures, as well as an enhanced partnership with management and a share of the profits; in addition to a marked improvement in housing and urban amenities. Workers were tired of *malgoverno*: the government's failure to address grass roots socio-economic issues, being more intent on retaining power for power's sake and feathering their own nests.

In 1948 the all-party trade unions confederation had split into three sectors which weakened its political clout to deal with the government's resistance to workers' demands. During the 1950s, national contracts were settled directly with the government, often excluding the Communist CGIL, the largest union which was strongest in the industrial northwest and republican Emilia-Romagna. Yet the PCI hesitated to stir up trouble since they feared a right-wing backlash. Although trade unions were legally allowed after their suppression by the Fascists, the government remained wary of them, as did employers for whom cheap labour was essential to exports and profits. Bosses discouraged CGIL membership: for instance Fiat pressurized workers to switch to the more moderate trades-based Catholic CISL union or face possible dismissal. The smaller UIL union, also more moderate, was composed of Social Democrat and Republican sympathisers: many of the latter were businessmen. Many in government accepted high wages as a moral condition for social harmony.

1962 witnessed the first signs of deep-rooted dissatisfaction, when the annual contract for the *Metalmeccanici* metalworkers came up for renewal. This was the largest labour sector with over one million trade union members by 1972, and the biggest at Fiat. A great surge of unrest welled up at Turin in many engineering firms that year, with southern workers taking the lead together with Marxist intellectuals, reaching a peak in 1963 with 2,782 strikes by 2.4 million workers. The metalworkers' unions claimed a reduction from 45 to a 40 hour/six-to-five-day week; a decline in pay differentials and greater freedom for trade union representation on the shopfloor. In that same year the workforce at Lancia Turin, with a strong southern element, struck for an end to short term contracts and a third week of paid holidays, with demonstrations in and outside the factory. They managed to secure many of their demands. On the other hand, a strike by Michelin employees, also in Turin, led to serious police clashes lasting 90 days, but ended in virtual failure.

Following these incidents, a national strike was called for on 13th June 1962 involving 100,000 workers. Significantly, the unions at Fiat had held back from the disturbances, since the management provided them with good social benefits. In the '50s the bosses had curtailed trade union activity, excluded troublemakers and employed few southerners. Yet much to the relief of the protesters, on 22/23rd June most of the Fiat workers decided to come out on strike, rising to some 60,000 and being most of the workforce. In July FIOM and FIM, respectively the metalworkers' branches of CGIL and Catholic CISL (the latter hitherto pacifist) called for a mass strike of all metalworkers in Turin, involving both northern and southern workers. Fierce clashes with the police ensued outside the vast Fiat factory at Mirafiori and other plants but, that same day 7th July, the right-wing UILM and Fiat's company union SIDA struck an agreement with management. In revenge some 6,500 workers ran riot in Piazza Statuto, Turin creating mayhem over two days, with police resorting to the use of tear gas. The unions, PCI and PSI claimed the ugly riots were the work of *agents provocateurs* having been paid to make trouble. In fact half of the protesters were Southern workers.

The tightening of the labour market forced bosses to concede wage increases and better working conditions. They carried out a programme of restructuring, replacing outdated machinery, introducing new techniques and automation; but with a resultant reduction in manning and an acceleration of work to achieve greater productivity and economies of scale: all of which only renewed pressure on workers. Increased piece-rate work accentuated differentials amongst employees. Management exercised control through the foreman who was responsible for job allocation and work surveillance. Shopfloor organisation, in the form of internal commissions, was run by the skilled who were usually immune to the concerns of the mass of semi/unskilled and female workers.

The arrival in 1963 of Moro's first coalition government with the Socialists raised workers' expectations of a better deal on work and living conditions. But they were to be bitterly disappointed. Moro was sympathetic towards employers' resistance to increased labour cost and, being a past master of procrastination, he resisted reform. Yet his conciliatory attitude only resulted in a fudging of the fundamental concerns and neutralized the Socialists. Throughout the '60s, the labour market continued to tighten, with southern migration peaking during the first wave from 1958 at 287,000 by 1963, but dropping to 120,000 per annum by 1967 and to under 100,000 by 1974.

The second wave from 1967 included some workers returning from Germany, Belgium and France. They were taken on by companies such as Fiat and Pirelli who preferred workers with foreign experience and qualifications. Yet their imported Socialist ideals made them potentially more disruptive. For their part southerners were also on a short fuse, unused to the pressurised working environment, and historically suspicious of their northern cousins. Furthermore, the educational reforms had reduced the supply of factory labour in Piedmont and Lombardy. Those who did take up such work were now better educated and more politically aware than the previous post-war generation. Consequently, bosses were now obliged to taken on an ever-increasing number of southerners but, with the economy slowing down after 1966 and with increased automation, jobs became scarcer.

With only meagre reforms enacted, 1968 saw a marked increase in the number of grass-roots factory protests and wildcat strikes, independent of trade union backing. Surprisingly, the first serious signs of worker agitation happened in the Marzotto textile factory in the Veneto, a SME family enterprise established in 1836 along the traditional lines of Catholic paternalism. Yet by the '60s the workers here were expected to work faster for lower wages, for which trade union representation was too weak to object. Redundancy loomed, as a result of which in April 4,000 demonstrators, including females, marched through the town and clashed with the police, who made 42 arrests.

In March 1968 the trade unions called for a general strike in support of higher pensions. As in 1962, the huge response was spearheaded by some 300,000 metalworkers from Milan, and significantly many white-collar workers took part. In a spirit of solidarity, students joined the factory picketing, believing that unity of leadership was essential for successful revolution. Blue collar semi and un-skilled workers came to realise that their grievances on the shop floor and outside work were similar to those of the non-union skilled technician and white-collar worker. These groups now amassed with the growing clamour from students and the non-parliamentary New Left, bypassing the ineffectual trade unions to present a formidable challenge to the vacillating government:

Contestazione confrontation. They consisted mainly of Leninist organisations, such as *Potere Operaio* Potop dominant in Turin and Porto Marghera (Venice); and *Avanguardia Operaia* AO based in Milan since 1969 and the best organised. The older far left intellectuals became involved with the smaller *Il Manifesto* group, which produced its eponymous newspaper, though many of its texts were too abstract except for the gifted few.

These radical New Left organisations were the largest in Europe and attracted thousands of militants during 1968-76. They arose out of disillusion with Russia's invasion of Hungary in 1956 and anger at the cosy political club of Socialists and Christian Democrats. Valuing their independence, they were both anti-capitalist and anti-trade unionist; yet they remained badly divided, ending up as subgroups of the mainstream parties. More worryingly they were all too prone to advocate violence, so common of the revolutionary movements in South America and Asia, but which sat awkwardly within West European society. They blithely assumed revolution would succeed in Italy yet failed to analyse correctly the Italian psyche.

The 1968 agitations were initiated by skilled workers who had previous experience of organising opposition to employers. Yet ironically it proved to be the Southern dominated *operai comuni* semi/unskilled who would take the lead and give the movement a tremendous momentum. The Pirelli factory at Bicocca in Milan set the scene for the confrontation. Here in late 1967 the trade unions struck for three days over the annual renewal of the contract for the rubber sector. In February '68 they secured only a modest rise in wages and no improvement in working conditions. In June 1969 a group of Pirelli blue and white-collar workers set up the *Comitato Unitario di Base* CUB United Base Committee which won over many semi-skilled workers, along with members of AO. Bitterly criticising the weakness of the trade unions and PCI, CUB eventually achieved a better deal for the workers at Pirelli. Other CUB cells sprouted up in Milan, and which came to be viewed as revolutionary workers' councils.

The Pirelli success, together with the momentous general strike in France of *mai 68*, spurred on workers elsewhere to achieve even greater gains to revolutionise worker-employer relations, such as an end to piece-work rates and slower assembly lines, reduction of pay differentials between white and blue collar, and abolition of differences amongst blue collar workers; promotion of semi-skilled labour to a higher category; an end to 'wage cages': different rates for the same job in different parts of the country; and a better health and safety programme, supported by many doctors. It was argued that wage increases should become an 'autonomous factor', in other words not tied to productivity, profits or the economic situation. In essence workers demanded more pay for less work. By 1969 wages had outstripped the cost of living and were double those elsewhere within the OECD area Organisation for Economic Co-operation & Development.

Workers were encouraged to take an active part in mass assemblies rather than leave the talking to trade union delegates. Strikes were now called during talks rather than held back. Mass picketing, with working/middle-class student support, gave way in 1969 to protests inside factories and so mirroring the university sit-ins. Various wildcat strikes were devised to disrupt production on the shopfloor. The *singhiozzo* hiccup had the factory partly on strike, whilst the *scacchiera* chessboard tactic involved different parts of the shopfloor at varying times; or *autoriduzione* go-slow action. Foremen became powerless against this snowball of new self-confidence, and were often threatened physically or even beaten up.

The climax of the confrontation was reached in the autumn of 1969, following an economic upturn thanks to higher exports and yet again with a tight labour market. The FLM metalworkers union downed tools throughout all plants over the renewal of their contract, such as at Fiat Mirafiori, where mainly southerners waged a series of strikes for better conditions, in tandem with a student/worker assembly which met at Turin University. The national trade unions organised a one-day strike in July in protest at high rents. That same day, another group of several thousand workers set out from Mirafiori and other factories, raising their own banner: '*Che cosa vogliamo? Tutto!*' 'What do we want? Everything!' Not surprisingly, the demonstrators clashed with the police in the battle of Corso Traiano, recalling the unrest in Piazza Statuto in this city in 1962. Mass assemblies followed at Fiat and other Turin factories. Revolutionary tension was now at fever pitch, and for a short while the protesters, both workers and students, fervently hoped they would achieve a new dawn. *Lotta Continua* believed a revolution along the lines of the Chinese protest was now imminent.

Amazed and encouraged by the strength of protest, and galvanized into action by the metalworkers, at last the trade unions CGIL and CISL sank their differences and seized the initiative. They now presented a united front of national solidarity: *Contestazione.* Trade unions enthusiastically supported the semi/unskilled workers' cause. *Autunno Caldo* the Hot Autumn had arrived, involving 1.5 million strikers. The outcome was the worst social and industrial unrest since 1947, and virtually brought the Italian economy to a standstill, with an intense series of disruptive strikes, factory occupations and demonstrations. The rise in trade union membership had increased the number of protesters from under 2.5 million in 1963, to 3.2m by 1968, and reaching some 5 million in 1969. The number of working days lost rose from 127 million in 1962 to 233 million in 1969.

Labour Reform

FIM, CISL's metalworker union, took on a leading role in the events of the Hot Autumn and at times was more radical than CGIL's own union, FIOM. Even the right-wing UILM joined in. The bulk of the unions sought reasonable reform, promised but not delivered by the centre left governments of the '60s under Moro, with only a minority seeking more radical action. The fact that action was channelled through the official unions made the bosses more amenable to negotiation. In December 1969, the new metalworkers' contract was signed, with an outright victory for the workers, though the New Left were unimpressed. A forty-hour week was introduced, with equal wage increases for everyone, a narrowing of differentials, special concessions for apprentices and worker-students, together with the right to hold mass assemblies during the working day for a maximum of ten hours a year, and paid for by bosses. Workers were offered 150 hours of paid study leave. Further worker disruption over renewal of the 1972 contract secured the abolition of lower grades, and achieving a single wage scale *inquadramento unico* for all blue and white-collar employees. This successful outcome put the trade unions firmly back in the driving seat and restored their credibility with their members. In Paul Ginsborg's words: 'The hot autumn, for all its later notoriety, was not a further development of the revolutionary trends of the previous year, but rather the reassertion of trade union leadership in the factories'.[27]

Confronted by critical unrest at Nanterre and Paris universities and a nationwide general strike by some ten million workers, General de Gaulle was spurred on by a favourable general election to crush the revolt within three months. In contrast, Italy continued to experience an unprecedented wave of agitation. The Moro government was incapable of gaining the upper hand due to

---

[27] P.Ginsborg op.cit. page 318

lack of decisive leadership and the tremendous support in the country for the strikers' grievances. During 1970-71, the fight for better working conditions and control of the workplace spread to the chemical and building sectors, the railways and elsewhere. Trade unions were now negotiating on the shopfloor direct with management, as opposed to national level, and so made them more aware of local issues, dealing swiftly with workers' grievances. Demonstrations sprang up at smaller workplaces and filtered into the tertiary sector, where numerous white-collar employees and technicians struck; on into shops, hotels and bars where many women worked; and even those doing piece-work at home. Public sector workers such as teachers, civil servants, hospital staff and postmen claimed higher wages to keep the differential with blue collar workers, and sought greater democracy in the workplace as well as greater efficiency in the public services.

Essentially, the ultimate success of the *contestazione* confrontation lay in its appeal across the classes and age groups. Miraculously, the extent and virulence of the protest had the desired effect in at long last goading the inert politicians into enacting desperately needed reforms laid down in the 1948 Constitution. In 1970 the *Statuto dei Lavoratori* Workers' Statute ratified article 39 of the Constitution, which granted the right to form trade unions and agree collective labour contracts at local level, over and above national contracts; but excluded SMEs and female home workers. Union participation at company board level was now permitted; together with the right of appeal to the courts against unfair dismissal, and which often found in their favour. The unions secured the setting up of a 150-hour paid education scheme for workers. Another welcome innovation was the appearance of female shop stewards *delegate* on the shopfloor. Women were also granted their own meetings and personal factory facilities.

During 1970-71, the trade unions accepted the new style factory councils, which replaced the internal commissions, consisting of delegates elected by secret ballot to represent workers in all matters and in a more direct manner, but with close links to trade unions. Bosses bowed to the inevitable, whilst the New Left sniffed that the new councils were not truly democratic. By 1972 there were 4,290 such bodies in metalworking, representing over a million workers. The prudent action of the trade unions helped them to restore their credibility. Membership of CGIL and CISL bounced upwards from four million in 1968 to five million by 1972, reaching 6.6 million by 1975. CGIL increased its share of the public sector workers by some 15%: for instance, 4,000 member teachers in

1968 rising to 90,000 by 1975. They won concessions on pensions, but failed to make any headway with reforms on housing, health and taxation.

Greater success was achieved with the inclusion of the unions in tripartite negotiation with the government and employers, which raised their profile with the ordinary citizens, such that membership rose markedly by over 60% during 1968-75, and helped to avert the threat of outright revolution. Workers gained more just and legally binding treatment together with a fairer and more relaxed working environment. The 1970s saw a huge increase in the tertiary sector from 40% in 1971 to 50% in 1981. Partly thanks to the expansion in tertiary education the number of teachers in CGIL rose from 4,000 in 1968 to 90,000 by 1975.

Another milestone was the setting up of the *Cassa Integrazione* state insurance fund in 1975, whereby workers were laid off temporarily and of whom some categories received up to 80% of their final salary in the first year. In fact, the concept of redundancy only recently entered the Italian vocabulary. Social security was overhauled, with improvements in pensions and health benefits, building upon Mussolini's measures which had granted early retirement, especially beneficial to civil servants, and which helped companies to re-organise. As from 1969, a generous increase in pensions was guaranteed to a worker after forty years of full-time employment, being 74% of their average annual wage over the last five years.

Student Protest

Factory workers were not alone in their *contestazione* of violent protest, since students, both from secondary school and university, also took to the streets to vent their deep satisfaction with the ills of Italian society. They were no less vociferous in their demands for better teaching and preparation for the world of work. In 1962 the government raised the school leaving age from 11 to 14 in a drive to combat mass illiteracy and so improve employment prospects. The first major reform since 1923, and one of the very few reforms of Moro's government, the *scuola media unica* single middle school was created in an effort to remove social discrimination by combining the academic and vocational disciplines of the previous *avviamento* and *media* streams. By the early '70s nearly 90% of 11-14 year-olds were in full-time education: *scuola media*, facilitated by urban proximity to a school and a better standard of living compared to remote rural areas. School attendance covered six mornings with the afternoons spent at home ostensibly doing homework. As a result, during 1959-69 pupil enrolment virtually doubled, as did consequently that of the *scuola superiore* upper school for 13 to 18-year-olds (changed to ages 14-19 in 2002).

At the *scuola superiore* students choose one of the following disciplines: *liceo* for classics, science or languages; art or music; technical/professional institute. Classes are held six mornings a week and finish at lunchtime. Assessment is on a yearly basis: if a student fails, they repeat the year. At age 18/19 students sit the *Maturitā*: two written papers (one six-hour essay and one specialist paper) plus an oral on two topics (changed for 2002 with three written papers and three orals). The orals are conducted by a mix of external examiners and the students' own teachers, but which favours subjective evaluation. The minimum pass for the oral is 60%. San Giuseppe da Copertino is the patron saint of examinations. Much emphasis is given to oral examination to minimise cheating which is rife in written examinations (for instance the use of cribbing belts) but is rarely penalised. A further drawback of the emphasis on oral questioning is that it tends to make adult Italians rather verbose and opaque in the presentation of their arguments. Facilities remained poor, with a lack of classrooms, trained teachers (only primary school teachers receive training) and books paid for by parents. Some 8-10% of youngsters attend private school, mainly Catholic, but they too suffer from poor teaching standards. Boarding is rare. Teachers retire after 15 years of service.

On a brighter note the post-war influx of younger teachers brought a welcome breath of fresh air into the classroom. Their fathers had perhaps served in the Resistance, likewise their pupils' fathers. They began to discuss the war, especially in the Communist 'red belt'; though the DC preferred to break with the past for the sake of national unity. Pupils welcomed open discussion of current and past affairs of both home and abroad. The increasingly popular television medium began to broadcast programmes on recent history, making youngsters more politically aware, and which encouraged them to question and criticise, a technique not usually practised in the classroom.

The 1962 reforms in secondary education paved the way for a surge in tertiary study, as elsewhere in Europe, hitherto viewed as a privilege for the rich and not a universal right. In 1961 students from technical institutes were granted access to science faculties to remove the distinction between manual and office workers, followed by the abolition of university entrance examinations in 1965. As a consequence, student enrolment soared from 268,000 in 1960 to over 450,000 by 1968, and which included a notable proportion of females. During

1962-75, university student numbers trebled. As with secondary education, the university teaching environment became dire, with inadequate administrative support, especially during examination periods with thousands of students to accommodate. By 1968 the universities in Rome (the oldest was established in 1303) Naples (dating from 1224 and Italy's oldest university) and Bari were catering for 60,000, 50,000 and 30,000 students respectively, on campuses designed for 5,000 apiece. Universities are divided into institutes or faculties grouped by similar disciplines.

Teaching both at secondary school and university remains highly passive, consisting of rote learning and minimal opportunity for open discussion and personal expression between student and teacher/tutor, with little emphasis on interpersonal teaching skills. Tutorials and seminars were non-existent until the introduction of the latter in 2002 at Uniroma University. Lecturers were scarce, and the few who appeared in the lecture hall were only contracted to teach 52 hours annually. Arrogant professors *baroni,* often lawyers, doctors or politicians, lived in ivory towers and were rarely to be seen, only descending occasionally with their retinue of assistants to give tediously long lectures full of irrelevant rhetoric and abstruse theory. At the Academy where I taught in Milan, I attended the inaugural year speech given by the Director: he was rather long-winded and repetitious. Usually political appointees, especially in the clientelistic South, a professorship *cattedra* is guaranteed for life, which holds back younger and more dynamic lecturers who are more in touch with their cohort of students. A recent survey revealed that 30% of top professors and 10% of lecturers are over 65, and only nine of the total of 18,651 are under 35 years; as against 7% in the US and 16% in the UK. Credits are now awarded to encourage regular attendance and public orals are conducted in a hall to prevent cheating.

During the 1990s, I lived in northern Italy and sent my two children to the *asilo* village nursery, which cared for and educated them very well; as did the primary school, as indeed confirmed by international studies. A major reason for returning to England was to give them a higher standard of education both at secondary and university level. Italian pedagogy is passively orientated which discourages individual development, as opposed to the more interactive English approach. Working as a university lecturer I went to meet my future boss at a highly respected university. I was ushered into a vast lecture hall where she was dictating a translation to a group of some 150 students, with no interaction whatsoever. My students, in groups of 20-40, were amazed and grateful for my more personal and inclusive style, taking the trouble to spend a few minutes with each one to briefly discuss some points of their essay. They also welcomed my seeking out their views and analysis on a wide range of topics in my study programme. Although I was only employed as a lecturer, invariably my students addressed me either as *Dottoressa* or *Professoressa,* which was heartening!

Students are reduced to teaching themselves or seeking external tutors. Ossified curricula remain unchanged for years, retaining the élite classics, history, philosophy and languages. There are no student grants except for a handful of scholarships, and so the middle-class parents pay. Poorer working-class students have to resort to part time jobs and miss what few lectures are offered. Students face an inordinate amount of dense academic reading, as well as the hurdle of 25-50 examinations to surmount to attain a degree. There is little discussion or case study work, and so little relevance to the world of work; let alone students reasoning for themselves. Minimum marks are 18/30, maximum 30/30 *con lode* distinction. A thesis is marked on a pass of 90-110 as well as distinction. A degree accords the title of Doctor and is essential for university teaching. University courses are designed for a duration of four to six years but usually take on average 7.5 years to complete. During the 65-66 academic year 81% of secondary students enrolled at university but only 44% graduated, of which only 15% completed within the requisite time limit; and with a drop-out rate of 56%. About a quarter leave at the end of the first year since they are ill-suited or ill-prepared for degree study. Robert Meade observes that 'Ultimately only about one out of four students ever triumphed over the obstacles and emerged from the chaos with a diploma in his hand.' [28] The upshot is that many students do not graduate until around the age of 28, which gives them a late start on the job ladder, let alone marriage and family.

On a more positive note, education opened young women's eyes to another life based on autonomy and career, as opposed to the traditional path of marriage, housewife, mother and subservience to male domination. Education broadened their horizon, giving them the confidence to campaign for financial and biological independence. Television revealed the outside world, in particular America and England, where young females were gaining immense freedom both in the workplace and in their personal lives. Newspapers and magazines presented an enticing new world of London and the Swinging Sixties, immortalized by Antonioni's film 'Blow-up'; together with the rise of American

---

[28] R.Meade: 20th Century Italy page 172

feminism and student sit-ins at Berkeley Univresity in California protesting against the war in Vietnam. The generation gap had arrived, creating a youth culture distinct from their parents' traditional lifestyle. Youngsters, dressed in jeans and sweaters, rode around on scooters and frequented bars with jukeboxes playing Elvis Presley rock music. Many young women joined the Feminist movement in Italy, which encouraged them to defy their parents and refuse to submit themselves to the stereotyped role of women. They set up the LID *Lega Italiana per l'Istituzione del Divorz*io pressure group campaign for divorce; and welcomed communal living without men. Other groups were *Lotta Femminile* and the more radical *Rivolta Femminile* who opposed marriage and family life.

The students' theme broadened into the world of work. The superabundance of graduates with raised career expectations devalued the possession of a degree; it also meant that many had scant hope of embarking upon a suitable career path. The absence of a strong industrial/commercial base made for a restricted Italian economy, where the main avenues for advancement rested in banking, insurance and accountancy; together with the law, medicine and the bloated civil service. In order to stand a chance of gaining a foothold on the job ladder, one either obtains a post through a *raccomandazione,* viz. a recommendation from a family relative or professional contact; or sits for a *concorso* competitive examination where hundreds or more take a competitive examination for a handful of posts. For instance, in 2015, a *concorso* was announced in a newspaper for a few state nursing positions, in response to which hundreds applied. Students felt cheated, robbed of a decent start in life. Workers' priorities centred on improved work, pay and living conditions; whereas many students were well fed and housed, coming from middle class backgrounds supplied by parents who had struggled in the '50s to make ends meet, and who encouraged their children to gain good qualifications in order to obtain a well-paid office job.

Boredom, bitterness and frustration led them to challenge the status quo of the political Establishment, seeking an alternative utopia of a simpler lifestyle and with direct democracy to achieve greater equality and participation. Disillusioned by the failure of the state to provide decent economic opportunities, they rejected university and political brainwashing, authoritarianism, pressure to conform, egoistic capitalist/consumerist values encapsulated in the smug nuclear family, but which their parents saw as a snug refuge from the realities of everyday life. They rejected the brutalist Stalinist PCI in favour of Marx's collectivist ownership of all goods and property. Previously popular with students and intellectuals in the 1890s, Marxism/Leninism made strange bedfellows with Catholicism in their joint denunciation of capitalism and consumerism; later embraced by the workers in the Piazza Statuto riots (see earlier) as the panacea to cure the ills of Italian society. They welcomed the New Left ideal of creating an inclusive golden age of direct democracy. Universities were transformed into revolutionary communes and sit-ins: Milan, Rome and Trento were in the vanguard of protest, with the *Movimento Studentesco* Students' Movement based at Milan's state university.

Students had moved beyond conventional Communism embodied in the PCI, since it was too feeble to fight the system. Instead, they welcomed the more vigorous Communist revolutions in Castro's Cuba and the Cultural Revolution in Mao Tse Tung's China, offering a brave new world for workers. Yet these models were ill-suited to the more advanced Western society. Students pinned up posters of the Bolivian revolutionary Che Guevara (he died in 1967), and accepted his cult of violence, also that of Mao. They sympathized with South American priests trying to reconcile Catholicism with Marxism. They opposed American involvement in Vietnam, for which they set up a peace movement; and opposed the US stance during the Bay of Pigs Cuban missile crisis 1962-63. They supported Afro-American rights championed by the Black Panthers in California. Yet although gaining a hold on much of Italy, the groups rarely collaborated, recalling the centuries-old individualism of the communes and city-states' regionalism.

Students rallied round workers in a merging of class, supporting their demonstrations and marching on picket lines, especially where trade unionism was weak. Increasingly vociferous in their condemnation of the political status quo, as elsewhere in America and Europe, they expounded their fervent ideas in pamphlets, journals and newspapers such as Il *Manifesto and Lotta Continua,* both of which fronted protest organisations. However, their text was generally too theoretical for the average reader or factory worker, and so failed to elicit mass broader support. Fortunately, professional investigative journalists, such as those at *Il Giorno* newspaper and the weekly *L'Espresso* magazine, had been attacking government corruption since the early '50s. They now seized the initiative to present the protesters' ideas in a more accessible prose. The most desperate students fell prey to radicalisation and slid into the tunnel of terrorism to force through change. The Hot Autumn opened up a frightening scenario of violence which would last a decade, culminating in the murder of Aldo Moro in 1978.

Students had used the opportunity of a visit in 1962 from Luigi Gui, Education Minister, to voice their grievances at a sit-in at the Great Hall of Sapienza at Pisa University. Gui proposed a limit on student numbers *numero chiuso* to reduce overcrowding; and three different types of degree from a one-year course to a full degree course, in order to cater for varying ability, but which downgraded qualifications. Students rejected these reforms as they were seen as discriminatory. Serious student protest flared up in the autumn of 1967 by the politically orientated UNURI National Union of Students, and so in fact anticipating *mai 68*, with a series of sit-ins and assemblies to offer a Marxist interpretation of the students' role in society. In 2017 more protests occurred over the *numero chiuso*.

Trento State University, located in a region of chequered history[29] was in the vanguard of the protests. Founded in 1962 by Catholic intellectuals and the sole campus at that time with a Faculty of Social Sciences, Trento objected to the Church's closeness to big business and the Establishment; as did the private Cattolica University in Milan, where many future DC politicians had attended. Trento had been the first university to accept technical students such as Renato Curcio, co-founder of the Red Brigades. Sociology was the largest faculty, unique amongst Italian universities at the time, attracting many radical students and accounting for 75% of the university's intake, since it offered good job prospects owing to its practical relevance to the world of work. Students, such as Curcio, developed the idea of a 'negative' university whereby students shunned lectures and taught themselves. In 1965 they were the first to demand the de-classification of degree status; together with the abolition of the elitist course for the upper echelons of the civil service. Their protest against Vietnam resulted in a strike on the campus: for the first-time police entered the conference hall and evicted all the students.

In November 1967, following an increase in fees, trouble broke out at the private *Cattolica* university in Milan with the discussion of world events. One of the students' leaders, Michelangelo Spada, had set up the *Lotta Continua* protest movement. The police were also called in to Turin University, where students had occupied the Faculty of Literature and, as at Trento, interrupted lectures and coerced professors into discussing the burning issues of poor teaching, course

---

[29] See Chapter Nine

127

content and examination strategy. The unrest spread to many other universities, including the South; and spilled over into urban secondary schools where youngsters agitated for greater equality and better didactic levels. Many university lecturers and school teachers sympathized with the students' call for change.

The climax occurred in March 1968 at the Battle of Valle Giulia at Rome University, in which the police evicted students at the Faculty of Architecture, only to be repulsed by the students who re-occupied the building. It was the first occasion in which students had resorted to violence, such was their anger and frustration with the system: 46 policemen were injured as well as students. Subsequently, relations between police and protesters took a turn for the worse with the killing of four workers by the police. During the 1940s, they had been legally permitted to kill protestors and did so. In fact, many policemen were sympathetic towards the cause of the students and workers, themselves carrying out illegal strikes in protest at their own working conditions. The film director Pier Paolo Pasolini sympathised with the police, many of whom came from humble backgrounds, and strongly denounced the students' behaviour; as did much of the press. After Valle Giulia student unrest waned.

Sympathy also emerged from the unlikely quarter of the Vatican. The liberal-minded Pope John XXIII had supported socio-doctrinal reform which, after his death in 1963, was undertaken by his modernising colleagues through the setting-up of the 2nd Vatican Council. Many members of *Azione Cattolica,* the Church's main lay organisation, deserted the conservative-minded Church members to join the youth movements; whilst defiant priests returned to the essence of their calling and set up community centres for the deprived in the south and centre, thereby creating the paradox that the Church was assisting the downtrodden more than the Communist party.

At secondary school level, in 1973 Malfatti, DC Education Minister, tried to set up consultative bodies involving elected teachers, parents and students. However, the parties concerned were unimpressed, and so control remained with the *provveditori* local education officers, head teachers and government bureaucracy. In 1996 the mini degree was introduced, with a basic three-year course followed by two years of specialization; with regular assessment, credits and repeats allowed (similar to the British Open University); and designed to offer a more relevant preparation to the practical demands of the workplace. In

2001 *Presidi* head teachers were granted greater autonomy in the mix of teaching syllabus and funding management.

There are now 77 universities as against 27 previously. The top university is Turin Polytechnic, followed by Trento, Pavia, Milan Polytechnic and Milan State universities. The southern univerisities are mediocre: Roma La Sapienza is poor on research; Roma Tre is bottom of a 2011 listing; whilst Rome's third university, Tor Vergata, is satisfactory. LUISS University for social sciences attracts over 9,000 students. La Cattolica and Bocconi, both in Milan, are private universities. Florence boasts the first European university; otherwise, no Italian university features in international ratings. Those who can afford it study abroad, particularly in Britain or America.

In 2012 a survey carried out by PISA Programme for International Student Assessment, and arranged by OECD, revealed that 15-year-old Italian students score below average in mathematics, reading and science; and poorly in literacy and numeracy amongst 16–24-year-olds. Prime Minister Renzi proposed financial incentives for the best teachers, closer liaison between schools and employers, and more finance for new school buildings and renovation work. In 2017 it was planned to take on 52,000 new teachers to improve teaching levels and lax class discipline. Teachers can retire after 15 years of service.

Educational reforms fell short of expectations, partly due to entrenched opposition from the university barons who continue to wield control. Access to upper secondary and tertiary education was made easier, yet inequality persists. University entrance examinations were simplified (abolished in France) yet working-class applicants remained modest. Overcrowding persists in the classroom and lecture hall, with minimum contact between lecturer and individual student. Ostensibly student unions became involved in the management of educational establishments, yet the traditional hierarchy continued to rule. In short, there was little change for the better: to this day graduate students continue to study for want of job opportunities, sniffing at more modest jobs available; whilst southern graduates go north in search of work since there remains precious little locally.

Other Reforms

During the 1970s, fifteen Regional governments were established (originally promised in the 1948 Constitution and which had been granted to just five regions at that time) with the aim of endorsing the inherent regionalism of the

Peninsula, bolstered by the continued use of hundreds of dialects, by transferring power from central government primarily to the regions. The smaller provinces set up by Napoleon were retained, which favours some degree of independence. Each region now has its own elected council with control over areas such as housing, health, transport and agriculture; but crucially, no power over taxation. In June 1971, the first regional elections were held, the main outcome being that the Communists predictably gained power in central Italy: Umbria, Tuscany and Emilia-Bologna. During 1971-73, fiscal reform was introduced, which established the principle of progressive income taxation, but at source only for dependent workers; whilst it remained the responsibility of the self-employed, such as shopkeepers and accountants, to declare their tax liability. To this day this sector suffers woefully from massive tax evasion: hence the importance of the more effective indirect VAT tax.

The right to hold Referenda, originally prescribed by the 1948 Constitution, finally became law in 1970. Half a million signatures, a request by five regional councils, or one fifth of either the Senate or the Chamber of Deputies, would activate the process. A referendum could not propose legislation, but it was allowed to repeal an extant law. This measure, together with regional government, acknowledged the strongly inherent regionalism of the Peninsula by decentralising the role of government; but in effect went against the concept of unity by turning back the clock to the local dominance of city states prior to unification in 1860.

Broader-based social reforms were achieved, in part due to Pope John's sympathy with women's desire for greater liberty, working outside the home and equality within marriage. Mass was now celebrated in Italian rather than Latin, thereby making it accessible to all Italians and indirectly promoting national unity. Non-Catholics were no longer discriminated against. In 1975 the 1930 Penal Code was suppressed, along with the 1942 Fascist civil code of Family Law, which abolished the concept of *capofamiglia* male dominance, but which persisted for many years. Women were now permitted to retain any inherited property rather than be obliged to transfer it to their husband's control. Dowries were abolished. Parents were accorded equal rights in the raising of their children; illegitimate offspring were treated equally to those born in wedlock. Civil marriage, rare before 1970, rose to 10% by 1980, of which a quarter took place in Rome. In 1956 70% attended mass regularly, falling to only 25% by 1985, and of which only one-third were DC members.

Despite vigorous opposition from the DC, the MSI and the Vatican, divorce was finally legalized in December 1970, largely due to the tenacious campaigning by the LID protest movement, and boosted by women's positive contribution to the Resistance movement. Napoleon had permitted divorce and civil marriage in Italy. Divorce would take five years if both parties agree, otherwise seven years. The divorce bill was passed by 398 to 283 votes in the Chamber of Deputies; then amended and approved by the Senate. Victory over divorce spurred the subsequent campaign and victory for abortion, for which women had previously faced five years' imprisonment. There ensued a fierce and protracted campaign to revise the old law. 800,000 signatures, pushed by Communists, were collected in favour of abortion. Pope Wojtyla spoke out forcefully, insisting on the basic tenet of the right to life, and as upheld by the Lateran Accords. The Communist party prudently decided that it was up to women to decide.

In May 1978 the new law finally came to pass, permitting free abortion on demand for women up to 90 days pregnant, longer if the mother's health was at risk; also for cases of rape. The DC insisted that parental consent be required for girls under 18, in order to 'defend the family'; but thereby prejudicing those females most at risk and so were still reduced to seeking a back-street abortion. Fascists opposed the law, also the strongly Catholic South Tyrolese. The law did make provision for conscientious objection by mostly male doctors which limited abortion especially in the South, where in fact many women supported the bill: a case of feminist triumph over Church indoctrination. Public dissemination of birth control was now allowed.

The newly-instituted referenda were implemented for the decisive ratification of both the laws on divorce (supported by *Azione Cattolica*) in 1978 by 60% and abortion by 78% in 1981. Such a resounding result shattered the DC, marking the beginning of their decline, together with the waning influence of the Catholic Church in people's lives. Generally, there was an air of increased informality, both at home and in the workplace, with more relaxed relationships. A referendum in 1978 on the state financing of political parties narrowly maintained the status quo, thanks to the Communists who were desperate to receive state funds now that help from Russia had tailed off. However, it was successfully repealed in another referendum in April 1993 in the wake of Tangentopoli. The overwhelming success of the divorce referendum encouraged other apolitical reform lobbies to take matters into their own hands and bypass the weak Parliament to press for change through direct democracy. *Magistratura Democratica* consisted of a pressure group run by judges and magistrates who strived to overhaul and accelerate the Italian legal system. They were to play a crucial role in the later corruption and Mafia scandals.

Other significant changes that improved the lot of women concerned the establishment of state nurseries in 1971; five months paid maternity leave with six months unpaid, and with the right to return to work; equal pay and job opportunities from 1977, including retirement at 60; and personal ownership of property. An increasing number of talented women entered the professions: medicine, law and the media. During the 1980s, women's clubs appeared: *Donne in Carriera* a professional women's club in Milan; and *Club delle Donne* based in Rome with some 800 members. Female workers at Fiat (40% of the total) were permitted to hold their own meetings and have personal facilities. Women writers became more prominent, for instance Elsa Morante and Dacia Maraini.

The radical organisation *Lotta Continua* LC was in the forefront of social reform. It was formed in Turin in 1970, after a split within Potop over the use of violence (the latter was dissolved in 1973) by O.Scalzone, F.Piperno and Toni Negri, the latter sociology professor at Padua University. LC felt it was necessary to broaden its appeal away from its worker base, and became increasingly involved in social issues. LC's supporters reached a peak of some 25,000, comprised mainly of women, students and soldiers. They established groups inside the factories of Fiat Mirafiori, Italsider steel and Alfasud Naples, particularly amongst those fighting for better housing conditions, a prime grievance issue for many years which involved many clashes with housing offices. Local area committees were formed to deal with amenities, infrastructure, sanitation and price increases. LC was proactive in Naples, a key area where living conditions were chronic. Here in 1973 a cholera epidemic broke out, which the officials attributed to mussels rather than the defective sewage system. Neapolitans sabotaged bread ovens due to the exorbitant price of bread on the black market; LC set up canteens for children. They also helped to improve the lot of the *leva* military service conscripts, especially in Friuli, Trentino Alto Adige and Piemonte.

Lotta Continua campaigned for improvement, but with scant success, over the dire state of ancient Italian prisons, usually medieval fortresses or monasteries which suffered dreadfully from gross overcrowding, with lack of food, hygiene and heating. On the verge of outright revolution, the prisoners organised two big revolts in 1969, one in San Vittore prison in Milan and the other in the Nuove Prison in Turin, both of which were brutally suppressed. In 1971 outbreaks of prisoner disruption involved 24 prisons. LC set up working groups with the inmates, but part of LC disagreed with the policy of the Prison Commission and broke away to form NAP *Nuclei Armati Proletari* which spread to various cities, and included not only prisoners but were joined by upper school and university students anxious to help these forgotten souls. 1974 was a tense year. Prison revolts again broke out in Florence; also Alessandria where 16 hostages were taken: the Carabinieri retaliated with seven dead and fifteen wounded, caught in the cross-fire. Demonstrations also flared up outside the prisons of San Vittore, Poggio Reale (Naples) and Rebibbia (Rome). Finally, NAP attacked the MSI offices in Naples, and raised funds of forty million lire by kidnapping a rich gynaecologist in that city.

Improvements in housing for workers were equally disappointing. By 1963 the public housing programme had virtually ground to a halt. In protest at the exorbitant rent rises, during 1968-70 tenants' committees organised major rent strikes in Milan, Turin, Rome and Naples, representing some 100,000 families on affordable (public) housing estates *case popolari*. They demanded decent housing, rent reduction and improved amenities: shops, parks, schools and transport; placing a limit on office building; and the renovation of old housing. In Turin squatters took possession of empty flats that had been allocated but not yet occupied. In 1969 the unions organised a one day strike which, being successful, brought the unions into direct talks with the government; but this was resented by politicians since they considered housing to be outside the unions' remit.

In October 1971, a law was passed assigning affordable housing to local authorities who would expropriate large tracts of land, for which 1,062 billion lire were made available. However, thanks to factional manoeuvring in Parliament, together with the addition of many amendments, and combined with the entrenched interests of local planners and developers, the law was too complicated to implement. By 1974 only 42 billion lire had been allocated and thus little was achieved. In 1978 the *Equo Canone* law on fair rents was passed, with tenants receiving a decrease. At the other end of the scale, landed property boomed thanks to massive tax evasion and much disposable cash since no-one trusted the novel concept of a national administration. Demand flourished for city centre living, leading to a revival of Renaissance living, for instance in

Florence and Siena, offering rented and luxury second homes which the many well-paid state officials could now afford. During 1953-60, rents rose 100% overall, and as much as 300% in northern cities such as Milan, Venice and Turin.

In 1978 a National Health System USL *Unita Sanitarie Locali* was instituted, under discussion since 1948 and subject over the years to interminable committees of enquiry. Designed to overhaul the old arrangements controlled by consultants and hospital administrators, the results were unsatisfactory, with lengthy waiting lists and expensive medicines which ate into the public funds and inflated the profits of the pharmaceutical companies. Furthermore, USL was bedevilled by the carving up amongst the political parties. In 1978 a law concerning mental health was enacted, thanks to a campaign led by Dr. Bassaglia in Gorizia and Trieste in the northeast, in an attempt to re-integrate patients into the local community. Sadly, the scheme offered insufficient places and so most patients had to fall back on family care as in the past.

With wages doubling during 1969-73, most workers were now content with having raised their standard of living since the *miseria* of the 1940s, with the possession of labour-saving household appliances previously undreamt of, and simply wanted a quiet life. Idealistic students, not having experienced the horrors of war and decades of deprivation, had overestimated the enthusiasm for revolutionary action. Anarchically clinging to theoretical models, they had opposed everything and won little; whereas the more realistic workers had targeted wages and working conditions, thereby achieving significant concessions. The mass of more mature and cautious Italians had little understanding or interest in politics and obscure political theory, remaining loyal to the trade unions and the left-wing parties, and looking to them for guidance. The more politicised workers were to be found in the large northern factories, as opposed to the SMEs smaller family firms in northeastern and central Italy where paternalistic owners usually offered a more congenial and personalized environment.

Revolution in the South was minimal, since the region had little industry; also because it was enchained to vested interests such as the landowners, criminal groups and political clientelism. In short, there was no outright revolution nationally because it simply was not wanted. Speaking in the 1980s, the writer Umberto Eco mused: 'Even though all visible traces of '68 are gone, it has profoundly changed the way all of us, at least in Europe, behave and relate to one another. Relations between bosses and workers, teachers and students, even parents and children have opened up. They'll never be the same again'[30].

[30] Oxford p27

Chapter Eight
Strategy of Tension

Following swiftly upon the events of the Hot Autumn, in December 1969 a bomb exploded at the Agricultural Bank in Piazza Fontana in central Milan, killing 16 people and injuring 88. That same day, right-wing anarchists exploded two bombs in Rome, wounding 18 people; as well as bombing in the South. The strategy of tension had begun. Initially, the police assumed it was an anarchist plot and arrested a dancer from Rome, who was imprisoned for three years before being cleared of the charge. Pino Pinelli, a railwayman, was also arrested on the day of the bomb attack and spent two days in police custody. One night, he fell to his death from the fourth-floor office of the police commissioner Luigi Calabresi, at the *Questura* police headquarters where he was being held, in the presence of five police brigadiers, although Calabresi was absent. Officially his death was described as suicide which apparently confirmed his guilt. A medical report suggested that he may have fainted due to fright and hunger, thereby losing his balance and falling out of the window. Pinelli's fate is immortalised in Dario Fo's play 'Accidental Death of an Anarchist'.

In 1988 Leonardo Marino, a member of Lotta Continua, confessed to murdering Calabresi in 1972, together with his companion Ovidio Bompressi; and also involving A.Sofri and G.Pietrostefani, the latter two being former LC leaders. The case dragged on for over a decade, based on flimsy evidence. Marino was eventually liberated; whilst the other three were declared guilty in 1997 and sentenced to 22 years in prison. Bompressi was later freed for medical reasons, whilst Pietrostefani fled whilst awaiting a further appeal. Concerning Piazza Fontana, eventually evidence revealed that a neoFascist group based in the Veneto, led by Franco Freda and Giovanni Ventura, had been responsible and that Ventura was in contact with Guido Giannettini, a colonel in the SID *Servizio Informazioni Difesa* Italian secret service and who supported the right-wing MSI party. With the Greek military coup d'etat of 1967 still fresh in their minds, revelations of a right-wing plot aimed at destabilising the centre left and reinstating authoritarian government triggered a wave of nervous tension throughout Italy. Fascism had not gone away.

Despite pressure from journalists and politicians to carry out a thorough investigation, the Milanese magistrates were forbidden access to vital documents. The *Corte di Cassazione*, Italy's highest court of appeal, eventually transferred the case from Milan to Rome, where the affair dragged on until 1981, when Giannettini, Ventura and Freda were sentenced to life imprisonment but subsequently cleared by the Court of Appeal.[31] In 2001 Milan's Second Assize Court sentenced to life imprisonment three terrorists still on the run: Carlo Maria Maggi, Delfo Zorzi and Giancarlo Rognoni.

In 1976 the Reale law was introduced to facilitate powers of arrest with an increase in restricted detention and more armed police. Furthermore, police could now detain suspects for 48 hours without advising a magistrate, or a week's minimum if advised. Interrogation was permitted without the presence of a judicial official or defence lawyer. In more serious cases suspects could be held up to over three years before trial, or if the case went to the highest court of appeal. So technically, a suspect could be imprisoned for up to a decade, given the snail-like process of the Italian legal system. The principle in English law of '*habeus corpus*' allowing the right to a trial does not exist in Italy, nor in other European countries for that matter. However, this rigorous approach was eventually relaxed to offer a lenient sentence for those who co-operated with the police, such that by the end of 1983, some 400 terrorists had benefited.

Mussolini's version of Fascism had been predicated upon tradition, elitism, order and nationalism. After the war some 7% of the population voted Fascist. Neofascism appeared in the 1960s, created by the younger generation who wanted to break away from the paternalistic version to form their own creed which was divisive and increasingly anarchistic towards heightened Communist activity, particularly in Milan/Lombardy and Veneto. About one hundred groups appeared of varying sizes, such as Mussolini Action Squads and the Italian Army of Liberation. In 1956 *Ordine Nuovo* ON appeared, set up by Pino Rauti,

---

[31] The Court of Appeal hears appeals against sentences passed by courts in both civil and criminal cases and can modify sentences. The Court of Cassation is the highest judicial authority and ensures that the law is correctly applied by other courts; and can order a retrial if appropriate.

attracting middle and upper-class youths in Lazio/Rome (especially in the areas of Monteverde and EUR) Veneto and Sicily. ON was heavily infiltrated by American spies, in particular Carlo Digilio under the code name of Zio Otto. An arms/explosives expert, he worked for US intelligence during 1966-88, as did his father. Arrested over the Piazza Fontana bombing, Otto supplied information concerning ON Veneto members who, in his opinion, were responsible for the Piazza Fontana massacre; yet they were all acquitted. Otto set up a link with a captain of the American Military Marine based in Verona. He also belonged to a network run by an ex-RSI (Salò Republic) man who, with others, were members of ON. Another agent was Gianfranco Bertoli, a Venetian, who had been a Sifar informer since the '60s under the cover name of 'Negro'. He was accused of an attack on the Milan Questura police headquarters but was acquitted. He was also involved with Count Sogno's activities (see Chapter 9).

Another prominent group was *Avanguardia Nazionale* AN, set up in 1960, which recruited middle class students in Rome and organised paramilitary training camps. AN and ON perpetrated most of the sadistic deaths and injuries between 1969 and 1980, the latter being charged with 74 bombings. Their members were tried in 1972, only to merge together in 1975 as *Ordine Nero*, which was later banned by Judge Occorsio, as well as SAMusso and AN. During the 1970s, a spate of bombings occurred, all the work of *trame nere* black terrorist plots. In July 1970, a train was derailed in Gioia Tauro (the location of an important steelworks) in Calabria, killing seven people. In May 1974, a bomb at an anti-Fascist rally in Brescia killed eight and injured 103, most of whom were *carabinieri* police (which come under the army). The perpetrators belonged to MAR *Movimento Armato Rivoluzionario* set up in 1969 by Carlo Fumagalli as the armed division of *Lega Italia* (begun in 1962) with 15 anti-Communist groups. In 1974, a bomb on the Brenner express wounded eight passengers. In August a bomb killed twelve and injured 105 passengers on the *Italicus* express, travelling between Munich and Bologna; followed by a similar incident in December 1984, on the Milan-Naples express, with 15 dead and dozens injured.

The climax of the bombings was the detonation of a 23-kilo bomb in the waiting room of Bologna station at the height of the holiday season of August 1980, leaving 85 dead and over 200 wounded. Symbolically, the large crack in the wall remains, beside a plaque dedicated to the 'Victims of Fascist terrorism' followed by a list of the dead. The Bologna massacre, the worst ever carnage, was perpetrated by the right-wing NAR *Nuclei Armati Rivoluzionari* founded by the Fioravanti brothers, who were child actors for television advertisements in the popular 'Carousel' programme, together with their pal Alessandro Aldobrandi. Growing up in the comfortable right-wing Monteverde district of Rome, the brothers' father worked as a RAI television presenter, whilst Alessandro's was a high-profile magistrate. NAR carried out some of the most savage attacks: during 1978-80 they exploded bombs on 90 buildings in Rome, leaving six dead. P.Musumeci, head of intelligence, was severely criticised for mishandling the Bologna investigation.

During the Hot Autumn of 1969, right-wing students harassed the left-wing university sit-ins. In retaliation *Lotta Continua* LC and *Autonomia Operaia* AO, rival left-wing groups, could swiftly muster up to 20-30,000 supporters in the Milanese hinterland to form well organised *servizi d'ordine* paramilitary groups with which to confront right-wing outfits such as SAM *Squadre d'Azione Mussolini* (SAMusso Action Squads). Central Milan in Lombardy had long been a prime location of left/right-wing conflict, centred on Piazza San Babila which lies at the heart of Milan, close to the Duomo, La Scala theatre and the Galleria Vittorio Emmanuele. Here *cani sciolti* young and lively neo-fascist bloods, members of AN and MSI's offshoot *Fronte della Gioventù,* would gather and let off steam, carrying out random attacks on newspaper and political offices. Although police were stationed in this area, they tended to turn a blind eye to the clashes.

For its part, the right-wing MSI political party seemed outwardly upright, but was probably involved with the bombing outrages. Furthermore, they proposed suspected terrorists as parliamentary deputies in order to benefit from immunity against prosecution, such as Miceli, Saccucci and De Lorenzo. Right-wing attacks benefited from State protection, and deterred the PCI from government despite gaining a third of the national vote. In 1969 Giorgio Almirante, formerly an official in the Salò Republic and now head of the MSI party, shifted it further right to merge with the ailing Monarchist party, and tacitly supporting the strategy of tension.

Right-wing youth was divided into about a hundred subgroups, such as the Spartiati which consisted of just 13 youths in San Babila, where left-wingers dared not tarry. The Sanbabilini ran with the anarchists based in Brera, an artists' haunt. Right and left-wing students clashed violently, during which many bars in the area were badly burnt. Fascist activists numbered about sixty (for which left-wingers held a list) who were always armed and wary, unlike their sympathisers who carried no protection. Both left and right-wingers hid iron bars and flick knives in bars, later supplemented by guns and hand grenades.

They set fire to Harry's Bar and blew up the Motta bar. In the words of Murelli, a Spartiato: 'We wanted to free ourselves from the bourgeois image imposed upon us by the media and our peers'.[32] Fabrizio Zani, a 17-year-old member of ON, described the atmosphere of Piazza San Babila in 1971: 'The violence is really fierce: using sticks of dynamite, throwing Molotov cocktails, burning entrance gates and cars: all was considered quite normal. At first I armed myself with a knife and later with a gun. The level of militancy had become impossible. You were a fool not to go around armed in that area. The days of leafleting and meetings were long gone.' A typical right-wing slogan was 'Ankara, Athens, and Rome next,' in response to which left-wingers retaliated: 'With the blood of black shirts, we shall paint our flags red'.

In December 1970, a year after the explosion in Piazza Fontana, Prince Junio Valerio Borghese organised a coup d'état. Member of the oldest Roman family, during the Republic of Salò he had served as a Fascist military leader and naval commander, organising the infamous Decima Mas battalion of forest guards and crack parachutists. In 1968 Borghese established the National Front organisation and schemed to take over the key ministries of the Interior, Foreign Affairs and Defence, Parliament and the broadcasting service. Members included high ranking officials, many of whom were linked to Licio Gelli, Venerable Master of P2 (see below). The plan also envisaged the arrest of the president, the assassination of the chief of police, and the deportation of left-wing activists to offshore islands.

Borghese organised a 200 strong team, consisting of his former forest guards and parachutists, led by Sandro Saccucci, previously an official of the Salò Republic and later an MSI deputy. On the night of 7th December, Borghese and his fellow conspirators entered the Viminale armoury and loaded up two lorries with weapons; and proceeded to occupy the Ministry of the Interior for a few hours. But at 1.49 am, a telephone call ordered them to cancel the operation, and the men withdrew without any shooting. In 1974 four generals were accused of involvement in the coup, of whom one General Vito Miceli who was head of SID. All were acquitted, including Miceli, at the subsequent trial. Borghese fled to Spain where he died in 1974.

---

[32] P.Sidoni/P.Zanetov: 'Cuori Rossi contro Cuori Neri' page 384

In December 2004, the *Repubblica* newspaper came into possession of some documents acquired through the Freedom of Information Act, which suggested that Graham Martin, the American ambassador to Italy at the time of Borghese's '*Immacolata*' coup (it occurred on 7-8th December, the feast of the Immaculate Conception) had been aware of the plot and that perhaps it was he who made the telephone call to cancel the operation. In fact, as revealed by these documents, the plot had been known to top military brass and the Italian secret service for some months; also by Mario Tanassi, the Social Democrat Minister of Defence (later involved in the Lockheed scandal) and so presumably by President Giuseppe Saragat. The documents consist of five reports, but with the omission of certain names, sent by Martin to the State Department in Washington during August-September 1970. The reports refer to the high state of tension in Italy at that time due to fear of a Communist takeover, hence the planned coup. Martin did not exclude the involvement of the CIA, given their independent approach at times; as indeed endorsed by Alastair Horne concerning the Suez crisis in 1956.[33]

The report reveals that James Clavio, an Italo-American military attaché to the US embassy in Rome, had engaged in talks with General Miceli, who spoke openly of the likelihood that something significant would occur around *Ferragosto* (the main summer holiday on 15th August). A young American businessman, whose name is not revealed in the report but was probably Ugo Fenwich, had also heard such rumours. Fenwich had been approached by an Italian acquaintance (possibly Adriano Monti, a doctor) who spoke to him about the project, asking whether the US government would recognise the new regime. Apparently, Martin gave Miceli $800,000 to be used carte blanche. According to a report issued in 1976 by the House of Representatives, since the war the CIA had contributed $75 million to the coffers of Italian parties and electoral candidates. In fact American officials had for years advised informally on Italy's coalitions and internal party affairs.

Equipped with a tape recorder Fenwich met one of the plotters, perhaps a Roman builder by the name of Remo Orlandini, who in turn reported everything to the Italian magistracy. Ambassador Martin listened to the recording which revealed that Borghese was indeed the mastermind behind the plot. Martin advised Borghese, whom he had earlier met at the embassy but mistrusted, that should the plot succeed it would destabilize the Mediterranean basin, and that he should exercise caution. Privately Martin reasoned that the coup would fail,

---

[33] Macmillan op.cit.page 435

provoking a shift leftwards. Fenwich told Orlandini that the US were not interested in supporting such a regime, but the conspirators pressed on regardless, spurred on by claims of support from Spain, Greece and Israel; whilst Germany's decision rested on how the US responded. Martin ordered Fenwich to refuse any further direct contact with Orlandini, which ends the report. If and when the remaining documents are de-classified, they may explain why Borghese and his fellow conspirators persisted with their plans, despite Martin having advised the highest Italian authorities of their intentions. The trial resolved little, Judge Guido Salvini writing years later: 'It is perhaps the only case of a trial in which, to soften the impact of an event, all have been absolved, together with the entire affair'.

In addition to the de Lorenzo and Borghese plots, there was *Operation Gladio*, another plan for a right-wing takeover of Italy, backed by NATO paramilitary groups, in the event of either a Russian invasion or the Italian Communists gaining power. Details of Gladio came to light when Felice Casson, a Venetian magistrate, authorised by Prime Minister Andreotti, uncovered evidence whilst dealing with the case of a neo-Fascist, Vincenzo Vinciguerra, convicted of killing three *carabinieri* in a booby-trapped car in 1972 in the Veneto. Vinciguerra revealed that all post 69 bombings could be attributed to an 'apparatus belonging to the state'. Questions were raised as to whether Gladio had been conceived to combat a Communist takeover and/or organise terrorist attacks attributed to left-wing activists.

In 1990 Andreotti, cognizant of widespread and persistent rumours, confirmed the existence of an underground force set up within NATO, ostensibly to defend the country not only from a possible attack by the Warsaw Pact countries, but also to combat subversive elements within Italy. Knowledge of Gladio's existence was restricted to just a few ministers. He played down its importance, describing the group as a small partisan network set up in the event of invasion. It emerged that in 1956 an irregular agreement had been signed between SIFAR Italian military intelligence and the American CIA. In December 1972, a meeting took place between the CIA station chief in Rome, Howard 'Rocky' Stone and his Gladio colleagues, in which he reasoned that Gladio existed to defend southern Italy against unfriendly forces.

Gladio (named after the short double-edged sword used by Roman gladiators) consisted of a force of some 600 specialists, arranged in 40 autonomous units to co-ordinate sabotage, escape routes, guerrilla tactics and intelligence. Trained in Sardinia by Anglo-American intelligence personnel, they set up 140 arms stores, principally near the Gorizia Gap in the north-east which was highly vulnerable not only to a Russian invasion, but also to an attack by Marshall Tito in Yugoslavia who coveted the north-eastern flank of Italian territory: Istria, Trieste (formerly a major cosmopolitan port for the Austro-Hungarian empire) and Venezia-Giulia, all with substantial Slovene-Croat populations. Gladio continued throughout the 1980s as a surveillance and information gathering outfit, and was wound up in 1990 by Andreotti. In 1991 President Cossiga openly admitted to knowledge of Gladio, which he viewed as a partisan organisation. He presented himself to the magistrates but no action was taken against him. In 1993 Prime Minister Ciampi sacked the heads of SISMI and SISDE and himself undertook direct control of intelligence.

In 1918, by the Treaty of Versailles, Trieste came under Italian rule, where the Fascists proceeded to 'Italianize' the citizens, repressing the Slovenian population. The city, with a significant Jewish population, contained the sole Nazi death camp in the Peninsula. In 1945 Tito wrested control of Trieste from the Nazis but, by the Treaty of Paris 1947, the Allies divided Trieste into a 'free territory' of military zones (as with Berlin and Vienna): American, British, French and Soviet, as part of a buffer against Russia. The dispute was resolved in 1954 with the permanent cession of Trieste to Italy, very much due to Macmillan's efforts. By the Treaty of Osimo in 1975, Italy renounced her claim to the territory and Italian population around Trieste but retaining control of the city. In recompense, the 1947 Treaty obliged Italy to cede Fiume, Istria and Dalmatia to Yugoslavia. In 1919 the town of Fiume (Rijeka) had been occupied by Italy for 15 months under the leadership of the flamboyant Abruzzese poet Gabriele d'Annunzio.

Yet another right-wing conspiracy, known as the *Rosa dei Venti* Weathervane, was supposedly concocted by Borghese. The intention was to kill over 1,600 people, mostly politicians, and set in place a neo-Fascist government. The plot was brought to light by a young magistrate, Giovanni Tamburino from Padua. Members included Salò veterans, secret service personnel and senior officers of the armed forces, who were possibly entangled with Gladio. In October 1974, Tamburino arrested General Miceli (involved in the Borghese coup) whereupon the Court of Cassation, Italy's highest court of appeal, promptly transferred the case to Rome (as with the Piazza Fontana bombing) and Miceli was soon released. Miceli's family, from Trapani in Sicily, had been previously mentioned in parliamentary anti-Mafia commissions. In November 1972, Arnaldo Forlani, a thoughtful young DC leader so presumably not yet tainted by the political world, had given a speech in La Spezia (Liguria) in which he spoke of evidence of a possibly critical right-wing plot.

Byzantine Intrigue: P2

Licio Gelli had fought with Mussolini in Spain and Albania, then in 1944 switched his allegiance to the Communists. A miller's son, as a child he had ambitions to be a puppet master. After the war he lived in Latin America, where he forged many contacts and became a pal of General Perón in Argentina. In 1971 the Grand Master of a major masonic lodge, the *Grande Oriente dell'Italia*, asked Gelli to reorganise the 19th century Propaganda Lodge. Gelli, now appointed as its Venerable Master, renamed the lodge Propaganda 2 (hence known as P2) and held its meetings at the prestigious Excelsior hotel in Rome.

Freemasonry, which apparently originated as a brotherhood of skilled masons in 14th century England, first appeared in Tuscany during the 1730s. Favoured by nobles and kings, the movement was banned in 1738 by Pope Clement XII since it was seen as a rival authority to the Church and State, although secret Catholic societies later emerged. Bastion of the *Risorgimento* movement, various sects appeared in Milan, whilst the *Carbonari* society spread to Naples and the South. Mussolini suppressed freemasonry, but it crept back after 1945, with the connivance of the Americans who viewed it as a means of keeping out Communism.

P2's members comprised high ranking secret service and armed force personnel, politicians and magistrates, businessmen and financiers, who were proposed for high level appointments through *raccomandazione*. They were a significant driver of the so-called 'strategy of tension', an expression coined by the 'Observer' newspaper. They obstructed official investigations into the right-wing bombing incidents, attributing them to left-wing anarchists, and called for a return to authoritarian government. They entertained schemes of a coup against the state, such as Borghese's. General Santovito, head of military intelligence, was a member of P2, together with his deputy. At the time of Moro's abduction by the Red Brigades, (see Chapter 11) all security leaders were P2 members. The conviction of two neoFascists for the 1974 Italicus bomb, together with other cases, were overturned. Following the fog of suspicion and connivance that enveloped the right-wing Establishment and the intelligence services, and suspicious collusion with right-wing terrorism, in 1977 SID and SIFAR were replaced by SISDE *Servizio Segreto Civile* under the Minister of the Interior, and SISMI *Servizio Segreto Militare* under the Carabinieri who are responsible to the Ministry of Defence. SISMI and SISDE were co-ordinated by CESIS which reported to the PM's office.

In 1981 two Milanese magistrates, Gherardo Colombo and Giuliano Turone, began an investigation into the activities of Sindona's bankruptcy (see Chapter 5). Enquiries led them to Gelli's home in Arezzo province, Tuscany, where they came across a list containing 960 names of P2 members. Giannini, head of the *Guardia di Finanza* GdF[34], urged caution since the document contained the names of all heads of intelligence (including Miceli, head of the former SID), 195 officers of the armed forces: 22 from the army, 4 from the airforce, 8 admirals and 12 *carabinieri*[35] generals and 5 GdF; as well as magistrates, prefects and *questori* police chiefs. The political membership included 44 deputies and senators, of which three belonged to the MSI Fascist party, whilst another three were cabinet ministers including the Social Democrat Pietro Longo. Neither Communists nor Radicals were listed, but Roberto Calvi's name appeared. Other walks of life covered businessmen, industrialists, diplomats, civil servants and judges. The numbering rose to 1,600 so presumably the balance was recorded on other lists not unearthed at the time. Possibly Gelli intended to use this list for blackmail.

Intriguingly, Colombo and Turone came across a transaction payment of $3.5million authorised in 1980 by Calvi into the account of C. Martelli, parliamentary deputy and secretary of the PSI, held in the Protezione account at the UBS bank in Lugano but on behalf of Bettino Craxi; and in accordance with an agreement with Dr Fiorini, finance director of ENI, the state energy company. The document advised of a further payment to be made for the same amount.

---

[34] The Guardia di Finanza derives from the Piedmontese army in 1774 and was responsible for defence of the frontiers. Numbering some 40,000 the unit is responsible to the Ministry of Finance.

[35] The Carabinieri originated in Piedmont in 1814 and became the royal guards; they now form the presidential escort. They were much involved in the suppression of banditry in the South following unification. Responsible to the Ministry of Defence, the force numbers some 85,000 men who receive nine months' army training. They are charged with policing the more rural areas; whilst the Polizia police come under the Home Office and patrol large towns. The Vigili Urbani town constables stem from the old police force.

The two magistrates discovered that one Silvano Larini, a Socialist and close pal of Craxi, was in fact the holder of the Protezione account and not Martelli or Craxi. Aware that they were on to him, and anxious to sever links with Craxi and Martelli, in 1981 Larini travelled to Lugano to withdraw all five million dollars in cash from the Protezione account, putting it in a bag which he passed to another Socialist politician; to be re-deposited elsewhere in separate tranches.

It transpired that the funds credited to the UBS Protezione account originated from an offshore unit of the Banco Ambrosiano, of which Gelli was chairman. By 1981 this bank had lent more than 11 billion lire to the PSI. Many of the senior managers at the state-owned BNL belonged to P2, one of whom was chief executive at one of Berlusconi's trust companies (which guarantee anonymity of ownership). The general manager at Monte Paschi di Siena, Italy's oldest bank, was a P2 member and financed Berlusconi's group. Berlusconi himself was a member, as was L.Di Donna, deputy chairman of ENI, along with senior managers.

In 1982, at Fiumicino Airport customs officers unearthed a batch of files hidden in a suitcase belonging to Gelli's daughter. These documents described schemes hatched by P2 to destroy Communism and trade unions by infiltrating key institutions. To this end, in 1977 P2 took over Rizzoli Publications (owner of *Corriere della Sera,* Italy's flagship newspaper), whose chief executive belonged to P2, increasing its capital from 5 to 25 billion lire, part of which came from the Vatican bank IOR. The evidence provided a clear link between P2 and the rogue banker Calvi.

The two magistrates tried to speak to President Pertini, but he was not available. They managed to secure an interview with the DC Prime Minister A. Forlani, who in 1981 ordered a parliamentary enquiry, headed by the DC deputy Tina Anselmi. The lodge was banned in 1982, and the new crime of secret association appeared on the statute books. In 1984 Anselmi produced her report, which for the most part confirmed the validity of the P2 members' list and condemning the lodge's subversive activities.

In 1982 Gelli fled to Geneva under a false appearance and bearing a transaction slip from a numbered bank account for $120million; whence he was arrested and extradited back to Italy. Awaiting trial in 1983, he escaped again, bribing a warder. He wrote letters to the Italian people declaring his desire to return to his native Tuscany to die. Gelli was sentenced to 6.5 years' imprisonment for his alleged involvement but it was annulled on appeal two years later.

The goings-on at the UBS Lugano account became public knowledge in 1994, when Craxi, Martelli, Larini and Di Donna were put on trial with Gelli for complicity in the Banco Ambrosiano bankruptcy. In 1993 Larini had confessed to his involvement in the receipt of bribes by politicians from contractors concerning the building of the Milan metro. Crucially, he also revealed that Craxi had requested his help in squirrelling away some funds into Switzerland, to which Larini obliged through the UBS Protezione transaction, thereby disclosing the vital link with Craxi's Protezione account at UBS ten years earlier, as well as his involvement in the *Tangentopoli* scandal.

In 1994 all four defendants were charged with fraudulent bankruptcy at the Ambrosiano, but Craxi fled to Tunisia where he later died. The case was a classic example of dragging out a legal affair, going thrice to appeal, until eventually by 2001 only two defendants remained, the charges against Gelli and Larini having been dropped. Di Donna was sentenced to seven years' imprisonment; whilst Martelli's sentence of 8.5 years became statute barred since it was outside the legal time limit: he just paid up for damages.

A definitive legal judgement over P2 was proving difficult to produce, so the case was taken out of the hands of Colombo and Turone and transferred from Milan to the Rome *Procura* where, predictably, it gathered dust for years on end until 1994, when the second assize court in Rome pronounced P2 to be a normal masonic lodge and not a secretive organisation. Finally, the Supreme Court of Cassation opined that P2 was not a conspiracy but simply a business committee. Only one person was sentenced, one General Maletti from the intelligence service, who was given an unsuspended prison sentence: he fled to South Africa. As a result of the revelations Forlani's DC coalition government collapsed, to be replaced by the Republican Spadolini as PM: the first time that small party had gained the premiership. In 2010 there were rumours of a P3 lodge in existence, of which one member by the name of Flavio Carboni, a businessman, had been tried for the murder of Roberto Calvi, but who was subsequently acquitted. He was however jailed for membership of P3.

Elections

In 1971 Saragat's lacklustre tenure as President ended, his PSDI party being judged too close to both right-wingers and the American CIA on terrorism. After

23 ballots the Christian Democrat Giovanni Leone, a Neapolitan lawyer, was at last elected thanks to MSI support. Militant Catholics had collected the legal minimum of half a million signatures to demand a referendum on the divorce law passed in 1970. Fearing a loss of support the DC opposed the referendum, Leone exercising his prerogative to dissolve parliament a year early and so postpone the referendum.

The results of the election in May 1972 revealed a certain shift to the right, coloured by recent terrorist events. The DC remained strong with 39% of the vote; previously 38% in 1963 and 39% in 1968. Significantly the neoFascist MSI-DN (of which Borghese was a member) and which now included the small Monarchist party, historically strong in the South, improved their standing with 9% of the votes cast, performing well in the South. In order to attract MSI voters, the coalition had offered generous early voluntary retirement terms to the Fascist hive of senior civil servants, as had Mussolini. Their candidates included De Lorenzo (leader of the attempted coup), Admiral Birindelli, formerly NATO commander in the Mediterranean; also, Saccucci (involved in Borghese's plot). The PLI Liberals lost votes to MSI and dropped to 4%. The PCI remained steady at 27%, whilst PSIUP (a far left offshoot of the PSI from 1968) dropped to 2% and returned no deputy: most of its members joined the PCI, whilst the minority, now PDUP, leant towards revolutionary groups. The election results allowed the DC to form a brief centre right coalition after many years: DC, PSDI and PLI and led by Giulio Andreotti. It was the first time the Liberals had served in government since 1957.

Yet all was not well within the DC. Rumor's Dorotei faction was on the wane, leaving six faction groups jostling for power, of which Fanfani's held 20%, the Andreotti-Colombo group 17%, and Moro's 9%. Membership remained heavily biassed towards the clientelistic South, with a low turnover of leaders and deputies, creating stalemate. *Azione Cattolica* and ACLI declined numerically and distanced themselves from the DC, as did the Catholic CISL union. Andreotti's administration failed to put together an effective strategy to deal with the heightened collective protest for reforms which, together with the looming economic crisis, led to his government's downfall in June 1973. Plans to revitalize DC party organisation and state industry were stymied by two scandals and the divorce referendum. Genoese magistrates had discovered that petroleum refiners and distributors had paid politicians, mostly Christian Democrats, in return for a more indulgent policy. A law was promptly passed allocating public finance in proportion to the electoral strength of parties; yet this use of taxpayers' cash infuriated the electorate, rightly convinced that nothing would change. The other scandal concerned the *Rosa dei Venti* plot discussed above.

Bolstered by the positive outcome of the 1972 elections, Fanfani decided to use the divorce referendum, now planned for May 1974, as the moment to relaunch the DC, again appealing to traditional Catholic values, and led by Mariano Rumor as PM, with Fanfani recalled as party secretary: in short, a return to the *status quo ante*. However, he and his party had badly misjudged the mood of the electorate. Many Italians no longer wished to be indoctrinated by either the Church or the DC, and demanded the right to end an unhappy marriage. Pope Paul VI remained wisely neutral, as did many of his bishops who declared the issue to be a matter of individual conscience. Some senior CISL leaders openly supported divorce; whereas the PCI shuffled its feet, trying to reassure voters of their support of family values. The result was 59% in favour of retaining the law, with 41% against.

Economic Crisis

1973 saw the beginnings of the world economic crisis, the worst since the Wall Street crash of 1929 and World War Two. Following Israel's victory over the Arabs in 1967, OPEC Oil Producing Exporting Countries quadrupled the price of crude oil and cut exports by 10%. At the time, Italy was 75% dependent on imported oil, as against 34% in 1955. A further critical factor was the decision of the United States to abandon the Bretton Woods system of fixed international exchange rates, established in 1944, in favour of floating rates and the dominance of the dollar. These two factors ushered in an era of politico-economic uncertainty and global stagnation.

Italy's economic miracle became well and truly grounded. She suffered from the highest inflation in Europe and America, peaking in 1974. The new system of floating rates allowed Italy to devalue the lira, making exports more competitive but imports became costlier, as did domestic products using imported materials. The Bank of Italy imposed a severe deflationary policy (last seen in Einaudi's post-war budget) and limited the money supply. As a result, many factories closed and unemployment shot up. 1973 was the first year since the war that Italians returned to their homeland due to a lack of job opportunities abroad. Germany's biggest bank, Herstatt, crashed. The trend over the next few years was one of a stop-go economy, as in Britain at that time, alternating between brief periods of buoyancy and recession, and underpinned by stagflation (stagnation with inflation); together with high prices, low profits and acute unemployment. In 1971, GEPI *Società per Gestioni e Partecipazioni Industriali* was set up to rescue ailing private companies.

Italy lagged behind France, Germany and Japan, facing increasingly stiff competition from third world manufacturers of shoes and clothing. Major Italian companies such as Fiat and Pirelli maintained their high level of investment and employment, reducing waste and inefficiency. Yet they faced workers demands for ever higher wages, now the highest in Europe, engineered by the powerful trade unions since the 1969 reforms and based on the 1952 *Scala Mobile* wage index. For these reasons, multinationals abandoned the Italian market.

National business confidence sank even lower after the chaos of the Hot Autumn. Larger companies either put a brake on investment and exported capital; or passed wage increases on in higher prices which fuelled inflation. Many decentralised production to the unofficial 'hidden' economy, especially in the northeast. Known as Third Italy, the region contained a myriad of SMEs smaller firms, of which many now took on the work previously performed by larger factories. Taking matters into their own hands, SME bosses exercised greater flexibility in tax evasion and non-payment of social security contributions, which particularly affected part-time females and youngsters. Further bolstered by the absence of trade unionism, they reaped the rewards of low labour costs and high profits. The unofficial sector at this time possibly accounted for some 15-20% of the total economy, and employing some 5-7 million workers.

Trade unions reverted to their traditional hierarchical organisation, replacing democratic workers' councils with nominated delegates. They attempted to co-ordinate action outside the factory through *consigli di zona* neighbourhood councils, but the PCI objected to their presence since they did not represent direct local democracy. In 1974 the metalworkers' union at one of Fiat's factories refused to pay the increases in bus fares and insisted on paying the original fare. Known as *autoriduzione,* the tactic spread to other factories in Turin and Piedmont, extending to non-payment of increases in electricity and telephone bills throughout the Centre and North. Trade union leaders and the PCI, out of touch with the rank and file, sniffed at such action which they considered illegal.

In 1976 the metal and chemical workers failed to secure their demands over contract renewal, thereby giving bosses the upper hand.

Another headache was the escalation in public sector debt, owing to the huge amounts paid out by the *Cassa Integrazione Guadagni* redundancy fund, which allocated 80-90% of previous wages in the first year. Furthermore, by 1970 recent reforms in health and education had pushed public expenditure from 38% of GDP in 1970 up to 44% in 1973, and rising to 55% by 1982, the highest in Europe. Revenue rose from 33% of GDP in 1970 to 43% in 1982 and so the public sector deficit grew significantly. The balance of payments deficit became critical owing to oil and other costly imports, plus the interest on international loans from the IMF and West Germany. By 1976 the lira had lost a quarter of its value against the dollar, the cost of investment borrowing was nearly 25%, and Italy was on the verge of bankruptcy. Given such a parlous state of affairs, it is small wonder that the IMF refused to make a further handout of $530m from its coffers. In the words of Gaetano Rasi: 'The devaluation of the lira still appears today, not just to have been an unfortunate choice but a mistaken one from the very beginning. The greater severity of Italy's economic recession in 1974-75, when compared to all other Western countries, without doubt has this as its dominant cause'.[36]

Coupled to this scenario was the increasingly dire state of the *enti pubblici* state industry, with massive losses in IRI and ENI. The 1950s had seen the heyday of public works development such as the motorways, electricity and steel. Yet during this period public bodies became increasingly autonomous, to the extent that their disbursement of state funds was not properly scrutinised by an independent body. This applied particularly to the Ministry of Public Works which was permanently in the pocket of a DC faction, such as Fanfani's during 1963-72. After 1963, IRI fell into loss until 1972; whilst ENI dipped markedly after 1969. The situation was similar elsewhere in Europe but the Italian situation was compounded by *sottogoverno*: political control of the state agencies, which resulted in *lottizzazione* parcelling out jobs for the boys within the state enterprises, which in turn led to professional incompetence and financial corruption. Even the lowliest posts were allocated to unqualified DC cronies and friends, with public cash ending up in private pockets.

The most glaring example concerned ENI, where Mattei was succeeded by Eugenio Cefis. Over time his empire stretched to newspapers, the funding of

---

[36] Ginsborg op.cit.page333

political parties and close ties with the secret services. Highly competent in finance and business, Cefis was close to Fanfani and the Dorotei leaders of Veneto and Trentino, both strong Catholic regions. Ever ambitious and arrogant, he took it into his head to acquire control of the huge Montedison chemical complex. The fusion of Montecatini and Edison in 1966 (partly in an attempt to challenge Fiat's dominance) was opposed by the left since it took control of 80% of the national chemical industry and 15% of the European market. Montedison suffered from poor management and a bag of loss-making firms. Cefis arrogated huge sums of state money within ENI to buy up a controlling share of Montedison, without anyone daring to question his strategy. Montedison went into the red 1970-72 due to poor management and an overlap of activities; similarly ENI which was mired in deep losses by 1972. Many other public managers abused the resources of the state, enriching themselves at the expense of the state patrimony, in a byzantine web of politics and personal gain.

Further bureaucratic problems concerned *residui passive:* the sums of un-allocated monies which reverted to the Treasury, due to the tortuous process of legal and juridical procedures to unlock them. The other obstacle was the plethora of laws which proved unenforceable due to the obscure wording, beloved of Southern lawyers, which made clear interpretation nigh impossible and so precluded any action. A prime casualty concerned EAGGF funding for structural projects by the EEC, where only 15% of the funds were disbursed over 1965-74. The reason given was that the foreign law had to be incorporated into the Italian legal code. Other EEC members drew the money directly from the Fund and so used far more of the cash made available. According to a survey in 1973, some 85% of senior civil servants had begun their careers in 1943 and who tended to be conservative and averse to any change whatsoever.

Berlinguer and the Historic Compromise

In 1972 Enrico Berlinguer, a quiet Sardinian aristocrat from a devoutly Catholic background, became the PCI's party secretary, taking over from Luigi Longo who had held the post since the death of Togliatti in 1964. He was honest yet ambitious, but more approachable than Togliatti, which endeared him to many. Resolved to breaking the PCI's political paralysis and the DC mould of factionalism, Berlinguer conceived the idea of a *'compromesso storico'*: the historic compromise of an alliance with the DC, the PCI and the PSI. His approach resembled Moro's recent alliance with the Socialists. Desirous of avoiding Chile's fate of a military coup d'état in 1967 over the Socialist President Allende, and with the Hot Autumn of '69 still vivid in his memory, Berlinguer wished to recreate the wartime alliance achieved by Togliatti, which brought together not only the working and middle classes but also Catholics and Communists in common cause to preserve Italy, in the words of Berlinguer, from 'unbridled individualism, senseless consumerism, economic disorder and the dissipation of resources'.[37] The goal was to extinguish the reactionary right of Fascism and unite the persistent rift in Italian society: a fault-line that stretched back to the medieval warring between Guelph and Ghibelline, clashes between Pope and Emperor, through to Fascist versus Communist and now Catholic pitted against Communist.

In 1974 Berlinguer began to distance the PCI from Moscow by challenging the hegemony of Russia in international Communism. This led to the 1975 Rome Declaration, signed by French and Spanish Communists, to create a brand of Eurocommunism which acknowledged a multi-party-political system, followed in 1976 by Berlinguer's support for Italy's membership of NATO. In 1981 he was concerned at the imposition of martial law in Poland and the suppression of the Solidarity movement. He thus decided on *lo strappo:* to break away from Moscow, thereby making a cautious rapprochement towards West European Socialism.

Unfortunately, Berlinguer's vision contained serious defects. His 'Proposals for a medium term strategy', presented in 1977, were too vague and crucially avoided the fundamental problem of root and branch reform. His appeal to belt-tightening and self-sacrifice fell on stoney ground: the Italians had no wish whatsoever to return to the post war years of struggle and deprivation and, as Paul Ginsborg rightly points out, it was family unity and tenacity that had been largely responsible for improving their lives, rather than the state. Berlinguer hoped that collectivism would replace consumerist values and capitalism, and which would protect democracy from authoritarian precepts; yet paradoxically he was proposing another form of authoritarianism.

---

[37] Ginsborg op.cit.page 356

Chapter Nine
Into the Darkness

In October 1970, the Brigate Rosse BR Red Brigades appeared, founded by Renato Curcio, Mara Cagol and Alberto Franceschini. Curcio was born in 1941 and lived in modest conditions with his mother. A serious young man, he attended a Catholic boarding school then studied chemistry at a professional institute. Refused a job by Pirelli-Bicocca in Milan, he decided to study sociology at Trento University, the sole university at that time which accepted technical students, and which was in the vanguard of the Hot Autumn protests. Sociology offered better job prospects and, like many of his fellow lower/middle class students, he managed on a modest grant and part-time work. Here he met Franceschini, his future BR co-leader. Curcio joined the Marxist/Leninist *Giovane Europa* Young Europe which dreamed of a united Europe. He disliked the rigidity of Maoist thinking and the constant arguments amongst the university's microgroups. He took part in the 'negative university', whereby students abandoned lectures and organised their own debates. Here Curcio met M.Boato and M.Rostagno, future leaders of *Lotta Continua.*

Curcio grew up in the region of Trento-Alto Adige, which has suffered a chequered history of ethno-political instability, and which possibly conditioned his political thinking. After Napoleon's defeat in 1815, the Congress of Vienna compensated Austria for her loss of territory in Germany and the Belgian provinces by according her the whole of Italy, ruled through a viceroy in Vienna, and so becoming part of the Austro-Hapsburg empire. The empire included German speaking Sud Tirol/Italian speaking Trentino, together with the Valtellina which was incorporated into the Kingdom of Lombardy-Venetia. In 1861 the Teutonic South Tyrolese refused to become part of the newly united Italy, insisting on their strong desire for independence.

In 1914 Italy withdrew from her 1882 Triple Alliance with Germany and Austria. Ostensibly neutral during the Great War, in 1915 by the Treaty of London she proceeded to make a secret pact with the Anglo-French allies, in return for the promise of the territories of Sud Tirol, Trentino, Istria, Trieste and much of Dalmatia; also the Brenner Pass for reasons of defence. In 1919 the Austro-Hungarian empire was split up, whereby the German speaking Sud Tirol region came under Italy, together with the Italian speaking province of Trentino; to be known collectively as Alto Adige. Numbering some 280,000 German speakers, Sud Tirol/Alto Adige projected a Teutonic lifestyle and was closely tied to Austria, such as schooling and education at Austrian universities.

Mussolini undertook to Italianise Sud Tirol/Alto Adige, suppressing the use of the German language and culture (also in the Slovenian speaking area of Trieste and its hinterland). He encouraged Italians to move into the area from Veneto and the South to work in the expanding public administration and new industry. A new area was built in Bolzano on the west bank of the river Adige to receive the new settlers, and where 70% are now Italian speaking. Disullusioned, some 75,000 Germans moved away from the area to Nazi Germany.

In 1946, by the Paris Peace Treaty, Austria renounced its claim to Sud Tirol/Alto Adige[38], on condition that Italy respected its Germanic language and culture. The region was now split into the provinces of Bolzano to the north and Trento to the south, the latter being the capital of Sud Tirol and housing some 100,000 Germans, with their own government and parliament, but with an Italian speaking majority. Alcide De Gasperi, the Italian prime minister at that time, was sensitive to the issue, since he himself was from Trentino and so had been an Austrian citizen for forty years; as well as having served as a deputy for Trento in the Austrian Parliament. He was wary of granting autonomy to the region since it risked destabilising the hard-won unification of Italy. Thus in 1948, De Gasperi deftly crafted an accord with Dr. Karl Gruber, Austrian Foreign Minister, whereby the mainly Italian speaking province of Trento would be combined with the province of Bolzano (Bozen in German) to create the region of Trentino-Alto Adige; thereby placing the Germans in a minority. The new region was accorded autonomy over matters such as taxation and legislation; as indeed granted to four other Italian regions at this time. German language and

---

[38] *Irredentismo* refers to Italy's refusal to cede Sud Tirol/Alto Adige and Trieste to Austria.

culture would be respected; whilst the area would remain under Austrian protection.

The arrangement created resentment and triggered an outbreak of terrorism acts during the 1950s/60s, with German speakers bombing railways and electrical power lines in their quest for autonomy. Trento University was instrumental in the student protests of 1969. That year, an agreement was reached to settle grievances, and eventually accepted by the SVP *Sudtiroler Volkspartei* South Tryol People's Party, the largest political party in the region. In 1972 two autonomous provinces were created, Bolzano and Trento, with the German speaking latter given full cultural and administrative autonomy. All 137 provisions were finally enacted by 1992 under the Andreotti government, with Austria continuing to act as a protector for the German speaking population. In 1973 the Italian foreign minister visited Vienna, the first from an Italian high official since the war. Since 1979 they have benefited from an Austrian law giving them some rights of Austrian citizenship, with a revision proposed in 2018 by the Viennese government. The Sud Tirol Freedom Party is claiming Austrian passports for German-speaking locals, supporting 'a Europe of national identities'; and seeks an eventual secession. In 2017 there was a flare-up over bilingual signage. The region receives an annual grant from Rome, as do the other regions.

As a consequence of the changes, many Italian speakers felt cold shouldered and moved away: the 1981 census records a drop in the number of Italian speakers, down from 33% in 1953 to 29%, with an increase to 66% of German speakers. There has been a recent boom in births to German families, for which they receive a cash gift. Sud Tirol is renowned for its Speck ham, which is marketed under that German name. Germans are usually bilingual, unlike the Italians (of whom only 30% speak German) and more enterprising, so they find it easier to secure jobs in the public administration, for which they are entitled to 67% of the posts, with 30% for the Italians and 3% for the small group of Ladino speakers (a neo Latin dialect). Sud Tirol is one of Europe's wealthiest regions. The two nationalities are better assimilated in the towns where there is more fluid mingling than in the countryside. EU membership has helped to improve the economy and diluted both Austrian influence and the tension between the two groups; so there is now less incentive to break away. A number of Germans now vote for Lega Nord or the Green parties rather than SVP.

Margherita Cagol, 'Mara' as she was known, was born in 1945 of a devoutly Catholic family from Trento. Volatile and resolute, she viewed Christianity as a duty towards helping the poor and suffering of Africa and South America, and joined the Catholic group of *Mani Tese*. She considered her commitment as a crusade for a better world, with a resort to arms if necessary, which sat awkwardly with Catholic pacifism. During this period 44% of revolutionary groups came from a Catholic background, 20% were Marxist and 15% from both. Mara's approach was not unusual: Harold Macmillan also viewed war as a crusade, and death in war as martyrdom.[39] During the summer of 1969, she and Curcio moved to Milan where they married shortly before the outbreak of the Hot Autumn. Mara had been awarded a study bursary for a two-year sociology course at the Milan *Umanitiaria* Institute.

In Milan Curcio became involved with the CUB group *Comitati Unitaria di Base,* active within Alfa Romeo, and taking part in the Hot Autumn protests. CUB collaborated with another outfit, GDS *Gruppo di Studio* set up by technicians at SIT-Siemens, a large electronics company in Milan, and supported by some 6,000 workers. GDS and CUB would form the base of *Brigate Rosse* BR Red Brigades and supply future leaders, such as Mario Moretti, who declared that GDS filled a gap left by the unions, whom the workers felt had betrayed them. For their part, the unions were hostile towards the semi-legal outfits who resorted to violence. The unions' slogan of *'vogliamo tutto e subito gia'* 'we want everything right now', also became the rallying call for BR.

Corrado Simioni was born in 1934, in Dolo (Veneto) into a well-off family. He attended the Bocconi University in Milan but never graduated. In 1954 he joined the PSI; only to be expelled in 1963 as a trouble maker and womaniser. He worked for Radio Free Europe in Munich, which also transmitted to Russia; and taught children at the upmarket Rousseau centres. Both organisations were financed by the USIS cultural organisation which was linked to the American CIA. He took up working in a commune for youngsters, organising holidays and training programmes. He then worked for Mondadori publishers in Milan, where he joined the local Maoists.

Similarly, to Curcio, Simioni grew up in a region of strong separatist feeling, which may well have coloured his future life. Venice itself boasts a proud history of regional autonomy since its medieval beginnings on the lagoon. A republic by 697AD, the city looked seawards, blossoming into a vibrant maritime trading

---

[39] Macmillan Vol.1 page 40

city on an international scale, venturing as far as China (where the Venetian Marco Polo stayed for several years) in constant search of new markets and products. Her republic stretched as far as the duchy of Milan until Napoleon ceded her to Austria in 1797. In 1815 the Treaty of Vienna accorded Venetia to Austria, coming under direct rule from Vienna through a viceroy. Over the years the Vatican had interceded with the Austro-Hapsburg rulers concerning their harsh treatment of the peasants, who in gratitude became staunch Catholics. In 1861 the new Kingdom of Italy excluded Venetia since, like Trentino, she insisted on her independence. Venetia was restored to Italy in 1866 by Austria ceding it to Napoleon 3rd of France, who in turn handed it over to Italy.

In 1918, by the 1915 Treaty of London, Italy at last regained Venetia which had never been redeemed by Austria: the area was the site of bitter Austro-Italian conflict during the Great War, with Italy's humiliating defeat at the battle of Caporetto, but vindicated by Italy's clinching victory at Vittorio Veneto. After 1919 Venetia was divided into the regions of Veneto and Friuli Venezia Giulia (Friuli had been part of the Venetian republic) with the port of Trieste as the latter's capital.

In September 1969, Curcio and Simioni teamed up to create CPM *Collettivo Politico Metropolitano*, which met in a disused theatre in Milan, and which they also used as a recreation centre. Simioni had developed excellent international contacts, especially with French Marxist/Leninist groups such as *Vive la Revolution* and *Gauche Proletarienne*, who explained how CPM could pass from a semi-legal to an underground movement. At CPM Curcio became the front man liaising with other groups, whilst Simioni operated behind the scenes on a military logistics network. During a demonstration the militant section of CPM would slip away to carry out their attack and then merge back into the crowd. Many of these activists were women, including Mara Cagol, and so were known as Simioni's *zie rosse* red aunts.

There were three main CPM groups, with a total of about 20 activists, the largest and best qualified of which was the GDS group of SIT-Siemens technicians, managed by Mario Moretti. Simioni ran the group of IBM engineers, whilst Franceschini led his Reggio group of some 10-15 members. CPM had a strong following with the engineers at Pirelli-Bicocca Milan, run by Simioni. They also enjoyed the support of students from Trent University. CPM included Marco Pisetta, an ex-smuggler who was also with GAP Trento and a future informer; Italo Saugo; and Franco Troiano who set up the Catholic group

Communione e Liberazione C&L. All of them later joined BR. CPM took as its model the Uruguay Tupamaros band of urban guerrillas, as well as the Brazilian theorist Carlos Marighella.

Alberto Franceschini, co-founder of the Red Brigades, was born in the small town of Reggio in central Italy. His father and grandfather both served in the Resistance which was very strong in Communist Emilia-Romagna. He joined the young Communists FGCI who were acquainted with some Resistance veterans; and in 1961 travelled to Russia. Franceschini knew Curcio whilst at Trent University. At the universities of Parma and Bologna, he came into contact with a far left revolutionary, who was a friend of the revolutionary triumvirate: the Cuban Fidel Castro, Ernesto Che Guevara from Bolivia and the Brazilian Carlos Marighella. In Milan Franceschini joined the CPM/SIT-Siemens cell for five months. Disillusioned by the PCI leadership's drift towards socialism, he abandoned the party and, together with like-minded companions, set up a commune in a large apartment in Reggio as a meeting point for about a hundred youngsters, who enthused over the Latin American revolutions. They enjoyed the liberating atmosphere and fulminated against capitalism and consumerism. Franceschini streamlined his group down to about a score of committed activists, with support from about a hundred sympathisers who later joined BR. His group was well-known in the small town of Reggio, financing itself with bank raids.

Franceschini forged contacts with former Resistance fighters, who had retained their cache of arms but were now too old to fight. They felt that the PCI had betrayed their Communist ideals, especially under Berlinguer's conciliatory approach promulgated in his 'historic compromise'. They passed the baton to the younger generation, who saw their mission as the embodiment of a new Resistance movement. Franceschini was given two pistols by a Resistance veteran: for him it was not just a transfer of weapons but a fight for a better world, epitomised in his Reggio group. The PCI tried to infiltrate Franceschini's group in order to ascertain their plans and dissuade them from action; also with other teams such as Curcio's CUB Pirelli which was involved in the Hot Autumn.

In August 1970, a meeting was held between Curcio, Franceschini, Simioni and Mara, when they gathered together a group of about a hundred youngsters near Reggio, most of whom were serious 'to the point of taciturnity'. Posing as a university group, they were spellbound by Curcio's talks, and enjoyed the enchanting woodland walks, imagining they were with Fidel Castro in his homeland, reading Che Guevara's diary and studying Marighella's manual of guerrilla tactics, and so following in the footsteps of Garibaldi who had indeed learnt his craft in South America. Romantic idealists, their jungle would be the towns and cities of Italy. Curcio and Franceschini rejected the hierarchical trade union movement, preferring a bottom-up democratic organisation; whereas Simioni and others wanted a top down approach like the Tupamaros, as well as infiltrating political centres and institutions. Much of the information on these foreign revolutionaries came from the widely travelled Feltrinelli. During the Hot Autumn revolutionary groups had worked within society to protest and fight for radical change. Now the revolutionary bands rejected the traditional protest tactics of the trade unions and adopted a strategy of unorthodox sabotage. They shunned society in search of more radical action, yet their isolation from the real world would eventually twist their perceptions of reality.

The four leaders decided to join forces since they possessed the same objectives of armed revolt and secrecy. In August 1970, CPM was disbanded and replaced by *Brigate Rosse* BR Red Brigades (at first briefly known as Proletarian Left and also harking back to Garibaldi's formations). The undercover organisation fluctuated between 70-100 members, most of whom agreed to a strategy of violence which would incorporate all existing groups. Disenchanted members of *Potere Operaio* Potop and *Lotta Continua* LC also moved over to the more radical BR. Simioni was attracted to BR since he knew Franceschini's commune was seriously dedicated to the cause and had already carried out attacks prior to joining CPM. Franceschini wrote two thought-provoking books: '*Mara, Renato ed io: storia delle BR'* Mara, Renato and me: story of BR' published in 1988 by Mondadori; and '*Cosa sono le BR'* 'What are the Red Brigades' published by Rizzoli in 2004, which reveal his seriousness of purpose and commitment to the cause, as indeed were many Brigade members. He declared that BR began in Reggio Emilia; that he and Curcio had already decided to set up BR prior to the Piazza Fontana bombing; but that attack had reinforced the necessity and justification for BR to resort to violence against capitalist exploiters. He went on to say that the civil war did not end on 25th April 1945, but continued to simmer below the surface until the Hot Autumn of '69.

In August 1970, BR appeared with a new poster in SIT-Siemens, designed by Mara, bearing the logo of hammer, sickle and rifle, and with the words: 'The organisation of violence is necessary for the class conflict'. Mara had been inspired by the Garibaldi Brigades of the wartime Resistance, the Vietkong flag and the symbol of the Tupamaros. Democratically organised, the first BR groups

160

were set up out of GDS at SIT-Siemens and CUB Pirelli in Milan; also at Fiat and Lancia in Turin. Other cells were set up in Milan, also in Reggio Emilia, Borgomanero (Novara province) and in the Lodigiano (south-east of Milan). There were about a hundred members of BR which, together with supporters, totalled around 1,000-1,500 people. The authorities had been aware of BR since December 1970. L. Mazza, prefect of Milan and a member of the right-wing Tambroni administration, sent a comprehensive report to the Ministry of the Interior (Home Office) detailing BR's tactics of promoting workers' independence from traditional trade unions by setting up cells in the factories. In March 1971, Curcio, Mara and Franceschini were held by the police for questioning by a magistrate but were released.

In order to obtain funds, in 1971 BR proceeded to carry out a series of bank robberies. Franceschini had serious doubts about his first bank raid, practising beforehand with a gun in his hand and repeating the classic words: 'Hands up! This is a bank raid!' In fact to his relief the raid went smoothly, giving him a sense of power: he concluded that the tone of one's words was sufficient to control some 75 terrified people. Bank raids were used as a test bed for recruits. The money was used to obtain false documents in order to rent flats, procure arms, explosives and vehicles.

During the first six months of 1970, supposedly anti-Fascist bomb attacks were carried out in Rome against the offices of MSI, AN *Avanguardia Nazionale* and Prince Borghese's office; the army barracks at Pavia and Rieti; also the American company Norton and Necchi sewing machines. The attacks were attributed to BR since the bombs were accompanied by BR leaflets. But in fact they were the work of the far-right group MAR (see Chapter 8). Against this highly charged atmosphere of civil conflict, in the autumn of 1970 BR retaliated by carrying out its first forays, targeting key capitalist enterprises. They set fire to the garage of SIT-Siemens' head of personnel; also the cars of the manager and security chief at Pirelli. They detonated three bombs on Pirelli's test circuit vehicles, followed in 1971 by the burning of some MSI vehicles. BR attacked many Fiat executives and kidnapped a close relative of the Agnelli family. Its boss Gianni Agnelli always travelled with a bodyguard and carried a cyanide pill.

Early in 1969, Simioni had set up a new organisation out of his IBM group of engineers at CPM. Simioni did not give the organisation a name since he wanted it to be ultrasecret, but BR called it *Superclan(destinitā)*. Its members knew it as *la Ditta* 'the Firm', many of whom were well-educated, working as professional people in publishing and translation. Organised in small cells of about thirty people, all controlled by Simioni, they were obliged to sever family relations and sometimes work commitments; as indeed was often the case with other terrorist groups. Moretti left CPM to join Superclan and assist Simioni in trying to take over BR. Italo Saugo already worked for GAP Trento but was probably Simioni's man too. Prospero Gallinari (later involved in the Moro kidnapping) mistrusted Simioni whose past was little known to the Firm. Run on military lines, a tense secrecy reigned within Superclan, where violent fights would break out and love-ins were organised by Simioni based on members' *curricula vitae*. Franceschini described Superclan as a sect that one could enter but not leave. Superclan was little known to the Milan police and the secret services, except for a series of robberies undertaken during 1971: in particular the robbery of 30 million lire at Savoia Insurance in Milan, for which two members were arrested.

Simioni led a high life of fast cars and fast women, with several villas and bodyguards, all of which needed a lot of financing. It seems that he had friends in high places, such as Roberto Dotti who possibly supplied him with funds. A mysterious chap, Dotti was a former Resistance leader. In 1952 he was in some way connected with the killing of a Fiat engineer in Turin, and so he transferred to Prague where he taught history and literature at the university. At that time Prague was the centre of international espionage, and where Dotti became involved in intelligence work. He possibly knew Feltrinelli there, who made frequent visits to that city and where he possibly owned a house. According to Franceschini, Dotti was probably working as a double agent, building up a network of informers, one of whom was connected to the Czech intelligence service STB.

Returning to Italy in 1954, Dotti came into contact with the Torinese Count Edgardo Sogno, who had been awarded a gold medal for commanding a Resistance group during the war, working with British intelligence. A freemason, Sogno too was probably a double agent: he developed intelligence links with the CIA, the French secret service and NATO (he was a friend of Manlio Brosio, its Secretary General); yet he was close to Dotti and Feltrinelli. He became involved with the right-wing groups of MAR and SAMusso. In 1953 Sogno set up the antiCommunist *Pace e Liberta* Peace and Liberty group (of which Dotti was a member) financed by Fiat, Pirelli, Confindustria, the Minister of the Interior and USIS (the latter probably financed Simioni).

In August 1971, Sogno planned a right-wing coup, backed by the US and NATO, but its revelation by a SID informer scotched the plot. He had planned to occupy the Valtellina zone in the north, cutting electricity cables. Such action would have called in the army, allowing Sogno to seize control. He planned to allocate greater powers to the head of state and Council of Ministers at the expense of Parliament, and offer popular referenda and majority elections. Sogno secured Dotti the job of running the upmarket 'Terrazza Martini' bar in Milan. Simioni introduced Mara to Dotti, who asked her to compile the *curricula vitae* on the Superclan people. Simioni advised her that she could approach Dotti for funds and other help. Mara was unaware of Dotti's background but Franceschini smelt a rat.

Simioni had criticised BR's initial attacks at Siemens and Pirelli, since he was intent on pursuing a higher profile campaign of activity aimed at politicians, businessmen and the judiciary. Given the heightened global tension caused by the Arab-Israeli conflict and the international economic oil crisis, Simioni conceived the ambitious scheme of launching not only a national civil war to unite revolutionary groups, but coupled with an international thrust against American imperialism: indeed, a strategy also envisaged by Feltrinelli and RAF/Baader-Meinhof. Over time Simioni's relationship with the other leaders deteriorated markedly. He tried to control BR from afar by infiltrating his men into other organisations as spies, such as Saugo and Moretti; and possibly working to the advantage of the intelligence services.

Simioni organised attacks without consulting either Curcio or Franceschini. Yet he confided in Mara, who in turn would tell Curcio. He suggested that they do away with Simioni; as did Franceschini who distrusted him; but Simioni disappeared along with some of his associates. After the deaths of Dotti in 1971 and Feltrinelli in 1972, Simioni became strapped for cash and his firm, already in a bad way morally and existing in a climate of fear, fell apart. Simioni and some of his associates left for his homeland in the Veneto, whilst others joined LC and Potop. Superclan later resurfaced as Hyperion, ('he who precedes the sun') a language school in Paris, with branches in London and Brussels, but possibly acting as a front for subversive activity which Simioni engineered from afar. Hyperion was financed by the French, such as the cultural Centre Pompidou; and came under the protection of Abbé Pierre who enjoyed high level contacts with the French political world, including the president Giscard d'Estaing. Investigation by the Italian authorities into Hyperion was met with obstruction from the French.

Franceschini, whose evidence and perceptive opinions appear trustworthy, offers a plausible interpretation of Simioni's convoluted motives. He strongly suspected that Simioni was a double agent (as with Dotti and Sogno) given his links with the CIA at the Rousseau centre and Radio Europe, and that he was in the pay of USIS (US Information Service) who wanted him to infiltrate BR. Franceschini reckoned Simioni was involved in a complicated spiderweb of international espionage, involving links with Mossad (Israeli intelligence), the Russian KGB and Franco-Czech spyrings. In 1970 he was responsible for a bomb attack on the US embassy in Athens, assisted by the KGB, in which the two perpetrators were killed by the bomb (possibly due to a defective Lucern timer), one of whom was Simioni's girlfriend. He had originally asked Mara Cagol to take part in the attack without telling her husband Curcio, but she demurred.

Simioni mooted plans to kill Prince Borghese, kidnap the US consul in Milan and murder two NATO officials at the US airbase in Naples, with the connivance of Anglo-Israeli intelligence. In fact Mossad had approached Franceschini via Aldo Bonomi, one of their agents as well as a SID informer and a pal of Curcio at Trento University (Bonomi was involved in a failed right-wing coup against Mariano Rumor, DC Secretary). They offered to co-operate with BR since Italy enjoyed a reasonable relationship with the Palestinians, and so hoped to exploit this link; but Franceschini declined. He concluded that, given the complexity of Simioni's case, it was virtually impossible to unravel the skein of secrecy he had craftily woven. Given the time now elapsed since then, the byzantine mysteries will probably remain shrouded in nebula.

Franceschini's suppositions are reinforced by the San Marco Dossier, compiled in 1974 by agent Z: Guido Giannettini (who had been arrested but released over the Piazza Fontana attack) and which he supplied to SID. Based mainly on German sources, the dossier should be treated with caution as to the accuracy of the agent's analysis. According to Z, international terrorism was being manipulated by foreign interests' intent on destabilising Europe, centred on Italy. Situated in a prime geo-political position, for centuries Italy had served as the cockpit of European conflicts and, since World War Two, had become the *'ventre molle'* soft underbelly of international intrigue. The Peninsula is strategically well-placed in relation to the Mediterranean and the Middle East, into which dipped foreign intelligence hatching their schemes.

According to Z, the main driver was Willy Brandt, West German Foreign Minister and later Chancellor, who had his sights on creating a Socialist European bloc as a bulwark against the Soviets: partly through BND West German intelligence; and partly by supporting and financing extra parliamentary left groups in France and Italy, such as *Lotta Continua*; together with Trotskyist outfits linked to Mossad which received American-Jewish money; and with ramifications through to ETA and the IRA.

Z considered Feltrinelli to be the *eminence grise* of the whole enterprise, especially bearing in mind his frequent visits to Prague, which harboured a nest of international spies. Following the Prague Spring of '56 and the descent of 4,000 Soviet tanks upon the capital to obliterate the uprising, Dubcek's Socialist government distanced itself from Moscow to align with East European Socialists. In December 2016 Anton Shekhovtsov, an expert on right-wing movements, stated that the KGB had supported not only Communist parties but also the Red Brigades, as well as extreme right-wing groups[40].

In his book *'L'Affaire Moro'* Leonardo Sciascia reveals that, apparently during the period 1948-79, some 2,000 young Italians were recruited by Czech agents in contact with various Italian groups such as BR; and of whom about 600 were known to SISMI Italian intelligence. The best were sent for paramilitary training in Czechoslovakia and elsewhere, then returned to Italy. He also refers to the existence at that time of a widespread traffic in armaments.[41]

Man of Shadows: Feltrinelli

GAP *Gruppi di Azione Partigiana* was the other major underground group, founded by Giangiacomo Feltrinelli. Born in 1926, Feltrinelli came from the South Tyrol, where his family had made its fortune in the timber trade during the 19th century. Feltrinelli's father was a rich businessman, president of many large organisations such as Edison and the *Credito Italiano* bank. Feltrinelli felt keenly the loss of his father in 1935 and became hostile towards his mother Paola and stepfather, Luigi Barzini, Fascist writer and journalist.[42] He became a partisan during the war, joining the GAP Legnano group near Milan; after which he

---

[40] Economist Dec.2016

[41] L.Sciascia: 'L'Affaire Moro' page 190

[42] Author of the classic 'The Italians' 1964

joined the PCI. Known as Giangi to his friends and family, he drove around in a luxury Buick cabriolet bedecked with Communist posters. Tall, slim and elegant, in 1967 he appeared on the front cover of the new 'Vogue for Men'. Serious-minded, intelligent and cultured, as well as heir to a vast family fortune, in 1947 he married a Communist girl, the first of several marriages, which belied his emotional instability.

In 1949 Feltrinelli organised a political camp at the family villa of Gargnano by Lake Garda, formerly the residence of Mussolini during his wartime Salò republic. Two participants were later arrested for armed robbery and pointed the finger at Feltrinelli for his influence and financial support; for which he passed a night in a prison cell, which raised eyebrows locally for his dare-devil attitude. Feltrinelli retained a fascination for the Resistance and became a firm friend of the former GAP leader Giovanni Pesce. In the early '50s Togliatti, the Communist leader, was a frequent dinner companion at the villa, partly in recognition of his host's financial benevolence towards his party. Feltrinelli set up a library which housed an important archive of the history of Communism. He established contacts with Russia, which he visited in 1954.

From 1949 Feltrinelli worked with UEC, an organisation set up by the PCI, to sell inexpensive popular paperbacks, which spurred him on to found his own publishing house in 1955, involving editing, distribution and a chain of bookshops. He published *Il Gattopardo* The Leopard written by Tommaso di Lampedusa. He set up an international archive centre to co-ordinate the various international groups, especially French and German outfits. In 1957 he issued 'Doctor Zivago' by Boris Pasternak, banned in Russia. He and many Western intellectuals were appalled by Pasternak's revelation of the atrocities of the Bolshevik Revolution in 1917, as well as later by Stalin's brutality, which radically altered their attitude towards the Russian Communists.

During the 1960s, Feltrinelli travelled frequently to Cuba where he became a close friend of Fidel Castro and one of his strongest supporters in Europe. Castro left a lasting impression on Feltrinelli, who relished being on first name terms with a world leader who dared to challenge the hegemony of America; and who achieved his revolutionary goals, unlike the Italians who, according to Feltrinelli, mostly discussed politics in an abstract manner. Castro presented Feltrinelli with a copy of the diary by the Argentinian, Ernesto Che Guevara, a Marxist theoretician who supported the revolutionaries in Bolivia and Cuba. Che was immensely popular at that time in Italy, with his dashing world-famous poster: the '60s reincarnation of Garibaldi. Feltrinelli held a meeting with him in Bolivia.

In 1967 Feltrinelli issued a cheap series of books on the South American revolution, (which arose from the ill treatment of shepherds) which included texts and diary by Che Guevara; books on the Tupamaros guerrilla fighters; also works by the French Marxist writer Régis Debray. One book discussed the organisation of solidarity in the 'third world' of Asia, Africa and Latin America, with a dedication by Castro: 'Tis the duty of every revolutionary to make a revolution'. Feltrinelli was in touch with Horst Mahler, future leader of the German revolutionary group RAF *Rote Armee Fraktion*, also known as Baader-Meinhof[43]; with Maoists in *Lotta Continua*; as well as the leaders of *Potere Operaio* (Potop): Oreste Scalzone, Franco Piperno, and Tony Negri from Trent university: the latter established AO. Many Potop members joined or supported GAP.

Feltrinelli embarked on an intense globe-trotting tour, involving over sixty meetings and innumerable encounters, in order to forge an international revolution. He and many others, such as Simioni, felt that the world was now poised on the brink of drastic change: the Cold War, Arab-Israeli conflict, *mai 68* in France, Prague Spring, Mao's Chinese revolution, Vietnam, and the American Black Panthers: a violent group who appeared in California in 1966, demanding civil rights and revolutionary war. Given the feeble Moro government and the failings of the State machine, the inward looking PCI and trade unions, together with the encouraging events of the Hot Autumn, Feltrinelli sensed the moment was ripe for outright revolution in Italy: 'Political warfare must evolve as the basic strategic element of the current fight by the Italian proletariat'. Feltrinelli announced his intention to devote himself to guerrilla warfare as practised in Vietnam, which he described in his essay on warfare and revolutionary politics: 'We must create a Vietnam!'

In 1967 the chief of Cuban counterespionage invited Feltrinelli to observe the trial of Régis Debray (who had been captured whilst on a mission for Che Guevara and Castro) to launch a campaign for his release. Already shadowed by

---

[43] For over twenty years RAF wreaked havoc in Germany, bombing, kidnapping and shooting of key figures. It was wound up in 1998. In 2007 Brigitte Mohnhaupt, a former leader, was released on probation after 24 years in prison. Three RAF members committed suicide in jail in 1977. Economist Feb.2007

the secret services, Feltrinelli was arrested by the CIA, who viewed him as Castro's main agent in Europe, but he was released after three days and expelled from Bolivia. His behaviour hit the international headlines. Shortly afterwards, Che Guevara was killed in Bolivia. Thus, began Feltrinelli's life as a 'man of shadows and influential agent'.[44]

Feltrinelli decided to revive the name of the wartime GAP organisation: *Gruppi di Azione Patriotica* but calling his men partisans rather than patriots. After his arrest in Bolivia, he struck up a close friendship with the lawyer Giovanbattista Lazagna, former Resistance leader of the Ligurian Garibaldi Brigade, and who was now working with a small group of partisans. In 1968 Feltrinelli first met Curcio and Simioni with a view to pooling resources. They appreciated Feltrinelli's invaluable international contacts, and embraced the Central/South American revolutionary experiences. As with Simioni's Superclan, Feltrinelli was keen to pursue a totally clandestine operation which would involve breaking family ties and shunning official movements; whilst Curcio and Franceschini preferred a semi-legal outfit in order to reach out to the masses, and only later develop an underground movement. All three groups would be self-financed through bank robberies and arms raids, in addition to funding by Feltrinelli. However, given their diverse approaches, they were unable to reach an agreement.

In 1971 Feltrinelli held further talks with Curcio and this time with Franceschini, during which Feltrinelli did most of the talking. A romantic idealist, his goal was to be overall coordinator of the entire armed revolt in Italy, eventually linking up with global revolution and employing Che Guevara's tactics. Feltrinelli now viewed the Italian traditional left of Communism and trade unionism as being too insular, and that they should look abroad for inspiration. He spoke of creating a proletarian army and of sabotaging mountain cables. His ideas seemed outlandish to his listeners, who felt that the battle for change should be waged in the towns and cities. Nor did they relish the idea of support from Russia and others behind the Iron Curtain; and so they could not accept finance from him. Perhaps they felt that Feltrinelli would dominate excessively and so they preferred to remain independent. GAP and BR did work together, albeit briefly, blowing up a Fascist's car, but there was too much rivalry between them to forge a longer relationship.

---

[44] 'Cuori Rossi' op.cit.page 263

The first GAP cell was set up in Genova under Lazagna. Feltrinelli also co-ordinated other cells in Milan, Veneto, Piedmont and Trento, the latter run by the Sardinian Italo Saugo with a small group of co-nationals, who dreamt of Sardinia becoming a Mediterranean Cuba. The Trento group included Marco Pisetta, the SID informer who also belonged to BR. Members totalled only about 65 of whom 70% were aged between 20 and 30 years, young and serious, made up of a mixed bag of activists: 22 liberal professionals, 11 manual workers and one soldier. The GAP Milan group of about 10 men, together with Feltrinelli, was the best organised team and a beacon for the others. Consisting of four cells, the members lodged in modest flats rented under false names, where they received visits from PCI Maoists and hid their cache of arms and explosives; all paid for by their leader. In 1970 they targeted the construction industry, known for its high accident/mortality rate, by setting fire to a company's concrete mixers.

The GAP Genova group worked briefly with the small 22 October group, founded on that day in 1969 by Mario Rossi in Genova, for centuries a left-wing stronghold due to the vast labour force at its port, and which included a rough band of former partisans and *Potere Operaio* (Potop) activists, many of whom much admired Feltrinelli. When Potop disbanded in 1972 many, including Valerio Morucci, one of their leaders (and later with BR) joined Feltrinelli whom they revered as an inspiring and charismatic leader. In 1970 22 October kidnapped the son of a wealthy Genoese family, who paid a ransom of 62 million lire. The group carried out two joint operations with GAP Genova, sabotaging the Alfa Romeo factory rail track and setting fire to the cars. Many 22 October members also belonged to the PCIm-l (Marxist-Leninist) group. The group received some finance from Feltrinelli but he considered them too leaky.

GAP and 22 October practised up in the Ligurian mountains, inspired by Che and using Marighella's warfare manual, which taught that knowledge of the terrain was vital to success: as indeed Garibaldi had well understood. In 1971 the two groups set fire to an entire warehouse stock of domestic appliances at Ignis Genova; also at a petrol refinery in protest at rising petrol prices and environmental pollution: both resulted in dreadful fires and extensive damage. They also ransacked ENEL cables. Radio GAP claimed responsibility for both actions as a concerted attack on capitalist exploitation with regard to sackings, and naively reasoned that their attack would force the bosses to re-employ workers they had sacked.

22 October also became involved in public housing problems. The council housing group *IACP Istituto Autonomo Case Popolari* was charging exorbitant rents and was accused of bad management and corruption (being in the clientelistic pocket of the Socialists). 22 October arranged a street snatch of IACP funds but a messenger boy was killed in the scuffle. This turned public opinion against the group, and the hard liner judge Sossi (later kidnapped) sentenced the culprits, which put an end to the outfit's activities.

Feltrinelli was questioned by the police about the Piazza Fontana bomb attack in Milan 1969, together with other incidents in that city such as at the trade fair. Afterwards, he decided it would be prudent to go into hiding, from where he issued his 'Summer 69' pamphlet. Well informed, he hinted at a possible right-wing coup with American support, resembling the Greek coup of '67 and the attempted coups by De Lorenzo and Borghese. Feltrinelli proceeded to set up a mountain base in Liguria, run by the Sardinians. Led by Saba, a serious young chap who became Feltrinelli's right-hand man, they stocked up with munitions and explosives hidden behind the wardrobe, in readiness for a counter attack. Feltrinelli was fascinated by technology and had acquired powerful transmitters in Germany in order to sabotage RAI Television, and which he housed in a Mini Morris. The Genova group was the first to possess a radio transmitter, with which they blocked the RAI Television announcement of the new Confindustria president, with their own news spoken by their leader in April 1970: 'Here is Radio GAP: stay tuned!' In 1970 Feltrinelli slipped out of Italy into Switzerland with help from the Potop Como group. The GAP group now adopted pseudonyms for greater security. Feltrinelli adopted the name of Osvaldo Ivaldi, the false name used by his Resistance hero G. Pesce.

GAP considered the possibility of abducting the German consul; also the banker Michele Sindona (a member of the P2 masonic lodge) who at that time was negotiating a business deal on behalf of Cefis, boss of ENI, and Cuccia, chief of Mediobanca. However, preparations were upset by BR activity, making Sindona suspicious. Feltrinelli's son Carlo vaguely recalled his father possibly hinting at killing Prince Borghese (as did Curcio and Simioni) whilst he attended an AN demonstration in Trento. Another project concerned a joint bank raid by GAP and Potop on the Saint Vincent casino in Val d'Aosta, similar to the one carried out by the Uruguay Tupamaros. Feltrinelli realised it would be tricky but declared he would have liked to try!

Early in 1972, Feltrinelli became seriously ill with pneumonia, and was at a low ebb physically and morally. Tense, and possibly prescient of his approaching death (there were rumours that foreign intelligence was planning to kidnap or even kill him) he made provision in his will for his son Carlo. Fearing for his life, Feltrinelli remarked to a few friends, including his former wife Inge, that 'if they find a dead man under a bridge, that man will be me'. His remark calls to mind the fate of Roberto Calvi. He was considered the grand organiser of international espionage, for which it would suit many state intelligence services to have him disposed of, since they perceived him as too dangerous. In the words of the lawyer Lazagna: 'The intelligence services: American, French, German or Israeli (the latter very proactive in Italy) will tolerate subversion on your own soil. But when it comes to the supply of arms to third parties you sign your own death warrant'.[45] Feltrinelli made many visits to Cuba: America viewed him as Castro's man in Europe. He also had close links with Franco-German terrorists such as Baader-Meinhof and *Nouvelle Resistance*; and was a frequent visitor to Prague, where he may have owned a house. He hoped that a suitable alliance could be made with Dubcek together with the Socialists in Russia and Eastern Europe. Feltrinelli's son is understandably vague on this aspect of his father's life, veiled in a 'shadow cone'.

Following the BR kidnapping of the SIT-Siemens manager in March 1972, which stunned Italy and the rest of Europe, Feltrinelli returned to Milan with the intention of ruining Berlinguer's PCI conference presenting his proposed 'historic compromise', by sabotaging ENEL's electricity cables at Segrate nearby. On 15th March Feltrinelli took with him two GAP members, mentioning that he was doing all this for his son. He was also accompanied by Gunter Grass, a shady character, who was a former Resistance fighter and explosives expert for GAP. At the site Feltrinelli, who had no experience of explosives work, climbed the four-metre-high fence to secure the time bomb onto a wooden board. Suddenly the bomb exploded, killing him outright. Perhaps the Lucern timer was faulty (as possibly with the Athens bomb) or had been tampered with. Gunter's timer did not work either; he disappeared and died in 1977, his true identity never known. Amongst Feltrinelli's personal effects were found his personal documents but no money. The true circumstances of his death remain a mystery. The Feltrinelli publishing house continues to thrive with over a dozen outlets. In 2016 it acquired Ricordi books and music.

---

[45] 'Cuori Rossi' page 317

Why did Feltrinelli's version of an Italian revolution fail? Possessed of immense charisma and deep conviction, he inspired many with his ambitious dream of an international revolution to improve the lot of common man. Yet it was an impractical vision. He ran a covert organisation and organised few operations, as with Simioni, and unlike BR's more proactive approach. There existed a lack of cohesion and joint approach, perhaps in part due to rivalry amongst the groups and Feltinelli's independent attitude. As Ginsborg argues[46], he failed to realise that what seemed a practical approach to Latin American problems was ill-suited to the political scenario in a modern West European country, with its diverse socio-economic development. 1969 seemed the ideal moment to challenge everything, given the conjuncture of widescale revolt overseas. Yet revolution challenged everything indiscriminately and so lacked precision. Many Italian workers were inert to opaque ideology imported from overseas which bore little relevance to their daily lives, especially in the centre and north-east of Italy where paternalistic family firms were the norm; whilst in the north-west many workers remained loyal to the Communist PCI party and CGIL trade union. The South remained dominated by the Mafia and clientelism, with weak trade unions. The initial euphoria was soon overtaken by the surge of the economic miracle which transformed the lives of so many Italians, giving them a hitherto undreamt-of decent standard of living. Economic well-being snuffed out the flame of revolution.

---

[46] Ginsborg op.cit. p340

Chapter Ten

Gli Anni di Piombo: Into the Chasm

Feltrinelli's death in 1972 came as a great blow to the Red Brigades BR, since he had been the sole person to unite the revolutionary left, reinforced by his invaluable overseas contacts and personal wealth. Bereft of its charismatic leader, GAP was virtually gone. General Dalla Chiesa's campaign against terrorism began to bear fruit, carrying out a wave of arrests, of which 19 were BR members, leaving just a rump of twelve BR activists who abandoned all, fled Milan by the skin of their teeth and went into hiding. Dalla Chiesa also arrested Lazagna of GAP and the informer Pisetta who was the only Brigadist not to be charged. Similarly the French and German police were having success in rounding up the members of *Nouvelle Resistance* and Baader-Meinhof.

Curcio, Franceschini and Mara took refuge with a supporter in the Lodigiano area south-east of Milan. Franceschini muttered that they now felt like 'blind cats'. He further mused that someone was protecting them since only their intermediary group had been disbanded, leaving intact their logistics network, despite Pisetta revealing all in a prepared confession to secure his release, and who took himself off to Germany. The historian De Lutiis agreed with Franceschini, declaring: 'The subversive left-wing groups in 1972 were very weak with no military structure and could have been neutralized in a few days... if only it had been wanted. But it was not.' Franceschini reasoned that their protector was the examining judge Ciro De Vincenzo. He had invited Franceschini and Curcio for a discussion to hear their interpretation of events, but they declined. Dalla Chiesa considered that Franceschini's supposition had some truth since De Vincenzo had appeared sympathetic towards BR; but he was cleared of any further involvement. The secret services and police relaxed their hold on BR and other groups to maintain the level of tension, in the hope that Andreotti's centre right coalition government (DC, PLI, PRI, PSDI) in 1972 would prevail and keep the PCI at arm's length, having held steady in the recent elections. Many people had tired of the severe upheaval since the Hot Autumn, which had achieved so little, and yearned for a return to stability.

BR re-organised itself into three main autonomous groups based in factories in Milan, Turin and Mestre (Veneto), the latter run by three recruits from Reggio; with smaller teams in Genova and Rome. The executive of Curcio, Franceschini and Mara were now joined by Mario Moretti, previously with Simioni's Superclan. Franceschini wanted to oust the newcomer since he was careless in operations and so put the team at risk; also because he knew he worked for Simioni who was keen to infiltrate BR. Curcio and Mara directed Turin, where they set up a cell at Fiat Mirafiori. Franceschini and Moretti returned to Milan to revive the old group destroyed by Pisetta's turncoat evidence. To the core of ten activists were added new 'irregular' recruits, many of whom worked in the key factories of Pirelli, Alfa Romeo, SIT Siemens and Fiat; and who urged BR to press on.

By 1972 BR were back in action, with a following of several hundred sympathisers, carrying out a series of bank raids nationwide to replenish their empty coffers in order to house recruits, restock on arms and pay their teams a modest wage. Their old partisan hunting guns, with their long barrels, were not suited to urban warfare, so they replaced them with modern guns bought in Switzerland and Liechtenstein through Valerio Morucci, a Potop contact who had previously assisted Feltrinelli in the procurement of weapons.

BR decided to target high level representatives of the state, 'who committed crimes against the people'. In January 1973, they broke into the offices, near San Babila, of De Cariolis, DC leader in Milan, to steal his list of business members. BR had planned to kidnap the politician but he received a tip-off and vanished. The incident raised Milanese eyebrows, especially as that same night there was a bomb attack on the *Avanguardia Nazionale* AN headquarters, succeeded by another on MSI at Lambiate, east of Milan. Further action involved a bomb on the Motta café in San Babila; as well as a bomb (defused) at the offices of the right-wing Cisnal trade union. These attacks were attributed to Far Left groups.

In June 1973, BR switched their base to Turin where there was much worker unrest at the annual renewal of their contract with Fiat. They occupied the Mirafiori factory, many of whom joined BR, and burning dozens of vehicles belonging to spies and agents provocateurs. BR organised raids on industrialists, for instance at Snia Viscosa and Singer sewing machines, which helped the recruitment of factory workers to the cause. That same year, Moretti organised the kidnapping of the Secretary of Cisnal, as well as the personnel directors of Fiat Milan and Alfa Romeo in Arese, as usual leaving them with a card around their neck and sending a photograph to the press. A close relative of Giovanni Agnelli, Fiat's boss, was kidnapped. Curcio remarked that 'in the feverish climate of those days it was easy to move on to more serious action', fomenting an atmosphere of civil war.

The Abduction of Judge Sossi

Against the background of growing economic crisis and increasing right-wing terrorism, BR raised its sights and crafted a plan for the abduction of Judge Sossi. The kidnapping occurred in April 1974, a few days before Fanfani's divorce referendum and on the very day Giovanni Agnelli became president of Confindustria (he hoped to make it more independent of politicians). The kidnapping was well organised, with Franceschini and Mara directly involved: capture, transport to hideout and interrogation. As a condition of Sossi's liberation they demanded the release of members of *Lotta Continua*, 22 October and Lazagna's GAP cell, all of whom had been arrested under Sossi's orders.

A difficult man, Sossi's independent approach was unpopular amongst the Genoese judiciary. The hardline public prosecutor for Genova, Judge Francesco Coco, refused to treat with BR and Sossi feared for his life, saying that Coco wanted to make a 'dead hero' of him. Since 1972 BR had conducted its own brief proletarian trial and sentencing of victims for crimes against the people. Sossi did feel some sympathy for his captors, and revealed to Franceschini, his interrogator, some well-informed goings-on within SID. General Vito Miceli, head of SID, was convinced that Lazagna was the leader of BR and should be arrested. General Maletti, his deputy, felt that someone above his boss was pulling the strings and who knew not only where Sossi was being held, but was also prepared to silence the awkward judge as well as his captors.

Moretti and Curcio wanted to do away with Sossi, whilst Franceschini wished to release him, convinced that his hiding place, some 70km from Genova, would soon be found. His decision prevailed: Sossi was set free after 35 days in captivity, and with no release of the terrorist prisoners. His first words to the press were of respect for the BR who had used no violence or torture, treating him civilly. He went on to say that his experience had made him realise that the independence of the magistracy was a 'utopia', and that BR shared his opinion.

Asked whether he had been afraid of the BR, he said 'Of the BR, no', but pressed further he said 'It's a vague thing, I can't say who. Perhaps you will understand'.

Franceschini assumed it was Marra who had informed the authorities. Marra, alias Rocco and a BR leader, had been a Fascist crack parachutist working for the PCI, and had offered to infiltrate the 'black' (right-wing) terrorists in Milan; but Franceschini, mistrustful, opposed the idea. Marra carried out operations with BR to prove his 'reliability', later helping to rescue Curcio from prison, but all the time working as an undercover agent for SID. Franceschini described Marra as a 'destabilising (double) agent'. In fact Marra was one of many who led a double life, for example Dotti and Simioni.

Thirty years after the incident, Franceschini revealed that Miceli probably knew from Marra the whereabouts of Sossi, and that BR had been divided on how to proceed with their captive. If Moretti, a violent man, had had his way, the authorities would have had no need to intervene and would have protected Marra. Indeed, of the 19 Brigadists arrested for the abduction, Marra was the sole member not to be sentenced. SID were relying on Marra to despatch Sossi to satisfy their expectations. Franceschini further related that the Sossi kidnapping had been a test run for the Moro abduction; and that someone was interested in the death of the hostage in both cases.

Bolstered by the political success of the Sossi kidnap, BR schemed to target top DC politician Andreotti; also Gritti, right hand man to the financier Cefis, in return for a better deal for the metalworkers' annual contract, together with the release of the 22 October members, as well as a BR man arrested during the Sossi incident. Franceschini went to Rome to shadow Moro's movements, who at that time was without an escort. But the plan was stymied by his arrest in September 1974, together with Curcio. The following February they were rescued by a group including both Marra and the informer Pisetta, presumably to cover their duplicity; and without firing a shot. General Dalla Chiesa was furious at the lack of security; though the rescuers probably received inside help.

During the attempted kidnap in June 1975 of the wine industrialist V.Gancia, Mara was shot dead near their country retreat in the Monferrato (south-west of Milan) where, posing as a group of teachers, they enjoyed relaxing weekends in the countryside, tending their orchard and vines. BR avenged Mara's death the following year with the assassination of the Genoese Judge Coco outside his home, together with his two bodyguards. He had been preparing the trial of BR's founders. It was the first murder organised by BR but, in Franceschini's words, he did not consider himself an assassin; rather that the bar had been raised and so deaths were now inevitable. Coco's assassination marked the beginning, in BR's words, of a 'new phase of class war': *gli Anni di Piombo*. The leaden years had begun.

After Mara's death, Curcio struggled to face up to the new scenario, and felt increasingly out of his depth. Moretti had now taken over at the helm, and was pursuing a more aggressive stance in place of Curcio and Franceschini's more moderate socio-political bias. Franceschini was unhappy about Moretti's role, especially given his link with Simioni. Having failed to secure a ransom from the Gancia episode, BR carried out a series of bank raids, climaxing in a raid on the savings bank of a large hospital complex in Genova, rendering 118 million lire unto the BR coffers. Later in 1975/early 1976, they kidnapped managers from Singer sewing and Ansaldo steel. They broke into the study centre of Confindustria in Milan; knee capped the Fiat doctor in Turin; and attacked the Carabinieri barracks in Milan and Genova.

In January 1976, following a shoot-out Curcio was captured for the second time and taken to the Nuove prison in Turin. By the spring his close colleagues had left BR, leaving an effective force under Moretti of just 12-15 activists who, having broken with Curcio and Franceschini, were all gung-ho on armed warfare against the State. The eminent lawyer F.Grande Stevens was assigned the unenviable task of defending Curcio.

Strategy of Annihilation

In December 1975, Mario Moretti arrived in Rome to head up a new phase of BR. He was joined by Valerio Morucci and Adriana Faranda, who together had run FAC *Formazioni Armate Comuniste*, and previously were with Potop which was wound up in 1973. BR were greatly encouraged by the strong support they found in Rome, such as NAP *Nuclei Armati Proletari* and the Tiburtaros group (a Potop spin-off), holding joint meetings involving the idealistic local middle/upper class youngsters in the quiet and respectable right-wing area of Monteverde. Moretti, formerly with Simioni, adopted the latter's strict rules of operating in a veil of secrecy. The Brigadist Prospero Gallinari also joined them, having escaped from prison for his involvement in Judge Sossi's kidnap. One day Moretti gave precise instructions to his comrade, 23 year old Anna Laura Braghetti, regarding the location and type of apartment he wished to rent, as ever under a false name. Highly nervous, she realised that the flat, no 96 Via Gradoli in Monteverde, would serve as a hiding place for a kidnapping.

Under Moretti BR's strategy became more extremist, intensifying their ever-violent attacks, paradoxically against a background of waning protest within society. Termed the 'strategy of annihilation', it was a last-ditch attempt to radically alter society, having failed through conventional avenues. In 1976 Moretti first organised two bomb attacks comprising eight kilos of explosive with steel shards: one went off in the capital, the other at the *carabinieri* barracks in Monza. Their target was Establishment figures, as well as policemen, magistrates and professionals such as journalists. That year they set fire to the cars of DC notables, killed eight victims and wounded 16. The following year the figures were 7 and 40 respectively, which included the highly respected Milanese journalist, Indro Montanelli, editor of *Il Giornale Nuovo*: he was wounded in both legs.

They carried out a series of kidnappings, for instance Enrico Rossi, TGI television director. They murdered F.Croce, President of the Bar Association; also Carlo Casalegno, assistant editor of *La Stampa* owned by Fiat, and whom older Fiat workers remembered for his opposition to trade unions. Indeed during the early years of BR's activities many factory employees and foremen were indifferent to the sufferings inflicted by terrorists upon their harsh bosses. They felt a certain sympathy for those who had resorted to extremism as a desperate attempt to confront the state's failure to remedy deep-seated ills within society. In March 1977, Moretti carried out the kidnapping of Pietro Costa, a naval engineer and member of the wealthy Genoese family who had made their fortune in armaments. He was held for 81 days strapped to a bed in a tent housed in a room. The family paid 1,350 million lire for his release, which financed BR's operations for a number of years, such as the purchase or rental of flats and hide-outs, together with Brigadists' wages and expenses.

In February 1978, the Brigadist Gallinari killed Judge Palma, who was preparing the trial of BR's leaders, Curcio and Francheschini. Palma was the fifth judge to be murdered, the others being Coco (the first), two by the Mafia, and Occorsio. The latter was murdered by the neoFascist P.Concutelli who ran the MPON group. Concutelli's other main exploits involved the kidnapping of a banker for a cash ransom of some 280 million lire; and a raid on the Ministry of Work & Pensions in central Rome: the take was a record 460 million lire in just 28 seconds. MPON folded in 1974.

Elections; Lockheed

Regional and local elections were due in 1975, followed by a national election the following year. Fanfani was still at the helm despite the outcome of the divorce referendum, and insisted on campaigning on traditional values and against Communism, together with law and order now reinforced by the Reale law passed in 1975, which restricted civil rights following the terrorist outbreaks. The entire DC party stood behind him. For their part the Communist party highlighted their moral probity in local government in central Italy, such as Bologna; and targeted DC's reputation of corrupt and defective government. Berlinguer tried to reinvent PCI's image as that of a responsible party of government, backing away from grass roots support and edging towards alliance with the DC. Now increasingly respectable, the PCI became a staunch defender of law and order, having voted against the Reale law but now objecting to youth's right to demonstrate for prison and other reforms, which only incited further violence.

The electioneering campaign was overshadowed by bomb attacks on trains, perpetrated by far-right activists, which prodded voters into upholding a moderate government and avoiding a Fascist/Communist polarisation. Nevertheless, the PCI managed to achieve an overwhelming gain in both the regional and local elections in June 1975, increasing its vote by some 6% since the previous regionals in 1970, which gave it almost one-third of the overall votes. The Socialists were content to take 12% of the vote, whilst the DC dropped slightly to 35%. The special status semi-autonomous regions were technically excluded from voting at these elections. The MSI-DN vote rose a little to 6.5%. Consequently, the PSI, now led by a pro Communist, agreed to ally with the PCI in order to create several new left-wing regional administrations. Previously, they had held the central regions of Emilia-Romagna, Tuscany and Umbria; to which were now added the labour strongholds of northern Lombardy, Piedmont and Liguria. All the main cities, barring Palermo and Bari in the south, fell under left-wing control, including Naples for the first time, where the Communists' proactive handling of the cholera epidemic in 1973 had paid dividends. Accounting overall for 47% of the total votes, miraculously the PCI was just 2% short of overtaking the DC, dominant since 1948, as the biggest party. *Il sorpasso* beckoned.

The DC reacted to this drastic state of affairs by replacing Fanfani with Benigno Zaccagnini, an honest and down-to-earth former partisan who, guided by Moro, would improve the DC's image and negotiate an alliance with the Communists; thereby fulfilling Berlinguer's *compromesso storico,* with the blessing of Andreotti and Moro. Unfortunately, the plan was upset by the findings of an American Senate enquiry which revealed that the US Lockheed aircraft company had bribed politicians worldwide to secure lucrative orders. The culprits included Mariano Rumor, former DC prime minister; Luigi Gui, previously the reformist Education Minister; and Mario Tanassi, a Social Democrat deputy. A parliamentary commission of enquiry removed the parliamentary immunity of the latter two and had them tried by the Constitutional Court. Gui was acquitted but Tanassi served a brief prison sentence in 1977. The commission was evenly split at 10-10: the casting vote of the president, Mino Martinazzoli DC, ruled in favour of Rumor not being tried. Moro staunchly defended his colleagues over Lockheed so as to maintain party solidarity; which annoyed Berlinguer.

A sequel to this incident reveals the convoluted rationale of Italian politics. At the thirteenth DC congress in 1976, a difficult affair, Zaccagnini enjoyed sympathetic support within the party membership in his desire to revive the party, and clean up the party image. He managed to stave off the challenge from the moderate groups of the Dorotei faction of Andreotti and Fanfani (particularly strong in the north-eastern Veneto and Trentino); only to see the 'new' national council dominated by the old guard of Moro, Rumor and Colombo. Zaccagnini was thus placed under Moro's thumb, who was hardly a reformist. Andreotti led the 'moderates' who included the Sicilian clientelist Giovanni Gioia. So much for the 'new look' DC.

In 1976 the political parties tried to reform the abortion laws without having to resort to a referendum. But the DC persisted in still defining abortion as a crime, thereby losing the vital support of the PSI, which triggered another national election one year early. The campaign was the most critical since 1948, waged against an international background of increasing tension, which raised the PCI's hopes of success. Portugal was convulsed by a Socialist revolution, Franco's tenure of power was ending in Spain, Greece and Turkey were at loggerheads over Cyprus, whilst a possible left-wing government hovered in France. During 1975 the French, Spanish and Italian Communist parties jointly proclaimed their commitment to social democracy and independence from Russia. America feared the looming of Euro-Communism and failed to see how it could square with Italy's membership of NATO. In Rome the American ambassador declared in a magazine interview that the United States would not accept the PCI within the Italian government; reaffirmed later by Henry Kissinger, US Secretary of State. Berlinguer hastened to assure the Americans that the PCI would support NATO.

Shortly before the national elections, violence broke out at a meeting held by a MSI candidate Saccucci (involved in the Borghese plot) in which a Communist was killed; also Judge Coco (see above). These attacks would have presumably played to the DC's advantage; yet the election results came as a great surprise to many. The PCI took 34% of the votes (as against 33% in the regionals) improving further on their performance of the previous year, having won votes from the Socialists. Berlinguer attributed their victory to winning over middle class voters, his historic compromise and his espousal of the NATO pact. The DC had remained steady at 39% and so remained the largest party, thanks to their traditional Catholic support combined with strong business backing, such as from Umberto Agnelli (Gianni's brother). The well-respected editor of Il Giorno newspaper, Indro Montanelli, urged people to vote for the DC to deter Communism and international consequences. Many Italians were content to be governed at local/regional level by Communists but not as a national government.

The PSI remained at its 1972 level at under 10%. In 1976 Bettino Craxi, a 43 year old Milanese, became vice president of the PSI. A protégé of Nenni, he was on the right of the party and became a decisive leader. Craxi's strategy was to abandon earlier attempts to draw the PSI closer to the PCI, and strike a more independent centre left path. The paradox was that, although the Left had received more votes, they suffered from the PCI-DC closet, failing to either build a partnership or an effective counterweight. The MSI vote declined to 6%, whilst the PSDI and PRI only managed 3% apiece, and the Liberals with barely 1% virtually vanished. These smaller parties lost ground to left-wing professional groups such as CGIL Scuola and Magistratura Democratica School and Democratic Magistracy who, combined with the PCI, aspired to carrying out effective reforms. The Radicals gained only 1.1% but it allowed them to enter Montecitorio (Parliament). They would later become a force to be reckoned with under Marco Pannella.

The PCI's outstanding success in the national elections was due to Berlinger's moderating historic compromise and support of NATO. He also attracted young first-time voters, together with many trade unionists. Yet the moment was lost. Berlinguer held back from building upon the PCI's electoral success and pressed on with his 'compromise', since as ever he feared a right-wing backlash following the Allende coup in 1967, and a return to Fascist authoritarianism; further aggravated by the judiciary dragging its feet on punishing right-wing offenders.

In August 1976, Andreotti formed a new government which was approved by the Chamber of Deputies, the PCI and PSI agreeing not to oppose it, being accorded a purely advisory role; yet it fell anyway. Andreotti resigned in January 1978, only to create his second government of so-called national solidarity (and his fourth administration) which lasted until January 1979, this time involving the PCI more directly, but still with no ministerial posts. Andreotti, a traditional Catholic yet a wily politician, was popular with the Vatican, and had held every major ministerial post over the years, especially that of Minister of the Interior. A disciple of De Gasperi, his electoral base was his native Rome/Lazio where he enjoyed a strong clientelistic following. His *eminence grise* was Aldo Moro, the master strategist, who planned to mould the PCI into the DC framework, thereby neutralising their power to maintain the status quo of DC domination

Left-wing Activity: *Movimento 77*

The economic crisis had increased unemployment for both manual workers and graduate students, whose numbers had swollen in recent years. The introduction of automation and computerisation, marking the transition from an industrial to a predominantly service economy, had further cut the jobs market which, with the push towards sending youngsters to university, had now produced a surplus of over-qualified youngsters. Jaded by lack of a job, they felt betrayed by the conventional political scene, in particular by the Communist party who now appeared irrelevant to their needs and concerns. The PCI had adopted a more pragmatic approach towards responsible government, such as adopting the Reale law. The new idealistic generation felt socially and economically excluded. By 1977 youngsters were organising self-help groups in some fifty centres in Milan, occupying empty buildings and involving some 5,000 youngsters. They put on social 'creative' events such as films and concerts, attended Dario Fo's alternative theatre with his protest plays, and organised photographic workshops and discussion groups. The centres offered a refuge for *emarginati* drop-outs and escapists fleeing from cold reality. A worrying number became drug addicts: heroin was especially popular. They refused to pay for pop concerts (another form of *autoriduzione)*, engaged in shoplifting, and listened to the free radio stations. In an effort to revive support, left-wing councils organised open air festivals in the town square.

Unsurprisingly, the New Left revolutionary groups were bitterly disappointed by the outcome of the 1975-76 elections since nothing had changed. Numbering about a hundred, these splinter groups, mostly Marxist inspired, achieved a modest success in the elections, desperate to make their voice heard under conventional conditions. Presenting themselves as the umbrella party of *Democrazia Proletaria* DP, an offshoot of Lotta Continua LC, they managed to poll half a million votes, representing 1.5% of the total, and so returned six deputies to Montecitorio. LC's second congress in Rimini was a shambles, illustrating how out of touch they had become with the new generation. Afterwards, the group broke up, leaving a rump of DP. Re-evoking the student protests of 1968, in February 1977 *Autonomia Operaia* AO organised a student sit-in at Rome University to protest against the reforms proposed by Malfatti, the Education Minister. Luciano Lama, CGIL's leader, attempted to address the assembly but was silenced and hounded out by the eruption of violence between AO and the PCI stewards, with spanners, clubs, iron bars and marble chips being hurled. Cossiga, Minister of the Interior, sent in the police with armoured vehicles to evict the students; some arrests were made. The fracas was shown on television: many viewers were appalled by the depth of violence. Two weeks later 60,000 youngsters demonstrated in Rome and shooting broke out in a four-hour conflict with the police.

The other major clash occurred in March 1977, at Bologna University during a meeting held by *Comunione e Liberazione* CL, a new young Catholic group who paradoxically supported both traditional Catholic values and youthful militancy. Halls were set on fire, and shops were looted. Youths carried guns inside their jackets and threw Molotov cocktails. As in Rome, Cossiga had no choice but to fight violence with violence, later declaring: 'Let's be honest, the situation was getting seriously out of hand'. Italy was poised on a knife edge. Cossiga again called out the riot police, using firearms and tear gas. Battle raged for three days, until ended by the police to cheers from residents. One youth and a policeman died. Violence broke out in other cities: in Turin 4,000 left-wingers attacked the headquarters of Cisnal and MSI; whilst an LC group clashed with young right-wingers in a bar, where a youngster died of burns. Two policemen were killed in Milan and Rome. Cossiga banned the victory celebrations of 25th

April and Labour Day on 1st May; also the celebration of the divorce referendum as requested by the radical Marco Pannella, but this one took place regardless.

In September 1977, thousands of youngsters poured into Bologna to attend a three-day festival of music, theatre and political presentations. Some 10,000 youths crowded together in the sports stadium, where about one thousand left and right-wingers clashed. The police dealt with the disturbance and Cossiga had the stadium destroyed. The incident snuffed out the so-called Movement of 77. Local authorities proceeded to cut off funds to the youth centres in major cities. Moretti from BR was nonplussed by the aimless gratuitous violence in Rome and Bologna, mirroring the lashing out of neoFascist youths which showed how far BR had distanced themselves from traditional working-class protests. Combative demonstrations also broke out in many other cities, involving numerous splinter groups, such as *Collettivo Autonomo* and *Policlinico* in Rome. *Prima Linea* protested violently against drugs, pornographic films, female exploitation, back street abortions and the high cost of living. Youngsters drifted back listlessly into the usual humdrum of conventional living. *Il riflusso* violence ebbed away.

Chapter Eleven
The Moro Affair

On 16th March 1978, the Christian Democrat Prime Minister Giulio Andreotti was due to present his new government in the Chamber of Deputies in Rome, which included the PCI: the 'historic compromise' promulgated by Berlinguer, albeit in a purely consultative role. The new administration was endorsed by Aldo Moro, epitome of the political Establishment, who had persuaded the PCI to join the administration and so maintain political equilibrium. That morning, the Red Brigades BR, led by Mario Moretti, ambushed Aldo Moro's car in via Fani, on the way to Montecitorio (Parliament), killed his driver and five bodyguards, and abducted Moro. Italy was seized with horror at the dramatic abduction on the very day of an innovatory political scenario. Hundreds of thousands of demonstrators thronged the streets of the key main cities, whilst trade unions called a strike. Moro was held for fifty-five days by the BR in Rome. Moro had been targeted because firstly he had failed to implement badly needed reforms; and secondly because he had brokered the historic compromise which BR saw as a betrayal of the people.

A moral dilemma arose: should the government accede to the terrorists' demands and save Moro; or should they stand fast as a matter of principle and sacrifice Moro's life. Judge Sossi had been released and so they hoped that Moro would also be liberated. Bettino Craxi, a prominent Socialist, argued for compromise, whilst the Communists reasoned that ceding to the kidnappers would only reinforce the cult of reform through violence. Eugenio Scalfari, editor of the new paper *La Repubblica*, was also of this opinion. DC deputies were divided: those close to Moro, together with his family and friends, pleaded for his life but were prevented from negotiating for his release; but they were allowed to send letters. Others led by Andreotti stood firm. Moro's wife refused to have her husband traded.

Despite five legal proceedings and a parliamentary commission involving forty members, three of whom were former prime ministers, and included Moro's close friend, the Sicilian writer Leonardo Sciascia, the Moro affair remains shrouded in a convoluted cloak and dagger mystery. Possibly ten Brigadists were involved (two being Morucci and Gallinari) of whom four fired their arms but they jammed. 49 shots were fired from another gun but to date it is still not known by whom. According to Sidoni and Zanetov, authors of *Cuori Rossi contro Cuori Neri* Red Hearts against Black Hearts, the sole certainty in the case was that the top echelons of the DC, together with high level civil servants and intelligence chiefs, would welcome Moro's elimination, many of whom were members of the far right P2 masonic lodge, and were involved in his 'rescue'. Moro's espousal of the historic compromise was anathema not only to the Communists but also to the Red Brigades, who saw it as a betrayal of Communist beliefs and of the Italian people, as well as a reinforcement of the political status quo.

Tommaso Buscetta, the mafioso *pentito* who had turned state evidence, declared that certain state officials had approached his organisation to assist in finding Moro, but then the request was withdrawn. The Mafia's cashier, Giuseppe Calò, apparently remarked to his boss, Stefano Bontate: 'But Stefano, you still don't understand: high level politicians in his party do not want him freed'. Raffaele Cutolo, another mafioso, told the authorities he knew of Moro's whereabouts; but he too was rebuffed and told to mind his own business.

On 16th March, the day of the abduction, the police found the Fiat 132 used, together with two other cars on the 17th and 19th inst. which suggested that the BR hide-out was nearby. On the 17th the police pulled in the Brigadist Moreno but released him three days later. Article 1 of the Constitution allowed Moro to have an élite escort since he had received death threats. However, its leader, Marshall Leonardi, was dissatisfied with the quality of his team and requested replacements. He knew he was being shadowed and feared something was amiss, which made him nervous and so he confided both in his wife and his boss. His driver Ricci, also sensing trouble, had requested a bullet proof car since the current one had become unreliable. Neither of these requests was forthcoming. More worrying is the fact that no record exists of their requests either written or verbal. A wall of silence reigned. On 3rd April some far left activists were arrested but they too were released.

The parliamentary Commission examined whether the police and security services had conducted a proper investigation. Sciascia, who served on the Commission, is scathing about the massive deployment of manpower which impressed the general public yet yielded scant results. Granted extended powers to stop and search, the police made over 72,000 road stops, of which 6,000 were in Rome; over 37,000 house searches (Rome 7,000); over 6 million people stopped and searched (167,000); and over three million vehicles checked (96,000). 150 arrests were made. The Rome Questor[47] was refused his request for just twelve men, yet the Roman police force totalled 4,300.

Nor could Moro rely on international organisations coming to his rescue, since he had made a hive of enemies abroad, and who would equally consider his death convenient. Israel was baying for his blood since, during his tenure as Foreign Minister, he had allowed the PLF Palestine Liberation Front to hold and transport weapons on Italian soil; in return for which they held off attacks on Italy. The PLF leader, Bassam Abu Sharif, who had never met Moro, declared that he had held meetings in Rome with Italian intelligence, together with the Beirut head of SID. He recalls that 'an understanding was reached which we have always respected'. Keen to help the Italian secret service through his links with BR, Sharif dialled a number but could only leave messages, which he thought strange for a special line. He declared: 'I could have saved Moro'.

The elimination of Moro suited the Russians, since his intention to include the Communists in the Italian government would distance the PCI from the Moscow orbit and reduce Russian influence in the Peninsula. The historian Giuseppe De Lutiis, who acted as advisory co-ordinator for the parliamentary commission on terrorism, stated that the historic compromise would have illustrated 'the feasibility of democratic Communism for countries such as Czechoslovakia, Hungary and especially Poland'. Achille Occhetto, general secretary of the PCI from 1988, endorsed De Lutiis' opinion by remarking that Moscow highly disapproved of Moro's strategy and the increasing independence of the PCI. Finally, the US Democrat President, Jimmy Carter, supported his predecessor, the Republican John Ford, in condemning any rapprochement whatsoever between the PCI and the Italian government. Germany also favoured a tough approach on the Moro abduction, since if Italy went Communist, that country could well come under Russian influence.

---

[47] The Questor is the public official responsible for the police in a provincial capital, and reports to the Prefect/Chief Constable.

As Minister of the Interior, Francesco Cossiga organised two crisis units: technical operations involving politicians, the police and the secret services, whose bosses were all members of P2; and a management crisis committee which included psychologists, behaviour experts and criminologists such as Professor Franco Ferracuti, also a P2 member; and Steve Piecznick, an international terrorist expert, sent by the Americans. An obscure character, Piecznick was invited to Italy by Cossiga, where he stayed in Rome for some weeks then left, declaring that the DC had no need of his services. Years later Piecznick, having refused to appear before the Italian Commission on terrorism, subsequently gave an interview to a French journalist in which he apparently revealed the truth surrounding Moro's captivity. Cossiga had not yet devised a plan of campaign, and confided to Piecznick that he feared a total shutdown of the Italian state, which would reverberate upon other NATO countries. It soon became clear to Piecznick that neither the state institutions nor the politicians wanted to save Moro; and that *ragion di stato* demanded the sacrifice of Moro to save thousands of other lives in a country, in Piecznick's words, 'besieged by indescribable chaos'. He realised that Andreotti and Cossiga were doing their utmost to obstruct attempts to locate their colleague. They reasoned that his death would prevent the Italian Communists from seizing power and block right-wing coups.

BR's sixth communication of 15th April, sent that same day to *La Repubblica*, declared that they had carried out a trial of Moro in the name of the Italian people and sentenced him to death. The seventh bulletin on the 18th inst. falsely announced his death, claiming that Moro's body had been thrown into the Duchessa Lake some 100km from Rome. Yet the body in the lake proved to be a red herring: the police and carabinieri dredged the frozen lake but found nothing. Andreotti and Cossiga both denied that the false document had been the work of the State, but Piecznick affirms that he did in fact discuss the false document with Cossiga, as well as secret service agents and Ferracuti, explaining that it was psychologically necessary to prepare public opinion both nationally and abroad. The false bulletin was perhaps the unforeseen move alluded to by Franceschini, so BR probably realised they were up against a psychological expert, forcing them to accept that the State had no intention of saving their colleague.

Leonardo Sciascia, writer and a close friend of Moro, was of the opinion that the false bulletin was a 'dark psychological manoeuvre'. Furthermore, it would explain why Franceschini suggests that Piecznick had tried to minimize his role but was in fact the key player. Two days later, on the 20th inst., BR's genuine seventh communication was despatched to *La Repubblica* newspaper denying Moro's death and displaying a new photograph of him: his last before dying and still showing his usual imperturbable demeanour. This bulletin proposed an exchange of thirteen terrorist prisoners, giving an ultimatum of reply by 22nd April. Panama offered refuge to the terrorists.

Likening the crisis to a game of chess, as did Sciascia (and incidentally Macmillan too on the Cuban crisis)[48] Piecznick smugly boasted that BR did not expect to come up against such a psychological expert as himself. 'If BR had liberated Moro, they would have become responsible heroes. I myself brought about their destruction.' He inveigled BR into believing that the State would negotiate for the release of Moro and some terrorist prisoners. The false bulletin wrongfooted BR into a trap, perhaps precipitating an abrupt end to negotiations; and from which their only way out was to do away with Moro.

Franceschini's comments on both the Sossi and Moro incidents are pertinent. He felt that someone high up was keen to have both men eliminated. When Moro was on the point of being liberated, that person upset proceedings with an unforeseen move (the false bulletin) but with a different outcome: Sossi lived, but Moro died. If the more moderate Franceschini and Curcio (imprisoned at the time) had still been in charge, rather than the more violent Moretti, the Brigadists may well have hoped that the government would release the prisoners and save Moro.

On 2nd April a séance was held, attended by Romano Prodi (a future prime minister), and two university lecturers from Bologna and Modena, one of whom hosted the meeting in the former town. Seated in the classic fashion around a table bedecked with a plate encircled by letters of the alphabet, the participants claimed that the spirit of Don Luigi Sturzo, a Sicilian mafioso, had indicated three locations where Moro might be held: Bolsena, Viterbo and Gradoli; which incidentally happened to be the three places suggested by *Autonomia Operaia*, and whom Bettino Craxi, the Socialist politician, had consulted. The police, who so far had been woefully negligent in their efforts to locate Moro, interviewed all the participants at the séance: they all confirmed that the spirit had indicated via Gradoli. So the police went to Viterbo, north of Rome, where they searched

---

[48] A.Horne: Macmillan Vol.1

high and low but to no avail. The séance seems a bizarre episode; yet Italians are very superstitious and attach a great deal of importance to such matters.

Whilst conducting their house searches, the police had visited the area of the BR hide-out in Rome at via Gradoli. However, since the neighbours advised that the occupants at no.96 were quiet people, the police did not bother to take further action, despite having been granted special powers to break in. In fact this was where Moro was being held. The street and so the hide-out, the two bedroom flat rented by Mario Moretti in December 1975, was later found by chance after Moro's death, due to a water leak attended by the fire brigade.

On 22nd April, shortly before the ultimatum deadline, Pope Paul VI, a close friend of Moro, received a brief note from Moro, just saying: *'Semplicemente senza emozioni:'* 'Simply without emotion'. In response the Pope sent a note of appeal to BR: *'Liberatelo senza condizioni'* 'Free him without conditions'; but his plea for clemency passed 'like water over stone' (Sciascia). The Vatican sent the letter to the press and radio, who published it since they felt that the people had a right to know what was going on, and perhaps hoping to sway public opinion to apply pressure on the government to save Moro. The Italian people thought the Pope showed more sense than the politicians.

The press played a crucial role in acting as a go-between, by allowing Moro and his family to correspond via the media, since he was given edited newspapers to read. Towards the end Moro received a letter from his children together with his wife's last letter via the press. Both the *Osservatore Romano* newspaper and Amnesty International made direct appeals to BR. Moro was particularly touched by the Brigadist who risked his life to deliver Easter greetings to his family. The action hints at a difference of opinion within BR as to how to proceed with their captive; indeed as with Sossi. Moro never received any written communication from his political colleagues in response to his letters: they had washed their hands of him, or been instructed not to communicate with him.

On 25th April, Kurt Waldheim, Secretary General of the United Nations, made an appeal on Italian television to BR. It was poorly received since he erroneously stated that BR had a *'causa'* legitimate suit when in fact, he meant 'purpose'. On the 28th, perhaps prodded by Waldheim's gesture, Andreotti also appeared before the cameras, and again on 3rd May, declaring his refusal to treat with BR, out of respect for those families who had suffered bereavement at the hands of the Brigadists.

The ninth communication on 5th May confirmed the execution of Moro. As he had requested, his family received a telephone call from BR advising the location of his body. On 9th May, it was found in the boot of a purple-red Renault 4 in Via Caetani, near to where Moro had been held, tellingly equidistant between the headquarters of the DC and PCI. He was buried the following day in a private ceremony; followed on the 13th by a public commemoration service at the Basilica of St. John in Lateran, attended by the political establishment but no family, and presided over by the Pope who solemnly intoned: 'Lord, thou hast not heard our prayer'. One hour later, a general strike was called.

During his fifty-five-day captivity in the 'people's prison' Moro apparently suffered no physical violence or submission to drug abuse, as confirmed by him in his correspondence. (Sossi also stated that he was quite well treated). BR's first communication sent on 18th March to the press acknowledged their responsibility for the abduction and enclosed a photograph of Moro with his usual opaque countenance. On 29th March BR sent their third communication to Cossiga, advising that the interrogation was proceeding with the total collaboration of the prisoner. Attached was Moro's letter to Cossiga, carefully couched as if encoded, since it offered veiled hints as to his whereabouts: for instance he mentions 'here' meaning Rome. Yet apparently Cossiga failed to have the letters analysed. Moro, being cryptic by nature, found it natural to encode his correspondence.

In his account 'L'Affaire Moro', Sciascia deduces from the missive that Moro is urging Cossiga to mobilise a search and rescue operation, and to negotiate an exchange of thirteen prisoners (including Curcio who was awaiting trial with other terrorists in a Turin prison) in order to gain time to locate his whereabouts. According to Sciascia, the number thirteen points to Moro's eventual demise. Moro is indeed already prescient of his own fate, hinting at a 'grave outcome': all ends in death. He requests Cossiga to appeal to the Pope to intercede.

In all his letters to the politicians, Moro refers to a great reciprocal emotion, in that not only do his wife and children have great need of him, but he too needs their solace. Yet his choice of words suggests a further code to Sciascia: that by extension he is referring to the concept of the nation as a family: in short that the Italians have great need of his guidance. Deprived of the physical and emotional presence of his family, psychologically his Southern (Puglian) pessimism exerts its inexorable pressure on a range of emotions. He feels lonely and anxious; as did Judge Sossi.

In his first letter of 4th April, addressed to the deputy Zaccagnini and sent to *La Repubblica* together with BR's fourth communication, Moro advises that he is not suffering physically, but he is already beginning to despair of ever being found. Speaking of his ordeal he believes that time is running out and expects to die. It begins to dawn on him that even his political 'friends' do not want him found. He has received no written communication from any of them, and feels abandoned. In this letter Moro mentions the eight politicians who hold his fate in their hands, and which include Andreotti, Cossiga, Fanfani, Leone (all DC) and the Socialist Craxi. Moro composes an open letter directed at senators Gui and Taviani, which reached the press on 10th April (respectively the former Education Minister and the latter imprisoned over the Lockheed scandal). Moro suspects that America and Germany are exerting pressure on Taviani, a US sympathizer, to urge the DC not to treat with BR over Moro, in order to prevent the Communists from taking power in Italy.

On 19th April, *La Repubblica* received a long and powerful letter from Moro addressed to Zaccagnini but in fact directed at all of the DC, in which he, the supreme politician, uses his powers of eloquence to save his life. He speaks of forty days of suffering, reminiscent of Christ's experience in the wilderness. Moro is astonished that his political 'friends' are all agreed on his death for *ragion di stato* the greater good of the nation. Almost as a veiled threat, in his despair he advises each one of them to think very carefully *pensateci bene,* since his death would only wreak havoc on Italy. He feels embittered by the lack of support for his DC-PCI alliance. In his last open letter received on 29th April by the Roman newspapers, he makes an ultimate appeal to Craxi, expressing his amazement at the DC's refusal to perform their Christian duty by saving him through an exchange of prisoners: *'Non l'avrei creduto possibile'* 'I would not have thought it possible'; yet adding with a hint of sarcasm 'unless the DC comes to its senses'. Having just read the final letters from his wife and children, he laments that he will enjoy no lasting embrace from them. He demands that none of the political establishment attend his funeral.

Both the politicians and part of the media defend the *ragion di stato*: Moro is a mere pawn for the greater good, and so they advocate his civil death *morte civile.* Fifty politicians issue a statement to the press declaring that Moro is no longer himself: 'We no longer know him'. Moro himself retorts that he is quite unchanged, as endorsed by Sciascia. Harshly the journalist Indro Montanelli declares Moro as being already dead politically. The few who wished to save him were the more moderate and humanitiarian Socialists, including Craxi who was much saddened by Moro's fate. On 21st April *Lotta Continua* launched an appeal in its newspaper which was signed by many, including the Communists, intellectuals such as Dario Fo, parliamentary deputies and two Communist bishops.

Throughout Moro's captivity, BR heightened the tension and applied pressure on the government by carrying out attacks and killings on various people. During April there occurred eleven attacks in a single day in Venice; the marshall of the prison guards in Milan was murdered, as well as a prison guard in Turin, an industrialist was kneecapped in Genoa; also a professor in Padua by another terrorist group. Valerio Morucci, one of the older Brigadists, remarked that 'the campaign began as a challenge that gradually became a bloody duel. The evil genie had now renounced its purpose and become out of control, becoming a nightmare for the apprentice wizards. An infernal web, which had swept away everything: both the good and the bad, especially the good, since there is little to cry about the bad; and that had grown back like a bad plant.'

Many of the self-styled intelligentsia refused to believe in the existence of left-wing red terrorism, blaming right-wing terrorists for the atrocities. They attributed Moro's death to the American CIA: in fact this was a rumour put about by the Russian KGB. They thirsted for Calabresi's blood following the death of Pinelli. The press insisted that Feltrinelli's GAP organisation was a fantasy and that he was killed by right-wing state terrorists. Older intellectuals had supported Mussolini, only to turn later to Communism and oppose the historic compromise: for instance the writer Dario Fo had served as a Fascist in the Salò Republic. During an interview in *Espresso* magazine between Oreste Scalzone, AO leader, and the writer Alberto Moravia, the latter proclaimed: 'I'm from that part of the proletariat that's called an artist'. Incredulous, the interviewer exclaimed: 'Moravia a prole?!' In fact most self-styled intellectuals had never seen the inside of a factory.

The roll call of left-wing sympathisers is legion, encompassing artists, writers, actors, film directors, painters, poets, psychoanalysts and architects. To name just a few: Michelangelo Antonioni, Bernardo Berolucci, Enzo Biagi, Umberto Eco, Federico Fellini, Carlo and Inge Feltrinelli (his son and wife), Dario Fo, Natalia Ginzburg, Primo Levi, Pier Paolo Pasolini, Cesare Pavese. The historian Giorgio Bocca published his article *'L'eterna favola delle BR'* three days after Curcio had escaped from prison, in which he observed: 'How can one now deny the existence of BR after these attacks?'

Since the early '70s, only a few journalists had understood the dangerous threat of left-wing terrorism: principally Giampaolo Pansa, Carlo Casalegno and Walter Tobagi. Writing in April 1972 in *La Stampa* about BR's first kidnap, that of the Sit-Siemens manager, Pansa opined that it would only encourage extremists to become Tupamaros type guerrillas, which paradoxically would only help the far right. Casalegno, deputy editor of *La Stampa*, spoke out against two Roman groups: *Collettivo Autonomo* and *Policlinico*. He was killed in November 1977. When Indro Montanelli, of high international profile, was wounded in both legs, the press simply announced: 'Journalist wounded'. Concluding his article on terrorism in *Avvenire* magazine in 1972, Tobagi declared: 'Terrorism, whether it be of the left or right, is always terrorism and always unacceptable'. He was murdered in Milan in 1980 by a terrorist who was the son of a film critic and editor.

Moro's assassination and the murder of Tobagi eventually shook some intellectuals and journalists out of their myopic torpor and induced them to revise their position. Those who had signed the document against the police commissioner Calabresi concerning the death of Pinelli (see Chapter 8) now became evasive, even haughty. One film producer said that one had the right to take up arms but that did not imply that they would actually do so. Another glossed over the matter, saying they remembered nothing. Another quipped: 'I signed the document but I don't want to go back over it'. Natalia Ginzburg limited herself to a terse 'no comment'. Some diehards persisted in their beliefs. Dario Fo, Nobel prize winner, proclaimed in 1996: 'The sole terrorism is that of the State'. The writer Domenico Porzio uttered: 'We were young and wild': he was aged 45 at the time. A former leader of the left-wing Katanga group, which beat up crowd controllers during the Hot Autumn, still denied the use of violence by the far left at that time, declaring that 'they (the far right) started it!' In the words of the authors of *'Cuori Rossi'*: 'The greatest crimes against humanity have been perpetrated with the ideological support of intellectuals who loudly proclaimed their desire to save the world of all its evils'. Let the historian Paul Johnson have the last word: 'Beware of intellectuals!'

End Game

Following the assassination of Moro, Carlo Alberto Dalla Chiesa, a Carabiniere General, was appointed to spearhead a counter offensive against the terrorist bands. Some 650 individuals were arrested. Assisted by recent legislation, he adopted the tactic of persuading disillusioned terrorists to repent, in return for which the *pentiti* were given short prison sentences, for instance Patrizio Peci, a prominent BR member. Toni Negri and other lecturers in his group at Padua University were arrested on suspicion of belonging to the BR. They were imprisoned for several years before being brought to trial, when most of the charges were dropped. Dalla Chiesa was later killed by the Mafia.

Following the assassination of Moro, BR split to form the offshoot of BR-*partitito guerriglia* warfare group. In December 1981, they abducted General James Lee Dozier, head of US NATO South East Europe. The terrorists simply rang his doorbell in Verona where he lived without a bodyguard, and took him to a people's prison in Padua, as with Sossi and Moro. They only questioned him once since nobody spoke adequate English. BR tried to play the international card but no organisation was interested in coming to Dozier's rescue. President Reagan was furious that, in his words, four ragamuffins had managed to abduct an American general. Yet again the public were stunned by the kidnapping.

In desperation SISMI military intelligence turned to the Mafia, as they did with the Camorra concerning Cirillo, to retrieve Dozier alive. They contacted M.Campione, Italian military attaché at the United Nations, who sounded out the Italo-American boss and notary A.Bove, who in turn arranged an appointment with D. Lombino, a lawyer who had illegally entered the US. Lombino met the mafioso F.Restelli, currently being held in an Italian prison, whose sources confirmed the precise address of the hide-out in Padua. The Ministry of the Interior denied having liaised with Lombino and Restelli; yet Bove confirmed that discussions had indeed taken place. Caught between the devil and the deep blue sea, SISMI were loth to manoeuvre for fear of risking the general's life and suffer stiff recriminations from the Americans. However, when the CIA threatened to act alone, they agreed to a joint operation and successfully rescued Dozier from his captors.

The discovery of the Padua cell, together with the confessions of a BR girl, Emilia Libera, led to the unearthing of eight cells in Rome and Sardinia (yet another area seeking independence) which brought about the arrest of a hundred activists, together with the questioning of another hundred in 1982, as well as details of the Rome network. The police, their forbearance now exhausted, resorted to strong force and torture to extract confessions throughout Italy.

Subsequent to the Dozier episode, BR signalled a 'strategic withdrawal', yet they continued to remain quite active, drifting in a changed socio-political scenario and far removed from reality. The 1982 elections signalled the replacement of Fanfani's DC administration by Craxi's Socialist *pentapartito* five party coalition, thereby shifting the DC and PCI into the background. People had had enough of terrorism disrupting their daily lives and yearned for a return to calm normality. M.Pannella, leader of the Radical party, gained a seat in Parliament, as did Liga Veneta. BR transferred to Turin where they carried out bank raids, killing two guards in the process. This incident annoyed Curcio, now in prison and who distanced himself from the new style BR. Even hardliners such as Mario Moretti, Valerio Morucci and Prospero Gallinari; as well as Anna Laura Braghetti and Adriana Faranda (she and Gallinari were involved in the Moro affair) together with many others, now renounced armed warfare. Hundreds of arrests were made of terrorists who now languished in prison, having shot, kidnapped, killed and raided, with precious little achieved.

Still with their heads in the clouds, in February 1984 the Communist arm of BR-PCC launched an anti-imperialist international front, reminiscent of Feltrinelli's dreams, hoping to team up with *Action Directe* and RAF (Baader-Meinhof). BR killed the American Ray L.Hunt, in charge of the multinational force operating in Sinai during the Arab-Israeli war. BR splintered into microgroups centred on Rome, re-forming under different names. They executed sporadic minor raids, for instance on the NATO base in Comiso. In September 1984, they seized 700 million lire from a post office in Rome.

The agreement on the revised *Scala Mobile* Wage Index, which favoured the employer, gave BR a new line of attack. They now had their sights on the consultants involved in the negotiations. In May 1983 they kneecapped Gino Giugni, a Socialist adviser to the trade unions and the Ministry of Labour. In March 1985, they murdered the economist Ezio Tarantelli, adviser to CISL Socialist trade union and a professor at Rome University. In February 1986, BR killed A. Da Empoli employed at the PM's Economics Department; also L.Conti, former mayor of Florence, simply because he held some military shares. Three Brigadists were imprisoned for life and another for thirty years. The following month, they killed L.Giorgieri, an aviation general responsible for armaments at the Ministry of Defence: four arrests were made.

Terrorism was now spearheaded by the newly reformed BR-PCC. In April 1988, they killed the DC Senator R.Ruffilli in Forli. BR lay low until 1992, when they carried out some minor attacks at the NATO Aviano base, and in 1994 at NATO's defence college in Rome, which led to 14 arrests. In May 1997 former terrorists signed an appeal entitled '*Storia infinita*' calling for an end to armed warfare. In December of that year, Moretti was granted partial liberty and Curcio temporary freedom.

The final flame of terrorism occurred in May 1999, when BR-PCC killed Massimo D'Antona, followed in March 2002 by the assassination of Marco Biagi in Bologna. Both victims were professors of industrial law at La Sapienza University in Rome and advisers at the Ministry of Labour. Biagi, a specialist in jurisprudence, was instrumental in effecting the much-needed labour reforms in favour of the employer. The new legislation offered flexible work contracts which permitted the sacking of employees, cancelling their right for reinstatement but offering financial compensation. Having received death threats, Biagi had requested an escort but this was refused. Many were deeply shocked at the turn of events.

Remand orders had been issued for six Brigadists involved in the murder of D'Antona: among them were Nadia Lioce and Mario Galesi. Their last stop occurred whilst travelling on a Florence-Rome express train. During a routine identification check, Galesi panicked, shots were fired, in which he was killed and his female companion arrested. So ended, in a somewhat muted fashion, the saga of the Red Brigades.

NAR: Postscript

In February 1981, NAR's right-wing co-founders, the brothers Cristiano and Valerio Fioravanti, together with Francesca Mambro and Gilberto Cavallini, planned to escape to Switzerland but, before doing so, organised a bank raid to raise funds. Whilst retrieving their cache of arms from a canal in Padua, the police came upon them: two policemen died. 39 NAR members were later arrested, including Massimo Sparti and Cristiano, who both pointed the finger at Valerio and Francesca as being responsible for the Bologna massacre. Sparti was released, whilst another NAR prisoner apparently confirmed his statement. The judiciary also accused five others of the Bologna incident. Cristiano's confessions led to the break-up of NAR, those not caught fleeing to Lebanon. In December 1981 Alessandro Alibrandi, fellow NAR founder, returned from Beirut but was shot dead by the police. Whilst NAR was carrying out a bank raid in March 1982, at the BNL bank in Rome, there followed a shoot-out with the police, in which Francesca was seriously wounded, but survived. Valerio perished, either shot or committed suicide.

Strange Bedfellows

The abduction of Ciro Cirillo provides a disturbing insight into the machinations of the Italian underworld. In 1980 the regions of Basilicata and Campania had suffered a massive earthquake centred on Irpinia, in which 3,000 people lost their lives and with thousands injured. The Red Brigades BR were disgusted at the lack of official measures to rehouse the 80,000 homeless, living in caravans, and with 280,000 evacuated. In April 1981, the BR Naples cell took their revenge by abducting Ciro Cirillo, DC Assessor for urban planning in the region of Campania, and in charge of reconstruction funds following the earthquake disaster. He was a member of the Dorotei faction led by Senator Antonio Gava, DC boss in Naples.

Cirillo's experience resembles Moro's ordeal. He was taken to a BR people's prison in *Ercolano* Herculaneum,[49] near Pompeii, where he was confined for 89 days in a restricted space with constant light and psychedelic music to disorientate him. Under interrogation Cirillo revealed to BR his extensive knowledge of shady DC deals and closely guarded secrets with the Camorra criminal organisation, dominant in the region since the war. This information was recorded at the time but the tapes later disappeared. Apparently, Gava and the secret services knew where he was being held, but chose to ignore the information. Cirillo tried to hint at his whereabouts (as did Moro) but his inferences were either not understood or ignored.

The DC bosses were desperate to secure Cirillo's release, since he held the DC pursestrings in the region, directing part into the DC coffers and part to the Camorra through his network of contacts. DC bosses decided to seek the assistance of Raffaele Cutolo, 'Don Rafele', Naples boss of the newly formed Camorra NCO *Nuova Camorra Organizzata*, which he organised along 19th century pyramidal lines, with 7,000 members at its peak and with his sister as cashier.

---

[49] The ancient site is well worth a visit.

A series of meetings was arranged with Cutolo at the maxi security prison at Ascoli Piceno (Abruzzo). Present were G.Criscuolo SISDE[50] agent, Musumeci SISMI[51] deputy head, a lawyer by the name of Madonna, R.Salzano, a carabiniere captain, and Granata, a former DC mayor and now Cirillo's right hand man. Negotiations opened with Cutolo and his personal assistant V.Casillo, an NCO businessman. Iacolare, Cutolo's brother in law and fourth in the NCO command, was also present. Although a wanted man, Iacolare's arrival was not blocked by the police since Cirillo's release was paramount. Cutolo agreed to open negotiations with BR for the release, for which he requested the transfer of several terrorist prisoners, including Brigadists, to Ascoli; which was duly effected. Moreover Cutolo revealed that he possessed the names of magistrates investigating BR; as well as policemen responsible for the death of Brigadists, including Mara Cagol, Curcio's wife and co-founder.

Cutolo was dragging his feet over brokering the release of Cirillo, so the politicians decided to exert pressure on him. The police set up road blocks and extra patrols to upset NCO's usual everyday business of drugs and cigarettes. The strategy virtually paralysed NCO's operations, with a decline in raids and a drop in killings, usually one a day, to 'only' three during this period. Caught between the vice of BR and the secret services, Cutolo sent a letter to BR suggesting they release Cirillo; at the same time telling them to quit Naples since they were ruining his business empire. A hint was dropped with the knifing of the Brigadist V.Moretti outside his high security prison in Cuneo, where he was detained together with Curcio and Franceschini. (Moretti had been on the run for ten years and finally caught, thanks to a DIGOS security informer). For their part, BR also forced Cutolo's hand by carrying out three kidnappings during this period: one concerned an engineer who was so severely battered during his six week captivity that he died. They killed the brother of Patrizio Peci, the first BR *pentito* to co-operate with the authorities, subjecting him to their usual proletarian trial which was shown on national television. The third victim, a PCI assessor for building works in Naples, was kneecapped.

The third and final meeting was held in Cutolo's cell, bedecked with Persian rugs and a Modigliani painting. The SISDE agent Criscuolo was replaced by one Titta, an aeronautics officer from SISMI military intelligence, and who had possibly been involved in shady deals with NCO. A. Bove, involved in the

---

[50] Servizio per l'Informazione e la sicurezza democratica: similar to MI5

[51] Servizio per l'informazione e la sicurezza militari

Dozier abduction, was also present. Apparently Gava, who maintained a low profile throughout the affair, had intimated to SISMI that he wanted Cirillo freed, which Titta now communicated to Cutolo. It seems that F.Paziena, a SISMI agent, agreed an 'arrangement' with Cutolo, whereby NCO would receive 5% on subcontracts for rebuilding works by major construction companies following the earthquake. Cutolo also secured a promise to have sixty of his men declassified to 'ordinary' prisons with greater liberty. Titta also offered Cutolo five hundred million lire in cash but he declined the money.

Eventually, in order to finalize the matter, BR settled for about half of their cash ransom, viz. 1.4 billion lira from Cirillo's family. A journalist, by the name of Zambelli, a friend of Cirillo, took the cash to BR, who proceeded to count it out there and then, note by note, all 29,000 in 50,000 lira notes. It took them three hours. The ransom was seen as a re-imbursement to the proletariat by the bourgeoisie: Robin Hood robbing the rich to help the poor, in this case victims of the earthquake. After 89 days in captivity Cirillo was released near Poggio Reale prison in Naples. He was picked up in the street by the police, who took him home to recover from the shock and avoid interrogation. Two days later Cirillo spoke to the press. Nobody whispered a word of involvement of the secret services, BR or the Camorra. A wall of silence reigned.

Cutolo and possibly others received some 1.4 billion lire from government tenders for lucrative building contracts through the Banco Ambrosiano (managed by Roberto Calvi) and the Vatican's IOR Institute for Religious Works which was directed by Monsignor Marcinkus. Apparently, Cutolo intended using part of his share towards Gava's election campaign. President Pertini had other ideas: Cutolo was transferred to an isolation cell in Asinara Prison, cut off from his men, which marked the wane of his career. In 1988 Judge Alemi, charged with investigating the Cirillo affair, declared he had come across a wasps' nest of *omertà* silence both by politicians and the secret services: for instance a trail of false names had been entered in the register at Ascoli prison. Cirillo's interview tapes (mentioned earlier) had disappeared without trace. Some of those involved in the affair were either silenced or died in suspicious circumstances. For his part Cutolo remained reticent, though he did allude to compromising documents in his possession; and hinted at the involvement of an important politician of Campania: possibly Gava, Scotti or Senator Patriarca. As for Cirillo, he left the world of politics. In 2001, during an interview with a newspaper, he revealed that he had consigned a lengthy account of the affair to his notary, to be released upon his death. In 1982 BR briefly joined forces with the Camorra in Naples to carry out some attacks. Their victims included the murder of Inspector Ammaturo, a soldier and three policemen. But the collaboration was short-lived, since the Camorra considered the BR approach too violent, which disturbed their usual business interests. [52]

---

[52] I am indebted to Messrs.P.Sidoni and P.Zanetov for the information contained in this section.

Chapter Twelve
The Craxi Years

In 1978 the Socialist Alessandro Pertini was elected as President of Italy, with a substantial majority of 832 votes out of a total of 995, facilitated by the support of the Communists and the DC. A former Resistance fighter, Pertini became a highly popular President, adopting a more proactive role in Italian affairs with his outspoken views, yet softened by his personal touch. Pertini was instrumental in the election of Giovanni Spadolini as prime minister in 1981, the first Republican to hold that post since Parri in 1945. That same year another noteworthy appointment was the election of the Pole, Karol Wojtyla, Archbishop of Cracow, as Pope John Paul II, and the first foreign pope since 1522. In June 1981, a *pentapartito* five party coalition government was formed amongst the Christian Democrats and Socialists, together with the smaller parties of the Liberals, Social Democrats and Republicans, thereby giving the DC a broader electoral base in return for minor cabinet positions. The coalition helped the DC regain control of many regions, provinces and cities.

In 1982 Ciriaco De Mita became general secretary of the DC, retaining that post until 1986, the longest ever for the DC. Like his predecessor Zacchagnini, De Mita was keen to modernize the ailing party, which was suffering from a lack of turnover at the top. De Mita wished to put an end to the melting pot of factionalism and clientelism, favouring the increase of regional power. However, the latter remained weak and De Mita retained his own centre left *Base* faction to stay in power. Local DC party organisation had become demoralized, exacerbated by a lack of grass roots support, especially in the cities where they were viewed as highly corrupt and out of touch with the younger generation. The DC had become top heavy in the clientelistic South, which accounted for 62% of its membership, especially in Sicily and Naples/Campania; but had suffered a decline in the north, where many moved left to Socialism and more modern ideas. As with Zacchagnini, De Mita welcomed free enterprise as promulgated by Thatcher and Reagan. He was anxious to reduce the public sector and promote a bipolar party system with the PSI.

DC policy is discussed by the National Council of 160 members of which half are parliamentarians, all of whom are elected by the biennial Congress of 1,200 delegates, which includes regional party secretaries, as well as faction leaders who effectively dictate party policy which is merely endorsed by Congress. Endemic in Italy since medieval times, with the rise of the city states, faction offers democracy within the modern party and deters autocratic leadership, but yields unstable national government. In the spirit of Catholic equality, seats in all the organisations are allocated strictly according to factional power. Day to day management is in the hands of the 45 member monthly executive Committee, elected by the national council. The post of party president is purely honorific. The party secretary is the chief executive, previously chosen by the National Council, but since 1976 by Congress. He has his work cut out trying to control the in-fighting, with the clans constantly jockeying for power. In 1986 the DC boasted six factions, little changed over the past two decades, and at that time dominated by the Base and Andreotti groups.

In 1976 the Socialist Bettino Craxi, a protégé of Nenni, became party secretary at the age of 42. In 1983 Craxi withdrew his support from De Mita's coalition government, which prompted an early national election that year. The DC experienced their worst result since 1945, due to the P2 scandal, losing the abortion referendum in 1981 and their waning image. Over twenty years their share of the vote dropped from 38% to 33%, especially in the Veneto where it fell from 50% to 43%, in part due to the rise of the *Liga Veneta* Venetian League seeking autonomy: the region has a strong history of independence. De Mita had failed to win the support of the middle classes and small business people since they mistrusted him as a Southerner; and because he too was immersed in the clientelistic system. Hailing from Avellino province in Campania, he headed the Base faction in Irpinia province. Furthermore he and his family were principal shareholders in the local *Banca Popolare* in Irpinia and had been accused of misappropriation of funds assigned to the earthquake disaster in 1981. The PCI remained stable at 30%, whilst the PSI rose slightly from 10% to 11%. The small Republican party rose a little from 3% to 5% thanks to Spadolini's election, becoming the third party in Milan.

The PCI Communist party had lost ground, partly due to the shift from a working class/industrial base to an increasingly middle class/service orientated economy. Berlinguer had engineered *lo strappo* moving the Italian Communist party away from Russia. Sadly his life was cut short by a heart attack in 1984: over a million Italians attended his funeral, not just Communists, essentially because he was a decent man amongst a hive of self-serving schemers. Berlinguer's historic compromise of collaboration with the DC had gained his party political and electoral respect. It was the end of an era.

Natta, an older and more traditional Communist, took over the party, moving closer to the non-Marxist Euroleft, and replacing worn Marxist rhetoric with more modern expressions such as 'reformist forces of the left'. In 1988 he was replaced by the younger Occhetto, vice secretary of the party and secretary of the FGCI youth movement. With the arrival of Gorbachev and the fall of the Berlin Wall in 1989, Occhetto decided to change the party name after seventy years to PDS *Partito Democratico della Sinistra*. 68% of party members supported him, whilst the 27% of hard liners (including the feminist writer Natalia Ginzburg) went off to found RC *Rifondazione Comunista*. The PCI had certainly shown itself more virtuous and less corrupt than the DC, for which it gained respect and votes in regional government.

A Milanese based in that Socialist controlled city rather than the power base of Rome, Craxi embraced the individualism and consumerism of the 'yuppie' 80s.[53] His reign lasted over two administrations until 1987, and was the longest serving government since 1945, ahead of Moro's and De Gasperi's. By 1985 the Socialists wielded power in 13 regions, 79 provinces and 69 cities. Having suffered for years from a viable identity since its inception in 1921, they were perceived as being too close to the PCI and dominated by the DC. To remedy this image, Craxi wished to place his party at the forefront of Italian politics by shifting it centre left, thereby coming more into line with the Eurosocialists such as Helmut Schmidt, Willy Brandt and Francois Mitterand. However, they fared poorly in the 1984 European elections. Craxi had broken the DC mould in becoming the first Socialist prime minister, the only other non-DC premier being the Republican Giovanni Spadolini.

In 1981 Craxi set about consolidating the power of his position as party secretary, switching his election to congress instead of the unwieldy Leninist central committee. In 1984 he replaced the latter with a 473 member national

---

[53] Young and upwardly mobile

assembly, which included over 100 deputies, senators and EC representatives, plus a hundred prominent people from all walks of life, embracing the new areas of media, sport and entertainment, in order to present a better image of contemporary society. Martelli, one of his lieutenants, took up the new causes of ecology and anti-nuclear policy. The sheer size of the assembly would hinder any effective opposition to him, thereby creating strong leadership which was welcomed by many. In similar vein, Craxi diluted the executive committee by increasing its membership from thirty to over fifty, making it difficult to oppose him. He attempted to neutralize factions by formally dissolving them, yet they persisted. Keen to minimize the influence of Communism and its trade union CGIL, he replaced the hammer and sickle emblem with a red carnation used previously at the turn of the century. He neutralized opponents by inviting them to join him: for instance Giuliano Amato, professor of political science at the Bocconi University in Milan (similar to the London School of Economics) who became his main adviser and Treasury Minister.

Craxi adopted an assertive and innovational approach to swift decision making: *decisionismo,* to combat the perennial lack of management and grass roots organisation within the PSI. He projected a populist image in tune with the younger post war electorate, introducing a new personalism into politics, in stark contrast to the DC's constant wheeling and dealing. Yet over time Craxi displayed a cunning Machiavellian instinct, intent on power for power's sake. He arrogated all decisions to himself, eschewing both divisive parliamentary debate and the consensual approach of the Catholic DC, to the point of arrogant dictatorship, seen in his resort to decrees to bypass Parliament.

A significant achievement by Craxi was the revision of the 1929 Concordat with the Vatican. After years of futile haggling through parliamentary commissions led by Andreotti and Spadolini, Craxi successfully nudged the Vatican into an agreement in 1984, thereby trumping the DC. Two accords were retained intact, whilst the third was revised, cancelling some provisions which had now become irrelevant, such as the legal disadvantage in not being a Catholic; whilst the 1970 divorce law had fundamentally altered the relationship between church and state. Against a backcloth of looming scandal concerning the Vatican bank finances (see Chapter 5) fourteen articles were signed by Craxi and Casiroli, Secretary of State for the Vatican, which crucially accorded the state supremacy over the Catholic Church. A church wedding now had to conform to the state's legal standards, whilst marital annulment came under the jurisdiction of the Italian courts. Crucially Catholicism was no longer the state religion, resembling the French policy of *laïcité;* whilst its instruction was no longer compulsory in state schools, which upset the bishops.

Craxi had achieved these ground-breaking reforms by excluding Parliament and the Synod (council) of bishops from the negotiations. However, he did set up a joint commission between the Vatican and government to tackle the thorny problem of tax exemption, whereby church property now became subject to taxation, including dividends on stocks, so these were sold off but without paying tax arrears. Church property, consisting of some 50,000 organisations, was split into two categories: those purely of a religious nature remained exempt, whilst by 1990 funding for church building would be phased out; together with stipends for the clergy, who by 1990 were to become self-financing through voluntary contributions. In 1989 some 26,000 priests cost the state £150 million. To encourage voluntary contributions from the general public, gifts of up to £800 were tax exempt; whilst taxpayers could donate nearly 1% of their taxes to one of four charities of their choice. The revised Concordat endorsed the spirit of Pope John XXIII's modernising reforms under the 2nd Vatican Council, and signalled a significant victory for the Italian State over centuries of Vatican hegemony.

Craxi's record is less convincing on the economy. Shortly after becoming prime minister, he managed a reduction in the *scale mobile* escalator clause to contain labour costs, especially for exports, and which he pushed through by decree to outmanoeuvre the PCI and CGIL; and which he had confirmed by referendum, gaining 54% of the votes. As elsewhere in Europe, the 1980s were boom years in Italy, with inflation dropping from 11% to 5% during 1983-87. High interest rates on state bonds attracted many private savers. Yet unemployment remained high, peaking at 15% during 1975-80, the highest in Europe and affecting 75% of the under-30s, but dropping to 8% after 1983. Craxi failed to effect an overhaul of the public finances. The annual government spending deficit remained stubbornly high, declining only from 14% to 12% of GDP; whilst public/national debt jumped from 72% to 93% of GDP. The South supplied only 18% of tax receipts, due to high unemployment and tax evasion. Research and Development R&D investment was one of the lowest in Europe.

There was no overhaul of the civil service, where salaries rose by a third during 1985-87, and with generous pensions (often with early retirement) representing a significant drain on resources. The public health service USL remained highly inefficient and corrupt, especially in the South. In 1983 a bicameral commission discussed reform of the political system but achieved nothing. The sole chink of change was the law, introduced in 1987 by Bruno Visentini, the Republican Finance Minister, which aimed at greater control over taxable income of shopkeepers, notorious for evasion and to which DC turned a blind eye because they constituted part of their faithful electoral base.

By 1987 Craxi was at the height of his power, a well-respected politician on the international stage, offering government stability and political credibility. Craxi dreamed of transforming the Republic into a Presidency as in France under Mitterand. The 1988 national elections saw a rise in the Socialist vote from 11% to 14%. The DC under De Mita took 34%, and the PCI remained steady at 27%. Two new parties appeared: the Greens with a modest 2.5%; and the Lombard League, run by the gruff Umberto Bossi from Varese (Lombardy) who became a senator, together with his close friend, Giuseppe Leone. *Liga Veneta* did well in regional government provinces and the traditional areas of Catholic SMEs such as Vicenza and Verona.

Disappointed by the election results, Craxi decided to step down and pass the baton to the younger Giovanni Goria. He only survived a few months, to be replaced in 1988 by De Mita, still underpinned by his strong *Base* faction. A new group appeared to challenge De Mita's autocratic leadership: the centrist *Azione Popolare* AP which included Enzo Scotti and Antonio Gava, the latter DC boss in Naples and now Minister of the Interior. Both were tainted by links with the Mafia and the Cirillo affair. They were joined by the old guard of Andreotti, Forlani and Colombo, and now reinvented as the gattopardian[54] *neoDorotei*: thus back to the *status quo ante*. At the 18th Congress in 1989, 37% of the delegates supported AP, with 35% in favour of De Mita. In the typical fashion of Italian skullduggery, Craxi and Forlani conspired to oust De Mita, replacing him with Andreotti as PM and Forlani as party secretary. Dubbed the CAF administration after the trio's initials, it was Andreotti's sixth term of government, which survived until 1992. A founder member of the DC, his first cabinet post was in 1947 as Under-secretary at the Presidency of the Council of Ministers. CAF marked a shift right with the *neoDorotei* close to the Vatican and the organisation *Communione e Liberazione* C&L, a Catholic university student organisation begun in 1969. The CAF administration proceeded to take over key positions in

---

[54] Meaning to change a little in order to remain the same. From 'Il Gattopardo' by Tommaso di Lampedusa.

the public sector, for instance Romano Prodi was replaced by F.Nobili at IRI, whilst the Socialist G.Cagliari headed up ENI.

Rome, his birthplace in 1919, was Andreotti's citadel of banks and town hall. At the local football stadium which catered for the two teams of Roma and Lazio, Andreotti would play host to clients on a Sunday afternoon, akin to a medieval monarch holding audience with his subjects. When in 1983 De Mita was asked by the editor of La *Repubblica,* Eugenio Scalgari, whether he trusted Andreotti, he eventually replied: 'Who is Andreotti, according to you? Do you know anything about him? Do you really know who he is? I don't.' Andreotti's friend, the film director Federico Fellini, portrayed him as 'the guardian of an undefined area, a person who has to introduce you into another dimension which you don't fully understand.' [55]

Andreotti's administration 1988-92 (in Italian terms consisting of two governments owing to a reshuffle) witnessed a flurry of reform, albeit in part due to an accumulation of pending legislation. Many were the result of individual efforts, usually designated by the proposer's name being given to the law, but many were whittled down to appease factional interests. Laws were passed on illegal immigration and equal opportunities; also on increased autonomy of the universities. A Republican, G.Galasso, Minister of Cultural Assets, had tried to introduce a law on protection of the environment, which had suffered dreadfully from the ravages of developers since 1945. But predictably progress was slight owing to the entrenched interests of property developers, pliant politicians and the Mafia. In 1989 G.Ruffolo, Minister for the Environment, introduced a law to increase the number of national parks to protect the land from yet more illegal building. Sadly his noble efforts suffered from a lack of funding and willpower.

On the debit side, there was no overhaul of public health or moves towards privatisation, and so a high public deficit contributed to a recession by the early '90s. With regard to public administration, individual civil servants were at last made responsible for their actions to the long-suffering general public, with time limits theoretically being set on procedure. There was no slimming down of the generous state pensions and early retirement. The CAF administration ran to full term, but scandal loomed.

Lastly, the Mammi media law of 1990, proposed by the eponymous Republican Minister for Post and Telecoms, confirmed Berlusconi's dominance in television, assisted by the tycoon's lobbying of Parliament. However, he was

---

[55] P.Ginsburg page 164

partly stopped in his tracks by Walter Veltroni, PDS mayor of Rome, a cinema lover, who attacked the business tycoon, joined by the support of many key actors such as Mastroianni, film director Fellini and the writer Moravia; with support also from the DC. They managed to secure an amendment to the law, limiting advertising during films shown on TV. Its support by the Senate secured its safe passage into legislation, leaving Berlusconi miffed.[56]

Finance

Fortuitously, this period was blessed with highly competent financial ministers and advisers to the government, offering a professional approach to the business of government instead of constant in-fighting. Heirs to a strong line of Italian bankers stretching back to medieval times, they removed the negative perception of Italian finance. As Treasury minister during 1987-89, Giulio Amato introduced a law to open up the public sector banks by changing their status from trust foundations and associations into joint stock companies. However, vested interests profited by securing 51% of the share stock which limited changes.

Amato was followed at the Treasury by Paolo Baffi and Guido Carli, the latter formerly the long serving governor of the Bank of Italy during 1963-75; as well as president of Confindustria in 1978. Carli, Treasury Minister to Andreotti, was instrumental in modernising the archaic finance and banking systems, bedevilled by massive national debt, a high current account deficit and weak balance of payments. The traumatic events of the Hot Autumn had led to high inflation and a huge budget deficit, partly due to the adjustment of the *Scala Mobile* (wage index) every three months to appease the trade unions, agreed in 1975 with Confindustria led by G.Agnelli. The index was abolished in 1984. In 1983 INPS *Istituto Nazionale Providenza Sociale*, concerned with social welfare, accounted for 21% of GNP.

Setting up a research team, Carli introduced the free flow of capital, implemented laws on antitrust and insider trading, and installed electronic trading and clearing systems (similarly with the City of London's Big Bang in 1986 under PM Thatcher), thereby accelerating share dealing and financial transactions overall. However, insider trading remained acceptable practice, as did share price manipulation. In 1981 the Bank of Italy was removed from Treasury control, leaving its governor free to set interest rates. At last the Bank

---

[56] See Chapter 17 concerning Berlusconi's media empire.

was liberated from factional meddling and nepotism, as scathingly described by Luigi Einaudi, post-war governor of the institution; and became a rare beacon of moral probity and professional expertise amongst a morass of inept and corrupt state institutions.

Carli's innovative reforms, coupled with a more buoyant economy during the '80s, improved corporate performance, helping to produce a surplus balance of payments in 1992 (net of interest repayments), coincidentally at the time of signing the Maastricht Treaty, though the annual public deficit remained high, mainly due to the demands of pensions and health. Italy's international credit rating rose, which led foreign investors, mainly the financially sophisticated British and Americans, to take a fresh look at the Italian finance market, previously dominated by the state. America launched its Italy fund, whilst in 1983 AT&T US acquired 25% of Olivetti.

In 1985 the Italian government opened up the Eurolire bond market to allow foreign investors to issue corporate bonds denominated in lira outside Italy, thereby placing the lira on an international footing. This initiative boosted trading interest on other stock market exchanges such as Paris and Frankfurt; as well as heightened activity in cross border joint ventures. Secondly financial institutions and private companies, such as Benetton, Fiat, Montedison, Olivetti, Pirelli and Mediobanca, began to issue corporate bonds on the international market. In 1983 the state-owned IMI *Istituto Mobiliare Italiano* set up Imigest to supply Italian funds, which later became a joint stock company and in 1994 was listed on the New York Stock Exchange. In 1998 it became an investment bank as *Banca d'Intermediazione Mobiliare* and later merged with Banca San Paolo. These bond markets assisted in the financing of the high government deficit, yet they were closely regulated by the Italian Treasury who feared a rise in value of the lira within the EMS.

Hitherto, the modest Milan Borsa stock exchange, founded in 1808 and supervised by Consob, had been dominated by a clutch of large Italian banks and insurance companies, with only a few of the quoted companies actively trading. In 1986 thirty companies were added to the existing list of around 300, against 2,500 at the LSE. In 1989, 75% of the Borsa was controlled by nine companies of which six were run by families. Fiat, Generali and IRI accounted for 60% of the top nine companies.[57] Family firms have always been reluctant to relinquish control and shunned debt, preferring to keep the business within the family, who

---

[57] The other six were Olivetti, Ferruzzi-Montedison, Pesenti, Pirelli, ENI and Orlando.

held many preference shares. However, the '80s did begin to see increased trading by them, for instance Benetton. In 1988 the ten firms with the highest market capitalisation were Fiat, Generali/RAS/Fondiaria/Alleanza insurance companies, Stet/SIP telecoms, Olivetti computers, Montedison chemicals and Mediobanca. That same year Fiat and Generali appeared in Europe's top ten.

Traditionally, Italians have been strongly cash orientated, debt averse and adopting a cautious approach to investment. Offering a rare example of Italians' faith in their government, many have traditionally invested in safe tax exempt state bonds *titoli di stato* CCT, BOT and BTP[58] issued in quarterly auctions, offering attractive interest rates and which help to finance public debt. The short dated three and six month BOT have been popular, offering a good risk/return ratio, with an 8-10% yield during the '80s. These high interest rates helped to shield the lira from devaluation prior to entry into the EMS system; yet at the same time contributing to the high public deficit.

The opening up of the *Borsa,* attracted many adventurous small savers (as indeed in Britain), numbering about 250,000 in 1985; by 1988 they had shot up to 2.4 million. About a quarter came from all walks of life, from professions and clerical workers to housewives, students and retirees. Mutual funds became popular, pooling investors' money and with profits paid direct to the individual unit holders rather than being re-invested in the fund. They also owed their success to being CGT tax exempt and marketed by local banks. Mutuals helped to increase liquidity on the *Borsa*, together with the similar unit trusts. Insurance workers struck for the right to buy stock options. There was a telephone number in Rome offering stock information; whilst even the Communist paper *L'unita* began to publish stock market data in response to demand from its readers.

The 1980s saw the increasing privatisation of banks, of which thirty were standard banks and ninety small savings banks *casse di risparmio* dating back to the 19th century, led by Cariplo. Traditionally, many Germans have deposited their money in such institutions, including non-profit co-operatives. 80% were state owned, such as Credito Italiano and San Paolo IMI, and were at the mercy of factionalism for senior posts, prey to nepotism, with poor staffing and inadequate systems. They were split into charitable/foundation status and commercial joint stock companies. In the past, banks suffered from strict exchange controls to stem the seepage of illicit funds abroad. Property

---

[58] CCT=Certificato di Credito del Tesoro; also now available as CCTEuro;
BOT=Buono del Tesoro; BTP=Buono del Tesoro Poliennale.

investment remains popular as ever since early times, and with mortgages now more widely available, mostly with a variable interest rate. Otherwise many Italians continue to save up to buy a house outright or build one. In the 1980s/90s, many Italians took out mortgages in ecus since they were cheaper than those in lira.

Italy and the EEC

In 1957 Italy was a crucial founder member of the EEC European Economic Community, particularly attracted by the prospect of employment abroad, raw materials, exports and funding, especially for the South. The ECSC European Coal and Steel Community, forerunner of the EC, had helped to stabilise steel prices for Finsider. Membership of the Euroclub also appealed in the absence of nationalist feeling following the Mussolini years, thereby returning the Peninsula to the European fold; and encouraged by the US, who viewed Italy as a bulwark against Communism. Italy's candidature was pioneered by the federalist Alfiero Spinelli (later elected in 1981 as President of the Commission). The European Investment Bank EIB and the European Social Fund ESF jointly contributed 4.5 billion lire, much of it destined for the South.

During the period 1958-68, trade grew by 500% and with a doubling of global exports. GNP shot up from $42bn to $72bn. During the 1950s, a million Italians moved elsewhere within the EEC, of which over half a million settled in Germany, which became Italy's prime trading partner. The ESF paid for half the costs of relocation and training. They settled with their families, who received a better education in their new country; and sent remittances home to their relatives, which helped the national balance of payments; and with a consequent dip in migration to the US. The years after 1962 saw a decline in the availability of EC core jobs, so many Italians returned home; yet there were still 1.7 million within the EC by 1982. At the time of writing, there are some 600,000 Italian residing in the UK.

Unfortunately the Italians got off to a poor start, being reluctant to assume a responsible role. Cold and cloudy Brussels was perceived as a dull place, attracting few careerists, viewed as an irritating distraction compared to the far more fascinating intrigue of national politics in sunny Rome. The few Italians who held key posts adopted a lackadaisical attitude, with low attendance at meetings to which they arrived poorly briefed. For instance, Franco Malfatti DC, was appointed President of the Commission in 1970, but stepped down in 1972 to resume his career in Rome.

Part of the problem lay in the fact that the disbursement and strict supervision of EEC funds stymied the diversion of monies to self-interested parties. The PIM[59] regional fund for poorer regions required that member countries contribute an equal amount, which upset local patronage, especially in the South. In 1978 Italy claimed only thirty million Ecus (economic currency unit, traded on the bond market and forerunner of the Euro) from the European Social Fund out of an allocated 209 million; whilst during 1989-91 Italy had spent only half of the Regional Fund, far less than Spain, Greece or Portugal. The bumbling civil service was overwhelmed by the deluge of legislation issuing forth from Brussels. Antonio Giolitti (grandson of the earlier premier) was a Commissioner in Brussels during 1977-85 and displayed a rare example of commitment to the European ideal. A keen EC player, he summed up as follows: 'The (Italian) administrative apparatus remained absolutely insensitive and impermeable to change, with unpropitious consequences for our efficiency, our economy, and the level and quality of our participation in European policies. In particular, I have in mind the agrarian, regional and Mediterranean policies of the Community.'[60]

The 1980s witnessed the appearance of serious and professionally competent technocrats. Convinced of the benefits of the EC to Italy, they were able to nudge the country along the straight and narrow path of economic and financial discipline. Guido Carli became a close adviser to Andreotti, who had the sense to listen to him and act upon his advice. Carli commented: 'The EU represented an alternative path for the solution of problems which we were not managing to handle through the normal channels of government and parliament'.[61] The EC also helped Italy to execute reforms relating to justice, the environment, human rights and equal opportunities.

In 1979 Italy, having miraculously managed a primary balance surplus, Carli negotiated her entry into the EMS European Monetary System. Based on the Ecu the system was designed to achieve exchange rate stability. A two-band system was put in place, one allowing limited fluctuations, and the other more leeway

---

[59] Regional Innovation Monitor Plus, based in the Netherlands.
[60] Paul Ginsborg op.cit. page 241
[61] Idem page 243

into which fell the lira. EMS membership brought Italy into line with the rest of the EC, thereby encouraging the business world to at last take Italy seriously.

In 1985 a meeting of the European Council[62] was held in Milan, chaired by its president, Prime Minister Craxi. Jacques Delors, a committed European and President of the European Commission[63] 1999-2004, was keen on greater convergence to complete the Single Market. Margaret Thatcher, Britain's Prime Minister, strongly objected to the policy. However, she was upstaged by the formidable Chancellor Kohl of Germany, who urged the delegates to attend an IGC inter-governmental conference to revise the founding Treaty of Rome. He was supported by President Mitterand of France, as well as Craxi who proposed a majority vote in favour of the motion. Only Denmark, Greece and Britain opposed it. The IGC laid the ground for the Single European Act which came into force in 1987, the most significant reform since the Treaty of Rome. Italy had shown her renewed commitment to the European dream and boosted Italy's prestige on the international stage. Concerning her relations with Britain, Italy had endorsed her candidature to the Euroclub, partly to counterbalance the Franco-German axis; and had supported Thatcher in her fight for a partial refund of Britain's contribution to the EC budget.

Henceforth, Italy knuckled down to taking the EC more seriously, such as better management of European legislation. The Fabbri law of 1987 set up a special department to co-ordinate EC policies within the PM's office; whilst the La Pergola law of 1989 declared that each year the Italian parliament must approve new EC legislation which listed all the EC directives to be translated into Italian law by the end of the same year. The first law was approved by the end of 1990, the second of 1991 by January 1992. Then matters began to slide in 1992, when only 52 of the 300 directives passed into Italian law; whereupon Brussels imposed infringement sanctions.

Italy's level of spending EC funds has continued to be mediocre. In 2017, halfway through the EU budget for 2014-20, Italy had only taken up 1.2% of her quota from the regional development funds, well below the EU average of 5.3%, and less than Spain & Portugal; and so having wasted over two billion Euros.

---

[62] The European Council consists of the heads of state, rotating on a six-monthly basis. It is not to be confused with the Council of the EU which consists of national ministers.
[63] The European Commission is the EU's Civil Service, which implements policy proposed by the European Council.

Most of this money would have gone to the South where, according to Svimez,[64] per capita income is 11% lower than in 2007. Part of the problem lies in the fact that the national government is also expected to supply funds, which would give about 50 billion Euros from the current EU budget for 2014-20. Yet politicians in Rome drag their feet due to factional meddling and interference from criminal organisations.

In 1990 Andreotti, a committed European, assumed the Chair of the European Council. With the Italian economy in buoyant mood, and encouraged by Carli, his eminence grise, Andreotti took the momentous decision to move the lira into the tighter band of the EMS/ERM currency system. In accordance with the concept of the Single Market, free short-term movement of capital was also introduced. The Italians, eager to show their enthusiasm, arranged a European Council meeting in Rome for October 1990, to discuss further integration, at which Gianni de Michelis, the extrovert Socialist Foreign Minister, attended. Backed by Kohl, Andreotti proposed that the Council proceed to Stage 2 of EMU Economic and Monetary Union; as well as an impromptu vote to hold an IGC on enhanced political union. Mrs Thatcher, who had formed a low opinion of Andreotti, found herself isolated in her staunch opposition to these manoeuvres. By contrast the 'Economist' newspaper was fulsome in its praise of Andreotti: 'He seized the chance to push for what may prove to be a historic decision. Winning agreement amongst the eleven members is a remarkable achievement. Only six weeks earlier a meeting of finance ministers in Rome had revealed huge differences over EMU's second stage'.[65] Andreotti's performance had left him triumphant and Thatcher out in the cold.

Foreign Policy in the Mediterranean

During the 1980s, Italy made a significant contribution to developing countries *cooperazione allo sviluppo*. Following demands from Catholic and left-wing pressure groups such as Marco Pannella's Radical party, a new Department for Overseas Aid was instituted, coming under the ruling Socialist enclave: nothing was safe from *partitocrazia*. Aid expenditure rose from 0.15% 1981 to 0.42% 1989, at a time when others were cutting back, and accounting

---

[64] Sviluppo per il Mezzogiorno: development fund for the South.
[65] Ginsborg op.cit.247

for over 6% of world aid. The FAI Italian Aid Fund was also set up. FAI[66] funds were targeted on the former colonies of Somalia and Ethiopia, along with smaller donations to lesser countries. The funds for Somalia were managed by G.Barre, the dictator's brother. In 1985 Craxi visited Mogadishu, together with his brother-in-law Paolo Pillitieri, and handed over 400 billion lire to Barre. Yet in return Craxi made no demands for the release of political prisoners, neither specifying that the monies be spent on the poor and needy, nor closer scrutiny of Italian military aid. Not surprisingly, much of the money ended up in Barre's coffers, or was squandered on useless projects, such as a fertilizer factory that never came into operation, and 3,000 silos that lay idle. Concerning the civil war in Mogadishu, Somalia, the Italians advocated a soft policy of negotiation, in contrast to America's more belligerent approach.

The Italian Peninsula protrudes deep into the Mediterranean basin, splitting it in half, with the Sicily Straits just 140km (90 miles) from the coast of north Africa. Italy had earlier possessed various colonies in the Horn of Africa: Abyssinia (present-day Ethiopia) together with the smaller states of Somalia and Eritrea, viewed as national aggrandizement as well as offering an outlet for emigration. The Romans exploited present day Tunisia for olive oil and grain supplies. In the ninth century, the Arabs settled in southern Italy and so their blood coursed through Italian veins. Medieval Venice enjoyed strong trading links with the Arabs. Post-war Italian policy in this area has been driven by economic needs, tempered with the Catholic tenet of appeasement, as opposed to America's more aggressive stance.

Almost devoid of indigenous energy sources, Italy became highly dependent on Arab oil and gas. During the 1950s/60s, Enrico Mattei, head of ENI state energy, pursued a commitment of friendly relations, brokering several agreements with Arab countries, and which allowed Italy to bypass the Big Seven of Anglo-American supranational oil companies. In the absence of stable government, hampered by factional control of the Foreign Ministry and a reduced defence budget since Musolini's forays, Mattei offered his own brand of a coherent foreign policy. Acting as a roving ambassador, he pursued a semi-autonomous policy in his support of Moroccan independence and the FLN in Algeria; as well as deals further afield with Iran, Egypt and Russia. By the 1990s,

---

[66] Not to be confused with FAI Fondazione dell'Ambiente Italiano Equivalent to the British National Trust.

Italy was importing 90% of her gas requirements, partly from Algeria.[67] The commercial arrangement has been reciprocal since Italy enjoys a high level of exports to these countries.

During the 1960s/70s, Libya, a former colony, provided work for some 15,000 Italians in the oil fields, also in construction and factory turnkey operations. Colonel Gadafy, the country's volatile leader, decreed that Italians returning home would not be allowed back. Craxi owned a villa here, where he sought refuge after the Tangentopoli crisis. The Libyan Arab Foreign Bank held 13% of Fiat's shares (subsequently repurchased by Fiat) and was the largest shareholder in Tamoil, an Italian oil refining company.

The Italians were anxious to protect Jerusalem and other holy Christian places; otherwise, they remained cool towards Israel, which annoyed the Americans, with their large and influential Jewish population. Nevertheless, Andreotti and his predecessor De Gasperi had backed the US as a counterweight against Anglo-French influence in the Gulf of Suez. In 1949 the US invited Italy to join NATO, viewing her as a bulwark against communism, thereby putting the country back on the international stage. In 1979 the Italians permitted the Americans to base Pershing missiles at Crotone in the South in order to combat Russia's SS20s. In the wake of France's exit from NATO engineered by De Gaulle, Italy allowed the American 6th Fleet in the Mediterranean to transfer to Naples. These installations boosted Italian self-esteem on the international stage. Craxi himself was at pains to maintain a cordial relationship with the American president Ronald Reagan, allowing the US to install Cruise missiles at Comiso in Sicily in 1984, subsequent to Spain's closure of NATO's frontline airbases on her soil. Yet with his growing self-confidence, in 1986 he refused to allow the Americans to use these bases for the bombing of Tripoli. During this period, the Italians acquired the new Tornado strike aircraft, together with the Garibaldi, a small aircraft carrier.

In a Catholic spirit of conciliatory diplomacy, Craxi and Andreotti were keen to maintain a harmonious relationship with the Arab states, gravitating towards the more moderate states of Egypt, Jordan and Tunisia. In December 1984, the pair met Yasser Arafat, leader of the PLO Palestine Liberation Organisation, when they managed to craft a preliminary agreement over Jordan. The 1980 Venice Declaration drawn up by the EC had acknowledged the right of all Arab

---

[67] Russia now accounts for one third of Italy's requirements.

states to self-determination, including Palestine and the recognition of the PLO; and later endorsed by President Reagan's Fez Plan of 1982.

Italian defence forces score highly on humanitarian roles. In 1982, 500 *bersaglieri* troops oversaw the withdrawal of the PLO from Beirut, and remained following local massacres until the Americans left in 1984. The Italian troops were well received and much preferred to their French and American comrades. Subsequent peacekeeping missions by the Italian army have concerned Lebanon, the Sinai desert, Afghanistan in 1981, and Iraq in 2003. In 1991 Italy sent aircraft and ships to the Gulf War.

The Achille Lauro Incident: A convoluted affair[68]

On Monday 7th October 1985, four Palestinian hijackers took control of the Italian cruise ship, Achille Lauro, which was sailing from Alexandria to Port Said in Egypt, carrying over 500 passengers and crew. The attack was possibly triggered by an Israeli bomb raid against the PLO Palestine Liberation Organisation headquarters near Tunis on 1st October. The following morning the Italians sent assault troops to Cyprus and ships towards Egypt, in case diplomacy should fail. The PLF Palestine Liberation Front in Tunis denied any connection and condemned the outrage; likewise the PLO in Damascus led by its leader Yassir Arafat;[69] as did most Arab countries. The hijackers demanded the release of 50 Palestinians being held in Israeli prisons, which suggested that the PLF had crafted the ship's hijacking: the first of its kind, since the hijacking of planes had become frequent in recent years. In exchange, they offered the liberation of the ship and its passengers. The following morning the hijackers broadcast on the ship radio that, if their conditions were not upheld, they intended to start killing the American passengers. Syria condemned the hijack, refusing the hijackers permission to land at Tartus: much to Italy's relief since, in Craxi's words, the hijackers were now politically isolated.

That same day, the United States Ambassador to Italy, Maxwell Rabb, declared the Americans' refusal to negotiate, hinting at a deadline by Wednesday for military intervention since they doubted the efficacy of a diplomatic solution. For his part, Craxi responded that he hoped for a peaceful solution to the crisis but, if necessary, Italy would take military action since the ship was Italian. By

---

[68] I am indebted to Frank J.Piason for the information concerning this affair.

[69] In Dec.1984 Craxi and Andreotti had met Arafat, when they managed to craft a preliminary agreement over Jordan.

Wednesday the ship was back in Egyptian waters, and the Italians advised the Egyptian foreign ministry that they wished to pursue negotiations to effect the release of the passengers; in response to which the ministry extended its full support. Arafat advised the Italians that the ship would be released without any conditions attached. In return, Italy promised that the hijackers would be provided with a safe conduct, provided that, in Craxi's words, 'no violent acts punishable by Italian law had been committed aboard the ship'. President Mubarak and Arafat had hoped that Italy would consent to the PLO taking custody of the hijackers, yet the Italians demurred due to pressure from the Americans.

That Wednesday afternoon the ship was liberated. Within an hour the Italian foreign ministry talked to the ship's captain, who advised him that he had regained control and that all was well. Shortly afterwards, the hijackers left the ship. A little later Craxi himself spoke to the captain, at which point he learnt of the killing and tossing overboard of a disabled American Jew, Leon Klinghoffer, in his wheelchair. Craxi sent condolences to President Reagan and held a press conference to update the situation. Many other countries had picked up the ship's announcement of a death on board.

Towards midnight on Wednesday, the US Ambassador to Egypt boarded the ship and had the death confirmed by other American passengers. Craxi advised Egypt and America that he would request extradition of the four hijackers to stand trial in Italy. Craxi reassured the US that 'no stone would be left unturned…until the guilty are identified and punished'. Craxi's handling of this delicate situation proved popular with the Italian media, public opinion and Arab sympathisers, raising both his and Italy's international profile; and judged far more worthy than the more aggressive American stance.

On Thursday 10th October, the White House informed Craxi that American jet planes had earlier that evening intercepted an Egyptian Boeing 737 carrying the hijackers, and forced it to follow them. (Tunisia and Algeria had refused permission for the aeroplane to land in their territories). Yet the American commander of the NATO base at Sigonella in Sicily, who picked up the plane by radar, had only advised his Italian counterpart an hour later. The White House requested permission from Craxi to land at Sigonella. The Boeing was ostensibly accompanied by two escort planes, but were in fact two transporters. The upshot was that Craxi was given barely forty minutes' advance notice, giving him precious little time to react appropriately, and suggesting that the manoeuvre was thus crafted to pre-empt Italian action. Craxi agreed to the landing only because of 'the almost certain killing of a passenger'.

Upon landing at Sigonella, the American soldiers, under orders to seize the hijackers, proceeded to encircle some fifty Italian troops who had already surrounded the aeroplane. It was a tense moment with an exchange of strong words, but apparently no military action occurred. There ensued a flurry of telephone calls, with the US Secretary of Defence, Caspar Weinberger, talking to his counterpart Spadolini, Defence Minister, with the Americans being intent on seizing the hijackers. President Reagan tried to persuade Craxi to allow the US to take control of them since they had killed an American citizen. Craxi responded that the act constituted a crime against an Italian ship and thus came under Italian jurisdiction, and which he could not countermand. Andreotti had previously made the same point to George Schulz, US Secretary of State; and had criticised the confusion of telephone calls.

President Reagan acquiesced to this argument, but now advised that he would have the hijackers extradited according to the Italo-American Extradition Treaty signed the previous year (at the time aimed at the Mafia and drug trafficking) and seek the custody of the two other Palestinians on board the ship: Abu Abbas (later viewed as organiser of the hijack and subsequently mediator); and Hani el Hassan, Arafat's personal adviser. Craxi ordered the four hijackers to be taken into custody, with apparently no objections from the Egyptians, together with Abbas and Hassan who would be treated as witnesses but whom the Americans considered guilty.

Abbas and Hassan refused to leave the plane and set foot on Italian soil. The Egyptian embassy in Rome claimed they were entitled to diplomatic immunity and so treated them as their guests. However, the Egyptians allowed Craxi's diplomatic adviser, A.Badini, to interview the pair on the plane, accompanied by an Italian SISMI (military intelligence) official and a PLO representative from the Rome office. Later that evening the two men were officially identified and the aeroplane was allowed to depart. Craxi received permission from Egypt to fly the plane to Rome's military airport at Ciampino in accordance with his government's agreement with Reagan.

At 10pm on Friday evening 11th October, the Boeing aeroplane took off from Sigonella for Ciampino, escorted by four Italian aircraft. Three minutes later an American military plane shadowing the Boeing flew below the airport's radar without Italian permission, requesting an emergency landing; whereupon Rome protested to Washington. In response, Rabb produced evidence of Abbas' past terrorist acts and formally requested his extradition. He passed on Reagan's personal request to the Italians that they continue to hold Abbas; Rabb himself at the same time personally stressing that he too had no wish to upset Italo-American relations. The Egyptians were still holding the ship at Port Said and threatened to put their troops aboard to protect Abbas from being taken off. The Italian government, albeit reluctantly, took the decision to release Abbas; whereupon Egypt liberated the ship. President Mubarak felt miffed at Italy's attitude towards his own efforts at solving the dilemma, yet the Italians insisted they were grateful for his mediation, and had released Abbas as a token of their long-standing friendship with Egypt.

There ensued a heated exchange of words between Craxi and Spadolini, a Republican in the PM's five party coalition, concerning the release of the hijackers. Spadolini, who inclined towards Israel, thought Craxi had been indulgent towards Reagan by releasing Abbas too quickly, since 'Italy was responsible for her international obligations'. The newspaper *La Voce Repubblicana* commented that the Italian government had been 'ambiguous' in its dealings. On 12th October Abbas left Italy on a regular Yuglosav flight to Belgrade organised by the Egyptian embassy in Rome. Rabb declared himself to be 'not at all happy'.

On 15th October Andreotti met Schulz in Brussels, remarking firmly that the American attitude towards Italy was 'unacceptable'. J. Whitehead, the US Undersecretary of State, travelled to Rome, where he declared that taking the plane had been right and legal; in response to which the Italians retorted that it was feasibly moral but against international law. Whitehead brought Craxi an emollient letter from Reagan, in which the US president took pains to smooth over the cracks, emphasising that he had every confidence that the Italians would resolve the crisis and deal firmly with the hijackers. He went on to stress the close relationship that existed between America and Italy. Much of the Italian press interpreted Reagan's statement as an apology. Later that month, Craxi and Andreotti flew to New York, as previously planned, for consultations prior to the Regan-Gorbachev summit.

After making a speech to the Chamber of Deputies on 17th October, Craxi resigned, declaring himself 'surprised and embittered' by the American attitude, and by their lack of appreciation towards Italy's conduct of the crisis, having allowed American planes to land in Sigonella and take the hijackers into custody.

Italy had respected both its own judicial authority, as well as international law, by not having retained Abbas since he carried diplomatic status, and given that the aeroplane was Egyptian. On 28th October the coalition government agreed to the drawing-up of a document, which included Republican observations on foreign policy. The points raised included Italy's refusal to cede to threats of blackmail by international terrorism, and the condemnation of the use of violence by such organisations; continuing to play an active role in the Mediterranean and the Middle East, working in harmony with the EU and US; and government unity in all affairs.

Two days later Craxi withdrew his resignation, whilst the Italian judiciary issued a warrant for the arrest of Abbas for having organised the hijacking. In his speech of 6th November in the Chamber of Deputies Craxi observed that he understood the 'legitimacy' of the PLO's use of weapons, dubiously comparing their struggle to Mazzini's fight for Italian independence. Such a comment naturally upset the Republicans, heirs of the great man, as well as the DC and the press; but his own party supported the remark, as did the PCI and the minor left-wing parties. Nevertheless Craxi secured a vote of confidence in the Senate, taking pains to rectify his *faux pas* by declaring that he had not meant to impugn Mazzini's reputation, pioneer of Italian independence. The Achille-Lauro affair set the stamp on Italian independence in foreign policy. In 1994 the ship, named after a rich Neapolitan shipowner, sank off the Somali coast.

Shortly after the Achille Lauro incident, in December 1985 Libya was implicated in PLO terrorist attacks on the Israeli El Al personnel at Rome Fiumicino airport: sixteen died. With Italy's own wave of terrorism still fresh in people's minds, Craxi issued a sharply outspoken statement and suspended arms sales to Libya. A few hours after America's attack on Libya in 1986, two Libyan missiles exploded 200 metres from the Italian island of Lampedusa, just 300km from Libya, being the location of Loran radar bases run by the United States.

Chapter Thirteen
The Judiciary

The Italian legal system derives from Roman law and the Napoleonic code. There is no case law based on precedent as in English common law. In 1931 Rocco, Mussolini's justice minister, rationalized the complicated criminal code, much of which remains in force, although the death penalty has been repealed. The judiciary was subject to control by the Fascist politicians until the 1948 Constitution, which provided for greater independence from the executive, despite opposition from Parliament and the Christian Democrat party who resented a rival force. The Constitution made provision for a fluid link amongst examining magistrates, prosecutors and judges, who are civil servants and together form the *Magistratura* magistracy, whose functions are diverse from those of the English magistrate. Defence lawyers are self-employed. There exist three branches of the Italian judiciary: civil, criminal and administrative.[70]

Most legal personnel, some 8,500 in all, belong to the Magistrates National Association ANM, which consists of various factions: the left-wing *Magistratura Democratica*, c.25%, the centrist independent *Unitá per la Costituzione* c. 30% and the smaller right leaning *Magistratura Indipendente*. There is also the lesser independent *Movimento per la Giustizia*. Members of all streams attest to being politically neutral when trying a case, yet remain prey to factional influences. For instance, the prosecutor who heard Berlusconi's appeal regarding tax fraud belonged to the third group, yet he quashed his appeal. All lawyers are governed by the *Consiglio Superiore della Magistratura* CSM Upper Council of the Magistracy, decreed by the Constitution and established in 1959,

---

[70] The administrative section includes TAR Tribunale Amministrativa Regionale which deals with inter-regional disputes; whilst the Corte dei Conti Auditors' Court handles state expenditure, such as pensions.

with an elected majority, mostly right-wing, to accord it a greater degree of freedom from political interference.

As the older Fascist members retired, the new intake of younger recruits to the junior ranks offered a fresher and more independent approach, advocating social reforms in the wake of the Hot Autumn. Known as *pretori d'assalto* fighting magistrates, some had links with the Red Brigades. Wider university access offered a better selection of recruits to the profession. After graduation prospective prosecutors and judges sit a stiff competitive examination *concorso* which few pass and so partly accounts for the shortage of lawyers, especially in the cities, and who are appointed for life. In 1992 there were over 10,000 applicants for 300 positions. Some 40% of qualified judges hail from the South, many of whom return there. Judges in Abruzzo struck in 1975 over their excessive workload and other grievances.

Taking the same examination provides them with a flexible interchange within the professions. Some magistrates start their career in the police, which offers them a good training ground for future legal work (for instance Antonio Di Pietro). Hence Italians and the media refer to magistrates equally as public prosecutors and judges, and which now include a few females, according to their role in a case, since they continue to have similar functions, despite the 1989 reform. Public prosecutors, known as *procuratore,* enjoy greater autonomy in civil law and are not just the mere corollary of prosecution lawyers under English common law. Indeed many consider they have retained the former power of the *giudice istruttore* examining magistrate, still leaving the role of defence in an inferior position.

The *Procura della Repubblica* is the public prosecutors' office, also called the *Pubblico Ministero*, based in the major cities and which, although under the tutelage of the procurator general, exercises a great deal of independence and freedom of action in assigning cases; though appointments can be political, with cases being switched to Rome. Newly qualified magistrates start practising as assistants *sostituti procura*. Once in court the state prosecutor is called the PM *pubblico ministero*; the phrase *la pubblica accusa* is also used.

In 1989 the new criminal code *Nuovo Codice di Procedura Penale* aimed to speed up the judicial process, limit the power of the magistrates and transform the criminal code from the adversarial approach to a more equitable contest between prosecution and defence, as in Britain and America. The process blends a mix of the old and the new, with the persistence of a fine line between the functions of judge, magistrate and prosecutor. In civil cases the defendant is now advised in advance of the charges, unlike previously, which made it rather difficult to prepare his case. S/he has the right to silence and not tell the truth, sanctioned by their counsel. The reform abolished annulment of a case for lack of evidence, which had allowed *mafiosi* to get off scot free. Moreover, the reform limited the period of preventive custody to just over a year. All cases are now heard in a public courtroom and magistrates are urged to speak less: a difficult challenge for Italians! Many trials are now televised, such as the Mafia maxi trials. Wiretapping is often used for collecting evidence against the accused. It is an offence to leak evidence *sub giudice* but the press frequently ignore this stricture.

In regard to criminal cases, the approach is still very much inquisitorial, based on the Napoleonic system, which weights the trial in the prosecution's favour. The investigating or examining magistrate *giudice istruttore* manages the overall investigation *istruttoria*, preparing the case for the prosecution, directing police enquiries and collating police evidence. He then proceeds with the trial *dibattimento* through questioning to establish the guilty party of a crime. Sentencing is carried out by the judge. The 1989 reform now provides the defence lawyer *avvocato* with the right to challenge or cross-examine witnesses, whereas previously his sole weapon was the submission of pleas in mitigation. Nevertheless the prosecutor retains the upper hand vis-à-vis the defence. The trial judge continues to be legally allowed to base a verdict on evidence not given in court. A verdict of not proven, akin to the Scottish verdict, was removed in 1989.

Both civil and criminal trials proceed in three stages. In the preliminary hearing the judge determines whether there is a case to prosecute. Magistrates are allowed up to two years to complete their investigation. Next one proceeds to the trial itself at the *Tribunale* regular court, presided by one, two or three judges, depending on the gravity of the case. There follows the right to two appeals: the first in a *Corte d'Appello* local court presided by five judges, led by the *procuratore generale* public prosecutor, and where the case is re-tried *ab initio*; and the second in the supreme and final Court of Cassation in Rome, where several judges, headed by the Attorney General, argue only points of law, and which can take up to three years. Lay judges are present at this final court and can outvote the professional judges by six to two. However it is the responsibility of the judges who disagree with the verdict to submit a written justification, known as a *sentenza suicida*. The verdict can be cast in a manner such that it can be over-ruled on appeal to the same court. The Supreme Court can ask for a retrial at appeal court level. The Constitution states that the defence is innocent until found guilty by the Supreme Court.

Trials are long drawn-out affairs since re-trials *ab initio* occur at each stage, taking up to seven years plus up to three years for the final appeal. Financial and commercial cases are fiendishly tortuous, as in Britain and America. In 2012 there was a backlog of 3.4 million criminal cases and over half a million civil ones. Throughout the trial the defendant remains at liberty except in the most serious cases. There are only one or two hearings a week, hence written evidence is essential to supplement fading memories. To give just one example, in 2002 a 16 year old teenager from Turin reported being raped by her father. Placed in a care home she suffered further sexual abuse. The trial commenced the following year, reached the first stage in 2007, went to appeal in 2013, with judgement being given in 2016. The Turin tribunal issued a public apology. In 2017 the case risked being closed out of time by the Statute of Limitations, so the perpetrators may have gone unpunished.[71]

Following the revelations of Tangentopoli in 1992, hundreds of people were held in custody, limited to just over a year by the 1989 reform; and with some 3,000 sent for trial. In 2012 over 40% of prisoners were awaiting final sentence, being the second highest rate in the EU, and of which many were embroiled in Tangentopoli; yet few were actually convicted. Bail is rare, whilst *habeus corpus* is non-existent. Sophia Loren spent seventeen days in prison for alleged tax evasion. The sluggish process allows the wealthy and powerful to play for time in the hope of having their case dismissed by the Statute of Limitations.

In 2002 M.Barbuto, appointed president of the main civil court in Turin, employed the simple technique of dealing with cases in chronological order, rather than on the 'last in/first out' approach: the oldest had begun 43 years previously. By 2009 the average length of a civil case had decreased from seven to three years. He subsequently moved to the justice ministry in Rome to head up the judicial organisation. Other methods now employed to speed up the procedure include the introduction of plea bargaining *patteggiamento*, whereby the defendant agrees to a financial settlement by the eve of the preliminary hearing, provided that the offence carries just a maximum prison sentence of two years. Another innovation is the omission of the initial and cross examinations,

---

[71] Grazia magazine October 2017

and limiting the prosecution's right to appeal, usually where the defence is sure that the case would be dismissed; or reduce the prison sentence if deemed guilty. These improvements also take pressure off overcrowded prisons and diminish the workload of the courts. In 1990 a building programme involved fifty new prisons, and were even implicated in the corruption scandal. Known as *Carceri d'oro* golden prisons, their final cost soared to 1,250% of the original estimate thanks to kickbacks to politicians.

The tortuously slow process is partly due to the interminable Catholic searching for absolute truth. The minute dissection of points of law becomes an intellectual exercise, entwined with the Catholic process of confession, forgiveness, and absolution. True penitence requires contrition, expressing a genuine regret for the sin committed. One cannot help feeling that this aspect does not figure highly in the conscience of many of the accused, though perhaps a number of *pentiti* repentants are nudged by their Catholic upbringing to confess a sin.

Mindful of the Catholic tenet of absolution, sentences are usually less than the stipulated term, for instance the penal code states 21 years for murder but incarceration is 12 years on average. Guilty parties over the age of 70 are not usually imprisoned: instead they can elect to carry out a year's community service, as in Berlusconi's first and sole conviction for tax fraud. Sentence reduction alleviates prison crowding; similarly with regular amnesties. Amnesties (expressing forgiveness) are frequent, partly due to over-crowding, there having been 13 during 1945-85, especially after the war, when they benefited Fascists. The *Condono* pardon, extant since Roman times, is often employed for building transgressions and tax evasion, and which conveniently fills the Treasury coffers with its fines.

Chapter Fourteen

In Terra Infidelium:
Mafia A Giovanni Falcone

The Mafia, strictly speaking known as *Cosa Nostra* Our Affair, probably goes back to Arabic times; whilst the term 'mafia' refers to other criminal organisations. The word mafia derives from the Arabic 'mahjas' for militancy. The locals fled to the hills and mountains to escape the invading Arabs and later the Normans. In the absence of effective national government, the Mafia filled a void in the South with its own brand of rough justice, for instance Fra Diavolo, the notorious 18th century bandit and his band of murderous followers. Basing their actions on a code of honour possibly inherited from the Normans, the Mafia defended the peasants against the wealthy landowners with their vast estates run by *gabelloti* managers.[72] Organisation of the Mafia resembles the pyramidal structure of their Norman ancestors with their baronial armies. Organised into family groups known as *cosche* (like the leaves of an artichoke) each consists of about fifty members, but sometimes as many as three hundred individuals; and governed by an elected *capo famiglia* head of each family who is assisted by a deputy and *consiglieri* advisers. Each group or clan has *comparaggio* godfatherhood in order to extend the influence of the clan leader.

The family chiefs collectively nominate the area chiefs, *capi mandamento* for the eight provinces[73], along with Palermo, and who exercise some degree of autonomy. The bosses sit on the Cupola, also known as the Commission, headed by the *capo dei capi* head chief of all the families. The groups of ten *picciotti* foot soldiers choose their leader *capo decina*. The Cupola organises strategy, issues orders and resolves disputes. Identity amongst the groups and the regional

---

[72] See Chapter 3 for earlier information on the Mafia
[73] Agrigento, Caltanissetta, Catania, Enna, Messina, Ragusa, Siracusa and Trapani.

bosses is secret to ensure greater security. There are about 5,000 *uomini d'onore* men of honour in Sicily.

With the Italians' predilection for secrecy and intrigue ever since medieval times, the Mafia resembles a masonic lodge, in that its rituals are based on a code of honour, secrecy, loyalty, *omertá* silence and revenge: the latter reminiscent of the Spanish *vendetta*, harking back to Spanish domination of the southern Peninsula over two centuries. In fact, during 1976-80 a number of Mafiosi joined the P2 and Gran Loggia, secret brotherhoods. Well organised and highly disciplined like a traditional army, Mafiosi are trained to obey and not question orders; and ever on the alert, even verbally, for fear of death hovers constantly. Death is only used as a last resort: hence the antipathy to Riina's murderous reign.

The initiation ceremony involves several novices swearing to obey the rules, such as not to take another man's woman (or at least be discreet) nor rob or kill, except in dire necessity; and above all never reveal anything about the Mafia. The index finger of the hand used for shooting is lightly pierced with a pin. Acting as men of honour they are always obliged to tell the truth. The Mafia epitomises the Sicilian sense of fatalism, endemic in the South, and resembling the Catholic resignation to death; and as evidenced in the writings of Lampedusa, Levi, Pirandello and Sciascia. In the absence of a strong state, and in today's superficial consumer society, the Mafia offers not only a sense of belonging in its strong familial clan base (a concept also embraced by most Italians), but also self control, reminiscent of the Englishman's stiff upper lip. Membership is for life, ending either in natural or violent death. The Mafia gives the appearance of a secular priesthood, indeed its patron saint is the Virgin Mary, and offering a sense of belonging, support and guidance. Judge Falcone observed that the Mafioso resembles a priest in his life-long commitment to his calling.

The Mafia is essentially male, patriarchal and fraternal, tied together by blood loyalties that go back a long way. Mafia families offer protection against the outside world, although inner conflicts do occur, just as with ordinary families. It has been unusual for fathers and sons to kill each other. The boss Calderone, from Catania, preferred no more than two brothers in the same family for fear of a conflict of interest, such as kinship taking precedence over the Mafia. Buscetta's two sons (not of the Mafia), as well as other relatives, were killed by the rival Corleonesi groups during the 1962-63 war, which finally led him to become a *pentito* turn state evidence. Women are excluded from the Mafia:

wives and mothers are considered saints, responsible for the home and family; whilst daughters are assumed to be pure until marriage, although female emancipation has loosened this perception. Calderone's wife was a classic model of loyalty and discretion; in contrast V.Buffa's spirited wife convinced her husband to retract his confession, as well as organising a wives' protest in the courtroom of the maxi trial.

Historically herdsmen and tenant farmers, during the 19th century the Mafia managed the great landed estates of the absentee nobles, and defended the rights of the peasants. Their interests centred on the *pizzo* protection of land and property, which all too easily slid into an extortion racket. Some were landowners themselves and controlled precious water supplies, for instance the Bontate and Greco families. During the late 19th century, many Southern Italians emigrated to the New World in search of a better life, out of which in the 1930s arose the American Mafia, adopting the Sicilian use of the word 'family' to offer security in a foreign country. Perhaps the Wild West cowboys and city gangsters made them feel at home.

In the 1930s Mussolini sent Cesare Mori, the 'iron prefect', to clamp down on the Mafia, since it posed a threat as a rival state. However, they recovered during World War Two, assisting the Allies who helped to defend them against the Fascists, for instance Lucky Luciano, top Mafia boss. The American troops set free thousands of Mafiosi who had been incarcerated by Mussolini, appointing them mayors and supplying them with armaments; thereby unwittingly renewing their power. The British SOE Special Operations Executive considered working with the Mafia but decided against the idea. In 1944 a law sanctioned the breakup of large estates to allow farm workers to take over the land for share cropping. Mafia landowners resented the reform: in 1947 they reminded people of their dreadful power by slaughtering eleven farm labourers and their leader during a rural festa at Portella della Ginestre.

After the war the Mafia became quiescent, to the extent of seeming non-existent; and so a false sense of security set in with little suppression by the authorities. During the 1950s convicted Mafiosi were transferred to the north *soggiorno obbligato,* yet this only contributed to their spread. About this time Mafiosi moved away from their traditional rural activities to become the 'new men' of city based enterprises. They came to control much of the building industry by exacting a high percentage cut *tangente* on commercial tenders and subcontracting, secured through intimidation and violence. They also profited from tax collection: in particular the unscrupulous cousins Ignazio and Antonino Salvo in Sicily, who during the '60s took a generous 10% rake-off; plus interest earnt from delaying transfer to the government. The Mafia insinuated themselves into national politics, supplying Southern votes to northern Christian Democrat politicians who, resigned to being unable to eradicate the Mafia, accorded them a free hand: *clientelismo* votes for favours, an arrangement which goes back to Roman times.

In 1958 a parliamentary enquiry was set up to look into the Mafia's nebulous activities especially in public works contracts, social security and banks; as well as exerting undue influence in the law courts. Yet politicians buried their heads in the sand, partly intimidated by the Mafia. Following the Mafia war in 1962-63, a commission proposed better coordination of the police forces, vetting state employees, exerting more rigorous controls over public works contracts, town planning and building licences. In 1971-72 a third parliamentary commission examined Mafia violence and its political links, but again achieved little.

During the 1970s, in the wake of many Southerners migrating north for work, criminal organisations also gravitated to Milan and Genoa, sinking their tentacles into bribery and corruption, skewing public works tenders by exacting their 2-3% cut, and later becoming involved in Tangentopoli. They demanded a 15% cut on the building of the *Autostrada del Sole*. Their nefarious activities were overshadowed by the unstable years of terrorism which occupied much of the magistrates' time, allowing the Mafia to flourish unmolested. During this period the Mafia rode high on the wave of the international drug trade, which encompassed Morocco, South America and Canada. The drug trade had begun in the 1920s/30s, displacing the cigarette business which, at its height, saw ships dock in the Bay of Naples, a major entrepot, with shipments of up to 40-50,000 cases, and which provided a modest income for the locals who unloaded. The boss Lucky Luciano had been expelled from New York after the war, and so returned to Naples where he moved into the narcotics trade, which was in full swing at the time. He died in 1962.

Heroin was shipped to Marseilles from the Far Eastern opium fields, (the south-western Golden Crescent and the south-eastern Golden Triangle) for refining either in Palermo or New York by their American cousins, in particular the prominent Gambino and Inzerillo clans based on an old Palermo family. During the 1950s, the highly respected Greco family, farmers of vast citrus plantations since the 19th century, became involved with drugs. With the decline of Marseilles, the Mafia centred the trade on Agrigento in Sicily, making use of the logistical setup from cigarettes to move smoothly into drugs.

Drugs often vary in quality, due to the addition of impure substances, such as benzoil-tropeine. French chemists refined the morphine base in Palermo which used to handle 30% of the trade, but by 1991 had dropped to 5% when other nations moved in, often tied in with arms deals. Since 1985 no new drugs laboratories have opened thanks to a crackdown with many arrests. In the past, co-operation with the French authorities has been good, but extradition has proved difficult since terrorism and the Mafia were not recognised by the French. Relations are excellent with the US, otherwise fair with Britain, Canada, Spain and Germany. Other foreign interests cover the sale of arms to Yugoslavia and Turkey, pornography, extortion, and prostitution (the latter apparently was not present in Sicily but was big business for the American Mafia). Since the 1980s, the Mafia has gravitated eastwards to cities such as Warsaw and Belgrade, as well as Russia where it has become entangled in administrative corruption. More recently, Italian mobsters have been muscling in on Maltese online gaming and drugs.

The heady concoction of fierce rivalry and immense wealth generated by the drug trade provoked a bitter two year war during 1981-83, between rival families as well as within families, headed on one side by the Corleonesi by Salvatore 'Totò' Riina and Bernardo Provenzano; and ranged against the ruling trio of Inzerillo, Stefano Bontate (one of the top businessmen during the 60s-70s) and Badalamenti with his drugs base in Detroit. The Corleonesi secured victory, settling old debts and feuds, with hundreds killed in open daylight. After the dreadful bloodbath the Mafia was regrouped into a more compact and rigorously controlled outfit. In 1984 the authorities retaliated strongly with the arrest of 366 Mafiosi: its first major onslaught.

The narcodollar business transformed Mafiosi from rural bandits into white-collar businessmen. Making colossal fortunes, Sicilian banks mushroomed to handle the revenues, with the Mafia investing their ill-gotten gains into tourism, property and casinos in the north. The money also financed the legal counsel of Mafiosi on trial. They made use of financial whizz kids who shunted the cash around the globe, recycling illegal funds to offshore tax havens, and possibly via the *Borsa* stock exchange in Milan. Mafiosi even acquired BOTs Treasury bonds, which ironically helped to finance the state. In 1993 the antiMafia parliamentary commission estimated that criminal organisations accounted for

4% of GDP, second only to the state organisation IRI. In Calabria citrus and bergamot groves (the latter was distilled for French perfumiers) were grubbed up in order to claim indemnity from Brussels' generous EU cohesion funds for poorer regions. One wonders what they will make of the new crypto currency, especially with the Bank of Italy's recent withdrawal of the five-hundred-euro banknote. In 1992 the authorities launched the international Green Ice operation to crack down on Colombian cocaine to break the link with America. The Cuntrera brothers, from Sicily, had run the operation from Venezuela during the 1970s, and involving a major importer based in London.

The Mafia also had in their clutches the highly lucrative health care sector, like bees round a honeypot: it seemed a logical move from drug dealing. The sector accounts for half of Sicily's annual budget viz 6.5 billion euros. In 2002 M.Aiello, head of the island's private health sector, was sentenced to 14 years in prison on grounds of corruption and complicity with the Mafia. Magistrates unearthed shady dealings over excessive hospital supplies purchased at inflated prices in the pharmacy at Messina university.

After World War Two, Messina, which lies at the northern tip of Sicily, had a flourishing industry and in 1955 hosted the preliminary talks leading to the Treaty of Rome setting up the Common Market. With the closure of the shipyard and military hospital during the 80s/90s due to public sector cuts, the university became an important employer, with some 6,000 teaching and support staff for 40,000 students. During the early '70s students went on the rampage, damaging property and attacking people. By the 1990s the campus had become a den of iniquity, with infiltration by the Mafia. Two people on the campus were murdered and two professors badly injured; two bombs were set off. In 2005, 66 people stood accused, of which 33 were sentenced for trading in courses, examinations and degrees during 1984-2001, and employing threats and intimidation. Other offences related to drug dealing, keeping illegal arms and being in receipt of stolen goods.

The Camorra, whose name derives from the Spanish denoting quarrel, shares several similarities with the Mafia. The organisation was largely responsible for much banditry in the 19th century. Based in the city of Naples in the region of Campania, the Camorra is a looser horizontal grouping than the vertical Mafia, but also based on families, and possibly older than its rival, perhaps with origins in a medieval society going back to Toledo in 1420. Its location in urban Naples makes it easier to extort, unlike the more rural Mafia and 'Ndrangheta. During

World War Two they too helped the Allies, controlling the black market for precious food, and afterwards moved into cigarette smuggling as well as post war construction. The newer NCO *Nuova Camorra Organizzata* was run by Rafaele Cutolo (see Chapter 11), which boasted about a hundred fluid bands organised by brothers, with youngsters and entire families involved in various activities such as drug peddling, gambling, prostitution and extortion. Cutolo recruited Apulian criminals into his band. The Camorra began trading in cocaine from Colombia through the Medellin barons, later taking on heroin with operations in Germany and the Netherlands. They also ran casinos and property on the French Riviera. In 1982 turf wars erupted between the NCO and its rival *Nuova Famiglia* NF, the latter in temporary alliance with older Camorra families. NF gained the upper hand, during which some 1,500 people died from the carnage. Women were accepted in key roles: for instance after the arrest of Cutolo his sister Rosetta took over the business. In 1995 there were some 7,000 members distributed amongst 145 families.

With the closure in 1961 of Tangier as a free port, during the 1970s the contraband trade in cigarettes run by the Camorra shifted to the Apulian mafia along the extensive Adriatic coastline. The port of Brinidisi is only 80 miles/130km from Albania across the Strait of Otranto. Cargoes of some 200,000 cigarettes from Montenegro were offloaded in Puglia, helped by the locals to earn a bit of cash. Following the murder of two *Guardia di Finanza* GdF finance officers in 2000, Operation *Primavera* spring was mounted, involving 2,000 personnel. They arrested 500 people and pulled in thousands of tons of tobacco; together with a large quantity of heroin and cocaine, as well as arms and explosives. During the 19th century, Naples boasted a thriving armaments industry to supply King Ferdinand's 50,000 strong army. Following this crackdown, smugglers switched to lorries and containers via the Balkan ferries or moving overland from the north. In the distant past Albanians had migrated to Italy; whilst following the outbreak of war in Kosovo in 1999, the Albanian mafia took to smuggling migrants. Other Balkan activities into Italy included slave prostitutes and arms from Croatia, illegal tobacco from Montenegro, and heroin from Kosovo and Bosnia.

A serious drug problem existed in Verona during the 1980s, where there were 3,500 regular heroin users, particularly amongst the well-heeled middle class rather than the down and outs. In 1987 police seized 100 kilos of heroin at a house near Verona and arrested two people. The heroin, along with cocaine, were brought in from Turkey and Syria by Yugoslav smugglers working with Italian dealers. Palermo and Milan were the main production and distribution centres, dealing in 4,000 kilos yearly of base heroin and morphine. At the time of writing Rogoredo, in the wealthy Brianza area north of Milan has the highest number of drug addicts, affecting some one thousand souls.

The ground-breaking Spartacus trial in 2005, presided over by Judge Tona, exposed how deeply the dominant Casalesi clan of the Camorra had penetrated into Neopolitan society and the Campania region. In 1981 the clan profited enormously from the earthquake centred on Irpinia (which registered 6.2 on the Richter scale) in which over 5,000 people died and some 8,000 were injured, with 250,000 left homeless. The Casalesi expropriated money from the disaster funds to launch their own construction firms, which included plant hire and building materials such as ready mix concrete, thereby hugely inflating the costs of rebuilding roads. They pressurized rival firms to cut them out of tendering. Costs for one road rocketed from 70 billion Lire to 240bnL thanks to their meddling; whilst the high-speed Naples-Rome train opened six years late.

Ever resourceful, with the decline of infrastructure programmes the Camorra slid into extortion at hotels, catering and food processing, creeping into Lazio, Tuscany and Emilia-Romagna, as well as Eastern Europe. With unemployment in Naples hovering around 50%, the Casalesi controlled jobs by infiltrating local firms. In 1989 a law was introduced to limit the concrete sprawl which ravaged the environment, causing mud flows, avalanches and soil degradation. During the 1950s/60s over 100,000 trees were felled for road construction. It is commonplace in Italy, including the north, to leave the remains of an old building as proof of former construction.

The Casalesi have made immense fortunes out of waste disposal, a thorny problem in the South. Untreated industrial waste from the north is dumped into holes and quarries conveniently exposed by road building. On average each year seven million tons of industrial waste is unaccounted for. A Camorra informant advised the authorities that he had refused to dump illegal waste in Mondragone (just north of Naples) since, judging by the money offered him, the material was extremely toxic, possibly nuclear. In the 1920s a chemicals industry developed in Crotone, Calabria, to supply the oil and gas industry: the site was closed in 1994. Over a period of 70 years, possibly some 90,000 tons of industrial waste was produced: mostly zinc but also mercury, cadmium and lead. 15,000 tons was transferred elsewhere in the region, notably to the Sibari Plain. The rest just simply disappeared. In 1959 ENI started extracting oil from Gela in Sicily. Over time an increasing number of cancer cases were reported. In 2018 *Espresso* magazine reported the dumping of toxic waste at Caserta province in the Campania region, giving rise to illnesses such as leukemia and cancer.

Domestic waste is another huge problem, bearing in mind Naple's population of one million. During the 1600s it vied with Paris and London for its sheer size, and already sprouting criminal gangs. Waste is dumped locally, giving rise to suspicion about the quality of fruit and vegetables grown locally, for instance on the fertile lava soils around Mount Vesuvius. The problem also deters tourists. Plans for the erection of seven waste treatment plants were blocked by the Greens, Radicals and the Church. In 2008, dioxin[74] was detected in the prized mozzarella cheese, made from buffalo and much exported to France, America and Britain. The Camorra control many dairies through the *pizzo* extortion, made easier by their remote rural situation; whereas in urban areas shopkeepers and artisans can club together to resist the menace. During 1991-2006, 41 town councils were disbanded in the province of Naples owing to corruption; compared with 23 apiece in the provinces of Palermo and Caserta: all due to mafia infiltration. In 2008 all the landfill sites for the rubbish from Naples were full, so some was shipped to Germany. The 1963 anti-Mafia parliamentary enquiry examined such abuse but no action was taken. More recently, the disposal of domestic waste in Rome has become a critical problem.

The other criminal organisation that came to dominance at this time is the *'ndrangheta* based in Calabria: the name derives from the Greek for virility. It too resembles its rival organisations in terms of fraternal solidarity and paternal blood ties. Numbering some 5,600 in 1993 (similar to the Mafia and the Camorra) it is more loosely organised into *ndrina* groups, grouped into a *locale* district (village or town) with a minimum of 49 people ruled by a *copiata* of three bosses. The most ruthless clans are based in Reggio di Calabria, the regional capital, where they are responsible for a high murder rate. The town suffered earthquakes in 1783 and 1908.

The *'ndrangheta's* earlier activities centred on extortion and bringing in hashish and heroin from Turkey. They dealt with Bosnia and Croatia in cocaine, cigarettes and arms, and so are well-armed themselves. These trades later financed their construction business, ruining much of the coastline in the process.

---

[74] In 1976 an explosion at a chemical plant in Seveso, north of Milan, released an emission of dioxin. The outbreak posed a threat to pregnant women.

They rose to power in the mid-1960s on the back of the construction of the Salerno-Reggio tract for the Autostrada del Sole, extracting a generous rake-off. During the 1970s they specialised in kidnappings of wealthy businessmen, including children. The *'ndrangheta* held their captives in the bleak Aspromonte area, their original base, which the Allies found a challenging terrain, with peaks up to 3,000 feet, dissected by deep ravines and fast flowing rivers. The area is now a national park, yet the *'ndrangheta* grow marijuana here. Sardinia was also a notorious area for kidnappings: the first occurred in 1960, reaching 583 by 1983 and latterly involving the Mafia. In 2007 six Italians were killed in Duisburg, Germany arising from a feud between two *'ndrangheta* clans. As with other mafia organisations, they have drifted north.

In 1981 a new group *Sacra Corona Unita* Sacred United Crown SCU emerged from the prison of Bari to set up a contraband business in the Bay of Naples. Later it dominated crime in Puglia during the 1980s, in league with the *'ndrangheta* and becoming entangled with Albanian criminal groups in Puglia following the collapse of Communist Yuogslavia. They have resorted to exploding bombs near Bari, also further north on the railway line to Ancona. Following Operation Galassia involving the round-up in Calabria of mafiosi in 1995, many shifted to Germany (a popular venue for many Italians in search of work during the 1950s) where they dealt in drugs and arms, car stealing and social security fraud.

All three criminal organisations share the common characteristics of territorial control and political power, with their hands deep into the local government till as well as international links. Yet many people deny their existence, perhaps because they prefer to airbrush them out of their lives. Men of the cloth also refuse to accept their existence, for instance Cardinal Ruffini. The enigmatic superpentito Buscetta was dismissive of these rival groups, declaring to Falcone that 'he did not wish to talk about the Camorra, who were just a bunch of clowns'. As for the 'ndrangheta: 'Are you certain, Signor Falcone, that they really exist?'

Emboldened by the crushing defeat of their rivals in 1983, the ruthless Corleonesi, now under the violent Totò Riina, began to target politicians and state servants, forsaking the earlier approach of *avvicinamento* mutual accommodation. They proceeded to murder three magistrates and two policemen. Stirred by the general feeling of revulsion at such atrocities both the state and the general public began to retaliate. One of the first politicians to mend his ways was the DC president of Sicily, P.Mattarella. He began a campaign of moral regeneration by refusing to hand over public monies to the Mafia, but he lacked substantial support since his new approach upset the status quo. He paid with his life in 1980 at the hands of the Mafia. Salvatore Lima, *assessore* alderman, and known as the 'viceroy of Sicily', drily commented: 'When agreements are made they must be kept.'

In 1982 General Carlo Alberto dalla Chiesa was nominated prefect of Palermo. A former Carabiniere officer, he secured exceptional success in the unmasking of terrorists, notably his outstanding rescue of the American General Dozier from the Red Brigades, of which naturally the Mafia were fully aware (see Chapter 11). Totally committed and highly professional, he realised that unbridled support from the government and politicians was crucial to success, given their tangled connections with the Mafia. In conversation with the writer Giorgio Bocca, he remarked: 'I believe I have understood the new rules of the game: the powerful government servant gets killed when two conditions intertwine: he has become too dangerous and at the same time he is isolated and therefore disposable.' He was not given a clear brief and so departed for Palermo, sent by Andreotti, beneath a cloud of foreboding. Three weeks later, in August 1982 he was dead, together with his dear wife (they had only just married) and bodyguard.

The omens had been inauspicious since he left for Palermo on the day the PCI deputy Pio La Torre was killed: he had presented a bill before Parliament concerning the first effective anti-Mafia legislation. It established as a criminal offence association with the Mafia, submission of the victim and the cult of *omertà* silence. Improving upon earlier and inadequate laws in 1956, 1965 and 1972, Article 416 was amended to distinguish between standard criminal associations with a one to five year prison sentence; and the new sub-section 416bis concerning mafia type organisations, whose members are liable to three to six years' incarceration. Crucially the Torre law accords magistrates and the police extensive powers to search bank accounts, including anonymous holdings, in order to seize Mafia assets. Furthermore the new law placed the burden of proof with the defence rather than the prosecution, demanding that the defence must prove that their clients obtained their assets legally. This procedure facilitated the seizure of assets in order to deprive the mafiosi of finance.

The nation was brutally shocked by the cold blooded assassination of La Torre and Dalla Chiesa, and marked a turning point in public attitudes towards criminal organisations. Ten days later, Parliament put aside its scruples and now hastened to enact the Rognoni-La Torre bill. In 1984 366 arrests were made. During 1993-2004, the court in Palermo seized around 2.5 billion euros in assets of which some 1.5 billion was confiscated. The power of the Mafia had been dented.

In 1980 and 1983 two magistrates were killed: G. Costa, chief prosecutor for Palermo, was gunned down, whilst his colleague R. Chinnici was killed by a car bomb, betrayed by a colleague. Chinnici was replaced in 1983 by the 63-year-old A. Caponnetto, also Sicilian, but had worked mainly in Florence. Living a quiet life, he put together a pool of four magistrates sharing information, which included Giovanni Falcone and Paolo Borsellino, who were childhood friends and attended schools which included future mafiosi. Both aged 40, they came from the Sicilian middle class, with a strong commitment of service to the state. They were supported by three DC ministers in Craxi's first coalition government: Mino Martinazzoli, minister of justice, Virginio Rognoni (co-sponsor of the Torre bill and head of CSM Magistracy 2002-06) and Oscar Luigi Scalfaro, all future Ministers of the Interior.

Giovanni Falcone was born in Palermo. His father was a local government official and his mother a devout Catholic. He cut his teeth as a *giudice istruttore* examining/investigating magistrate in Trapani, south-west Sicily, then in 1978 moved back to Palermo, the heart of the Mafia, where he joined Chinnici's team which included Costa. Taking over from Chinnici, Falcone's first important case dealt with an international heroin ring based in Palermo, for which he employed up to date scientific methods to unravel money laundering and banking records (the first trawl occurred in 1979), tracing money trails in America and Switzerland, and which revolutionised investigation procedures (as did Magistrate Di Pietro with his skilful use of the computer during the Tangentopoli crisis.) Falcone observed that the six month limit for investigations set by the 1989 penal code was insufficient.

In his book, '*Cose di Cose Nostra*' Concerning the Mafia, Falcone stresses the absolute need for international co-operation to combat the deviousness of parts of society. He presents the following case as an example, though without revealing the culprit. In 1986 he liaised with Carla Del Ponte, the Swiss chief prosecutor in Lugano, to investigate three Swiss bank accounts, through which had passed sporadic and significant movements of five million dollars during 1981-82, possibly from drug trafficking. The Swiss authorities granted him permission to examine their documentation, only to discover that the accounts had vanished. Delving further, he discovered that the monies had ended up in the account of a Panamian company, of which half went to a bank in New York and the other half to one in Montreal. The monies finished up in a Guernsey company, which received instructions to divide the five million dollars amongst five bank accounts, and which ended up in two banks next door to each other, one of which had attracted the Italian magistracy in the first place. The Swiss advised him that the original sum had now grown to $15 million; of which in 1991 a Swiss magistrate ordered its confiscation.

For fourteen years, Falcone lived in the shadows of the courts and prisons, working for six years on the anti-Mafia team, and returning home late to dine and sleep. Highly intelligent, he possessed an excellent retentive memory and possessed tremendous dedication to his daunting task. His transfer to Rome, where many politicians and mafiosi live, offered him a more congenial working environment where he set up an improved support base for future magistrates. Fully aware of the risks he took, in the end Falcone was eliminated because, like Dalla Chiesa, he had become a serious threat, not just to the Mafia but to people in high places. Falcone described himself as 'simply a servant of the state *in terra infidelium'* (untrustworthy territory). Falcone believed that the root cause of distortion of the Sicilian soul lay in a lack of sense of state.

Counter Attack

Miraculously, in July 1984 the anti-Mafia team won a breakthrough with the confession of a senior Mafioso boss, Tommaso Buscetta, the first *superpentito.* Aged 65 he was arrested in Brazil that year and brought to Rome. He decided to co-operate with the police since the Mafia had killed two of his sons during the 1981-84 carnage and who were not members of the clan; as well as ten other relatives. Buscetta decided to speak out since he was disgusted by the culture of money, drugs and greed that had washed away the traditional code values of honour and loyalty. Married to a Brazilian woman, he enjoyed widespread contacts in the Americas and Europe, being highly involved with coordinating the international cocaine and heroin markets. Falcone's book includes a series of highly informative interviews between the magistrate and Buscetta, covering a period of 45 days, and offering an invaluable insight into the Mafia psyche. In Falcone's words: 'Buscetta gave us a global vision... of the phenomenon; an essential key into reading the Mafia, its language and code'. Buscetta's confessions led to the conviction of over 350 mafiosi. He also gave evidence in America concerning the sale of heroin through pizza restaurants, which led to the conviction of 22 people.

Falcone conducted a series of painstaking interviews with Buscetta, forging a sensitive relationship with his enigmatic interlocutor. Possessed of immense patience and tact, Falcone slowly gained the confidence of the *pentito* informant and absorbed a profound insider knowledge of the Mafia phenomenon: its organisation and its raison d'etre. Falcone carefully read the Sicilian code of the look in the eyes, the tone of voice, the gestures, in order to tease out the precious information; along with valuable evidence extracted from other informants *pentiti*.[75] Falcone, let us not forget, was Sicilian too and understood the workings of the Sicilian mind. By 1990, 35 Mafiosi had come forward to co-operate with the authorities, later rising to some 250, including some from abroad. The stream of pentiti revealed the Mafia's vulnerability, eroding its existence. Crucially Falcone broke the Mafia rule of *omertà*, being the first to venture into the no-man's land twixt State and Mafia, trying to understand their need for order in an unstable and ill-disciplined society based on a nascent state. Perhaps Falcone was imbued with a Catholic sense of duty to coax the Mafiosi back into the fold of decency. These conversations revealed to Falcone that the Mafia was not invincible; yet he also doubts the State's current ability to conquer the rival state.

Buscetta responded to Falcone's respect towards him as an equal, holding the magistrate in high esteem and so deciding to speak, saying: '*Ho fiducia in Lei. Ma non mi fido di nessun'altro*'. 'I trust you. But I trust no-one else.' Buscetta considered Falcone to be an honourable man, the highest accolade accorded by a man of honour. He addressed him as *Signor Giudice* and with the courteous *Lei* (to do otherwise with Italians would cause offence). Thus, a remarkable relationship was forged between Falcone, servant of the state, and Buscetta, enemy of the state. Buscetta paid the highest price for his revelations: his entire family of thirty-three relations was murdered.

Antonio Calderone was another key informant who supplied detailed information. A native of Catania, he was arrested in Nice in 1987 and supplied vital evidence on the Mafia's political connections, for instance Lima (see below); also on thirty families in Palermo who controlled half of the total 360,000 votes on the island. Calderone stated that the Mafia's top priority is survival not power. Intriguingly, he disclosed that in 1981 five masonic lodges

---

[75] Also known as 'collaboratori di giustizia'.

were set up in Trapani, known jointly as *Circolo Scontrino* Ticket Club, founded by Licio Gelli, venerable master of P2, and who offered the Mafia a possible entrée into politics. In 1985 the head of the flying squad in Trapani ordered a search: he was later transferred. An investigating magistrate unearthed a link with East European drugs smuggling through the Mafia into north-east Italy, following upon the discovery of a heroin refinery in Trapani with East European equipment. An attempt was made on his life but failed.

The Mafioso F.Mannoia gave himself up to the FBI in the States, declaring in Catholic fashion that he had repented of his life of crime. Significantly he revealed that the government had approached Cosa Nostra to intercede in the abduction of Aldo Moro by the Red Brigades. He also alluded to the collusion of the Bishop of Naples. The boss S.Bontate, who was close to the DC, favoured intercession, whilst the tougher Corleonesi were opposed and over-ruled him, saying: 'Political matters are their affair not ours.' Mannoia also spoke of vote-rigging in the 1987 elections. Contorno, a *picciotto* humble footsoldier, dismissed the Mafia as nothing more than a bunch of cowards and assassins. Magistrate D. Gozzo, working in Palermo, observed that true repentance is rare: usually an informant makes a purely rational choice to speak, as a means to a shorter sentence.

The pool gleaned a wealth of insider information from Buscetta and his fellow informants, which led to the *maxiprocesso* maxi trial held in 1986-87 in a custom-made underground bunker in Palermo. Caution is always exercised when dealing with informants' evidence since the confessor may be trying to wreak revenge on a rival. The trial established that the Mafia possessed a definite hierarchy, and was not simply a loose affiliation. Some 700 people were questioned, of which 450 were accused, and of which 344 were found guilty (including 12 of the 13 members of the Cupola) and with 19 life sentences being imposed. Amongst the indicted were Salvatore 'Totó' Riina, *capo dei capi* top boss of the Mafia, and his deputy Bernardo Provenzano. Both being fugitives from justice, they were sentenced in absentia. The trial marked a definitive moment in the fight against the Mafia, and encouraged greater hope for its eventual defeat.

Crucially Buscetta did not reveal the close links between the Mafia and high ranking politicians, and so the investigating team broke up. Borsellino went to Marsala, whilst Caponnetto was replaced by a mediocre chap. Falcone was appointed Minister of Penal Affairs at the Ministry of Justice in Rome by Claudio

Martelli, Minister of Justice and a prominent Socialist, where he could exert pressure on the Mafia who, naturally, had their nose put out of joint by this appointment. Hiatus reigned: people doubted that the higher courts would uphold the sentences.

About this time, local government took a turn for the better in Palermo, with the election in 1985 of Leoluca Orlando, a young and radical politician as mayor and promoted by the Christian Democrat De Mita. He lovingly restored the city's *Teatro Massimo*. Tired of the DC's hob-nobbing with the Mafia, Orlando left the party to found the left-wing anti-Mafia group *La Rete* network and, provided with a round the clock police bodyguard, won most of the preference votes in the 1992 elections; though sadly he later lost out to Berlusconi's Forza Italia. A local branch of La Rete was managed by Nando Dalla Chiesa, son of the murdered General. Known as the shortlived Palermo Spring, it was a time of optimism, with various elements campaigning for an end to terrorization by the Mafia and other criminal organisations. People had tired of living in an atmosphere of fear and suspicion, ideal for criminal elements: *mafiosità* in Sciascia's description. University students organised demonstrations; whilst bishops, priests and Jesuits openly defied the Mafia, including Pope John Wojtyla. Many priests received threats: two were killed.

Unsurprisingly, various appeals were made over the convictions, held in Palermo during 1989. Mafia bosses blithely assumed that their connections with the highest echelons of the political world would absolve them thanks to Lima, Andreotti and their cronies in Rome. In particular they were counting on Judge Corrado Carnevale, President of the first section of the highest court of appeal *Corte di Cassazione*, who had let off some 400 mafiosi in the past through legal niceities, and who now overturned the sentences of four Mafia bosses. He declared that the Cupola did not exist and that the Mafia was run just by a group of families. Close to Andreotti (as was Judge P.Dell'Anno) he was later put on trial for association with the Mafia. Thanks to the concerted efforts of Falcone at the Ministry of Justice, supported by his boss Claudio Martelli (who as Justice Minister was now in the Mafia's sights; and later head of DIS intelligence), together with objections from the Higher Court and parliamentary anti-Mafia commissions, Carnevale was relieved of his role in order to ensure a fair hearing. The final decision of the court's composition lay with the senior judge, Antonio Brancaccio, who was also the First President of the *Corte di Cassazione*. He appointed Alfonso Valente as president of the appeal hearing, known for his impartiality. In January 1992, the year of Tangentopoli, all the original sentences were upheld.

In 1989 Giulio Andreotti became President of the Council of Ministers (prime minister) till 1992, with Antonio Gava as his Minister of the Interior till 1990, who enjoyed links with the Camorra in Naples. Born in Rome in 1919, Andreotti was a founder member of the DC in 1942, and a protégé of De Gasperi. He held his first cabinet post in 1957, holding all major offices and serving as PM seven times; and elected life senator. Known as Don Giulio, Andreotti's faction was notorious for their association with clientelism, corruption and the Mafia. General Dalla Chiesa remarked that the Andreotti faction was the 'most compromised political family' of Palermo. Astutely bowing to public pressure, the ambivalent Andreotti supported the fight against the Mafia, presiding over the enactment of laws, mostly prepared by Falcone, to protect informants, reinforce police powers over kidnappings, better police coordination, and revising rules on subcontracting. A past master of Machiavellian manoeuvring, he would defer decisions to maintain the status quo. He was acquainted with Sindona and Calvi, the rogue bankers. The journalist Pecorella was killed since he possessed incriminating evidence on Andreotti. The Mafia probably had some 70-80 deputies and senators in its pocket.

Andreotti had another motive for playing his double game, since he aspired to become President when Cossiga stood down, for which he needed cross party support from the Communists and Social Democrats. In 1991 he flew to Sicily to support his pal Lima and other candidates in the regional elections, of whom one was probably a mafioso, as endorsed by local carabinieri. Baldassare Di Maggio, Riina's driver, accused Andreotti of being responsible for the death of Dalla Chiesa, whom he had expressly sent to Sicily. Di Maggio further revealed that he had witnessed his boss Riina kiss the politician on the cheek whilst in Palermo in 1987. The gesture symbolized the power over the recipient of the gesture. Andreotti denied both the moment and the charge. In 2002 Andreotti was sentenced in Perugia, charged by Magistrate Gian Carlo Caselli with *odore di mafia* association with the Mafia; also complicity in murder, for which he received a 24 year sentence; only to be overturned by the Supreme Court the following year. He had previously been under investigation 26 times. The judiciary had never managed to secure a conviction; partly because all his cases were cancelled by the Statute of Limitations; and partly due to Andreotti being shielded by parliamentary immunity (as with Berlusconi), secured by deputies in article 68 of the post-war Constitution, since Mussolini would invent fake charges on which to arrest any opposition. Upon learning of the acquittal of Andreotti, Berlusconi uttered, doubtless with an inner sigh of relief, that the verdict was 'the beginning of the end of judicial revolution that has been the cancer of public life.' He followed Andreotti's footsteps into Southern politics.

In 1968 Salvatore Lima became a DC deputy, having won 80,000 preference votes in Palermo. Mayor of that city during the heyday of post-war construction as Assessor of public works, he freely granted illegal building licenses to all and sundry, including the Mafia, regardless of consideration for the environment which suffered dreadfully from the ravages of pollution and degradation. The 1963 anti-Mafia parliamentary enquiry examined such abuse but no action was taken. Berlusconi later issued several amnesties concerning waste water pollution, with derisory fines being imposed: hardly an incentive for deterring the Mafia. Lima fell out with his former patron, Giovanni Gioia, Fanfani's deputy, and so offered his services to Andreotti who was keen to expand his factional base beyond the environs of Rome/Lazio. Lima declared he would come with an army of supporters.

In 1972 Andreotti appointed Lima to various posts, in particular as under secretary at the Ministry of Finance and as regional tax collector until 1984. Lima acted as an intermediary between the Mafia and Andreotti, who later denied such a relationship. The economist Labini resigned in protest at his appointment, whilst eleven submissions were made to incriminate Lima but were ignored, until he was eventually shunted to Strasbourg as a Eurodeputy; but his past followed him. Buscetta declared that Lima's father had been a man of honour, whilst other substantial evidence testified to Lima's links to the Mafia.

Following the maxitrial verdicts, the Corleonesi, led by Riina and Provenzano, wished to reassert their authority over Cosa Nostra, at about the time when Falcone transferred to Rome and the anti-Mafia pool was disbanded. They soon wreaked their revenge. In March 1992, their man F.Onorato murdered Salvatore Lima since he had failed to block the maxi trial sentences; though he spared his escort. In 1996 Onorato confessed to the killing.

Lima's successor as mayor of Palermo was Vito Ciancimino. Born in Corleone, and associated with the Corleonese clan, in 1959 he became chairman of Palermo city council, and in 1964 was nominated mayor. During their twenty year reign over Palermo the pair proceeded to ransack the western area of the city, destroying the lovely Liberty style (Art Nouveau) architecture and eradicating the citrus groves. When Judge Falcone returned to Palermo he was appalled by the devastation of what had once been a lovely city. In their place they had thrown up shoddy tenements and charged exorbitant rents for offices; with many of the building licences being issued in the names of three pensioners acting as a front for the Mafia. A major culprit was V.Piazza, a mafioso close to Ciancimino, from whom the city court eventually confiscated assets valued at over 2,000 billion lire (c.£650 million) from his property empire. The Mafia used Piazza as a conduit for laundering their proceeds from drug trafficking. Ciancimino was convicted for mismanagement of the city's municipal contracts and sentenced for 13 years, but he was deemed too old to serve it. He died a natural death in 2002.

Next in the Mafia's sights were the prosecuting magistrates Falcone and Paolo Borsellino, engineered by Riina and Provenzano, who convinced the Cupola, the Mafia's governing body, that they must be eliminated, especially given Falcone's powerful position at the Ministry of Justice. A previous attempt on the judge had failed in 1989, when he invited the Swiss public prosecutor, Carla del Ponte, to his seaside home near Palermo: she too was also on their hit list since she had become a dangerous adversary. Buscetta had warned Falcone: 'First they (the Mafia) will try to kill me, and then it will be your turn. They will go on until they succeed!'[76] In May 1992, at the height of the Tangentopoli scandal, Falcone and his wife were blown up in their car at Capaci close to Palermo airport, which he was driving contrary to regulations, with two other cars in front and behind. Cars are usually just bullet proof but not protected from explosives: Riina's men had placed 300 kilograms of explosive in a large metal drainpipe. The huge explosion gouged out a huge crater and was registered on seismographs in the south of the island. The three carabinieri accompanying the Falcone couple were killed outright, whilst one driver survived badly wounded and with the three bodyguards receiving minor injuries. Falcone and his wife died shortly afterwards in hospital. An impressive monument now marks the location of this atrocious tragedy. Forty thousand people in Palermo attended Falcone's funeral. Words are inadequate to express the horror: his death hit at the soul of Italians. On the eve of his assassination, Falcone was in line for a new top job as *Super Procuratore* Chief Magistrate for the whole of Italy, although there was opposition from men in high places. That same month Oscar Scalfaro was chosen as the new president of Italy.

---

[76] G.Falcone: Cose di Cosa Nostra p10

In July, Borsellino arranged his usual visit to his mother, full of foreboding. The moment he pressed her doorbell a bomb exploded, killing him outright. Prime Minister Amato ordered the posting of 7,000 troops to Sicily, whilst the Camorrista Alfieri was arrested, as well as G.Madonia, Mafioso boss. Palermo airport was re-named Falcone-Borsellino, as was a piazza. Following upon the deaths of Falcone and Borsellino, art.41bis of the criminal code 6/1992 was amended to impose *carcere duro* high level confinement: within a week 300 Mafiosi were locked up.

Held in Caltanissetta, Sicily, in 1996 the trial began relating to the assassination of Falcone, and concerned 42 accused. Verdicts were promptly given the following year: eight were acquitted, 24 received life sentences, raised to 29 at appeal in 2000. Two had died in the meantime. In 2002 the Supreme Court of Appeal confirmed 14 life sentences, whilst the rest faced retrial. Concerning the car bombings, it emerged that it was top boss Riina who had issued the order to kill Falcone and Borsellino. The court confirmed long term incarceration for him and his deputy Provenzano (both still on the run), together with Leoluca Bagarella, one of Riina's deputies and also his son-in-law; as well as the Graviano brothers.

As deputy chief prosecutor, Judge Anna Maria Palma presided over the three trials for the assassination of her colleague Borsellino and his bodyguards. A Sicilian by birth, and whose father had been a magistrate, Anna Maria began work as *pretore* assistant magistrate working with Chinnici, then with Falcone and Borsellino on bankruptcy cases. Borsellino supported her transfer as judge to Palermo in 1992, where she began her work just a fortnight before the assassination of Falcone and his wife (who was her friend and a fellow magistrate). Understandably her husband was reluctant for her to undertake the role.

In 1996 the first trial concerning Borsellino found the four accused guilty. The second trial dealt with 18 accused, with the first appeal in 2002, handing down 13 life sentences including Riina and G.Graviano. The third trial also dealt with the death of Borsellino, for which 27 were accused, including G.Brusca who set off the bomb for Falcone's car; also Provenzano. In 1999 all were found guilty, the minimum sentence being 12 years' imprisonment; whilst 17 received life, reduced to 10 at final appeal in 2002.

The defence lawyers contested the prosecuting magistrates in a menacing fashion. They addressed formal complaints through the criminal bar association in Palermo, whose chairman was Nino Mormino, who defended those accused of Mafia crimes. In 2001 he became a parliamentary deputy in Berlusconi's Forza Italia party. Costs for the defence were funded by illicit sources such as international drug trafficking. Despite the tense and hostile atmosphere in the courtroom, those who fought for justice could be reasonably satisfied with their achievements.

Intent on holding the state to ransom, in May 1993, at the instigation of Riina, the Mafia continued to retaliate with a vicious car bombing campaign in major cities. There followed in quick succession a series of murderous attacks. The popular presenter, Maurizio Costanzo, who had denounced the Mafia on television, narrowly escaped death in Rome due to a switch in vehicle, but twenty were injured and causing damage to many buildings. In Florence, early one morning five died and forty were injured; and with serious damage to precious works of art at the Uffizi Gallery. Next in line was the centre of Milan where, late one evening in Via Palestro, five bystanders were killed and many were injured, as well as damaging the Pavilion of Contemporary Art. In July the fourth bomb was detonated in the heart of Rome where several were hurt, with extensive damage to the Lateran Palace, the Pope's historic residence as Bishop of Rome. An innocuous Fiat Uno was used for all four of the outrages.

Trials relating to the car bombings were carried out in Florence during 1996-98, at the same time as the trials in Sicily relating to Falcone and Borsellino, so it proved a busy time for the courts. In a lower assize court, two judges and a jury sat through 190 hearings relating to charges of cold-blooded slaughter *strage* and devastation. The proceedings were facilitated by the confessions of Brusca, who furnished a detailed insight into their lives; together with twelve Mafiosi. P.Carra, a lorry driver who hovered on the fringes of the Mafia, also gave vital evidence. The verdict was 14 life sentences and 10 long term, all confirmed by both levels of appeal and supreme appeal in 2001/02. Amongst those found guilty were Riina, Provenzano (both still fugitives from justice), Bagarella, Brusca and the Graviano brothers.

In 1993 Totò Riina was at long last caught by the RAS *Raggruppamento Operativo Sicurezza* (similar to the SAS) under the orders of magistrate Ilda Boccassini (who was involved in Berlusconi's trials) after 35 years on the run, followed two years later by L.Bagarella. Riina's driver, B.di Maggio, had blown the whistle on his former boss. Born in Corleone and head of the Madonia clan, he had been a key link with the United States and South America. He had been living in a bungalow on the outskirts of Palermo, yet the police had held back, reluctant to take action since the DC government was reliant on Riina's influence in local elections. The authorities came to realise that Mafiosi usually respond to their homing instinct, hiding amongst family and friends for moral support and to manage their business.

Known as '*la belva*' beast, Riina's speciality was killing off victims by strangling them, immersing them in a bath of sulphuric acid *la lupara bianca* and finally, disposing of the body in a deep pit. Another favoured method is *incaprettamento* goat tie, wherein the binding of the wrists and ankles enables easy transport. If the victim struggles he will strangle himself. Some victims were buried alive. Previously the Mafia used the *lupara* sawn off shotgun; later they came to prefer the short-barrelled Magnum 38 and 357 with explosive bullets. The Kalashnikov is used for bigger jobs. Poison is a discreet method. Riina was responsible for some 150 killings, of which 40 personally.

Following the arrest of Riina, many *pentiti* came forward since they were fed up with Riina's autocratic and violent rule. In June 2017, the Supreme Court suggested an early release for Riina so that he could 'die with dignity'. Close relatives are now allowed into a mafioso's cell, whilst other visitors must remain outside by a glass window. In 2017 the breakdown of mafia inmates detained under art.41bis is as follows: Camorra 37%, Cosa Nostra 27%, 'Ndrangheta 26%, SCU 3%, others in Puglia 3%, others in Sicily 3%. The highest incidence of mafia crime is in Sicily at 48%, followed by Campania 21%, 17% Calabria, and 6% Puglia. Crimes are committed by 90% men and 10% women, in age groups of 31-60 years at 42%, 23% 18-30 years, 11% 0-17 years, and 6% over 61 years. The total number imprisoned as at 3/2017 was 729, with twelve male sections and one female. [77]

Following upon the car bombings and extensive trials, the Mafia lay low, biding its time. It remained strong in Agrigento province, centre of the international drug trade, and ruled by 32 families grouped into eight *mandamenti* areas where predictably the cult of *omertà* is particularly well entrenched. A young magistrate by the name of R.Livatino had been working in the province, site of ancient Greek temples. Without police protection, he was ambushed and killed. The *Stidde* stars, an offshoot of the Mafia, held sway in Agrigento, often feuding violently with their rivals, especially during 1991-94; and with close links to the Mafia in Palermo and Trapani. They have since appeared in Genoa.

---

[77] Source La Repubblica 3/2017

Libero Grassi owned a thriving pyjama factory in Palermo, employing one hundred workers. Here there existed a tight mesh between businessmen and the Mafia who controlled 180,000 votes. He refused to pay the *pizzo* protection money and not only publicised the situation in a local newspaper, but also denounced the Mafia on television. Furthermore, a secret register *Libro Mastro* was discovered, which detailed *pizzo* extortion payments made by about five hundred local manufacturers and businessmen. Grassi was murdered in cold blood outside his home. Extortion is deeply engrained, of which in 2002 there were 183 cases in Palermo and 104 in Agrigento; and with some 450 reported cases during 1997-2002. Potential victims from all levels of society are enticed into their confidence then trapped into fearful silence: *mafiosità*.

Not all was doom and gloom, since the magistracy did enjoy some degree of success over the years. Following the deaths of Falcone and Borsellino, Gian Carlo Caselli was appointed chief prosecutor for Palermo, staying till 1999. President Cossiga, a man of mercurial temperament, accused him of 'an illness' in his pursual of Andreotti. Caselli came from the Torinese working class, a left-winger yet a devout Catholic like Caponnetto, so a northern outsider which perhaps made him more objective. In 1996, 24 mafiosi were brought to trial, followed by 49 in 1999. 251 life sentences were handed down in 2001-02. In 1999 Caselli was followed by Ignazio de Francisci as chief prosecutor, who restored morale and authority to the legal department. A native of Palermo, he had served with Caponnetto, Falcone and Borsellino, and so provided professional continuity.

In 2002 the Mafioso A.Giuffre was caught. Close to Provenzano *capo dei capi* top boss, Giuffre had been responsible for rebuilding the Mafia after the spate of trials and arrests. Hidden away, Giuffre gave evidence from a secret place onto a court screen regarding the trial of Marcello Dell'Utri accused of association with the Mafia. Giuffre thought it was Dell'Utri who had persuaded Berlusconi to go into politics so that he could protect the Mafia. Unfortunatey Giuffre could not reveal more, since at that time Berlusconi's government passed a law in 2001 imposing a six months' time limit on confessions. A similar situation arose in 2002, when the wife of the magistrate Caponnetto, who took over from Chinnici but was murdered by the Mafia in 1983, requested an extension from Berlusconi's justice minister: he flatly refused, despite widespread support from Parliament and the general public.

Another notable success following the confessions of Buscetta was the running to ground in 2006 of Bernardo Provenzano, who had been in hiding since 1963, thanks to the tipoff given by Giuffre. He had been found near his home in Corleone, as with Riina. He had previously crept away to go to France for a cancer operation, part of which was paid by the Palermo health authority. As *capo dei capi* head of the Mafia, Provenzano had adopted a low-profile policy after the recent activities, putting a stop to the carnage perpetrated under Riina, appointing new leaders of smaller groups for those now imprisoned, with himself managing a tighter knit group based on isolated cells as before. He controlled the rival clans and resumed the traditional approach of operating alongside the state: *avvicinamento*. Provenzano died in 2016 and was replaced by Matteo M.Denaro from Trapani.

With violence on the wane for the time being, sadly the national media in the north lost interest in the South, except for high profile cases. Repulsed by the dreadful car bombings on their home ground, people preferred to forget. Yet under Provenzano it had simply slipped underground, as after the war. Magistrate Ingroia, who had worked closely with Borsellino, lamented that the state failed to take the initiative after the deaths of his colleague and Falcone, that Cosa Nostra was still as strong as ever.

Berlusconi's government sought to divert attention away from the Mafia by addressing the problem of *clandestini* illegal immigrants drifting into Sicily and the island of Lampedusa by boat from North Africa. This priority drew resources away from the police and magistracy, who now found themselves ill-equipped for fighting the battle against organised crime. Berlusconi and his powerful associates rubbed salt into the wound by bitterly criticising the magistrates, accusing judges of prejudice and invention of evidence by the prosecution. Judge Palma commented that people now had only a faint memory of the sacrifice made by Falcone, Borsellino and their colleagues: their heroic stand against evil seemed to have been in vain.

Carpe Diem: The Fight Back

The most effective way to stem mafia crime is to deprive them of their financial lifeline. To this end, a law was passed in 1996, whereby confiscated property becomes an asset of the state, assigning local authorities to designate its eventual use, such as a co-operative, voluntary association or rehabilitation centre. There has been encouraging progress in this direction. Land confiscated from mafia organisations has been transferred to agricultural co-operatives, the first appearing in 2005 in Gioia Tauro in Calabria, site of the ill-fated steelworks, abandoned due to mafia meddling. The young workers grubbed up old orchards to grow chilli peppers, aubergines and olives, aided by a Tuscan organisation which donated machinery and cash. They also produce pasta made from their durum wheat, as well as wine. They make a modest living by selling the products through Libera, a voluntary organisation in Turin, set up in 1995 by the priest Don Ciotti in the wake of the assassination of Falcone and Borsellino. This initiative offers an encouraging sign of the north and south pulling together against the common enemy. Another co-operative in Corleone, in the heart of Mafia country in Sicily, contains land expropriated from the *capo* boss Provenzano. Assets elsewhere have also been sequestered from Riina and Ciancimino. The farm revives the productivity of the land and contributes to the local economy. Fruit farms have also been established. The *Casa dei Giovani* Youth Shelter provides a refuge for drug addicts and ex-prisoners, who work the land in return for a modest wage.

Predictably, the Mafia attack these small and isolated farms, burning crops and damaging machinery. Other worthy initatives suffer from threats. The owner of a tuna processing factory in western Calabria employs armed guards to patrol his business at night to deter the 'Ndrangheta from setting fire to the place; as happened to a clothing business close by. In the same area a farmer was shot and his car set alight: his assassins had demanded payment of the *pizzo* extortion money which he refused to hand over.

Etna valley in eastern Sicily has become a high tech area, having miraculously managed to attract top companies such as Canon, Alcatel, Ericcson, Nokia and Omnitel. ST Electronics, a Franco-Italian group, has established itself in the Palermo area, employing over 4,000 operatives; yet water and power supplies are a problem, with frequent supply interruptions. Municipal authorities struggle to secure payment from users, for instance EAS regional water company has only received two-thirds of the money owed by customers, mainly by town councils. A private bus company sued a regional authority to recover 80mE of arrears. ST took it upon itself to set up a second-high voltage line from the power grid, but managed to persuade the local council to lay water pipes.

A disturbing trend is the gradual creep northwards of criminal organisations, lured by even richer pickings. The trend is partly due to the establishment of two high security prisons in Umbria, central Italy, as part of a post-war policy to move mafia prisoners away from their homeland. As a consequence, relatives of prisoners move into the area to live. In 2014 police arrested 61 people in Perugia (Umbria).

Two investigations unearthed 24 'Ndrangheta *locali* clans holed up in Lombardy, which in 2011 led to 110 arrests, mainly concerned with arms dealing. A third investigation in Piedmont resulted in the dissolution of a town council and 172 arrests. A worrying trend is the muscling in by some 300 Chinese on money laundering in textile firms in Prato, Tuscany. Some 40,000 Chinese live in the area, mostly illegals, working in the sweat shops and sending some E4.5 billion back home during 2007-10.

Moving southwards, in 2014 officials in Rome were arrested for accepting bribes from a waste management company and involving politicians, including Renzi's PD party. In 2015 police raided twenty pizzerias in the capital, supposedly owned by the Camorra, along with three restaurants under the thumb of the 'Ndrangheta. In 2009 it emerged that the Café de Paris in the smart Via Veneto in Rome, with the posh Harry's Bar at the top and just a stone's throw from the Villa Borghese gardens, was a meeting place for the 'Ndrangheta. In 2011, 22 local authorities were disbanded due to mafia infiltration, of which four were in the north.

The 'Ndrangheta may have become a more powerful force than the Mafia, proving a hard nut to crack. Members are thick with drug cartels in Colombia, also Mexico, centred on lucrative cocaine. In March 2019, the police secured an important coup with the arrest of Marco Di Lauro, known as *Il Fantasma* the ghost, one of Italy's four most wanted gangsters. He had been in hiding for some 15 years, close to his home (not an uncommon ruse). He seemed particularly worried about the welfare of his cats. His father's exploits as a member of the Casalesi clan inspired the book Gomorrah (the writer R. Saviano had to go into hiding due to death threats) and later made into a popular film. The Di Lauro clan was involved in the largest drug outlet in Europe, raking in at its peak some 300 million euros a month. Predictably the clan split in half and feuded, with many deaths. The clan, which includes several prominent female activists, has since shifted from drugs to counterfeit and more legitimate business, but remains strong.

In 2010 police arrested Giò Tegano, the most senior mobster of the Camorra, in the regional capital of Reggio Calabria and a key leader during the 1985-91 turf wars, when some 6,000 died. Worryingly the organisation has sprouted gangs with members as young as twelve years old, partly due to the high unemployment rate (90%) amongst the 15-24 age group, and who run amok firing arms. One boss is aged just 16, whose father is in jail over the receipt of funds from drugs. Unsurprisingly, Italy ranks poorly on the EU's index of transparency in international corruption. Hopefully more sophisticated computer software, such as the use of algorithms, will help beat the scourge.

An encouraging development is the increasing resistance to paying the *pizzo*. Extortion exerts power over the victims, who are coerced into hiding firearms and drugs, and keeping silent over crimes witnessed. A hint at compliance is left, such as a bottle of petrol by the victim's premises. One businessman paid out over 245,000 euros over 17 years. In Palermo an organisation called *Addiopizzo* 'goodbye protection racket' are urging businesses to resist paying, display window stickers and report the perpetrators to the authorities. Previously around 70% of commercial outlets paid the pizzo, now there are over a thousand pizzo free businesses; thanks also to the legal interception of telephone calls since 1978. Breaking the cult of *omertà*, the campaign is having the desired effect, with the take on turnover down from 10% to 5%, whilst the crime rate has dropped from 50% during the early' 90s down to 20%, especially since 2014.

In 2015 the Libera group organised a demonstration, the largest ever, in Bologna (where the 'Ndrangheta are present), led by its founder, Don Ciotti. A roll call was read out of the one thousand innocent victims killed by the mafia. He urged P.Grasso, President of the Senate, to oppose the watering down of a new law against corruption. Rosy Bindi, president of the anti-mafia commission and a judge in Berlusconi's corruption cases, was also present; along with G.C.Caselli, former chief prosecutor of Palermo, and the former Prime Minister R.Prodi. This event was followed up in 2017 by President Mattarella's visit to Locri in Calabria, in the bleak Aspromonte area (his brother, a former judge, was murdered by the Mafia) to commemorate the 22nd day of annual remembrance of setting up Libera. Once more, the long list was read out of the victims sacrificed to the criminal organisations, of which one hundred were children, along with many women. Mattarella remarked that the absence of a strong state allowed such organisations to thrive; a comment echoed by Judge Falcone.

The battle to overcome the criminal organisations will continue to be long and arduous. Over the years, the Mafia, a dark force for too long, has been weakened by the wave of arrests and the flow of informants who have come to doubt the validity of the organisation, perhaps tinged by Catholic doubt, and which suggests a greater force than the Mafia. Other measures concern higher level international co-operation, as well as better protection for magistrates; together with improved liaison between police and politicians. However, the risk of the latter's collusion with the enemy of the state will not disappear quickly: 'tis the weakness of human nature, having been endemic for so long and older than the state itself. It is crucial to have greater respect for the rule of law, coupled with the united defiant action between the people and the commitment of the authorities and politicians to fight back and change defeatist attitudes. Falcone compared the Mafia to a human body, with a beginning, a middle and an end: whether it will be vanquished eventually, only time will tell.

Chapter Fifteen
Tangentopoli

Corruption in the form of financial bribery has long been endemic in Italian society. In the 18th century, Bartolomeo d'Aquino and his associates reaped huge profits from farming the duties and taxes of the Neapolitan economy. After the war the banking swindlers Calvi and Sindona made huge fortunes; whilst the Economic Miracle multiplied opportunities for securing lucrative cash rewards, especially in construction. Government officials and politicians were now lured by the apparent ease with which they could profit ever more financially and professionally from the spoils of the state, and get away with it. Previously content with the more modest *bustarella* of cash in an envelope, they now demanded ever greater cash rewards to enjoy a luxurious lifestyle and provide for their retirement.

Over time corruption grew on an increasing scale, reaching a peak in the 1980s during the Craxi era, viewed as a way of life against the background of a vibrant economy and the confident young and upwardly mobile generation who sought ever higher rewards, both materialistic and financial. The system revolved around the awarding of local government contracts which were vital to the livelihood of contractors and subcontractors. In order to secure these contracts, they were obliged to pay a generous *tangente* percentage to government officials and politicians, who met discreetly in clubs, offices, masonic lodges and on the golf course to hatch their illicit deals.

Corruption pervaded all levels of government: local, urban, provincial and regional. Those who refused to oblige were excluded from tender lists and insider information. Payment veered between the classic stuffing of wads of notes into cardboard boxes tied up with string, and collected by the boss's *portaborse* bag carrier; and the more sophisticated route of substantial bank transfers to discreet *paradisi fiscali* offshore havens. It was the sheer extent and depth of the contagion that finally destroyed the system.

An early case concerned Salvatore Ligresti, a wealthy financier from Catania in Sicily who had made his money building shoddy flats in Milan to the tune of some five trillion lire (£2.2 billion). In 1976 Don Salvatore acquired the SAI insurance group from Fiat. He enjoyed close links with Enrico Cuccia, the opaque Sicilian chief of Mediobanca, Italy's major merchant bank. Close to Craxi, during the '80s Don Salvatore was often charged with planning irregularities but always evaded prosecution. The DC prime minister Ciriaco de Mita and his family were charged with siphoning off a substantial sum from the funds totalling 51,000 billion lire assigned to damage repair caused by the Irpinia earthquake in 1980 (the town came within his power base). The Camorra and the Mafia likewise benefitted financially from the disaster. De Mita's brother Michele did well out of road building contracts.

In 1990 the Bonifica services company, a subsidiary of Italstat, a huge state construction company, planned to build a new administrative centre in Reggio di Calabria. A meeting was held in Rome in which the DC politician G.Nicolò and A.Licandro, ex-mayor of that town, demanded a payoff from De Camillis, boss of Italstat. He managed to whittle down the amount of the payoff to 300 million lire (some £120,000). An assistant appeared with a tin box containing the cash, which Nicolò counted outside the office. A third of the monies was earmarked for the Socialist party, another third for the municipal councillors, and with a lesser sum for the small Republican party. Private donations to Italian political parties are illegal, unlike in Britain, but it was not illegal to pay bribes overseas.

Another case involved corruption at the Fatebenfratelli hospital in Milan, concerning the appointment of a consultant by a committee. Candidates paid up to £40,000 in bribes to take part in the frozen ball lottery, whereby one ball holding the name of the favoured candidate wold be frozen so that it could be easily drawn. Judges alluded to a clan mentality, a mesh of acquaintances across the professions and social networks.

Central state corruption, based in Rome, was widespread but scantily investigated, since magistrates hesitated to probe too deeply, or were warned off. Such an attitude was partly due to Italy suffering from a 'blocked' democracy, in the sense that there was no viable alternative to the Christian Democrats, the Communists being quite unacceptable in government. There was no wish to upset the status quo. The few who dared to ask pertinent questions were met with a wall of silence. The *Corte dei Conti* Audit Office was powerless to stem the flow of unabated corruption.

In 1978 Guido Carli, head of Confindustria at the time, tried to push through a Statute for Business to rein in corruption, with enhanced clarity in company accounts and shareholding structure. It was thrown out by Parliament and the business lobby, led by Craxi and his Socialist clan, being seen as too close to home and as an unjustified encroachment on their cosy way of conducting business deals, as well as involving criminal organisations in the South. Paolo Pillitteri, Craxi's brother-in-law and former mayor of Milan, remarked forcefully that those who failed to understand the system were 'cretins who still do not understand how the world goes round'. The PCI, despite a good track record of regional government, was not immune, although Berlinguer asserted that his party was above such things. In 1982 a Communist vice president stated that the average payoff was a modest 3% split between the PSI and DC, with a lesser rate for minor culprits such as the PCI. Smaller parties such as the MSI, Radicals and Greens were virtually immune.

During the Craxi years, the judiciary was on the back foot dealing with corruption, receiving scant political support. Many magistrates turned a blind eye, tantamount to passive corruption, whilst some actually profited from misdemeanours. Michele del Gaudio, a young Neapolitan magistrate keen to serve the state democracy and root out corruption, was responsible for the trial of A.Teardo, former Socialist president of the Liguria region. In 1983 Teardo was arrested, together with his associates, and convicted for corruption over building contracts. Del Gaudio was assisted by his fellow magistrate, F.Granero, and N.Bozzo, a Carabiniere colonel. In an effort to protect the Socialists, Craxi had the temerity to criticise them of political prejudice. They succeeded in convicting the defendant but were transferred elsewhere, at a cost to their careers.

Nepotism, a form of soft patronage involving families (the word derives from *nipote,* referring to the favouritism bestowed by popes on their 'nephews') has long been prevalent. In 1986 Craxi visited China with a retinue of 52 people, accompanied by his family menage of eleven members at the taxpayers' expense. Andreotti was not amused. Furthermore, Craxi assigned a publicity budget of 500 million lire, celebrating the first flight from Malpensa, to Gabriele, the brother of Paolo Pillitteri, city mayor of Milan. As with the Mafia most wives remained discreetly in the background, quietly tending the hearth and home, apparently oblivious to all around them and content to enjoy the spoils of their husbands' work. However, not all women were meekly submissive. Gianfranco Rosci, a DC member of Andreotti's faction, was an administrator at the USL hospital in Rome. Enjoying a luxurious lifestyle, he had divorced his first wife for a younger woman, and had neglected to pay alimony to his former wife. Reporting her ex-husband to the police, she threw 13 million lire out of the window, shouting at the police that she had another 90 million indoors as laundered money brought home by her husband every evening.

A major victory was the un-masking of the payoff racket at the Milan Metro scandal, run by ATM *Azienda Tranviaria Municipale* city authorities. In 1984, whilst the magistrates Antonio Di Pietro and Piercamillo Davigo were investigating a case of fraudulent bankruptcy, a director of that company declared that money had been siphoned off to pay public officials, including the Metro's chairman. Craxi visited the chairman, now in prison, on the pretext of being a close friend and to discuss party politics. His visit aroused the magistrates' suspicions, which were proved right: in 1992 they discovered that Craxi had been a major beneficiary of the missing Metro cash, for which he was convicted in 1996.

Construction of the Milan Metro proved to be a hideously expensive project thanks to the political machinations to steal taxpayers' money. Payoffs were priced at 4-5% for construction contracts and up to a hefty 14% for equipment on the new underground Line Three. The company managers collected the bribery money from the contractors and distributed it to the party bosses and faction leaders, perhaps in an effort to allocate a fair distribution of spoils to assuage their Catholic consciences. A good part of the cash ended up in the pockets of local bigwigs to fund his local citadel for buying votes, jobs and favours; and pocketed for personal gain to lead a high level lifestyle.

The DC received a 20% rakeoff for building Malpensa Airport, whilst the Socialists, as rulers of Milan, took 30%, and their Republican allies 10%; with lesser amounts for the PSDI Social Democrats and PDS (formerly the PCI). Davigo remarked: 'They were like the thieves of Pisa, pretending to argue during the day but ganging up together at night to rob'. Colombo commented: 'If opposition parties are in bed with the governing parties in accepting corrupt payment, what kind of opposition is it?' The politicians cynically retorted that such blatant corruption was the price of politics. Twas a pity they did not expend their energies on governing the country more efficiently.

Towards the end of the 1980s, Di Pietro and Davigo received a tipoff from a state employee concerning the percentage firms had to pay to secure contracts for building prisons, and even having to pay retired staff. Known as the 'golden prisons' affair, the PSI took over a third of the cut, whilst the DC raked off about half, with the rest to the Social Democrats and Republicans. There was also the lesser scandal of the costly 'golden bed sheets' supplied for the overnight sleepers, which forced the head of railways to resign. Local politicians even dared to exact a higher percentage for exceptional works, with taxpayers' money being frittered away on grandiose projects, such as the World Cup Italia 90 at the San Siro stadium in Milan and the 1992 quincentennial festivities for Christopher Columbus. A substantial part of this money funded the high payoffs demanded by the politicians from contractors.

It was the shenanigans at a Milanese old people's home that triggered Tangentopoli: Bribestown. Mario Chiesa was the manager of an old people's home, the *Pio Albergo Trivulzio*. The original hospice was built in 1767 thanks to the generous bequest of the palazzo's owner, Prince A.Tolomeo Trivulzio, one of Milan's leading families. During the 1970s the home came under USL, Italy's new national health service, becoming the city's largest geriatric hospital with a thousand beds. The hospital's president at that time was Mario Chiesa who, in hock with the Socialists, demanded and shared the commission of 5% on building work, up to 10% on materials and as much as 15% on cleaning. Furthermore, Chiesa controlled some 700 votes for Carlo Tognoli, the local Socialist politician and a mayor of Milan, later switching his vote to Craxi's son Bobo (later denied by him), then to Craxi's brother-in-law, Paolo Pillitteri.

Chiesa owned over a thousand flats in the centre of Milan, along with shops and offices. Early in 1992, one Luca Magni was negotiating an industrial cleaning contract with Chiesa worth 140m lire, the latter demanding a cut of 10% which would have halved Magni's profit. So he reported Chiesa to the police, who referred the case to the magistrate Antonio Di Pietro. His suspicions had already been aroused since he had known about an earlier funeral racket at the Pio Trivulzio home, with 100,000 lire being demanded of the undertakers for the burial of each corpse. Di Pietro had Chiesa's telephone tapped and searched his bank accounts, safe deposits and investments. Larger contractors informed him that over the previous five years Chiesa had demanded kickbacks from them. He had in fact received his first payoff in 1974 when working at another hospital.

Di Pietro carried out checks at other hospitals where some heads admitted to paying bribes to obtain business. Di Pietro realised Chiesa was their man.

Di Pietro arranged for Magni to be wired with a microphone in a ballpoint pen and equipped with a camera in a black briefcase, together with ten marked banknotes each 100,000 lire. Magni handed over to Chiesa the agreed sum of seven million lire, being about £3,000, for his half of the cut. Suddenly the police burst in and found Chiesa flushing wads of banknotes worth 37million lire down the toilet. The police discovered that Chiesa had deposited some 12 billion lire (£5 million) in various personal bank accounts in the name of his secretary/girlfriend, who had spoken to the police.

Chiesa confessed he had received substantial bribes in order to further his political career. He had raked off part of the money due to the PSI in order to fund his high lifestyle, and spoke of a cartel operating to block market competition. Political power had become dependent on financial power, with businessmen feeding off a synergy of interests with politicians. Chiesa was sentenced to six years' imprisonment and a six billion lire fine, still leaving him with another six billion upon his release. Significantly, amongst Chiesa's possessions the police discovered a floppy disk containing some 700 names of contacts who had received payoffs. Whilst Chiesa languished in prison Di Pietro spoke to his wife who, wishing to divorce her husband, referred to his Swiss bank accounts.

Now spurned by Craxi, upon further questioning Chiesa revealed corruption at AEM, Milan's electricity and gas utility, which was seeking damages from previous directors for paying bribes: by 1996 the utility had recovered over eight billion lire. Similarly, in 1999 corrupt directors at AEA, Rome's electricity and water utility, were brought to trial, part of the monies having ended up in the hands of criminal organisations.

Another scandal concerned one D.Poggiolini, head of the pharmceuticals department at the Ministry of Health, a major responsibility of regional government and highly prone to corruption. He had siphoned off ten million lire of Treasury bills, part of which was discovered stashed away in a footstool at his flat in Rome. He had also squirrelled away some 120 million dollars in his other homes and 14 Swiss bank accounts. Part of his ill-gotten gains came from approving sub-standard medicines manufactured by drug companies. Poggiolini commented that, like many Italians, he was simply bending the rules a little.

The judiciary now possessed a substantial body of evidence to corroborate what had hitherto been hearsay. Judge Francesco Saverio Borrelli, chief prosecutor for Milan, set up the *Dipartimento* Pool to investigate Tangente. His team, commonly known as *Mani Pulite* Clean Hands, consisted of a core of six magistrates, with Gerardo D'Ambrosio, assistant chief prosecutor, as his deputy, together with the junior prosecuting magistrates Gherardo Colombo, Antonio Di Pietro and Piercamillo Davigo. They were nicely balanced politically, the first two with right-wing leanings and the second two more left-wing. Davigo's first case of corruption occurred in 1979, a year after becoming a magistrate. An IVA (VAT) tax official had secured a bribe of 250,000 lire, worth about a monthly salary for a junion civil servant; also a gold watch from a jeweller for being lenient on his tax inspection. The young man justified his action by stating that all his colleagues were on the take and that his refusal to join in would have prejudiced the security of the group and their livelihood. In 2002 Davigo was appointed a judge in criminal cases at the court of appeal in Milan.

Antonio Di Pietro was born in 1950, near Campobasso in the region of Molise, where his parents were modest farmers. He worked in Germany for a year, sending money home to his mother, to whom he was devoted, telephoning her every day later in life. Back in Italy he worked for six years as an electronics technician for the defence ministry, testing computer guidance systems for warplanes. His computing experience later stood him in good stead in his judicial work. In his spare time he studied law and entered the police force, where he dealt in drug trafficking and fraud. He passed the *concorso* competitive examination for the judiciary, this being a common transition from the police force. He spent a year in Bergamo as an assistant magistrate, preparing cases for the prosecution, and then returned to Milan, where he worked with Judge Falcone, offering an objective and methodical approach. Highly intuitive, Di Pietro was adept at winkling out information from suspects, as indeed was Falcone. In Borrelli's words: 'I gave Di Pietro his head, and he did not fail me.'[78]

Di Pietro's first three cases in the 1980s concerned fraud. With the aid of the computer, he managed to discover that local officials were passing un-qualified candidates from local driving schools. Computer records also helped him detect false names on the USL national health services file, as well as off book donations to a PSI official of 150million lire. He worked principally with Gherardo Colombo, another young magistrate who had been involved in the P2

---

[78] P.Ginsborg p257

affair; also money laundering to secret Swiss bank accounts involving Berlusconi.

There had been occasional cases of malfeasance in the past, as elsewhere in Europe and America. What was now unacceptable was the sheer scale of collusion between politicians, civil servants and businessmen, driven by the relentless determination to secure ever dizzying amounts of cash. The proceeds of Tangentopoli possibly amounted to some 17,000bn lire or £7 billion per annum. During the first year of Tangentopoli, about a thousand people, including one hundred deputies, received *avvisi di garanzia* i.e. that they were under investigation, as per the new Penal Code of 1989, and which implies guilt under Italian law. Magistrates had the power to lock up a suspect for three months (preventive detention) or even up to a year if need be.

The first to be arrested were Paolo Pillitteri and Carlo Tognoli. During the decade up to 2002, over 3,000 people were detained, of which about a third were based in Milan. Here they appeared before the preliminary hearings, which decide whether there is a case to answer. 600 were sentenced by the higher courts through the fast track procedure or plea bargaining *patteggiamento* (where the accused agrees to a financial settlement), introduced to speed up the judicial process and ease prison crowding; whilst under 300 were dismissed for insufficient evidence. A number of cases were dropped by the Statute of Limitations, being out of the time allowed. In regard to the parliamentary culprits, 228 deputies and 93 senators received *avvisi di garanzia*, out of a total of 630. Many requested immunity by the 1945 law, but most were refused. At the height of the *Mani Pulite* investigation some 2,000 accused were incarcerated in the rat infested San Vittore prison in Milan, built in the 19th century, and housing HIV positive inmates. Full to the gunnels, a short spell here worked wonders to tease out confessions. Many festered up to six months, were at last interrogated and then released with no formal charge.

In December 1992, Craxi received his first *Avviso di Garanzia* and was subjected to 17 investigations. His son Bobo was also questioned. Craxi claimed it was a plot to bring down the Socialists, and that he only did what everyone else was doing. Forced to resign, in 1993 he retired to his villa in Tunisia to escape prosecution, where he died in 2000. Over one hundred city councils were disbanded by 1994. For instance, in Varese, north of Milan (near to where I lived) the entire council of some forty DC/PSI officials were suspended, charged with receiving kickbacks amounting to billions of lire: they spent just a few days in the newly built town jail for which they had received payoffs. Gianni de Michaelis, the extrovert Socialist Foreign Minister and known as *Doge* leader from his native Venice, was charged with receiving bribes valued at some $500,000 concerning the construction of a motorway near Venice airport.

The graft grinds on. In 2008 Ottaviano Del Turco, Socialist finance minister in Amato's 2000-01 government, as well as centre left governor of the region of Abruzzo, was accused of receiving kickbacks to the tune of E15 million from Vincenzo Angelini, a private health businessman. Placed in solitary confinement and denied access to his lawyers, Del Turco's defence (according to Angelini) was that part of the money was destined to persuade senators to shore up the centre left government. Angelini claimed to have passed the money over in bags stuffed with banknotes at Del Turco's home, amounting to some six millions euros just for the minister. Another regional centre left leader had told Angelini to pay up, otherwise they could not prevent a hospital inspection. Angelini decided to co-operate with the magistrates and took a tape recorder to register the meetings with Del Turco, and had his driver photograph the cash payments. In 2018 the Bank of Italy withdrew circulation of the five hundred euro banknote in an effort to clamp down on money laundering.

In 2015 *La Repubblica* newspaper interviewed Pietro Ciucci, president of ANAS since 2006, concerning a defective viaduct at Agrigento in Sicily. He denied any instance of bribery, nevertheless he admitted that they were hostages to the companies over tendering for the roadworks. To place Italian affairs into perspective, in 2014 Airbus France admitted to receiving bribes from third party consultants to secure sales, reporting to both the British Serious Fraud Office and its French equivalent. Moreover, the company acknowledged that it may have possibly infringed American regulations on arms exports since it had paid fees to sales agents to win orders. Austro-German authorities are looking into possible bribery over the $2bn sale of Eurofighter jets in 2003. In 2017 Rolls Royce paid a fine of £671 million concerning its alleged involvement in payments to third party consultants to win orders. In 2006 Boeing too was fined $615m relating to corruption over the award of military contracts from the Pentagon.

Tangentopoli involved even greater fish. In 1993 Carlo De Benedetti, key *condottiere* captain of industry, began his career at Olivetti, the blue-chip computer, office equipment and telecoms giant, and which he took over in 1978. The company came under the CIR holding, which also held interests in the

Repubblica and *Espresso* news media. At a shareholders' meeting De Benedetti denied any involvement in corruption concerning the financing of political parties. Yet three weeks later, he appeared before the magistrates, explaining that he had previously refused to pay any bribes but eventually relented in order to protect his business, employees and share-holders. He admitted to contributing some 20 billion lire (£8.5m) to the DC and Socialist parties to guarantee contracts from the Ministry of Posts, a highly competitive sector, and to which he was paying 2% commission in 1988. This enabled him to increase his turnover one hundredfold from two billion lire to 200bnL (£85million) per annum. He explained that he had to prove his worth in the home market in order to attract lucrative Swiss and German export orders which accounted for two-thirds of his business. One has to consider the Italian perception of corruption. Spending just half a day in prison, De Benedetti remarked that he did not feel guilty, but was simply an innocent prey of systemic extortion, which Italians describe as '*concussione*'; as opposed to outright *corruzione* corruption between two consenting parties.[79]

Raul Gardini, another captain of industry, was an international playboy, with an extensive ranch in Argentina and a penchant for large yachts. He married into the Ferruzzi family which had founded a cereal and commodities group. In 1985 Gardini diversified into Montedison chemicals, merging it with Ferruzzi to create an agro-chemical conglomerate and the second largest industrial group after Fiat. Next, he brokered a joint venture with the state-owned chemicals giant Enichem to create Enimont. However, the venture was short-lived and was wound up, with Gardini offloading substantial Ferruzzi debt onto Enimont, which subsequently passed to ENI.

Having incurred immense losses of some $200 million at Montedison from the Enimont merger, Gardini conjured up the ruse of bribing a range of political parties in order to neutralize any combined factional reaction, thereby protecting himself, but which was later construed as complicity. In 1991 he paid out a grand total of thirteen billion lire (about £4,000 milllion). To the DC party he donated 4,750 million lire to the Forlani faction (party secretary); L5,000 million to the Naples faction; and L2,477million to Andreotti's clan based in Lazio/Sicily. He donated lesser sums to the smaller parties: L205m to the Liberals and L300m to the Social Democrats; as well as L200m to the Lega Nord. His ruse discovered, he hung himself in a prison cell shortly before receiving the *avviso di garanzia*,

---

[79] De Benedetti was implicated in the Banco Ambrosiano affair: see Chapter 5.

leaving his empire in smithereens. Shortly after Gardini's death, Gabriele Cagliari, former chairman of ENI, also took his own life.

Even Fiat, king of Italian industry, ranging from cars to defence and aerospace interests, was tainted. By the 1990s, the company employed 250,000 workers plus two million in feeder industries, and accounting for 5% of GDP. The group included banks, insurance, defence and aerospace, along with print media and advertising. Two executives from Cogefar-Impresit, Fiat's construction subsidiary, were accused of paying commission for their involvement in an extension contract for the Milan metro. Fiat denied the existence of a slush fund operating through *paradisi fiscali* offshore tax havens. In 1987 Cesare Romiti, Fiat's forthright MD for many years, and reporting direct to Agnelli (both of whom were not directly involved with any bribery) publicly blamed the system, claiming that Fiat was paying excessive bribes to politicians on many lucrative contracts. He proceeded to issue a code of ethics to employees, forbidding the donation of money or goods in favour of the Fiat group.

In the end, the system blew itself out for various reasons. Business politicians became too greedy and over-reached themselves, thereby creating a momentum for people wishing to speak out and confess. People became tired of the whole affair, perhaps tinged with embarrassment. During the recession that followed the '80s boom, which had partly been financed by the corruption, companies could no longer afford to pay 10-15% in kickbacks, and so refused to pay up. Italy's massive national debt had now reached 115%, bloated by the deep-seated bribery, and which had to be reduced to 60% in order to meet the convergence criteria of joining the Euro in 1999. In 1992 Italy was obliged to exit the ERM system, although devaluation helped exports. The fall of the Berlin Wall in 1989 led to the reunification of Germany, which involved heavy expenditure and a consequent dip in imports from Italy. On the credit side, reunification scuppered the Communist threat in Italy which had created a so-called blocked democracy, in other words no alternative to the perennial centre right DC, and so now loosened up the political stage. In 1992 Italy reached its nadir, with the assassination of Judges Falcone and Borsellino by the Mafia. Judge Borrelli, a realist, commented that Tangentopoli altered little since corruption persisted. Fabric being woven into the Italian fabric.

Chapter Sixteen
Interlude: Post Tangentopoli

This period shows the usual series of short governments, but with a more professional approach. Following his fall from grace in 1992 as prime minister, Craxi put forward three Socialist candidates: G.De Michaelis, the extrovert foreign minister till 1992, C.Martelli[80], deputy PM under Andreotti, and Giuliano Amato, Treasury Minister during the late '80s. Exercising his constitutional prerogative, President Scalfaro chose the latter. Born into a Sicilian family living in Turin, Amato taught constitutional law at Rome's La Sapienza University during 1975-97. He served as Under Secretary in Craxi's Council of Ministers (Cabinet) during 1983-87. His administration was the first of technocrat styled governments, strong on finance, with six professional 'new men' as ministers. Amato set about dealing with the national finances which, with the budget deficit standing at 10% and public (national) debt at 103% of GDP, were way over the limits imposed by the EU's Convergence Criteria of respectively 3% and 60%; and with inflation at 7%. These figures raised a question mark over Italy's tenure in the narrower upper band of EMS currencies. Ratification of the Maastricht treaty was under threat, since Denmark had voted against it, and with France hovering. Within a week of taking office, in an effort to improve the public finances Amato authorised spending cuts and tax increases to achieve savings of 30,000 billion lire. Many people realised the importance of the EU to Italy, and so resigned themselves to the austerity measures.

The tighter currency band brought into play stiff constraints on the Italian economy, leading to the ERM Exchange Rate Mechanism crisis in 1992. That

---

[80] In fact Martelli had to resign as Justice Minister owing to revelations about his involvement with the P2 masonic lodge, as well as receipt of $7million paid into a Lugano bank account by the rogue banker Calvi on behalf of Craxi.

year high inflation in Italy, well above the EU average, caused speculators to sell off the Lira, despite support from the Bank of Italy. They also bought heavily into the Deutschmark which had shot up in value, due to the reunification of Germany in 1989, which demanded a high level of public expenditure. This brought about a 10% rise in German interest rates to combat the consequent hike in inflation, and which in turn forced the Italian rate up to 12%. The Italians imposed a 7% devaluation on the lira, and with the Bundesbank offering support; yet all to no avail, though exports and tourism benefitted. In Britain the Bank of England tried desperately to shore up sterling. On 17th September 1992, the lira exited from the ERM, with a consequent devaluation, stabilising at around 15% of its previous value (and later dropping to 25%). Sterling had left the previous day, known as Black Wednesday. The ERM crisis sent shock waves through the Italian economy. That month saw a low take-up of BOTs Italian treasury bonds, a major source of state funds, so the Bank of Italy bought in heavily to maintain public confidence. Furthermore, there was a strong withdrawal of cash from personal bank accounts.

In his 1993 *Finanziaria* annual budget Amato again drastically reined in public spending, and raised taxes to save over 93,000 billion lire. Using decrees to reinforce the urgency of the situation, he imposed cuts in health and social insurance; a new tax on house ownership, and a minimum tax for the self-employed. That year, Italy fell into recession, albeit experienced elsewhere in the EU. A more positive area was the start of privatising the public sector entities IRI, ENI, INA and ENEL in an effort to introduce greater efficiency, bring in much needed cash into the nation's coffers, as well as break the decades-long political meddling by becoming shareholding companies; and supported by Confindustria. Sales involved RAI television, Alitalia/airports, motorways, Telecom and Finmeccanica. Rosy Bindi, health minister, endeavoured to improve the performance of USL, the national health service. Significant reform also concerned public administration, introduced by decree law and against widespread opposition; and long overdue since Napoleon set up the system. Contracts were now subject to private administrative law, which ended the long era of jobs for life, and with sacking now allowed. Public offices now stayed open in the afternoon and trade union power reined in; but softened with performance related pay.

A welcome innovation was the direct election of city mayors, which was popular with voters, and which would prove a useful stepping stone to central power, for instance Veltroni and Rutelli. Notably Antonio Bassolino, the left-wing mayor of Naples from 1993, revitalized its historic centre, though the city remained heavily infiltrated by the Camorra. Rosa Jervolino was elected mayoress of Naples, the first woman to hold such a post. Italsider's old steelworks at Bagnoli became a park and seaside resort.

A notable success was Amato's agreement concluded with the trade unions CGIL, CISL and UIL, Confindustria and the government to renounce the *scala mobile,* the hallowed safeguard of workers wages since 1962. B.Trentin, the Communist CGIL leader, was instrumental in securing this major post-war victory, although predictably there were significant street protests. This measure would ease pressure on the public finances, raise international confidence in the Italian economy and restore membership credibility in the ERM.

Having weathered a challenging administration, Amato's government was finally brought down by the fallout from Tangentopoli (he had been viewed as Craxi's man, although not directly involved in the scandal). In an effort to stem the contagion he, together with G.Conso, minister of justice, in April 1993 issued four decree laws to depenalize the illicit financing of political parties, downgrading the offence to a purely administrative one; and allowing plea bargaining for bribery and extortion which would help businessmen avoid prison. This provision would shift control of the police away from the magistrates to the government. The public response was total uproar at the politicians trying to save their own skins. Borrelli, chief of the Mani Pulite team, naturally opposed the leniency. Sensitive to public opinion, President Scalfaro (who had previously favoured an amnesty) refused to sign the decrees, thereby upholding the will of the people.

In March 1993, Andreotti had been issued with an *avviso di garanzia* placed under investigation by Gian Carlo Caselli, chief prosecutor in Palermo, for association with the Mafia, and likewise the following day to Antonio Gava, former Interior minister, for association with the Camorra. Following the assassination of Judges Falcone and Borsellino in Sicily, Amato despatched 7,000 troops. It was a busy time, since in April 1993 a referendum was held regarding changes to the voting system proposed by the Sardinian, Mario Segni, son of a former president and who had formed the centre left *Patto* Pact party. 75% voted (a 50% minimum is needed) of which 83% called for change. The pace did not slacken.

Ciampi's Caretaker Government 1993-94

Once more, it fell to President Scalfaro to nominate a new prime minister to replace Amato. He designated Carlo Azeglio Ciampi, a Tuscan by birth and wartime partisan. Governor of the Bank of Italy since 1979, he was strong on finance and economics. A keen European, over the years he had become highly regarded both at home and abroad. He was also sensitive to social issues. Notably Ciampi's administration included professional ministers, as with Amato's, which rendered it relatively faction free, since they were more interested in serving their country than feathering their own nests. Ciampi's technocrat government included three ministers from the left-wing PDS, also F.Rutelli from the Green party who took the relatively new portfolio for the environment, and who was later mayor of Rome. Ciampi was immediately confronted by the refusal of the Chamber of Deputies to lift parliamentary immunity on Craxi and three other ministers so that they could stand trial in Milan for corruption. Fortunately the PDS and Greens forced the issue by demanding the resignation of all four, which they duly did.

Ciampi considered his main success to be the accord on labour costs in 1993, following on from Amato's ground-breaking abolition of the *scala mobile*. A new incomes policy was set up which eased inflation; together with regular meetings between the trade unions, Confindustria and the government. Ciampi continued Amato's reform of the civil service, now under the aegis of S.Cassese, who achieved savings of some 2,500 billion lire. He moved briskly to produce a charter of public services; transparency and simplification of administrative procedures and *autocertificazione,* whereby citizens could declare their civil status without recourse to time-consuming procedures to obtain certified certificates. He drew up a Code of Behaviour for civil servants which would interface with EU regulations. During his tenure of office Ciampi quietly worked towards meeting the Maastricht criteria in preparation for the common Euro currency. Lastly, Ciampi sold off two banks: BCI Banca Commerciale Italiana and Credito Italiano.

Finally, Ciampi's government enacted the people's desire for electoral change. Segni proposed changing the voting system from total proportional representation (with the voter choosing four candidates) to the British style FPTP first past the post majoritarian system, in order to create a tighter political spectrum. There was a 62% turnout, of which 96% supported the abolition of multi preference voting which had given rise to much vote rigging. Henceforth,

75% of the Senate and S. Cassese Chamber of Deputies would be elected by the FPTP system, for which 707 single member electoral colleges were created. The balance of 25% remained as previously under proportional representation. Female deputies remained scarce but Rosy Bindi, health minister, became Speaker of the Deputies; and later followed in that role by Irene Pivetti.

Chapter Seventeen[81]

Berlusconi

Early Years

Silvio Berlusconi was born in 1936 in Milan. In 1943 his father took refuge in Switzerland to escape the Germans. During this period his mother worked as a secretary at Pirelli to make ends meet. Berlusconi attended the Liceo Sant'Ambrogio, a religious boarding school in Milan, where he did well in Italian and the classics. He already showed signs of being an extrovert, self-assured, a smooth talker and popular with the girls. He graduated in law at Milan University, where he met Bettino Craxi, winning a prize for his thesis on advertising contracts. He joined forces with his university friend Fedele Confalonieri (who later managed the Fininvest group) to entertain cruise holidaymakers, with Berlusconi as singer.

Attracted by the post-war property boom, Berlusconi went into partnership with P.Canali, who owned a small building firm. They set up CRM Cantieri Riuniti Milanesi, and obtained a small mortgage from the Rasini bank, a small family credit institution, in order to buy a plot of land west of Milan's city centre. Berlusconi's funds came from his previous earnings as a singer, together with money from his father who had returned to the Rasini bank after the war. Berlusconi managed both the financing of the building project and the bureaucratic requirements. They sold off plan with buyers paying instalments as work progressed.

Boosted by the success of their first venture, in 1963 they embarked on another project at Brugherio, in the upmarket Brianza area north east of Milan. Berlusconi set up Edilnord, a limited partnership in which he was a working partner; and with capital funded by a private Swiss company FFR *Fin für*

---

[81] I am indebted to David Lane for the legal and financial information contained in this chapter and elsewhere on Berlusconi.

Residenzen, registered in Lugano. Ownership of the shares and name of the nominee director were not disclosed. The project proved disappointing, partly due to lack of public transport. In 1965 he married Carla dell'Oglio, by whom he had a son and a daughter. In 1990 they separated and Berlusconi married the actress Veronica Lario, by whom he had two daughters and a son. He bought the Manzoni theatre where he met her.

In 1968 Berlusconi embarked on the Milano 2 project of creating a garden city located in Segrate, east of Milan towards Linate airport. Again the land was purchased through Edilnord, headed up by Berlusconi's brother Paolo, and which received additional funds from A.I.R., a Swiss Company in Lugano whose owners were anonymous. Completed in 1979, the development proved popular with young professionals, and for which Berlusconi received a knighthood, with the title of *Cavaliere*. He pressed on with a third project, Milano 3, a mixed residential-office development south of Milan, but it proved disappointing partly due to its location.

Tireless as ever, Berlusconi now set his sights on the publishing world. In 1977 he took a 12% share in the unprofitable newspaper *Il Giornale*, taking full control in 1999, and later splitting the equity 51:49 between himself and Fininvest. In 1992 he sold the newspaper to his brother Paolo to avoid a conflict of interests under the new Mammi law (see below). In 1991 Berlusconi took control of A.Mondadori, Italy's foremost publisher with nearly a third of the book and magazines market, as well as school textbooks and quality titles such as Einaudi. Magazines included the ever-popular Panorama and women's *Grazia*. The battle with Mondadori caught the attention of the anti corruption magistrates in Milan (see below).

Another new venture for Berlusconi was his entry into the world of television. In 1973, in tandem with his brother Paolo, he set up Telemilano which broadcast locally via cable for his Milano 2 development, linked to a central antenna to minimise the blight of television aerials. He bought up other local stations throughout Lombardy which, with Telemilano, merged into Canale 5, the largest private station. By 1980 he controlled over 1,300 local stations, with his Mediaset television company based in Milano 2. He built up an extensive film library which was highly popular, with its American drama such as Dallas and Dynasty; also the British MI5 series 'The Professionals'. Berlusconi signed up stars such as the likeable quiz presenter Mike Bongiorno, an American by birth. Berlusconi achieved high audience levels for the transmission of football matches; whilst his news channels were considered more professional and with superior content to those of his rivals. His media empire was now second only to Bertelsmann in Germany. In 1980 Berlusconi purchased Italia 1 from the Rusconi publishing house, followed by Rete 4 from Mondadori; and bundled with lucrative advertising contracts.

In 1976 the Constitutional Court had decreed that private television should be allowed to transmit locally since there were sufficient frequencies available, and which led to a mushrooming of local channels. Parliament demurred, unconvinced. Not content with being limited to local broadcasting, Berlusconi retaliated by having copies prepared of master tapes for all his local stations, along with advertising, which gave the appearance of national broadcasting. RAI state television looked on askance at Berlusconi's invasion of their monopoly. Part of the spoils system *partitocrazia,* RAI 1 came under the control of the DC, RAI 2 under the Socialists, and RAI 3 under the Communists. Their factional in-fighting prevented them from presenting a united front to the newcomer, who now rivalled them with a similar audience and advertising share, the latter coming under the control of his Publitalia company set up in 1982.

Matters came to a head in 1984, when three magistrates from Turin, Rome and Pescara ordered the blackout of Berlusconi's three 'national' channels, pronouncing them illegal. Craxi promptly nullified the Court order, bypassed Parliament and issued another decree allowing the resumption of his friend's channels, including pre-recorded programmes; as well as for all other private stations. Craxi also proceeded to place one of his men, the Socialist E. Manca, as chairman of RAI to muffle opposition from that quarter. One month later the Chamber of Deputies rejected the decree as unconstitutional. Undeterred, in 1990 Craxi bamboozled Parliament into accepting the decree, to which the governing parties acquiesced; only to again be stopped by the Constitutional Court. The upshot was the Mammi law, to which again Parliament rose up in opposition. Craxi threatened to pull out from Andreotti's coalition; whereupon the PM advised his deputies to support the new law, which was duly approved; although there was strong opposition from the DC coalition deputies, and with the resignation of five cabinet ministers. Mammi confirmed Berlusconi as the king of television and in control of 60% of its advertising. In 1996 his TV business was floated on the Borsa stock exchange.

In 1985 Berlusconi descended onto the football field, acquiring AC Milan, founded in 1899, and which was on the verge of bankruptcy. A keen football fan

274

like most Italians, and which offered him light relief from business and political affairs, he turned round the club by using Fininvest money to improve the management and acquire better players. The club went on to impressive results, winning the Italian league in 1987-88 and European Champions' Cup in 1989; but it continued to struggle financially. Furthermore, the venture was blotted when Milanese magistrates came across an illegal payment in 1992, concerning the transfer contract of a player from Juventus in Turin (arch rival to AC Milan and owned by Gianni Agnelli) for 18.5 billion lire. This proved to be an early clash for Berlusconi with the law. As chairman of AC Milan he was charged with false accounting and sent for trial. Although the chairman of the Turin club admitted to receiving over ten billion lire, Berlusconi and his co-defendants were acquitted in 2002. This arose from Berlusconi's first government changing the law in 2001 on false accounting, decriminalising some offences as well as limiting the conviction period i.e. statute barred thus out of time. In 2017 Berlusconi sold AC Milan to a Luxembourg sports company for 830million Euros.

Toghe Sporche:[82] **Mondadori, IMI-SIR and SME**

This section concerns three commercial cases, in which Berlusconi endeavoured to influence the verdicts to his advantage, and illustrates the lengths to which he would go to exert pressure on judges to ensure a favourable outcome. Furthermore, the cases reveal the antagonism and difference in degree of probity between the Roman and Milanese judges. They also throw light on the financial traffic between Italy and Switzerland.

In 1988, Berlusconi and his arch rival Carlo De Benedetti, joint owners of Mondadori publishing at that time, each made a bid to gain control of this major publishing group. The Formenton family, descendants of the publisher's founder, Arnoldo Mondadori, agreed to sell to De Benedetti, then switched their sale to Berlusconi. Legal arbitration upheld De Benedetti's claim, but an appeal court in Rome, for which one of the judges was V.Metta, overturned this decision and upheld Formenton's sale to Berlusconi.

Magistrates Gherardo Colombo and his female colleague, Ilda Boccassini, had been piecing together a convoluted money trail involving Swiss banks. Lugano, with a population of some 30,000, is just one hour from Milan by train. It was a hive for SOE operations and other foreign agents during World War

---

[82] Besmirched Robes

Two. The charming town has long been popular with wealthy Italians wishing to squirrel away their money, licit or otherwise, into discreet Swiss banks. *Spalloni* bag carriers would be hired to take cash there. During the 1960s/70s strict exchange control regulations were in force to underpin the weak Lira, so businessmen began to employ more subtle methods of exporting capital, such as over-invoicing imports or under invoicing exports. In 2001 Berlusconi's government introduced the *Scudo fiscale* law: a tax shield to enable Italians to repatriate assets anonymously. As a result, some 55 billion Euros were returned (the currency was introduced in 1999) of which 60% came from Lugano, and out of an estimated 500 billion Euros stashed away there.

The magistrates' investigation involved All Iberian, an offshore company in the Channel Islands which was used as a shell company by Fininvest for the clandestine movement of monies. All Iberian was owned by G. Foscale, MD of Fininvest and Berlusconi's cousin. The banks were usually told not to mention the instructing party. Thanks to assistance from the Swiss authorities, the magistrates had found evidence of Judge Metta having received funds from Fininvest and so wished to place him on trial.

The magistrates discovered a circuitous route of cash movements during February 1991. All Iberian had an office in Lugano which received c.4.6 billion lire from Libra Communications, yet another of Fininvest's offshore companies. The next day All Iberian proceeded to credit c.3 billion lire to the Ferrido account used by Fininvest at a bank in Chiasso; and which sped onwards to the Mercier account held by Previti with a Genevan bank; whence 1.5bnL was moved to a Luxembourg bank for a company account linked to Judge Acampora. 425mL were later moved from the Luxembourg bank to Previti's Mercier account, whence sums of 225mL and 200 mL were paid into an account held by Judge Pacifico with another bank in Lugano. Pacifico withdrew two cash sums of 225mL and 300mL. He was alleged to have passed 425mL to Judge V.Metta, who possibly intended the money for the purchase of an apartment for his daughter. Metta enjoyed a close relationship both with Judge Acampora and Previti.

SIR *Societa Italiana Resine* was owned by Nino Rovelli, a powerful industrialist. His business empire collapsed towards the end of the 1970s with colossal debts of over 3,000bn lire (£1.3m). In 1982 Rovelli sued IMI *Istituto Mobiliare Italiano*, a major state investment bank, for having refused to honour pre-agreed loans. In 1986, at a court in Rome Judge F.Verde ruled in Rovelli's favour, but in 1990 Judge V.Metta in the appeal court overturned the judgement in favour of IMI, awarding 1,000 billion lire to Rovelli; later confirmed in 1993 by the supreme court of appeal.

IMI paid up but pursual of the case by the magistrates had thrown up murkier dealings concerning substantial transfers of clandestine money by the Rovellis to various judges. In 1991 Rovelli's wife and son (Nino Rovelli having died that year) transferred 1 billion lire from a bank account in Zurich to Judge Pacifico's bank account in Lugano. He withdrew 450million Lire in cash, having previously transferred 133mL to a bank in Bellinzona under Rowena Finance, a Panamanian company owned by Judge Squillante, a former legal adviser to Craxi. Pacifico also transferred 133mL lire to Previti's bank account in Geneva.

In 1994 Mrs Rovelli and her son executed a second transfer of funds. They sent 29m Swiss Francs CHF to Pacifico's accounts in Switzerland and Liechtenstein; also 18 millionCHF to Previti's account in Geneva. Previti eventually admitted that the money was for his professional fees, and so was liable to taxation. That same year the Rovellis forwarded 11m CHF to Judge Acampora's accounts. In total they had transferred around 58millionCHF to the three judges between March and June 1994 (c.67 billion lire). It seems that this sum was a debt owed by Nino Rovelli to the three judges. Evidence showed widespread telephone and personal contact amongst the defendants. The two cases would be heard simultaneously since some of the accused were implicated in both.

Tangled Pasta

The third case concerns the SME and Buitoni food companies, in which De Benedetti was once again locked in a legal battle with Berlusconi over SME. Originally in the electricity sector, SME became a pan European food conglomerate, with up to 15,000 employees. In 1985 De Benedetti, who already owned the prestigious Buitoni group, entered into a contract with Romano Prodi, chairman of IRI, to take over SME, which was part of IRI the state controlled corporation, and so subject to political meddling. Craxi, prime minister at the time, put pressure on Prodi to revoke the deal, and encouraged his pal Berlusconi to have Previti organise a counter offer through IAR, a bidding vehicle which included Barilla, another major pasta manufacturer. In the end, Judge Verde blocked the acquisition of SME by both parties.

Magistrates, who happened to be investigating Barilla's business affairs, discovered that just after rejection of the Buitoni case, Barilla had transferred 750m lire from a Zurich bank to Judge Pacifico's bank account in Bellinzona; from which a week later he apparently executed a transfer of about 200m lire to Judge Verde for his account at the Bank of Rome. In 1988, just after the appeal court judgement, one billion lire was transferred from Barilla to Pacifico, whilst Previti's account in Geneva was credited with 850m lire. Judge Squillante received 100m lire from Pacifico into his Lugano account. Significantly 434,404$ reached Previti's account from the Chiasso bank of All Iberian (see earlier); whence it passed through two transit accounts, then into Previti's account, and onwards to the Rowena business account of Judge Squillante.

Blocking the Course of Justice

Having received scant satisfaction from the Milanese courts over the SME case despite employing an army of lawyers, Berlusconi, now prime minister (2001-06) and Previti decided to have the SME trial transferred to the more sympathetic jurisdiction of Brescia east of Milan, although it was ill-equipped for such work. In March 2002 they had a bill proposed by Cirami, a Sicilian magistrate and deputy for Agrigento province (where he had turned a blind eye towards the devastation of the environment by the Mafia). Cirami's eponymous bill proposed that, in order to guarantee a fair trial, and where there existed 'legitimate suspicion' of a prejudiced court, defendants could request a transfer of jurisdiction. Such a ruse would mean starting the trials *ab initio,* playing for time in which to throw up semi-legal obstacles. Berlusconi's cronies pushed through the bill during the summer holidays, hoping to slip it through unnoticed. Surprisingly, the Senate's Speaker, just one step below the president and ostensibly apolitical, agreed to waive through the bill, resorting to all night sittings. In September 2002, the presiding judge suspended the trials of the SME case involving Berlusconi, together with the IMI-SIR and Mondadori cases since the same defendants were implicated.

Many senators objected to the bill, including an elderly lady senator, recipient of a Nobel prize. S.Passigli, an opposition senator, declared that the bill 'is the exploitation of legislative power in the private interests of the PM and Previti to escape from the trials in Milan.'[83] The centre left were dissatisfied with the bill nor, interestingly, were former supporters of Berlusconi, who now began

---

[83] D.Lane: 'Berlusconi's Shadow' page 188

to drift away from his circle. V.Dotti, a prominent Milanese corporate lawyer involved with Fininvest for the period 1980-95, and previously FI leader in the Chamber of Deputies during Berlusconi's first administration in 1994, wanted to prevent the 'devastation of justice'. MPs questioned the independence of the government in this matter. F.Mancuso, an elderly Sicilian FI deputy and previously a magistrate at the Ministry of Justice, presented a lengthy document suggesting that Previti was applying pressure on Berlusconi over the bill, but the Speaker of the House would not allow his comments to be placed in the official archives. In desperation, Pecorella, Berlusconi's man and Chair of the Judicial Affairs Committee, threatened to dissolve Parliament if the bill were not passed.

The CSM magistrates' governing council, having grown wise to *Il Cavaliere*'s machinations, were concerned as to the precise definition of 'legitimate suspicion', which could favour organised crime. Furthermore, the suspension and transfer of trials would lengthen them even further, sapping confidence in the judicial system. The upshot was that five CSM members from Berlusconi's political party, House of Freedoms, boycotted the CSM meeting so there was no quorum to continue. Back from their holidays in September, Romans took to the streets, outraged at Berlusconi's manoeuvring to save his own skin. Demonstrators included Borsellino's sister Rita, the playwright Dario Fo and his actress wife Franca Rame. In the Senate's final vote some twenty senators were recorded on video pressing the voting buttons of absent colleagues: the Speaker claimed that parliamentary procedures had been properly observed. The bill was passed back to the lower house.

Nano Moretti, film director, organised a vigil to urge Ciampi to reject the Cirami bill: it became law that same night. Inexplicably Ciampi signed, as later with the *Rogatoria*. Fudging the issue, the Supreme Court referred the matter to the Constitutional Court who, ten days after the Cirami law was passed, opined that the existing law already covered legitimate suspicion and so in fact the Cirami bill had proved superfluous; thus a waste of parliamentary time and public money. The trials remained in Milan. Berlusconi haughtily declared that Parliament alone could judge him.

Since legitimate suspicion had been insufficient to secure victory in his legal battles, in June 2003 Berlusconi now hit on another blocking tactic, driving through changes in the law on parliamentary immunity covering five prime state positions, in order to give him protection from criminal proceedings whilst he was in office. Having always been allowed to freely express their opinions, prior to 1993 deputies were not liable to criminal proceedings except in cases of *delicto flagrante*. This legal arrangement was prompted by Mussolini's tendency to prosecute opponents on trumped-up charges. For instance MPs refused to lift the immunity on Craxi who was charged with corruption. When almost 200 MPs were placed under *avviso di garanzia* concerning Tangentopoli, the judiciary seized their chance to amend the law. In 1993 the Amato government passed a law whereby magistrates no longer required Parliament's consent to start proceedings against deputies; but they did now require its permission to access correspondence and telephone calls.

Pending the outcome, the presiding judge suspended all Berlusconi's trial proceedings. The general public and protest groups such as *Girotondi* and *Liberta & Giustizia* were again up in arms. Yet the Constitutional Court still had a card up its sleeve. In January 2004, the court declared that the new law violated the constitutional right that all Italians were equal before the law and thus had the right to defend themselves, including Berlusconi. He had secured a pyrrhic victory: the trials would resume shortly.

In April 2003, the three Milanese judges, led by Rossato, (who had heard the preliminary hearings regarding the summary of evidence in 2000) at long last delivered their verdict on bribery of judges in the Mondadori and IMI-SIR cases. The hearings had taken over three years to wend their way through the courts, having commenced in November 1999. The court ruled in favour of the prosecution on the charge of corruption. IMI was awarded damages concerning corrupt judgements of 516 million Euros; whilst CIR, De Benedetti's holding company, received 380millionE. Judge Verde, close to Previti, was technically absolved of guilt for lack of proof, but the presiding judge dismissed him as a 'judge on the payroll'. Judge Metta received a 13-year prison sentence, whilst Judge Squillante received 8.5 years. Sig.ra Rovelli was sentenced to 4.5 years and her son six years. Pacifico was sent down for eleven years. Judge Acampora, just for the Mondadori case, was granted the shorter procedure since he pleaded guilty, and was sent down for 5.6 years. Previti received an eleven-year sentence for bribing judges both in the Mondadori and IMI-SIR cases. The magistrates consulted F.G.Stevens, an eminent lawyer for the Agnelli family, and who had represented counter parties to Fininvest, for his valued opinion of Previti. He denied all knowledge of the man. When Previti threatened to sue him Stevens reiterated his earlier statement. [84]

All charges were dropped against Berlusconi of having bribed Judge Metta on the Mondadori case, since his liability was now barred by the legal niceity of the Statute of Limitations (due to the length of time having elapsed) which he had hastened to enact upon becoming PM in May 2001. Another reason given was that indirect bribery via an intermediary does not qualify as an offence. Other mitigating circumstances were Berlusconi's decision to split Mondadori with De Benedetti, together with his responsibilities as leader of a political party and as a major businessman. For the same reason, he was let off the hook over the All Iberian case, although technically he was guilty. He was not involved in the IMI-SIR case.

Concerning the SME case, in November 2003 Judges Verde, Pacifico and Previti were cleared on charges of corruption due to insufficient evidence. The court of appeal was obliged to drop the charges against Berlusconi since his case was now statute barred. Concerning magistrates Boccassini and Colombo, they became embroiled in a smear campaign, accused of exceeding their brief, but were eventually cleared of professional misconduct.

London Link

This incident throws interesting light on the different approach between the workings of English and Italian justice. In 1996 the Serious Fraud Office SFO in London had been approached by the Italian judiciary to assist in an extensive fraud relating to secretive offshore operations, concerning the removal of some 100billion lire from Fininvest for possible illegal use. The relevant documentation, previously kept in Switzerland, was now in the possession of CMM (Carnelutti Mackenzie Mills) Corporate Services, an Anglo-Italian law firm based in London, acting on behalf of Berlusconi and his close associate F. Confalonieri, president of Fininvest since 1991. Fearing that the incriminating documents would be spirited away, SFO had obtained a search warrant. Berlusconi and Confalonieri submitted a request to the Queen's Bench Division of the High Court in London to prevent the transfer of the incriminating documents back to Italy.

---

[84] F.G.Stevens was assigned the unenviable task of defending the Brigadist Renato Curcio.

The British judges took a dim view of the plaintiffs' objections and manoeuvres. In a four day hearing, Lord Justice Simon Brown, in consultation with Mr Justice Gage, brushed aside Berlusconi's claims of unfair treatment by the Italian judiciary for political reasons: in their opinion the Italian magistrates were acting in a professional and unbiassed manner. In conclusion the judges ruled against the submission, the case being dismissed a week later by the House of Lords appeal committee (Britain's highest court of appeal) barring further action by the plaintiffs. Justice had been upheld.

David Mills, co-partner in the Mackenzie Mills' practice and married to Tessa Jowells, British MP and cabinet minister, received $600,000 via a hedge fund from the Swiss bank account of a company registered in the British Virgin Islands, an offshore tax haven. Apparently, he had assisted Fininvest set up an off the books web of offshore companies, as later revealed in Berlusconi's trials. Italian magistrates questioned Mills, who asserted that the money had come from another client, D.Attanasio, but the latter denied the deed. In 2009 Mills was sentenced to 4.5 years' imprisonment, on charges of bribery relating to Berlusconi's affairs.

Into Politics

With the old guard parties of the DC and PSI in disarray following the Tangentopoli débacle, Berlusconi perceived a void in the political spectrum. A number of Italians spoke of a Second Republic given the drastic political changes, together with the introduction of the majoritarian voting system; yet technically Italy is still in the First Republic. But it proved to be a false dawn since people were soon disillusioned. Berlusconi saw his chance to set up a right-wing counter force to create a new look government and apply his Midas touch to turning round the Italian economy. He was encouraged by his close colleague Marcello Dell'Utri, MD of Publitalia advertising company; whereas Previti and Letta were dubious about entering the political field. Perhaps the business tycoon viewed the late entry of a new party on the political scene as a marketing ploy to capture the majority of the electorate.

Treating politics as an advertising campaign, Berlusconi called upon the services of a senior manager who worked at Fininvest and Standa, a key department store he had purchased in 1988, to organise telephone market research to see how the electoral land lay. A poll of some 20,000 people indicated that many were tired of the old guard tainted by Tangentopoli, and that 75%

wanted a new face and a strong man to govern the nation. To this end Berlusconi set about harvesting the talents of some 60 managers and regional bosses from Publitalia, making use of their networking system to recruit suitable parliamentary candidates. Some 4,000 local business people were selected, which were whittled down to 276 parliamentary candidates. Even a former boss of Saatchi, Roberto Lasagna, was recruited as a campaign manager, and later became a senator. He commented that they had filled a 'market niche'.

In January 1994, the new party appeared: *Forza Italia* Come on Italy!, adopting a populist football cry to curry favour with ordinary voters. In fact the name had previously described a wartime Fascist group. Berlusconi now brought on board Publitalia's sister company, *Programma Italia,* organising a political induction course for its team of financial consultants, who were in touch with the general public. Adopting the concept of football clubs, FI clubs were set up, the first being in Brugherio, site of one of Berlusconi's building projects. Italians were dazzled by the new face of politics. At rallies, Berlusconi's persona and fine words galvanised people: almost overnight he transformed Italy after the woes of Tangentopoli.

Berlusconi's next task was to cast around for suitable allies to widen his electoral net to trawl sufficient votes. Tangentopoli had thrown up an array of new political parties to choose from. It was a time of reappraisal for the DC. Having held the country together for half a century, only to disintegrate under Tangentopoli, the DC was recast by Mino Martinazzoli, adopting its former name of *Popolari.* Another new party to appear was Leoluca Orlando's anti Mafia *La Rete* which was doing well in the South. The highly acclaimed magistrate, Antonio di Pietro, saviour of Tangentopoli (for which he had suffered a smear campaign) had launched a new party *Italia dei Valori.* The new centre left PDS *Partito Democratico della Sinistra* was led by Achille Occhetto, who had defeated Mussolini's grand-daughter in Naples. *Forza Nuova*, a new far right party, later appeared in 1997.

Berlusconi proceeded to make overtures towards Gianfranco Fini, leader of the post Fascist *Alleanza Nazionale* AN (National Alliance), formerly the MSI run by Mussolini, and which had since languished in the political doldrums. AN's traditional strongholds were based in Rome and Naples, where in the 1992 elections its leader G.Almirante had secured 5% of the vote. During the early '90s much internal bickering ensued between the radical Pino Rauti, hostile towards America and capitalism, and the more moderate Fini, Almirante's protégé, who turned out to be quite a success story. Following Tangentopoli Fini took 47% of the vote in the municipal elections in Rome, appealing to a large section of Roman society, but he lost out to the popular left-winger Rutelli with 53%. As with Berlusconi, Fini portrayed an attractive image and was a fluent speaker on television, which helped to boost his party's vote: indeed in 1994 Fini topped the opinion polls. In February 1994, Berlusconi and Fini, both to the right of the political spectrum, agreed to hitch their wagons together in the *Polo del Buon Governo* PBG Alliance of Good Government.

Berlusconi's other ally was quite a contrast to Fini. Umberto Bossi, gruff and down to earth, was the leader of *Lega Nord*, an umbrella group of regional independence groups that appeared in 1991. Formerly the *Lega Lombarda* based in Brescia and Bergamo east of Milan, and extending to Padua and Venice as *Liga Veneta*, all strongly Catholic/ex DC areas, the party took its name from the medieval League of communes that in 1176 defeated the Imperial army of Frederick Barbarossa at Legnano just north of Milan, and which is celebrated annually with a politico-historical pageant. A former rock singer, salesman and laboratory technician, Bossi advocated federalism, hoping to create the northern state of Padania. In the 1987 elections he was elected as a senator for Varese, Lombardy. Many admired Bossi's straight talking: many of the people I spoke to at the time supported him.

Bossi's party supported the self employed and small businesses, who were tired of seeing their hard earnt money being taxed by *Roma ladrona* thieving Rome to subsidise the South, and from where many came north to seek work. Lega Nord also resented the arrival of immigrants *extracomunitari*. He dismissed the European Union as 'a nest of freemasons and communist bankers'. Both Bossi and Berlusconi promulgated the importance of family values (ever a vote winner for all parties). Yet a black mark stood against Bossi: in 1995 he was charged with the illegal financing of Lega Nord, since in 1993 his party treasurer, A.Patelli, had been arrested for having received 200million lire from Enimont. Berlusconi and Bossi struggled to get on with each other, presenting an incongruous duet: the suave showman beside the abrasive Lombard. Nevertheless they agreed to stand together in the *Polo della Libertà* Freedom Axis, in tandem with Fini's party, demanding liberation from state bureaucracy and high taxes.

Election campaigning began in earnest in January 1994, with Berlusconi taking full advantage of his grip on Italian television by bombarding his screens with some thousand publicity 'spots' over the next ten weeks as if he were advertising a brand new product. Using state of the art mass communication techniques, in January 1994 he had his personal video beamed over his television channels as well as RAI. Using simple language, he proclaimed his wish to help the country and improve the functioning of the state. His all-inclusive manifesto proclaimed his intention to improve the economy by reducing taxes and bureaucracy, and creating a million jobs. He spoke of upholding Catholicism and western democracy against the left-wing parties, especially Communism; although it was on the wane since the fall of the Berlin Wall in 1989, and the rise of the more liberal Mikhail Gorbachev. 'We must create for ourselves and our children a new Italian miracle': fine words which went down well. Women fell for his salesman's charm, whilst men envied his wealth, power and success. All had to be stage-managed, with image being paramount to his success: Berlusconi avoided open-ended interviews with unprepared questions, and took exception to being heckled in public. He was also fussy about lighting.

The elections in March 1994 were the first to be held under the majoritarian (first past the post FPTP) system promulgated by Segni's referendum for the single preference vote. The triple alliance of FI/AN/LN polled 43% of the votes which gave them 58% of the Chamber of Deputies, being 366 seats out of a total of 630. FI was the largest party, polling 21% of the vote, doing well in the north, though less than Berlusconi's personal polls had predicted: many middle class voters held reservations about his conflict of interests as a businessman and politician. Half of his voters were female, along with many youngsters and self-employed, such as shopkeepers and artisans, whom he had wooed during the campaign. FI also acquitted itself well in the European elections shortly afterwards. The Alliance did less well in the Senate with 49%, since only over 25s can vote for the upper chamber, and representing 156 seats of the total of 315. 27% of FI parliamentarians were businessmen, with 28% lawyers and doctors; and with Publitalia supplying 50 deputies.

Second in close position was Occhetto's centre left PDS with just under 21%, doing well in central Italy. One third of its support came from the progressive liberals such as teachers. Fini's AN did remarkably well, standing in third place with 13.5% of the vote (compared to 5% in 1992), picking up many former DC voters in the South. As expected, Lega Nord performed nicely in the north, securing just 8% of the votes but which constituted the largest party with 118 deputies thanks to Bossi's stiff bargaining. *Rifondazione Comunista* RC fared reasonably with 6%, especially in Genoa with its strong working class element in shipbuilding. FI held Sicily against the newcomer *La Rete*: perhaps because the Mafia had persuaded voters to support Berlusconi in the hope of currying favour with him, since he had criticised the anti-Mafia magistrates. The Catholic rump of the *Popolari* took 11% of the votes, securing seven seats. Smaller groups such as the Greens predictably fared more modestly, whilst Segni's *Patto* party gained 5%. In short, Parliament presented a new look after this election, with 70% of the deputies and 60% of the senators as newcomers, and with 29% as professional politicians. Yet despite the new voting system, Parliament remained highly fragmented, reflecting the inherent individualistic nature of the Italians.

A Taste of Power

In his first address to Parliament in May 1994, Berlusconi laid out his government's programme to create new jobs and reduce employment costs; as well as encourage investment and privatisation, which appealed to the business/financial sector, as well as Bossi. Yet he backtracked since Fini preferred the power fiefs such as Mediobanca to control the economy. Not surprisingly the state civil service opposed attempts at reforming their comfortable working life. Berlusconi took the opportunity to praise the magistrates for their valiant efforts in fighting corruption in public life.

Yet no sooner had Berlusconi installed himself at Palazzo Chigi than he had his justice minister, A.Biondi and FI member, prepare legislation extending greater leniency towards suspects and criminals, substituting house arrest for imprisonment. Amato had attempted a similar process but backed down in the face of strong public opposition. Suggesting a hint of leniency, the decree was quickly dubbed *salvaladri* save the thieves, since it obliged magistrates to advise people they were under investigation; whilst those suspected of financial crimes such as false accounting, corruption and extortion would no longer be retained in custody. This was an open door for those flouting the law: within days some 3,000 people were released from prison, many of them involved in Tangentopoli. Extradition procedures ground to a halt. Berlusconi had tried to appear inclusive in the election campaigning but, once in power, he proved to be autocratic, just like Craxi and Mussolini, trying to run a country as if it were a business, coupled with his twisted sense of priorities.

Issued at the height of the summer holidays Berlusconi had hoped to slip through the Biondi decree almost unnoticed without opposition. But within days there were mass protests, for instance in Milan, with 75% of Italians opposed, together with Bossi's Lega Nord. Magistrate Antonio di Pietro appeared on television to criticise the decree. Berlusconi was now swiftly grounded, with his Minister of the Interior, R.Maroni, on the point of resigning; and with Bossi threatening to withdraw his support (also because he had lost votes in the north to Berlusconi). Fini demurred, waiting for developments. By July Berlusconi was obliged to drop the decree in order to hold the alliance together and stay in power, his administration now sorely dented.

Events moved in quick succession to bring about Berlusconi's downfall. The crunch came when he proposed in his September 1994 budget to raise 50,000 billion lire from spending cuts and taxation, partly by reducing workers' pension benefits, yet granting concessions to the self-employed sector. As a result, some five million trade unionists took to the streets, of which 1.5 million protested in Rome; and with the support of Bossi. Against the backdrop of a falling lira, Berlusconi was forced to climb down and accede to trade union demands.

In November 1994, Berlusconi was hosting a United Nations summit meeting in Naples, basking in the international limelight, away from the bustle of party politics and populist criticism. Whilst hobnobbing with fellow world leaders, he received an *avviso di garanzia* i.e. that he was under investigation for corruption. Foreign office officials and diplomats had been at pains to paint a rosy picture of their master, wrestling to present his conflict of interests and embroilment in legal disputes. Berlusconi acknowledged that he had made illegal payments to the GdF *Guardia di Finanza* financial police, but as a victim of *concussione* (an argument used by De Benedetti for his involvement in Tangentopoli). The following month, Bossi, now a force to be reckoned with, and who now referred to Berlusconi as *Berlukaiser,* withdrew his party from the PBG coalition, and so the government promptly fell apart after only seven months in power. It was not an auspicious start to the business tycoon's political career.

Chapter Eighteen
Centre Left Interlude: Prodi

Following the fall of Berlusconi's first brief government, President Scalfaro again exercised his prerogative to appoint another caretaker government under Lamberto Dini. A Roman by birth and an economist by profession, he was Berlusconi's Treasury minister and a former general manager of the Bank of Italy. Dini was supported by Bossi; the centre left *Ulivo* olive tree coalition led by Romano Prodi, along with the CCD and CDU, offshoots from the old DC. Massimo D'Alema, another Roman and leader of the former Communist party, also lent his support to Dini, since he was keen to break with the party's Communist past and present a more modern image, thereby appealing to a wider electoral base. To that effect, the party was now known as PDS *Partito Democratico Socialista*. It was the first time the Communists had enjoyed power since Togliatti participated in post war governments. The PCI rump, *Rifondazione Comunista* RC, was led by Fausto Bertinotti, who took over from Achille Occhetto.

During his brief tenure, Dini managed to persuade the trade unions to accept the pension reforms and tax increases previously rejected under Berlusconi. Dini proposed to finance inflation-linked pay rises through a drop in subsidies for health, rail, post and roads; as well as freezing new staff appointments in the public sector and reducing overtime pay. However he increased funding to the South and family benefit for the poor. Dini pressed on with Amato's and Ciampi's programme of privatising the major state organisations, which poured much needed cash into the nation's coffers; though Alitalia resisted his efforts to contract out its catering and bag handling. Given the existence of over a thousand banks, many of which were small and linked by cross-holdings to industry, tax breaks were awarded to encourage bank mergers to improve economies of scale and profitability. Dini also cracked down on the perennial tax evasion.

Fresh elections were held in April 1996, in which the centre left Ulivo coalition of Prodi and D'Alema's PDS won by a small margin, with a strong majority in the Senate, thanks to the new FPTP uninominal system (voting for just one candidate instead of four) despite polling fewer votes than the centre right; but dependent on the Communist RC rump in the Chamber of Deputies, that party having secured 9% of the votes. A minimum 4% of the votes are needed to sit as a deputy. The PDS became the largest party in the coalition, having made a good showing in the central 'red belt', gaining 21% of the vote. Next was Forza Italia FI with just under 21%, in coalition with AN and CCD/CDU. Fini had changed the MSI name to *Alleanza Nazionale* AN to distance the party from its Fascist roots, thereby securing a respectable 16%, better than in 1994 and which now made it the third force. A small MSI rump was led by Pino Rauti. The Popolari (former DC) was left with 7%; whilst the CCD-CDU took 6% and Dini 4% centre left. Forza Nuova now represented the far right flank.

Defiant, the Lega Nord stood alone and gained 10% of the vote, taking many votes from the centre right FI. The magistrate Antonio Di Pietro did not stand for election, since he was being investigated by the Brescia *Procura* Public Prosecutor's Office, involving some opaque goings-on, but he was not charged. He joined the Ulivo and later set up his own party *Italia dei Valori* Italy of Values. The government's slant reflected a surge to the centre left across Europe: Jospin in France, Schroder in Germany, Aznar in Spain and Blair in Britain. Prodi's administration was the first centre left government since the war, and the longest tenure until his rival Berlusconi's during 2001-06.

Following upon Berlusconi's bumbling efforts at governing, Prodi's administration, the 55th government since 1945 (against Britain's twelve, though the Italians include reshuffles) was like a breath of fresh air, offering a more professional approach to the business of government. Dini served as his foreign minister. A native of Bologna and an economist by profession, and so known as *Il Professore*, Prodi was a former president of IRI. During 1982-89 he had sold off 29 companies, the largest being Alfa Romeo; along with Finsider steel and Finmeccanica. In 1997 Dini, now Prodi's foreign minister, sent troops to Albania to quell the unrest, whence 14,000 refugees sailed to Italy. In 1990 C. Martelli and G. Napolitano had passed the first law to tighten immigration.

The jewel in Prodi's crown was his handling of Italy's entry into the EMS/Euro system in January 1999. A staunch Europhile, Prodi viewed the EU as Italy's lifebelt; as indeed did many Italians. Since the ERM crisis in 1992, when the Lira was forced out of the Eurocurrency system (see earlier), a two tier Europe had emerged. The stronger northern economies, led by Germany and the Netherlands, advocated a strong adherence to the convergence criteria, backed by Hans Tietmeyer at the Bundesbank, and Theo Waigel, Germany's Finance Minister. Chancellor Helmut Kohl was more emollient, intent on the grander European canvas. They were sceptical about Italy's commitment to reducing welfare and pension costs to rein in the stubborn public debt; combined with an historically unstable lira and which, with Spain and Greece, represented the Mediterranean EU. President Chirac sniffed at including Italy in the upper tier owing to her lack of performance; but his Socialist successor, Lionel Jospin, welcomed Italy, and who acted as a counterweight to Germany.

With Italy at a low ebb in European circles, against a background of the Tangentopoli fallout and a stagnant economy, Prodi began the stiff climb back to financial rectitude. He vigorously set about knocking the parlous economy into shape to meet the EU convergence criteria, with its maxima of 3% on the budget deficit (currently 6.5%) and 60% on the public debt deficit (124%). Prodi reduced inflation from 3.9% to under 3% but still well above the EU average of 1.5%. However, in the light of the ERM crisis, the Maastricht Treaty had been amended by article 104c(2) to allow some leeway in meeting these figures, provided that the excess was definitely diminishing. Prodi created a fiscal adjustment of over 32,000 billion lire, plus a progressive Eurotax, aimed at the wealthier, of some 13,000 billion lire which, combined with spending cuts, brought in some 60,000 billion lire to the nation's coffers. In 1997 Prodi introduced the 35 hour week to appease the trade unions over his austerity programme; and liberalized shop hours and licences. Berlusconi organised a rally in Rome objecting to Prodi's economic measures.

Fortunately, Prodi was supported by Ciampi as his Treasury minister who, thanks to his invaluable input, had Italy readmitted to the ERM club in November 1996. Prodi also received immense support from D'Alema, PDS leader, and Walter Veltroni, deputy PM and member of the Ulivo; along with the leaders of the three trade unions who had convinced their members to support the PM's austerity measures. Aware of the greater good, Fausto Bertinotti, leader of the RC rump, refrained from upsetting the apple cart. In return, Prodi wisely resisted the temptation to tinker with pensions and welfare. Boosted by his success at the recent polls, Bossi threw a spanner in Prodi's works by again flexing his secessionist muscles for Padania. The threat was averted by the irresponsible antics of a few individuals who occupied the *Campanile* in Saint Mark's Square, Venice, for which they were duly arrested, and which put paid to a more serious espousal of the independence cause.

By 1997, of the fifteen countries waiting at the Euro gate, five had reached the 3% budget deficit maximum, with another eight making good progress; but with Italy and Greece lagging behind. Italy's public debt was still too high (also in Belgium). Yet in the interests of European unity, some flexibility was allowed, and so she was welcomed into the Euroclub; further assisted by vigorous lobbying from Emma Bonino and Mario Monti, keen EU commissioners. Britain, Sweden and Denmark abstained from joining. Prodi's fear of a run on the lira never transpired. Italy had come a long way since 1945. The EU leaders had sensibly fused idealism with reality to ensure its continued existence.

In 1998 Prodi was abruptly brought down to earth by a loss of confidence by just one vote thanks to RC, who refused to agree to his economic measures. He was replaced by D'Alema and appointed President of the European Commission, though he would have preferred to stay in Italian politics. He had his revenge: D'Alema's reign was brief since two years later he had to resign owing to poor regional election results, to be succeeded by Giuliano Amato. During 1981-2007, Italy was served by 16 prime ministers, as against four in Britain.

Back at the helm, Amato's brief second administration during April 2000-March 2001 continued with Cassese's reforms, now under the aegis of Franco Bassanini, a technocrat and member of the DS, having resigned from Craxi's party. The civil service was decentralized to regional and local level except for national functions such as foreign and monetary policy. Administrative reform simplified budget procedures, reduced the number of central ministries based in Rome from 18 to 12, with cutbacks in staff, such as at the finance ministry, and with some move towards taxation at regional and local level. Senior officials now came under review and were subject to transfer. Procedures were simplified and accelerated for the benefit of the general public. The installation of *sportelli unici* single counters were introduced for a third of Italian communes (local councils) covering 70% of the population. This innovation rolled into a single procedure the setting up of a business entity (previously involving 43 steps), with swifter confirmation of enactment, and vastly reducing paperwork. Nevertheless, the reforms remained very legalistic, as anyone dealing with the Italian authorities will attest. In 2013 Amato was appointed to the Constitutional Court.

Chapter Nineteen
Back Again: Berlusconi

Out of the Limelight

By the 1990s, Berlusconi was the richest man in Italy, worth 22,500 billion lire (c.£7.5bn) covering the Fininvest and Publitalia companies. Yet financially he was in a bad way, his business empire having reached a hiatus, overstretched and mired in huge debts, much of it short term, of some 840 million lire according to an audit in 1983 by Arthur Andersen; and rising to 4,500bn lire by 1992. Berlusconi was awarded the honorary title of *Cavaliere*, yet he was viewed by the *salotto buono* business establishment as a parvenu, cold shouldered by the likes of Agnelli, De Benedetti and Cuccia, the latter being the *eminence grise* of the Italian business world since the war. His pal Craxi had been charged with corruption, which left Berlusconi increasingly vulnerable to criticism of his media monopoly. As financial and judicial investigators probed ever more deeply into malfeasance, Fininvest came under heavy pressure, with Berlusconi fearing for his questionable business dealings.

In 1994 Berlusconi took the decision to spin off his television and advertising business from his private company, Fininvest, into a new public subisidiary, Mediaset, and which would promote his political career. He organised a rights issue of 1,800bn lire (c.£650m) for Mediaset, of which 10% was taken up by German business, 6% by South Africa/Netherlands and 4% by a Saudi prince. Nominated board directors, they were accorded control over Mediaset in order to ring-fence Berlusconi's asset trading. A television referendum revealed overwhelming support for his retaining a majority interest in order to keep the company in Italian hands.

In 1996 Berlusconi organised a television advertising campaign to sell off 288 million shares of Mediaset, as well as a further 145m shares offered from 29% of Fininvest's holding in the company. The sale raised 990billion Lire (c.£350m) for the company's coffers, and with a similar sum for himself. Finally, he floated his Mediolanum insurance business on the Milan Borsa. Set up in 1984, the company had grown rapidly, moving into banking and private pension funds, with a sales network comprising some 6,000 agents by 2000; as well as operations in Austria, Germany and Spain. Since Mediaset had now become a public company, together with Mondadori, Berlusconi was legally obliged to declare his financial interests. By 1999 Berlusconi was out of the woods, having succeeded in placing Fininvest on a more secure financial footing, and ready to campaign for the next election.

Berlusconi's second government 2001-06

Against a background of tortuous legal trials, Berlusconi's second election campaign, following the fall of Amato's caretaker administration, was run under the banner of the centre right coalition *Casa delle Libertà* CL House of Freedoms, harking back to his previous catchword. His allies again included, albeit reluctantly, Bossi of the *Lega Nord* and Fini's AN; also UCD/CCD. Very much a re-run of his previous campaign, Berlusconi's manifesto reiterated the mantra of tax cuts, now sugared with the proposed abolition of gift and inheritance taxes, which appealed to the middle class. Berlusconi further proclaimed reform of the civil service, education and health, together with an increase in the monthly pension to a million lire (c.£320) to satisfy the public sector workers. New public works jobs would be created to reduce unemployment, especially high in the South. The most original idea was the building of a bridge across the Messina Straits to link Sicily with the mainland (still under discussion at the time of writing, the project forms part of a grander rail express network stretching across Europe to Malmo in Sweden). The coalition would be tough on crime and clandestine immigration. His buzzwords remained liberty and choice, which appealed to the business and financial world. Predictably he vowed to curb the power of the magistrates, which upset law-abiding citizens. Solely his face appeared on posters; whilst his Autobooklet was sent to all Italian households.

Berlusconi had long been subjected to criticism, levelled at his autocratic style of leadership, creating a top down party and peppered with too many Fininvest managers doing his bidding. There was little grass roots involvement which voters had expected from the FI clubs. Eventually bowing to pressure, Berlusconi appointed Previti, his defence minister and business confidant, as party co-ordinator. Yet this proved to be a smoke screen offering little effective local power since Berlusconi continued to rule as chairman, smug in his strong electoral support.

Berlusconi profited from disproportionate airtime, even on state television, to the disadvantage of his centre left opponent Francesco Rutelli. Yet he refused to participate in a television debate with his rival, perhaps because his rival presented well on the media and would have put the media king on the back foot. A former mayor of Rome and supporter of NATO, Rutelli was now leader of the *Ulivo* OliveTree coalition (Prodi being now based in Brussels) and in charge of the *Margherita* Daisy party, which campaigned in coalition with D'Alema's DS. Bertinotti, leader of the Communist RC, stood alone; as did the magistrate Antonio Di Pietro with his new *Italia dei Valori* party; also Emma Bonino's Liberal party, former EU commissioner. Tellingly, during the campaign the Economist newspaper weighed in, supported by *Le Monde* and *El Mundo*, by blazoning on its April cover 'Why Silvio Berlusconi is unfit to lead Italy'[85], owing to his legal trials and overlap of interests in business and politics. Berlusconi sued *La Repubblica* (owned by his arch rival De Benedetti) for publishing much of the Economist critique, but the Court dismissed the case. Indro Montanelli, the eminent journalist writing for the independent *Corriere della Sera*, heartily endorsed The Economist's stance.[86]

Berlusconi bounced back into power, his FI/AN/LN coalition taking 46% of the vote with 367 seats in the Chamber of Deputies: FI 196, AN 99, UCD/CCD 40, LN 30; others two. The Ulivo secured 248 seats, being 44% of the vote; and with *Forza Italia* as the largest party with 29% of the votes, against 17% for the Ulivo. With the House of Freedoms holding 177 seats in the Senate, Berlusconi boasted a strong majority in both houses, having performed well in Lazio and Puglia, and particularly in Sicily. The Margherita/Ulivo coalition secured 14.5%, performing well in Basilicata and Campania, in part due to Antonio Bassolino who was the popular left-wing mayor of Naples. AN with 99 seats dropped from 16% to 12%; similarly the Lega Nord with 30 seats from 10% to 4%, having lost out in the Veneto. In the local elections held at the same time, the centre left Veltroni became mayor of Rome, whilst the very first female mayor, Rosa Jervolino, was elected in Naples. The Communist RC gained 11 seats, whilst Di

---

[85] Written by David Lane

[86] A public garden in Milan is now named after Montanelli.

Pietro's party secured one seat. In 1999 FI had joined the Christian Democrat division of the European People's Party EPP in the European Parliament.

Berlusconi's outright victory at the 2001 elections raised suspicions of Mafia assistance in the South (with a third of the population). He had taken all 61 of the first past the post seats in Sicily, split between 41 deputies and 20 senators; thereby representing 37% of the island votes, making Forza Italia the largest party there. FI had replaced the DC as co-ruler in Sicily, with its promise of jobs and cash in exchange for votes. Indeed the FI clubs on the island had been subject to Mafia influence since their inception. In 1993 the Mafioso S.Cancemi, *capo mandamento* area chief in Palermo, advised the *carabinieri* of 'important people' having been involved in the assassination of Falcone and Borsellino; and alluded to exploratory talks between top financial managers at Fininvest and V.Mangano. Imprisoned twice for drug trafficking, Mangano was Cancemi's man at Berlusconi's villa in Arcore, Lombardy. In depositions made to Judge Tona in 2002, four other Mafiosi confirmed the links between the Mafia and northern businessmen.

L. Bagarella, an important Mafioso on the run, charged T.Cannella, one of the four informants who had sheltered Bagarella, with the task of setting up a new party, *Sicilia Libera.* Ostensibly in the cause of independence for the island, it would act as an intermediary between the politicians and the Mafia to give the latter a legal patina, as well as to ease pressure on investigation into their affairs. However this scheme was nipped in the bud by the emergence of FI. Totò Riina, *capo dei capi* top boss, had been casting around for a fresh political source to cultivate in order to cramp the authorities' war on the Mafia. E.Cartotto, a journalist, revealed that Marcello Dell'Utri, MD of Publitalia, had spoken of the need for finding 'new political reference points' for Fininvest. Thus a synergy of interests arose between FI and Cosa Nostra: a new version of the status quo ante with DC clientelism. To this end, in 1990, Riina dispensed with Mangano's liaison services at Arcore to deal direct himself with Berlusconi and Dell'Utri, proclaiming: 'I have Dell'Utri and Berlusconi in the palm of my hand and this is good for Cosa Nostra'; and naturally expecting some recompense. F.Giuffrida, a senior official at the Bank of Italy, provided evidence in the Dell'Utri case. He had earlier delivered information regarding Berlusconi's financial operations.

Cancemi's evidence led to Berlusconi and Dell'Utri being placed under preliminary investigation for their alleged involvement in the assassination of Falcone and Borsellino. In 1996 Dell'Utri was already placed on trial for complicity with the Mafia thanks to evidence culled from telephone tapping, bank documents and eight of his diaries for the period 1984-93: a careless habit for such a person. Dell'Utri's brother was also involved. At the trial, the informant A. Giuffre disclosed on a secret video link that the Mafia were keen to join forces with FI, and that Provenzano, Riina's deputy, had ordered the Sicilians to vote for FI. Giuffre was prevented from revealing further information due to a law introduced under Berlusconi's government imposing a six month time limit for such disclosures. Nine months before Giuffre gave his evidence, Judge Tona (involved in Berlusconi's trials) strangely declared that Borsellino had been eliminated as a 'precautionary measure'; and furthermore rejecting the evidence of Giuffre, Cancemi and other Mafiosi as being unreliable. Based on this contorted reasoning Tona dismissed the case against Berlusconi and Dell'Utri.

In December 2004, Dell'Utri was given a nine year prison sentence by Judge L.Guarnotta, one of the four members of the original anti-Mafia pool in 1984 and who wound up the Mafia maxi-trials. Dell'Utri was also convicted of fraud to the tune of eleven billion lire (c.£3.7 million) perpetrated during 1988-94, part of which he had used to rebuild his villa by Lake Como. Despite his protests he was obliged to relinquish his seats in the Chamber of Deputies and the European Parliament.

Back in power, with his charm and gift of the gab, *Il Cavaliere's* first parliamentary speech proclaimed respect for rules and plans to extensively modernize the country. Yet the glitz soon wore off. Set against the backdrop of his legal tussles, his second tenure as PM was at best lacklustre, devoting most of his energies to battling in the courts, at the expense of neglecting the economy which was in severe difficulties. Contrary to his electoral promises, as in his previous administration, he imposed heavy budget cuts, with higher costs for medicines, refuse and local transport, which did not go down well with the electorate.

During his second term of office, (the first post-war administration to run to a full term) the economy stagnated, mired in massive debt borrowing, with sluggish growth averaging around 0.7%pa, well below the EU average; and with high inflation. Public debt stood at 106% of GDP thanks to a bloated public sector; with a 4% budget deficit, well above the EU's 3% ceiling in the Stability Pact; and weighed down by a heavy pensions burden, being 15% of GDP. Unemployment stood at 9%, the highest in the EU, exacerbated by rising labour costs which made it increasingly difficult for family SMEs to compete with cheap imports from Asia and China, coming in through the ports of Genoa and Trieste, and which hit traditional sectors such as textiles and shoes, also white goods which had been a key player in the Economic Miracle.

In 2001 Berlusconi introduced the *scudo fiscale* tax shield to encourage the anonymous repatriation of illicit assets held abroad (see earlier). Perhaps with an eye to self-interest, Berlusconi resorted to amnesties on taxation and foreign exchange in an effort to balance the books, but this only pushed the PSBR (Public Sector Borrowing Requirement) up from 1.8% to 2.3%. Eurocrats were not impressed. As ever, to avoid loss of popularity, Berlusconi shelved problems rather than bow to market discipline. He had promised to continue Dini's sell-off of state organisations, but the plans now lay in the doldrums. Finally, many were put off by his contempt for justice, with his stinging attacks on the magistracy. Anyone hoping for a serious approach to the business of government was sorely disappointed. In 2006 he reinstated the PR proportional representation system which facilitated vote rigging.

One of Berlusconi's few achievements was the introduction in 2003 of short term contracts, which allowed employers to circumvent article 18 of the 1970 Workers Statute, and decreed the right to reinstate a long term/permanent employee if they were unfairly dismissed. Such a provision made it virtually impossible to sack workers and hindered youngsters from climbing onto the job ladder; further aggravated by the scarcity of jobs. His other success was the introduction in 2004 of new pension rules, to come into force as from 2008, which lifted the retirement age from 57 to 60, and with a lower pension for those who retired earlier. The intention was to raise the retirement age every three months; whilst rising for females from age 60 in 2014 to 65 by 2026. 14 billion euros would be poured into private independent asset managed funds to further lift the state burden on pensions, which accounted for 14% of GDP at the time.

Berlusconi encroached even further on state television, his vanity piqued by those who dared to criticise him. For instance, Enzo Biagi, the well respected writer and journalist, accused the great man of going into politics to save his business empire and avoid arrest. A similar comment was uttered by Prodi. Many at RAI, especially TG1 and TG2 news channels, bowed to the PM's hegemony, broadcasting favourable programmes of him and his cronies; although the traditionally Communist TG3 offered a more balanced view. Berlusconi meddled with RAI board appointments, with contracts not being renewed. Since

RAI's inception it has been said that whoever runs RAI runs the country. Two directors resigned under pressure in protest at the lack of editorial independence. In an effort to reduce the PM's hold on the media, the Constitutional Court had decreed that his Rete 4 channel should cease broadcasting after 2003. Berlusconi proceeded to steamroller through the Gasparri bill to circumvent the decision. Thankfully, President Ciampi had the sense to block it, one of his reasons being that such a scenario would lessen choice of news source. Berlusconi arrogantly refused to read the President's ruling. Italians sensibly began to consult the foreign press for more impartial reporting of their national affairs.

Berlusconi's army of lawyers were further kept busy by his intention to gag opposition from the print media, of which he already owned *Il Giornale*. The independent *Corriere della Sera* had closely reported the trials of the PM and Previti, so he tried to silence it: in 2003 the editor resigned in protest, only to see Agnelli acquire its ownership. Berlusconi's machinations mirror those of Roberto Calvi, the corrupt banker who in the 1980s also tried to control *Corriere*. He was a member of the P2 masonic lodge; as indeed was Berlusconi.

Legal Problems Anew

There are many lawyers in Italy, especially in the South. The profession is well remunerated and much in demand. Berlusconi decided that the best way to solve his legal problems was to pack his own men, criminal lawyers by profession and now FI deputies, into a parliamentary legal team. They included G. Pecorella from Milan and N. Ghedini from Padua. They had defended Berlusconi in his bribery of judges' cases. Both sat on the deputies' justice commission, with Pecorella as chairman. The commission included A. Mormino from Palermo who specialised in defending Mafiosi. M.Saponara from Milan, who had defended Previti on charges of bribing judges, was now FI leader on the constitutional affairs commission. He had previously served on the judicial affairs commission, of which 13 members out of the total 44 were FI members: an arrangement which dovetailed nicely to press their master's suit. Saponara also worked on the deputies' smaller legislative committee whose chairman was E. Trantino, a Sicilian lawyer defending the Mafioso M. Dell'Utri. The dual role of these men as deputy and lawyer to promote Berlusconi's cause gave rise to a moral conflict of interests between the legislature and judiciary, which the post-war Constitution had endeavoured to keep separate; albeit not a technical conflict according to the eminent lawyer F.G.Stevens. Once in power, instead of directing his energies to governing the country, Berlusconi busied himself with sorting out his legal entanglements.

A major task for Berlusconi was to clear himself of false accounting, a crime which formed the bulk of the magistrates' work in Milan, and which served as a useful key for sorting out more serious offences such as bribery and extortion. Berlusconi's first case in 1997 concerned false accounting over the acquisition of the Medusa film company, involving ten billion lire of illicit funds. Berlusconi protested his ignorance of such a transaction; nevertheless he was sentenced to 16 months' prison, but was later acquitted by the supreme court of appeal. Berlusconi was also embroiled in the recruitment of a footballer for the AC Milan team owned by Fininvest; as well as the SME and Mondadori cases 2001-3 discussed earlier. Businessmen have habitually kept various sets of accounts to evade detection, which lack of transparency worries their foreign peers, showing Italy in an unfavourable light and discouraging inward investment.

To this end, Berlusconi's team, directed by Pecorella, drew up a parliamentary bill, downgrading false accounting from a criminal to a civil offence. The maximum prison sentence was reduced from five to four years for stock market companies and to three years for non listed firms. To rub salt into the wound the new law would allow false accounting for up to 5% of pre tax profits or 10% of net assets. Furthermore the crime would become statute barred after seven years for listed companies instead of 15 years and 4.5 years for non-listed, so magistrates had less time to prepare a case. This revision got Berlusconi nicely off the hook over the footballer case and with a similar charge in the SME case. Crucially, magistrates would no longer be able to avail themselves of telephone tapping facilities. Magistrate G.Colombo opined that the amended law was contrary to the 1968 EU directive, which applied penalties for non compliance. Berlusconi had made nonsense of the judiciary, considering himself to be above the law.

Berlusconi's younger brother Paolo was also enmeshed in legal irregularities. In 1979 *Guardia di Finanza* GdF finance inspectors had carried out an inspection at Edilnord, Berlusconi's construction company and of which Paolo was managing director. Accused of bribery, Paolo confessed to the crime but which his lawyers described as *concussione*, suggesting that the defendant is a victim of extortion (the same argument was propounded by De Benedetti over Tangentopoli). M.Berruti, leading the Edilnord enquiry, resigned and became an FI deputy as well as one of Berlusconi's lawyers. The GdF later probed into the tax department of Fininvest, and as a result arrested its head S.Sciascia (and other staff) who admitted to having paid $200,000 to the GdF out of a $2million slush fund created by Paolo, to ensure a favourable ruling of the accounts. 40 GdF officers were arrested, of which three committed suicide.

Switzerland was waiting for Italy to ratify the European convention of 1998 on *Rogatorie:* international judicial assistance. In 2001 Berlusconi's team drafted some adjustments, for which Dell'Utri was one of the signatories, as ever in an attempt to hamper investigation into accusations of the bribery of judges by Berlusconi and Previti in the Mondadori, IMI/SIR and SME cases. Crucially evidence would now require original documents or certified copies, even for existing cases, which was highly impractical, given the mountain of computer information and paperwork involved in every case. Berlusconi hastened this bill through Parliament. Inexplicably, (as previously over parliamentary immunity) President Ciampi rubber stamped the bill, despite widespread protest from the general public, who now began to perceive which way the wind was blowing with their leader. The Swiss chief prosecutor, Carla del Ponte, who had been involved in drafting the 1998 treaty, was incredulous at such action. She had worked assiduously both with the anti Mafia magistrates in Palermo and the Clean Hands team in Milan. Indeed in 1989 she had been staying at Judge Falcone's seaside villa near Palermo, where they narrowly escaped an attempt on their lives by the Mafia with the placing of fifty sticks of dynamite. Mercifully magistrates declared the law unconstitutional, which was upheld by the Supreme Court in 2002; and with confirmation of the existing practice permitting the use of copies. Details of Berlusconi's Swiss accounts appeared in the Italian press.

In 2001, just one week into Berlusconi's government, a G8 meeting of key nation states held in Genoa cast a cloud, where riots broke out for a week, reminiscent of previous trouble in Naples, badly handled by the police due to excessive harassment of the crowds of 'No global' protesters, and involving *tute nere* Fascist Blackshirts, to the extent of drawing official complaints from Amnesty International. Berlusconi appointed R. Ruggiero, a former career diplomat in Brussels and highly respected, as his foreign minister; only to brusquely shunt him to one side so that he himself could bask in the international limelight, only relinquishing that incumbency at the end of 2002. Foreign officials were aghast at how he praised key rulers, regardless of their political actions, such as Gadafy and Putin, slanting his opinions according to his interlocutor, which led to confusion as to his true beliefs. Perhaps he was simply being diplomatic, tinged by his Catholic upbringing of fairness.

In 2003 Berlusconi was gung ho for invading Iraq in alliance with the US and Britain, but he held back in the face of two million protesters in Rome, together with a poll showing 75% against invasion. Traditionally opposed to military intervention since the Second World War and mindful of Mussolini's risky foreign campaigns, as well as being influenced by Catholic pacifism, Italy just sent a 3,000 strong peace-keeping force, the third largest after the US and UK, and of whom 19 sadly lost their lives. Italy spends only about 1% of GDP on defence, compared to Britain 2.5% and America 4%; and with a stock of out-dated equipment and transport. Yet in recent years Italian peacekeeping has acquitted itself well, usually establishing a good rapport with host nationals: in Lebanon and during the first Gulf war; also Ethiopia and Eritrea, two former colonies in the Horn of Africa. In 2002, 7,000 troops were posted to Bosnia.

Berlusconi's tenure of the EU presidency (a six month incumbency) was not a success in international diplomacy, displaying a distinct lack of tact and sensitivity. Many foreigners disliked his close relationship with the post Fascist Dini and the xenophobic Bossi. Equally unpalatable were his perennial legal problems which many considered made him an unsuitable leader. He caused great offence in the European Parliament in Strasbourg when he uttered a crass comment, comparing Martin Schulz, the German social democrat member, to a Nazi concentration guard. Insensitive, he rubbed salt into the wound by refusing to make an apology. Fini was present at the occasion and was shocked. EU foreign ministers were annoyed that, on a visit to meet Putin, Berlusconi did not discuss the Chechnya crisis. As with running his political party and business empire, Berlusconi was not a team player, preferring to control everything himself. All show and no substance, his review at the end of his presidency was poorly prepared and ill received. His tenure was a shabby indictment of the Italian nation on the international stage.

Prodi's Second Government 2006-08

2006 saw a fresh electoral contest between Prodi and Berlusconi, against a background of 39 political parties. They took part in two television debates, in which Prodi made the better showing, ironically so bearing in mind that Berlusconi was hot on image creation as a media mogul. Talking about the future, Prodi engaged the viewers' attention by speaking to camera, which helped him win undecided voters, with 47% of viewers favouring him. In contrast, Berlusconi harked back to the past in lacklustre speeches. On the day Prodi launched his political programme for the electoral campaign, Berlusconi proclaimed: 'I am the Jesus Christ of politics. I'm a patient victim. I endure all, I sacrifice myself for everyone'. He also compared himself to Napoleon. He walked out of another televised debate, haughtily objecting to hostile questioning. An increasing number of FI members, tired of their master's dictatorial approach and now viewing him as an electoral liability, wanted a vote on a change of leadership before the election. Prior to voting Berlusconi introduced new rules whereby ballot papers only showed candidates' names and without any mention of a criminal record.

Berlusconi's Forza Italia once more campaigned under the PDL Pole of Freedoms banner, in alliance with Fini's AN and Bossi's Lega Nord; and now joined by UDC led by Pierferdinando Casini. Prodi's Olive Tree coalition comprised Rutelli's Margherita group, the Refounded Communists RC led by Bertinotti and the PDS Communist party run by Piero Fassino (former mayor of Turin). With its working class base now eroded, the Communists now turned towards the young jobless and immigrants for support. Prodi's coalition won by a wafer thin majority of just 25,000 votes, for which Berlusconi demanded a recount but it was rejected. Ironically, thanks to Berlusconi's reintroduction of PR in 2005, Prodi received a bonus of 50 seats in the Deputies for being the party with the most votes, giving a total of 220 seats against FI's 140 seats, AN 71, UDC 39, RC 41 and LN 26. Prodi benefitted from the support of four life (unelected) senators out of a total of seven, who were mostly left-wing.

Prodi's brief second administration was a mere shadow of his brilliant first. With D'Alema as deputy PM, Prodi headed an unwieldy centre left coalition of nine parties. Keen on the Anglo-American two party political system which creates stronger administrations, Prodi decided to merge the DS with Rutelli's Daisy party to form the Democrat Party PD. His finance minister, Tommaso Padoa-Schioppa, a Milanese tax lawyer, contributed to the government's unpopularity by raising taxes and clamping down both on public expenditure and tax evasion, partly to satisfy EU national and budget deficit limits; yet tempered with an amnesty for undisclosed tax returns which brought in much needed cash to the Treasury coffers. In the end, Prodi was forced to resign owing to lack of Communist support for his despatch of 2,600 peacekeeping troops to Afghanistan in 2007: one thousand soldiers returned home. The Taliban captured the Italian journalist Daniele Mastrogiacomo, but mercifully liberated him upon payment of a ransom. Furthermore, the troops eventually sent to Iraq by Berlusconi were now withdrawn.

In 2006 a trial took place in Milan, leading to the conviction of 22 alleged CIA[87] officers and agents, an American air force colonel and two Italian agents. They were accused of having assisted in the kidnap of Abu Omar, an Egyptian cleric, in a Milanese street in 2003. Jeff Castelli, head of the CIA in Italy at the time of the abduction, and two other Americans, were acquitted on grounds of diplomatic immunity, but were in fact given sentences in absentia (the US government having blocked their extradition) of respectively eight and five years. General Pollari, head of SISMI intelligence, mused whether he too would be charged in the affair. Prodi and the Constitutional Court tried to hush up the incident. However, the prosecuting magistrate, one A.Spataro, happened to come across the case when looking into Omar's links with Islamist militants (magistrates had a similar piece of luck with the Gelli/P2 case). The incident offers an example of American influence in Italian affairs, as indeed they have had with other European countries.

In the light of these revelations, in 2006 Prodi took drastic action by replacing the existing intelligence operations with AISI *Agenzia Informazioni e Sicurezza Interna* (national security) and AISE foreign security; both overseen by CISR Interministerial Committee charged with the security of the republic, again chaired by the PM. RIS *Reparto Informazioni e Sicurezza* co-ordinates the technical and military/police forces with the overseas armed forces.

Ignominy: Berlusconi's Third Government 2008-11

Berlusconi campaigned once more under the PDL *Polo della Libertà* banner in alliance with LN and AN, though the latter's leader Fini had become increasingly critical of Berlusconi's dictatorial approach. The Forza Italia party was now joined by the small Independence for Sicily party. Berlusconi vanquished the lacklustre PD party now led by Walter Veltroni, and bounced back into power, taking 384 Deputy Seats against Veltroni's 246, and holding 174 in the Senate against Veltroni's 134. As with Prodi, Berlusconi secured a bonus as the winning party, giving him a 98 seat majority. P.F. Casini's UDC gained 36 seats but still refused to join Berlusconi, hoping to found a new centre right party. LN almost doubled its vote, making it the third largest party and

---

[87] US Central Intelligence Agency

holding the balance of power in the Senate. Small radical parties such as the Greens were routed, as was *Rifondazione* RC, so Bertinotti resigned. Tellingly, FI later performed badly in Milan's local elections in 2011, which was *Il Cavaliere's* home area.

Berlusconi had won the election by concentrating his attack on Prodi's poor handling of a parlous economy. Yet as ever, he proved to be long on pledges and short on delivery. In a 380 page long programme, and without consulting his allies, he offered his usual catch-all ragbag of promises to increase pensions, cut taxes, reduce the number of temporary jobs, sell off state enterprises, decrease expenditure to bring down the national debt, and hypocritically crack down on tax evasion. Furthermore, he promised an end to long hospital waiting lists, the issue of free school textbooks, better policing and the sale of public housing to tenants. He promised to clear up the rubbish scandal in Naples/Campania, which had contributed to Prodi's downfall.

Berlusconi now began his third term with the national debt standing at 1.9 trillion Euros, being 130% of GDP, with high yield government bonds (high interest rates to compensate for the risk) and with growth expected to be at rock bottom 0.3% in 2008-09, the lowest within the EU, and compounded by the worst recession since the war, looming against a backdrop of the Eurozone and global financial crises during 2008-13. This scenario was in stark contrast to the mid 1990s when Italy, the EU's third largest economy, had fared better than either France or Britain, and was second only to Germany in manufacturing.

Berlusconi's sole achievement was reaching an agreement with Colonel Gadafy of Libya, whereby the president would endeavour to control illegal migration to Italy, in return for five billion dollars' compensation for Italy's former colonisation of his country. A rare bright spot in Berlusconi's final administration was his decision to hold the G8 summit, of which he was leader 2009-11, in the Abruzzese town of L'Aquila which had suffered badly from an earthquake[88]. Following the resignation of that region's PD governor, accused of having accepted a six-million-euro bribe, Forza Italia comfortably won the regional election there in December 2008.

Berlusconi's finance minister, Giulio Tremonti, a tax expert, proposed an emergency budget for 2011-12, but scrapped the unpopular property tax, and

---

[88] In 2012 seven scientists were sentenced to six years' imprisonment on grounds of manslaughter, having failed to give adequate warning: 29 people died. They were acquitted on appeal except for one.

schemed to take some forty billion euros from the Southern fund in order to plug the budget deficit. Many foreigners were highly sceptical of Berlusconi's ability to pull round the Italian economy, based on his past performance and entanglements with the judiciary. The UDC opposed the tax reforms, whilst the IMF refused Italy a loan, in response to which Berlusconi later accused Christine Lagarde, its boss, of conspiracy against him, in collusion with Chancellor Angela Merkel and President Nicolas Sarkozy.

The upshot was that Berlusconi lost the vote on passing the austerity budget and so was forced to resign. Seeing which way the wind was blowing, a host of FI deputies deserted the party, like rats from a sinking ship, moving over to the up and coming M5S Five Star Movement. It was the end of an era. News of his ousting was greeted by a host of Italians, with dancing in the streets, jeering '*buffone*' and '*mafioso*' at him as he sneaked out by a side door of the Quirinale presidential residence. The scales had at last fallen from their eyes at his duplicitous nature. Many had objected to his re-instatement of PR with the majority bonus, which allowed party leaders to choose the lists of candidates and so manipulate the outcome. However, Berlusconi continued to enjoy strong support in the Senate.

Il Cavaliere's affairs rumbled on. His private life had become swathed in a fog of sleaze, with the tawdry affair of the Ruby case, allegedly having paid for sex with an underage (17-year-old) Moroccan girl. In 2013 he was given a jail sentence of seven years for this offence; together with a lifetime ban from politics, yet was acquitted in 2015; but the mask had slipped. In 2013 he was at long last convicted of tax fraud with regard to false accounting over film rights at Mediaset, for which he was handed down a four-year prison sentence. It was his first case ever to clinch a sentence, out of a total of 32, secured by Prosecuting Magistrate Fabio De Pasquale and confirmed by the court of appeal. Thanks to an amnesty, it was reduced to one year with house arrest or community work, since he was now over 70 years old (he worked in an old folks' home); together with a six-year ban on holding public office until 2019, as per a new law passed by the Senate. President Napolitano was loth to grant him a pardon. In short, he was expelled from Parliament, in disgrace. He had the effrontery to appeal to the European Court of Human Rights in Strasbourg. Of his legal record to date, six cases had expired by the Statute of Limitations, whilst two lapsed due to his changing the law. In over twelve trials, he was either acquitted or ruled out of time by the Statute of Limitations (the latter also protected Andreotti from prosecution). The Italian judiciary deserve a medal for their forbearance with the man.

Berlusconi ran in the 2013 elections, back under the FI label, but thankfully he lost out to LN and M5S. In 2009 his second wife, the actress Veronica Lario, sued him for divorce, fed up with his philandering at erotic 'bunga bunga' parties, for which his accountant reimbursed the girls for their services. She received $48million by court order in 2012, whilst her former husband kept their $100million mansion at Arcore. In 2016 he suffered a severe stroke.

Berlusconi was now gradually passing over control of his business empire to his children, who took steps to consolidate their father's business empire and reduce the huge debt held by Fininvest. His daughter Marina took over the running of the latter, along with Mondadori, still Italy's largest publishing house, of which Berlusconi retained half, together with 30% of Mediolanum insurance. His son Pier Silvio took charge of Mediaset, with the family reducing its holding to a 38% stake, and now accounting for just 40% of Italian terrestrial television, as well as a stake in Spanish television. Mediaset had come under heavy pressure in recent years from weak advertising revenue, partly due to the rising popularity of Murdoch's Sky Italia Premium pay TV. Vivendi France, whose boss had been a chum of Berlusconi's, tried to acquire 20% of Mediaset but the deal failed. In 2016 Berlusconi sold AC Milan to a Chinese company, only to acquire the Monza football club in 2018 for three million Euros: a return to his old passion. It was the beginning of the end.

Mario Monti

Following Berlusconi's resignation in 2011, President Napolitano invited Mario Monti to form an administration, but it was short-lived. An economic liberal and a life senator, Monti left his post as president of the private Bocconi university in Milan (similar to the LSE in London) to put together a strong technocratic team of 18 ministers, with an overall average age of 64, the highest in the EU. It included three females, and with the chairman of NATO as defence minister. Offering a serious approach to the business of government, they put forward an emergency budget, implemented by decree. Acting as finance minister, Monti's budget covered the refinancing of 300 billion euros of debt, with tax breaks for females and the young. He planned to extend shopping hours, as well as liberalise the licensing of notaries, taxis and pharmacies. However, in the face of stiff opposition from existing holders, he was obliged to scale back these reforms. He re-instated the unpopular property tax, whilst an increase in excise duty on diesel annoyed lorry drivers. Refusing a salary himself, Monti froze public salaries, reducing that cost from 166 billion in 2011, down to 159m by 2015.

Monti implemented his budget against the background of a three-year recession (technically two consecutive quarters without growth), the longest since the war, with minimum growth since joining the Euro in 1999, and saddled with high borrowing costs; Berlusconi having been ineffectual on his watch. Manufacturing was now in the doldrums following its post-war heyday, when Italy was second only to Germany. During 2009-12, nearly 20% of firms shut down, battered by the 2008 financial crisis and two recessions. During 2008-09, output fell by 24% followed by a brief recovery, only to again sink into crisis in 2011, with a further drop of 10%, and with productivity now 26% below its 2007 peak. Textiles were in the doldrums with production down by 35%, although luxury clothing continued to perform well, pandering to the world's pampered rich. Electrical goods were also down by 35%. Car manufacturing fell by 45%, with Fiat, driver of the post-war Economic Miracle, still the largest car maker but with its output dropping from 911,000 in 2007 to 397,000; and with vans' output at 207,000, 18% below the pre crisis peak. Since 2009 some 11,000 Fiat workers, out of a total of 41,000, had come under the state *Cassa Integrazione* scheme which pays up to 80% of salary whilst laid off, technically just for three years but which was extended.

Domestic appliances, once a key player in Italy's post-war recovery, were also in the doldrums, with just 130,000 workers. Candy, Ignis, Indesit and Zanussi were used as successful case studies in 60s/70s business models. Production plummeted from 24 million 'white goods' in 2007 to 13 million by 2012. Washing machines were down by 52% to 4.4 million, similarly dishwashers by 59% to 1.1million, refrigerators by 55% to 1.8 million and cookers by 75% to 300,000. Increasing competition from abroad, combined with expensive home labour, contributed to the decline. In 2018 China bought out Candy for E475 million: founded in 1945, its third generation will remain on the board of directors. The slump in car and domestic appliance sectors has badly hit supply chains for parts, which in turn has pushed production abroad to cheaper locations. Italy is low down on the international list for doing business, in particular on competition.

Monti's financial programme was backed by Mario Draghi, who holds an impressive track record, and the latest in a long list of competent Italian bankers. He was Executive Director of the World Bank during 1984-89; then Director General of the Italian Treasury during 1991-2001. Afterwards he was appointed Governor of the Bank of Italy, during which time he sat on the governing and general councils of the ECB European Central Bank in Frankfurt, where he gained first hand experience of the negative effects of high inflation on the Italian economy. He was a member of the board of directors of the BIS Bank for International Settlements: the bankers' bank, from 2002 to 2005. He was appointed vice chairman and MD of Goldman Sachs International. In 2006 he was nominated chair of the G20 Financial Stability Board.

In October 2011, at the height of the Eurozone crisis, Draghi was nominated President of the ECB, taking over from Jean-Claude Trichet who had been at the helm for eight years, during which time he apparently failed to heed the warning signs of a deep-seated crisis, let alone take any action. Like many Italians, Draghi is passionate about the EU, since it has been the prime mover of the Italian post-war economy. Pragmatic and dynamic, Draghi promptly declared that he would 'do whatever it takes to save the Euro', at the same time upholding the independence of the ECB, as well as impose a 2% limit on inflation, the keystone of ECB policy. In 2015 he implemented a programme of Quantitative Easing QE (also called large scale asset purchasing) to galvanize the Euro economy by boosting the money supply in order to encourage lending and investment, through the ECB's regular purchase of substantial quantities of government bonds and other securities at low rates of interest. Since 2015 ECB has bought some 2.6 trillion Eurozone bonds; in December 2018 it began to gradually wind down QE, and still paying negative interest rates on deposits.

Throughout the crisis, Draghi has carefully and painstakingly striven to find common accord with his colleagues and other EU/international bodies, in a herculean effort to save the Euro and put the Eurozone countries back on the straight path of financial discipline. He established a harmonious relationship with Chancellor Angela Merkel (no mean achievement). Draghi is due to step down from the ECB in 2019: he will be a hard act to follow.[89]

Monti's programme for improving economic growth and reducing spending by regional authorities met with approval from the centre left PD, though he

---

[89] Stop press: Draghi is to be succeeded by Christine Lagarde, head of the IMF and a former French finance minister.

failed to win support for his highly unpopular property tax on first homes, even with Brussels who considered the tax insufficiently progressive. Monti hinted to Chancellor Merkel and others that a lack of economic stimulus within the Eurozone was creating strong populist militancy in Italy. A keen European and popular able diplomat, Monti had served as EU Commissioner during 1995-2004, both for the single market and competition; together with Emma Bonino and Romano Prodi. However, Berlusconi withdrew his party's support since Monti had put forward legislation to prevent certain classes of convicted criminals from holding office or running in elections; and so Monti was obliged to step down.

During the election campaign in 2013, Berlusconi's PDL, in coalition with LN, promised to reimburse the hated property tax payments, which helped him to secure 125 Deputy Seats and 117 in the Senate. Monti made a poor showing, gaining respectively just 47 and 19 seats. Yet it was the PD that secured victory, now led by P.Bersani, gaining 345 Deputies and 123 in the Senate, but 35 short of an absolute majority. Since both Houses hold equal powers Bersani[90] also needed a majority in the Senate, so he considered allying with Beppe Grillo, leader of the new M5S party, which had made its first appearance on the political stage. Grillo took 47 seats in the Deputies and 19 in the Senate. However, due to a stalemate, it fell to Bersani's deputy, the centrist Enrico Letta, to form a more centrist government than Bersani's offering, and with a younger cabinet than Monti's.

Letta, aged 46, a native of Pisa and a technocrat like Monti, entered into coalition with PDL (his uncle Gianni had been a close adviser to Berlusconi) but the alliance was short-lived. Berlusconi persisted in his opposition to Monti's property tax which Letta suspended rather than cancel. So Berlusconi pulled out his support and Letta's brief government promptly fell in 2014.[91] He did manage to cut ministers' salaries, and appoint an African lady, Cecile Kyenge, as education minister.

---

[90] In Feb.2021 Draghi became Prime Minister of Italy.

[91] In Feb.2021 he became Prime Minister of Italy.

Chapter Twenty

Renzi: *Il Rottomattore*

Born in Florence in 1975, in 2001 Matteo Renzi joined Rutelli's Daisy party, and in 2009 was appointed mayor of his city, where he streamlined the town hall administration, reduced taxes and raised expenditure on education and welfare. In December 2013, he secured two thirds of the votes of an internal contest for the leadership of the centre left PD Democratic Party, thereby supplanting the incumbent Bersani, leader since 2012. In 2014 Renzi, aged 39, led the party to electoral victory in the European elections (sugared with an 80-euro tax break for the lower paid) gaining 41% of the national vote, against Forza Italia's 17%. Thanks to the earlier merger with the PCI his party did well in communist Emilia-Romagna for the 2014 regional elections. Full of reformist zeal, he described himself as *Il Rottomattore* demolition man, since he was intent on transforming Italian politics and reviving the moribund economy.

His youthful and dynamic cabinet of twelve ministers, of which seven were females, were brimming with ideas and promises to reform employment, taxation, public administration and infrastructure such as school buildings. His coalition partners included Monti's Civic Choice party, together with NCD New Centre Right, a small splinter group from PDL formed by Angelino Alfano in 2013. Formerly Letta's deputy PM, Alfano had tired of his master Berlusconi's antics, having hoped to succeed him.

The Italian economy, the EU's third largest, remained in a parlous state, labouring under a double dip recession, following two consecutive quarters of minimal growth, with barely 0.8% growth in 2014, and with a poor performance for five of the previous eight years. In 2012 house and car sales were down. The 2015 quarter figures proved sluggish, dipping from 0.3% Q1 to 0.2% in Q3. The IMF estimates Italian growth to hover around 1% over the next few years, against a possible world downturn. American growth is expected to slide from 3.5% in

2018 down to 2%. The budget deficit stood at 2.4% which, although below the EU ceiling of 3%, remains worrying because of Italy's huge debts burden of E684 billion in 2013 (nett of interest payments) and possibly rising to E691billion by 2015; and which includes some 350bnE of NPLs bad loans at the banks. Exports have declined since Italy joined the Euro in 1999, since she is unable to devalue to increase competitivity.

Italy's lacklustre economy is not alone. Spain has also suffered a double dip recession, but has managed to cut costs to boost exports. Germany has suffered some contraction in her economy by 0.2% in the third quarter of 2018, resulting in fewer imports from Italy which previously accounted for one-sixth of the total; together with its own heavy pensions burden which is guaranteed until 2040. German exports are down, especially for automobiles, which is partly due to the forthcoming EU Directive on carbon emissions standards.

Working with Pier Carlo Padoan, his finance minister who previously had served as chief economist at OECD, Renzi envisaged cuts of two billion euros to public expenditure, of which one billion would be slashed from healthcare; also social services and education, withdrawing plans for early retirement for teachers and lecturers. In fact, health and education spending of respectively 7% and 4% are roughly in line with the EU average, whilst pensions at 14% are markedly higher. Renzi did manage some tax breaks to stimulate corporate investment; along with cuts to the property tax on first homes (which had contributed to Monti's downfall). He planned to pay off E100bn of state debts to private suppliers, arranged for the auction of ministers' cars, and capped by 25% the pay of top managers. Yet despite these cuts, public expenditure remains critically high, largely due to public transport subsidies and the pensions burden, the latter now costing an extra 25 billion euros in 2016, compared to 2012, and despite Monti's other reductions. The ECB continued to maintain borrowing costs at a low rate of interest to soften the blow. Nevertheless, both the Italian Court of Accounts (Audit Office) and the EU Commission told Renzi to revise down his budget: he responded by criticising the German approach to handling the EU. Britain is not alone in resenting interference from Berlin and Brussels bureaucracy.

Renzi confirmed his government's intention of putting Letta's privatisation programme into effect, in order to increase competitivity and rationalize assets. Building upon the privatisation programme of the 1990s under Amato and Dini, Renzi expected to yield some E8-10 billion unto the state coffers and thereby lower the public debt now standing at 130% of GDP. Finmeccanica's rail assets were to be sold, but with the state retaining a 30% interest; the company would henceforth concentrate on aerospace and defence. *Grandi Stazioni*, responsible for the 13 largest railway stations and part of FS *Ferrovie dello Stato* State Railways,[92] would be sold off, with *Ferrovie* itself possibly later. Privatisation of state holdings has encouraged the appearance of private travel companies. *Nuovo Trasporto Viaggiatori* NTV, partly owned by SNCF France, is Italy's first high speed operation in Europe. Begun in 2012, it has since acquired 20% of the travel business, though FSI state railways controls its track. NTV's Nugo application allows passengers to travel with fifty other companies, including ferry and car sharing. NTV-Italo is another private rail company, in which the chief executive of Tod's, an upmarket shoe maker, holds shares. Trenitalia has recently made its entry into Britain.

Finmeccanica is a major world arms manufacturer, and owns Agusta Westland helicopters based in Lombardy. The company is now working with Airbus over the production of the pan European Typhoon fighter jet. In 2019 the Leonardo company joined the consortium, which includes BAE Systems and Rolls-Royce, to build the Tempest fighter plane. In 2016 Beretta Arms Company opened up a factory in America. ChemChina is now a principal shareholder in Pirelli. Half of Fincantieri, Europe's largest shipbuilder and a major employer in Trieste, has been put up for sale; also *Sace,* Italy's export credit agency. Other sales envisaged include *CDP Reti* responsible for gas and electricity networks.

Having been in serious difficulties for some time, Alitalia filed for bankruptcy in 2008. The flagship airline was purchased by the CAI consortium *Compagnia Aerea Italiana* which involved some of Berlusconi's pals taking over the more profitable areas, such as AirOne; and burdening the debts onto the Italian taxpayer. CAI subsequently sold 25% of the Alitalia shares to AirFrance-KLM. Now known as the Alitalia Group, the company leases most of its aeroplanes from an Irish company owned by the previous owner of Air One. Yet again in trouble, in 2017 the company filed for bankruptcy protection, following the employees' rejection of cuts to recapitalise, and with the government refusing to bail it out. In 2019 there was talk of a possible joint venture with AirFrance-KLM.

The largest privatisation since 2000 was the sale in 2015 of 40% of *Poste Italiane*, hoping to raise some eight billion euros and attract foreign investment.

---

[92] Now known as Ferrovie Italiane, the company began high speed travel in 2008.

Poste is a prime example of a former state organisation reinventing itself in a challenging environment. The blow was softened by offering shares to its 140,000 workers, as arranged with the partial sale of ENEL and ENI in the 1990s (the latter has had a female Chair since 2017). Postal services were down to 14% of revenue by 2014, so deliveries are now just every two days. Italians have never been keen letter writers, preferring to talk on the telephone and send cheaper e-mails. Over the years, parcel sales have held up, now working with Amazon, especially from the expanding sector of e-commerce, such as in Scandinavia. Trading on its trustworthy brand recognition and its 13,000-branch network, Poste has diversified into financial services, especially insurance, through its 10% acquisition of Anima, an Italian asset fund manager, aiming at higher bond yields than the state bonds (the latter accounts for 13% of savings compared to the EU average of 5%). Both revenue and profit are now nicely up, and with a generous dividend.

A further 3% of the ENI oil and gas behemoth, partly privatised in the 1990s, may be sold but with the government retaining a controlling share. ENI has made a significant offshore gas discovery in Egypt: encouraging news since Italy is one third dependent on Russia for its gas supplies, and with Algeria as another key supplier. Italy is now involved in the last section of the EU's Southern Gas Corridor, designed to import gas from the Caspian region, and expected to come on-stream in 2020 via a pipeline beneath the Adriatic Sea. ENI too has been hit recently by scandal, concerning its boss Descalzi and four other executives who made a deal with Royal Dutch Shell in Nigeria in exchange for backhanders disguised as retrocessions; corruption with Saipem drilling contracts in Algeria; also concerning lax environmental standards at an Italian power station. They were tried by Fabio De Pasquale, the magistrate who secured the sole conviction against Berlusconi for tax fraud. In 2016 G.Orsi and B.Spangolini, respectively former bosses of Finmeccanica and Agusta Westland helicopters, were tried for corruption and false accounting.

As we enter an era of low carbon emission with cleaner and renewable energy, over a period of five years ENEL, currently run by F.Starace, is switching to green energy by decommissioning 23 power stations with a total capacity of 13 gigawatts, the first being in Venice. Enel is currently the second largest producer of renewable energy in Europe. They may convert some into cultural centres, as happened successfully with London's Bankside power station, now home to the Tate Modern. Enel Green Power was sold off partly to decrease its parent's debt burden, and is now listed on the Milan *Borsa*. A leader for many years in geothermal power, it has expanded into hydro and wind power both at home and abroad, such as Brazil and Chile where energy demand is high (the latter is strong in geothermal power). The high load factor of green energy (most of it is used) contributes towards a regular cashflow. Enel Green has entered into a joint venture with Sharp Electronics for solar cell production. Green power is also prominent in Spain with Iberdrola, which leads in this sector; EdF in France; RWE and E. On in Germany, the latter with a strong presence in Italy. The Padana Energia Company in northern Italy may have provoked two earthquakes in the area in 2012, by pumping high pressure water into oil wells. 27 people were killed and hundreds injured.

In 1966 Giovanni Agnelli took over FIAT, Italy's flagship company and driver of the post-war economic miracle, and led the group as Chairman until his retirement in 1996. Following the 1973 hike in oil prices car sales dropped, so Agnelli targeted public transport, making buses and trains till the late '80s. The Fiat Auto Group included Lancia, Ferrari, Maserati, and Alfa Romeo (previously under IRI) with its popular Giulietta, and so dominated the Italian car market. Furthermore, the company was the largest world producer after GM and Ford, and ahead of its European rivals Renault and Peugeot-Citroen (it had a brief merger with Citroen). It boasted a strong presence in Poland and Germany, together with factories in Russia, India and Argentina. The group also produced CNH Iveco trucks, construction and agricultural equipment, later diversifying into print media and advertising (Agnelli was chairman of La Stampa newspaper, printed in Turin) as well as telecoms and pharmaceuticals. In 1971 Agnelli agreed with Luciano Lama, the Communist trade union leader, to link wages to inflation. In 1974 he became chairman of Confindustria, partly to defuse political interference. In 1976 he sold 10% of Fiat shares to Colonel Gadafy of Libya.

In 1979 Fiat suffered severely from militant trade unions, enduring high absenteeism and culminating in a 35-day shutdown at the Mirafiori plant, and with the loss in production of 200,000 cars. Factories suffered fire and destruction of machinery. The company was also subjected to attacks by the Red Brigades, who killed two managers and wounded another 27 managers. Fortuitously the company was saved by the remarkable anti trade union march of the 40,000 managers and non-Communist workers who urged a return to work. 61 workers were fired. Fiat achieved a turnaround with the introduction in

1983 of its Fiat Uno model, produced by robots, and which brought the company back into healthy profit.

In 1996 Agnelli handed over to Cesare Romiti, formerly with Alitalia, who proceeded to sack 23,000 workers, ended a five-week strike and installed more robots to streamline the business. The group had dipped in the early '90s with unpopular models such as the Stilo, but its fortunes were revived with the launch of the Fiat Punto and later the Bravo, which boosted profits. Agnelli died in 2003: it was the end of an era.

The business was once more revived in 2004, with the arrival of the Italo-Canadian Sergio Marchionne, with the successful launch in 2009 of the new version of the highly popular Panda car, as well as a revamped 500 the following year. The Grande Punto hatchback was well received, along with the Alfa Romeo Spider and Mito, also a new Lancia model. Success lay in the innovative styling from a new design team; and a shorter lead time from design to market through the introduction of virtual engineering with computer simulated models. In the light of forthcoming EU regulations on carbon emissions, a new type of engine has been introduced, which reduces emissions partly by eliminating camshafts and valve gear.

In 2005 Marchionne deftly crafted the timely termination of a disappointing five-year partnership with Chrysler US (which involved sharing of platforms, engines and purchasing) by paying the Americans $2 million to cancel the 'Put' option (which gave Fiat the right to sell its car business to Chrysler). In 2009 he set up a new partnership with Chrysler, leading to the establishment in 2014 of FC Automobiles, with its holding company based in London. Marchionne died in 2010. The combined group is currently looking into the electric vehicle market, though current battery costs pose a stumbling block. In 2016 Fiat sold Ferrari at an IPO in New York; the team used to invest heavily in Formula One racing. In 2019 Fiat Chrysler decided against a merger with Renault. Mike Manley, a Briton, currently heads up FC's British Jeep division.

In 2003, Chancellor Schroder carried out the Hartz labour reforms to boost German exports, concentrating on wage restraint rather than trying to increase productivity. Impressed by Schroder's success, and encouraged by President Macron's similar plans, Renzi was determined to overhaul Italy's labour market in order to loosen up the jobs market and dent the power of the trade unions. As in Germany, productivity remains low which, compounded by high labour costs, renders exports uncompetitive. During his first year in office, Renzi passed the

Jobs Act, with 158 for (including FI), 9 against and with 45 abstentions which included M5S and LN. Aimed at liberalising the world of work and the decentralization of collective bargaining, the Act did away with protection for unfair dismissal as per article 18 of the sacrosanct Workers' Statute of 1970.

Predictably, the decision met with a mass protest in Rome of a million people, organised by the Communist CGIL; followed by another demonstration involving 100,000 workers. 33 PD deputies opposed the bill, although unfairly dismissed workers would receive compensation anyway. Berlusconi had in fact allowed short term contracts to boost employment, but with few of the benefits available to permanent workers. Labour reform is a poisoned chalice: two lawyers working on greater flexibility were murdered by the Red Brigades: Professors Massimo D'Antona in 1999 and Marco Biagi in 2002.

The Jobs Act vastly improves upon employment regulations for the self-employed, putting them on an equal footing with standard workers who enjoy the benefits of job security and generous pensions of up to 80% of final salary. In the words of the Act's author, M. Del Conte, the Act aims to bring work into the 'third millenium'. 'Smartwork' allows them greater flexibility in working hours and workplace, with the right to 'disconnect' for breaks. The Act offers them the same economic and legislative treatment as standard workers. Late salary payment beyond 60 days is now subject to compensation. Secondly, in the event of illness or accident that requires absence beyond 60 days, health contributions will be suspended for up to two years, after which an employee can pay the arrears by instalments. Females are to receive five months' maternity leave whilst working from home. The self-employed will now be allowed to compete for jobs in the public sector. Italian youth unemployment in 2018 stands at over 30%, against an overall figure of 12%, and 4% in the UK. A similar situation exists in Spain, where the percentage of jobless youngsters is 35%, with 27% of jobs being short term, and taking them up to ten years to secure a permanent job, partly due to job protection by the unions. Pensions are 80% of final salary as in Italy.

In May 2016, the Civil Unions law concerning same sex partnerships was passed in the Deputies, with 369 in favour and 163 against, whilst in the Senate the vote was 173 in favour with 71 against. The law brought Italy into compliance with the European Court of Human Rights in Strasbourg, supported by PD and FI but many were opposed, especially Catholics, also Renzi's ally NCD, an offshoot of PDL. Renzi's government was keen to speed up civil justice due to the complexity and costly legal fees which have hitherto discouraged divorce, the second lowest rate in EU (there are currently five million lawsuits of all types in waiting). A majority of 398 to 28 in the Chamber of Deputies passed the raft of reforms to liberalize further the 1970 law. Couples can now divorce after a year's separation if the divorce is contested, otherwise six months if not. Previously a three-year separation was necessary. There is now available even a DIY divorce handled by the parties' lawyers without going to court. An increasing number of couples simply cohabit *'coppie di fatto'* and have children outside wedlock; Italian marriages are now the fifth lowest in the EU. In 2017 new regulations were introduced, whereby a former wife is accorded 'self-sufficiency' but not her former (luxurious) lifestyle. Finally, Renzi had hoped to carry out far reaching reforms in education but needless to say they were strongly opposed by teachers and students.

Renzi was keen to carry out administrative reform. Italy has a triple layered bureaucracy at regional, provincial and municipal (local) level. Such an unwieldy arrangement makes it highly prone to patronage and excessive spending, exacerbated by a plethora of costly and time-consuming counter checks and balances, leading to inertia. He intended to decentralize power away from the 21 regions, especially with regard to infrastructure, health and energy, except the five original regions which had been granted autonomy after the war. In 1970 the remaining regions were accorded limited power.

Another of Renzi's projects concerned reform of the electoral law for the Chamber of Deputies, which had changed in 1993 from PR to FPTP, only to be reinstated to PR by Berlusconi, and with a bonus for the winner. Renzi now proposed in his Italicum law a revised PR system presenting lists of candidates and allowing two preferences in a two round ballot, with a majority bonus for the winning party gaining over 40% of the votes, who would thus receive 340 of the 630 seats (based on 32 electoral colleges for both chambers, plus seven life senators). The changes are designed to hopefully create a stable long-term administration, moving away from the system of *trasformismo* shifting alliances that has bedevilled Italian politics ever since Italian independence. Managing Italian politicians is akin to herding cats. Smaller parties, who need a minimum of 3% of the votes to sit as a deputy, objected to the idea, though they can pick up votes on the second ballot. A drawback persists, in that voters still cannot choose the candidates nor their order on the lists since it remains the decision of the party bosses. In 2015 Renzi put forward a vote of confidence on electoral reform: the bill was strongly supported, with just 61 against and four abstentions, and which included a PD faction, along with the party president who resigned in protest. Berlusconi and his FI party supported the bill, except for 13 members led by Raffaele Fitto from Puglia, who later formed a new party. So the Italicum bill passed into law, strengthening the powers of the Chamber of Deputies, and to the advantage of the incumbent PM and his party.

Renzi was determined to reform the Constitution set up in 1948. There had been earlier attempts by D'Alema and Letta, with the support of President Napolitano, now aged 90. Renzi proposed that the current balance of equal powers twixt the Deputies and the Senate, established in 1948, should now be weighted in favour of the Deputies, and with a smaller Senate of just 100 members, of which 95 would be selected by the regional and municipal representatives and five by the president. The new look Senate would fulfil a purely advisory role and offer a restraining influence: somewhat akin to the English House of Lords. The Senate would have the power to veto but not block new legislation, in order to accelerate law making and become a regional chamber, taking back regional responsibility for energy and transport. Many bills never become law owing to stalemates, aggravated by frequent changes of government, of which there have been 55 since 1945 (but which include reshuffles). Under a secret ballot the bill was passed in the Senate by 179 voters (including former FI lawyers) with 61 against, and predictably with many abstentions. As with the Italicum Law the constitutional changes were designed to offer stronger and more stable government, which appealed to a large sector of the business community intent on stable economic growth.

Many, both in and outside Parliament, opposed Renzi's bill since it would accord far greater power to the PM, harking back to Mussolini's dictatorship. Renzi had already come under fire from his colleagues for his autocratic approach, akin to Berlusconi's, and preferring Bersani's inclusive approach. With mounting opposition from the electorate, in December 2016 Renzi decided to put his constitutional proposals to a public referendum, but he lost his gamble: they were rejected by 59% of the voters, with 41% in favour. Despite being legally disqualified from attending Parliament owing to his conviction for tax fraud, Berlusconi had supported Renzi, but now changed tack since the PM had outwitted him over the appointment of Mattarella as President in 2015, following Napolitano's resignation. Mattarella was voted in on the fourth round with 665 of the 1009 votes. He had entered politics because his brother was murdered by the Mafia. As he had promised in such an event, in December 2016, Renzi promptly resigned three days after the result, to be replaced by Paolo Gentiloni, a Roman aristocrat. Some PD members defected to M5S. Another contributory factor to Renzi's ousting was his mishandled bailing out of four small banks.

Bank Crisis: Bail-in or Bail-out?

In 2015 Renzi, perhaps inspired by the Spanish government's creation of a 'bad bank' to solve their banks' debt crisis, hatched a rescue plan, governed by Italian solvency law, to save four small banks which had become insolvent, saddled with huge debts owing to the protracted recession: Banco Popolare di Vicenza and Banco Veneto, together with the Popolare in Milan and Banca Popolare di Milano.[93] Vicenza's share issue to meet required capital ratios had failed, despite being underwritten by Unicredit, a major bank. In 2016 Renzi proposed the state purchase of the banks' debts at near face value, and so at the taxpayers' expense. Renzi decided that the four banks sell their NPLs non-performing loans at a high discount, with the consequent losses borne by thousands of small retail savers who have traditionally invested their precious savings in conservative bank bonds and who constitute a significant mainstay of the Italian economy.

Renzi was rapped over the knuckles by the EU Commission, who called a halt to his scheme, declaring that it was tantamount to state aid, thereby infringing their new BRRD rules. He retorted that he did not take orders from Brussels. In 2016 the Bank Resolution and Recovery Directive came into force, which puts failed banks into 'resolution' i.e. bankruptcy rules, and creating a bail-in system whereby only senior bondholders and depositors with balances exceeding 100,000E are liable for 8% of the debts before resorting to public money, and so circumventing a bail-out by the state using taxpayers' money. The Directive was designed to avoid a repeat of the bail-outs in Spain and Eire, following their housing/property boom and bust during the 2008-11 financial crisis, where 'bad banks' took dud loans off banks' books and compensated bondholders and depositors with taxpayers' money.

The Directive stipulates that banks must be solvent, hold sufficient reserve funds and that capital shortfall is to be identified by a stress test. Separately the Basel Committee drew up their global regulations, with the aim of tightening up

---

[93] The many Popolari began as savings banks and are municipally owned, mutual (non profit-making) institutions.

on financial cushions, placing a restriction on banks' own estimate of RWAs risk weighted assets (an important indicator of a bank's strength) since they are too subjective. The Bank for International Settlements BIS remarked that banks had paid out too generous dividends during 2007-15, and should have retained a greater part of their earnings as a cushion. Even Deutsche Banke had been in difficulties and was obliged to increase its ratio of common equity to RWAs.

With Brexit looming, which has hit Italian bank shares, not to mention mutterings of an Italexit, the EU was keen to tread warily, since Italy was a founder member and its economy is too big to allow it to sink. Perhaps mindful of Germany's many small banks[94] and modest depositors, the EU decided to sidestep the issue by declaring that thousands of small retail investors had been 'mis-sold' bonds to the tune of 200 billion euros, unaware of their greater risk and enticed by favourable tax terms, and thus were eligible for compensation. Brussels would therefore allow a 'precautionary and temporary' recapitalisation to compensate them, by allocating shares which would be swapped for new safer bonds.

The solution came too late for Renzi: his mishandling of the affair contributed to his downfall in December 2016. At least that year saw the first drop in NPLs since 2008, though interest rates remained at rock bottom as elsewhere in Europe. In July 2017, the Vicenza and Veneto banks were both declared to be on the point of failure, and so were placed into the insolvency procedure under Italian law and thus not subject to BRRD. The Intesa San Paolo Bank would take on part of the banks' assets and liabilities for a token one euro; whilst the Italian government was to provide state aid through the Atlante guarantee scheme, amounting to a 4.8bnE cash injection, and backed by financial institutions. Banco Popolare and Banca Popolare di Milano were later merged into BPM.

Monte dei Paschi di Siena MPS is Italy's oldest bank, founded in 1472 by the town's magistrates, acting as a key player in medieval finance, along with Genoese and Lombard banks. The bank is the largest employer in the town, home to the renowned annual *Palio* horserace. Previously one third owned by a local

---

[94] German banks bear some resemblance to the Italian system, with a total of 1,580 banks which include 385 *Sparkassen* savings banks largely municipally owned; and six *Landesbanken* regional banks which act as clearing houses for some 875 local co-operatives which themselves are cleared by DZ Bank, which is also a corporate lender and second largest by assets.

non-profit foundation, major shareholders included the Treasury with a 4% holding, a French insurer and a Mexican asset manager. MPS has some 40,000 customers who hold deposit accounts and two billion euros in bonds. In 2007 MPS bought the Antonveneta bank from Santander for E9 billion in cash. Furthermore, MPS lost billions of Euros in obscure derivatives transactions.

In 2016, MPS made two attempts at raising capital sums of 5bnE and 8.8bnE in order to stay afloat, but failed due to lack of investor confidence. In December 2016, an attempt to dispose of 28bn NPLs was brokered by JPMorgan and Mediobanca, and possibly involving a Qatar sovereign wealth fund. The initiative was opposed by the EU as being contrary to its 'resolution' rule and so was rejected. The share price plummeted, bringing its stock market value tumbling down to 600mE, and so trading was suspended.

Following the bank's failure in the ECB stress test (it came bottom of the list of 51 lenders) it had no choice but to go cap in hand to the government asking for a bailout: E8.8bn according to the ECB's estimate and E6.6bn by the Bank of Italy's reckoning. As with the four small banks, the argument was based on the reasoning that small retail investors had been 'mis-sold' their bonds, attracted by favourable interest rates. It was decided that two billion euros of the compensation money would be used to convert their junior bonds into shares, which could then be swapped for new, safer bonds. MPS would be obliged to sell its *sofferenze*, the worst category of bad debts, being 24% of all loans. The Atlante state guarantee scheme would purchase most of the junior and middle tranches of the debts for E1.6bn; whilst senior debt would be sold on the open market. The bailouts have stymied the German hope of a European banking union, since the concept of one size fits all simply does not work, given the present state of affairs.

In 2017, MPS' CEO chief executive officer, Marco Morelli, put forward a restructuring plan, subject to approval by the Commission, to streamline the business within three years, which involves over 2,000 job cuts out of a total of 25,500, the closure of 500 branches, computerizing the lucrative wealth management business, and capping bosses' pay at ten times the average staff salary. In 2016 MPS had returned to the stockmarket in better shape, with its E28bn of NPLs down to 13%, its lowest since 2008, against the EU average of 5%. In January 2019, MPS issued a one billion Eurobond, guaranteed by residential mortgages, and which was heavily oversubscribed. Italian banks are not alone in the new era following the Eurozone crisis: facilitated by the greater use of computers, ING in the Netherlands has shed 7,000 posts, whilst Commerzbank in Germany has dismissed 9,600; and with staff reductions at Credit Suisse. Even Deutsche Banke is now struggling, with recent talks of a merger with Commerzbank having come to naught. The more frugal Scandinavian banks are holding up. The crisis has seen consolidation amongst the myriad of small banks, also some reduction in the number of non-profit making foundations/charitable trusts.

Much to his relief Padoan, the finance minister, remarked that the finance sector was at last turning over a new leaf. Yet the economy remains sluggish, against a drop in global growth coupled with a dearth of profits and rising regulatory costs. Most banks still need to cut costs and rid themselves of bad loans, a difficult challenge given the current low interest environment.

Unicredit, Italy's largest bank, languished in the doldrums for years, partly due to the poor economy and fifty billion Euros of bad loans, of which E18bn were taken over and sold by the Atlante state rescue fund. In 2006 it acquired Capitalia (which owned Banca di Roma), Italy's third largest bank at that time. Since 2016, Unicredit has turned itself around, written down bad debt, and improved its RWA ratio. It has shed some 6,500 jobs and closed 944 branches in Italy, and is operating well as a pan European bank, currently run by a French CEO, with default rates down and a E13bn share issue to inject new capital. Blackrock, a world leader in asset management, is currently its largest shareholder after the government, having doubled its initial investment since 2016. Unicredit has rationalised its retail operations in the EU, having sold its Pioneer asset management business to Amundi, a French asset manager, as well as its holdings in a Polish bank; also Fineco, an Italian online bank. It still owns a bank in Germany and one in Austria.

Under the aegis of Enrico Cuccia, for half a century Mediobanca lay at the heart of Italian industry and finance. A Sicilian by birth, Cuccia began his career at the Central Bank of Italy, and then moved to IRI after the war where he managed the BCI bank. In 1946 Mediobanca was set up and which Cuccia transformed into Italy's first merchant bank under his management from the 1960s, and as chairman until 1982, making it the cornerstone of post-war investment. The *eminence grise* of the business world, he became a genius at saving troubled banks and companies. He drew a modest salary, shunned interviews and publicity, living quietly with his family.

Over the years, Cuccia wove a dense web of cross shareholding pacts amongst major industrial concerns, thereby locking in control and mutual support with the *salotto buono* top businessmen's club. A prime example of a cross share-holding was Generali, Italy's largest insurance group based in Trieste: Mediobanca was its major shareholder, whilst in turn Generali held 2% of the bank's stock (and was also responsible for managing 25% of national savings). Berlusconi's Fininvest and Mediolanum also held shares in Mediobanca. Major bank shareholders were BCI, Credito Italiano and BNL (the latter was bought in 2003 by Banque Paribas for E9bn). Mediobanca was also entwined with Unicredit and Intesa San Paolo banks. Cuccia arranged loans and deals, such as the Pirelli-Dunlop merger in 1970, the sale of Fiat shares to Libya in 1976 (with a handsome profit for Colonel Gadafy) and brokering Agnelli's increased control of Fiat.

During the 1980s, Mediobanca faced increasing competition from the development of Italy's financial markets under Craxi. In the wake of Big Bang in London in 1979, Cuccia was implicated in various corruption enquiries but was always acquitted. In the 1990s, he won control of Credito Italiano and BCI banks; and brokered a hostile takeover of Telecom Italia by Olivetti, for which he received $70m. Following the demise of Cuccia in 1999, Mediobanca was wound down and its operations rationalized, reverting to its core business; as did Generali with its own restructuring plan. The bank's shareholding in Telecom was sold and its holding in MPS reduced in 2014. A similar transformation has occurred with Berlusconi's Fininvest, having been streamlined by his children. The issue of the Basel 3 regulations requiring greater business transparency has led to a diminution of cosy shareholder pacts, with a reduction from 57 to 43 on the Borsa. In 2013 Mediobanca put up for sale all its equity holdings and exited various pacts; and reduced its stake in Generali. Moving with the times, in 2017 Mediobanca opened a private bank and arranged a cross border deal through its 69% acquisition of RAM Active Investments, a Swiss investment management firm.

Italian Finance in the 21st century: A Second Renaissance?

Since the upheavals of the Eurozone crisis and within its national banks, the Italian business world has witnessed a transformation of state and privately owned companies into publicly quoted entities controlled by institutional investors, mainly pension and insurance funds, along with foreign companies and private investors through the *Borsa* stock exchange.

Deluded by the bank failures and threat to their savings, retail (private) savers, which account for about 85% of the Italian financial market, are moving away from the traditional bank deposits and government bonds. Italians now just invest about 8% of their income in bonds, compared to 20% in 2010, but still higher than France at 1.2% and Germany at 2.6%. Their managed assets have now soared to over two trillion Euros: ironically about the same amount as the national debt. In the hunt for a good return, they have taken up the challenge to diversify into investing on the riskier stock market through professional asset managers, and with an increasing number of shareholders taking a keen interest in AGMs.

Some two thirds of Italian firms are family owned SMEs, of which 60% are now listed on the Borsa, hitherto a minor player on the European stock market, but now with a total of some six hundred companies, as against 2,500 at the London Stock Exchange. SMEs employ some 70% of the Italian labour force in firms with fewer than 50 employees, as indeed similarly in Britain and Germany (*Mittelstand*) as against a third in America. The recent financial crisis has made businessmen and women realise that they must move with the times in order to survive: expand, diversify and look abroad for new business markets. Italians have struggled to make the transition from the post-war manufacturing boom to a digital services era, as well as rise to the challenge of globalisation and emerging market demand.

High taxes such as IVA (VAT) currently 22% and high wages involving social security contributions, hinders employment and encourages tax evasion. New business start-ups are discouraged by time-consuming red tape, for instance expensive notaries who are essential for drawing up legal documents, as in France and Germany. In 2011 the European Court of Justice took a step towards liberalising the profession by ruling that notaries are now free to practise in other countries, as well as increasing their number to expedite transactions. The new EU MIFID2 regulations in 2018 aim to ensure greater clarity on banking costs, which are particularly high in Italy. Banks are responsible for 70% of investment sales and so will endeavour to negotiate lower fees with asset managers.

Many family businesses now have ageing bosses: first generation founders who relied on traditional cashflow and bank loans for finance, but which now need a fresh injection of capital. Amongst the second and third generations some are losing interest in the family business and wish to sell out, or revive the firm by bringing in new talent, as well as offer share options to attract high calibre managers. Younger sons and daughters, looking to reinvent the family firm within the more sophisticated scenario of the 21st century, have studied abroad and secured internships, especially in Britain and America, to hone their technical/professional skills in computer literacy, corporate management and new sources of finance; and so returning with a fresh approach. Cross border deals are in greater evidence: for instance, Luxottica is planning to be listed on the Paris Bourse in a merger with Essilor.

In response to this scenario, in 2012 the *Borsa Italiana*, now part of the London Stock Exchange, established its Elite programme designed to introduce SME owners and managers to a more sophisticated approach to the art of raising capital from the finance markets and prepare for an IPO stock market listing. Elite offers them expertise in working internationally and introduces them to powerful backers, such as the expanding pool of private equity funds. 2017 saw 33 IPOs new share issues, of which 24 were made by SMEs. SMEs have also benefitted from the introduction in 2017 of tax friendly PIRs *piano individuale di risparmio.* 70% of the Plan must be invested in Italian based firms, of which a minimum of 30% is to be placed in SMEs. PIRs can also invest in private equity funds such as offered by Equita SIM *società italiana mobiliare.* Since their inception PIRs have raised over E11bn. SMEs have also benefited from private equity buyouts, which have increased from E1.7bn in 2012 to E5.8bn in 2016. The innovative SPACS Special Purpose Acquisition Companies, mostly run by investment banks and private equity firms, are interested in purchasing mid-size SMEs in the region of 100-150mE in value.

With finance becoming more international, as in medieval times, Italians are moving into the more sophisticated forms of alternative investments such as venture capital and hedge funds from a low base. For instance, Indosuez, the wealth management unit of Credit Agricole bank, acquired the private Leonardo bank in Milan in order to introduce alternative investment to retail customers, such as the newer ethical/environmental stocks, though they still present a rather risky sector. In regard to more challenging investments, in 2005 Milan City Council got its fingers burnt through being enticed by a joint proposal from UBS, JPM and Deutsche Banke. The Council arranged a Swap, a type of Derivative, whereby it paid out E1.6bn to switch from an existing fixed interest to a floating rate, thereby hoping to save E60m on its borrowing costs. However, interest rates in fact fell and so they made a huge loss of E298m but the banks possibly raked in E100m of illegal profit. They were charged with mis-selling, apparently having failed to disclose the negative aspects of the deal. Derivatives have possibly involved some 600 Italian city councils; many German local authorities, as well as the Austrian state railways, have suffered likewise.

Banca Etica offers a refreshing approach to banking. Harking back to the older non profit *Popolari* banks, and supported by M5S voters, the bank shuns casinos, pornography, finance, tax havens and commodities, oil and arms. Etica was the first bank to lend to co-operatives run by youngsters who are farming land confiscated from the Mafia. To date, Etica has opened 17 branches with 230 staff, and with executive pay limited to six times the lowest bank salary. With up to loans of a billion euros, in 2012 it made a profit of some E1.6m.

Chapter Twenty-One

Sic Transit Gloria Mundi: The Vatican

In 2005, white smoke issuing from the Sistine Chapel signified the German cardinal Benedict as choice of Pope (and Bishop of Rome) having secured the requisite two thirds majority from the Conclave (electoral college) of 140 cardinals, of which 75 live in Rome. Successor to the highly popular Polish Pope John Paul, Benedict was a scholarly man, more concerned with the inner soul rather than the here and now. Yet he harboured a shadowy past, having been a member of Hitler's Jugend youth brigade and served in the Nazi armed forces. Writing his own speeches without consulting others, he lacked diplomatic communication skills. On a visit to Israel he expressed sympathy for victims of the Holocaust, yet he reinstated Cardinal Williamson who had denied the event. A conservative in religion, he reversed some of the modernising changes effected by the Second Vatican Council 1962-65 under Pope John XXIII, such as reverting to the Tridentine Latin mass rather than keeping to the vernacular Italian. At the age of 85, in 2013 Benedict stepped down as pope, the first ever to resign, and perhaps setting a precedent that the job is not for life.

Benedict's concern with spiritual matters distanced him from grass roots thinking, such as on contraception and same sex marriage. More open-minded prelates, such as Cardinal Martini, a former Archbishop of Milan, defended the use of condoms in the fight against AIDS. Since the '80s many Italian Catholics, especially women, have resented male domination and turned away from the Church's traditional teachings on personal matters, now opting for contraception and abortion. Just about a quarter of Italians now attend monthly mass, as opposed to 40% previously. Women in particular feel the Church is out of touch with the changing times, which has contributed to the sharp fall in nuns. The litmus test remains the recognition of female and married priests, which receives some support, such as from Cardinal Burke on the latter.

To his credit, Benedict appointed 24 new cardinals in order to create a more universal version of modern Catholicism. Acknowledging that the centre of spiritual gravity had shifted from its Rome/European base towards emerging countries, seven hailed from sub Saharan Africa, Asia and Latin America, which now accounts for two-thirds of baptised Catholics, out of a global figure of 1.2 billion souls. Brazil is now the largest Catholic country, with some 3.5million believers in Rio de Janeiro; although the faith is strongly rivalled here by Pentecostalism, which preaches the presence of God through the Holy Spirit.

Cardinal Jorge Mario Begoglio, a native of Argentina and previously runner-up to Benedict, was eventually selected as Benedict's successor, being a compromise between the diehard establishment and the modernist Anglo-German grouping. The cardinal chose the name of Francis in honour both of Saint Francis of Assisi and the first Jesuit missionary, Saint Francis Xavier. Francis himself became leader of the local Jesuits at the age of 36. Son of an Italian immigrant railway worker, Pope Francis was the first non-European pope since the eighth century.

Ambivalent towards the right-wing military government during 1976-83, apparently Francis hid fugitives on church property, yet refused to answer allegations of complicity with the Junta. A warm man and a good communicator, unlike the more aloof Benedict, he displayed sympathy towards the poor and down and outs of Buenos Aires: wastepickers, slum dwellers, drug addicts, homosexuals and young offenders. At his last mass in Rio de Janeiro, one million attended and his final press release there was well received. A benign and informal pope, he chose to live simply in a hostel amongst fellow clerics rather than amidst the grand isolation of the apostolic palace by Saint Peter's Square. Like Benedict, Francis holds conservative views on social issues, but has been leaning towards contraception.

Vatican Finances

The Vatican bank, formally known as IOR Institute for Religious Works, is a relatively small bank with assets of some 6.3 billion euros, over 33,000 accounts and 13 ATMs with instructions in Latin. Operating as a tax haven within the Vatican City State, IOR has a long history wreathed in secrecy, hitherto immune to outside regulation and inspection.[95] There had been little reform since Paul VI's pontificate during 1963-78. Pope Benedict strongly

---

[95] See Chapter Five.

disapproved of financial malpractice such as money laundering, and in 2010 set up the FIA Financial Information Authority to improve standards and ensure greater transparency. Yet it lacked legal authority to inspect bank accounts for suspicious cash transfers. Moneyval, the Council of Europe's money laundering group, carried out an inspection and passed IOR on only 9 of its 16 criteria; and rating it weak on reporting dubious cash movements.

In 2006 Benedict appointed Tarcisio Bertone, hitherto Archbishop of Genoa, as Secretary of State, making him head of the Vatican diplomatic staff and the Pope's deputy. With his eye on the top job, Bertone placed his cronies in key posts such as the Vatican Treasury. However, on account of his being an outsider, along with his brisk management style and lack of diplomatic skills, and speaking neither French nor English, he proved unpopular with the Vatican establishment and made too many enemies. Senior officials held him responsible for Benedict's public relations faux pas, such as the speech given at the University of Regensburg and hosted by Muslims, in which he insensitively quoted a Byzantine ruler who had criticised Muhammad.

Bertone brought in Ettore Gotti Tedeschi to head up IOR. Eventually the pair fell out, partly because the latter objected to Bertone augmenting his own power at the expense of the FIA. Another contributory factor was the Vatileaks affair, in which a secret file drawn up by Benedict was revealed by his butler Gabriele in an effort to unseat Bertone. The file also contained letters written by Archbishop Vigano relating to financial corruption within the Vatican. Tedeschi was placed under investigation by Naples prosecutors concerning allegations of money laundering unearthed by Moneyval, concerning 23 million euros taken from the Vatican account with a Rome bank. The case was dismissed but the IOR Board accused Tedeschi of negligence and relieved him of his post.

In 2012 Tedeschi was replaced by René Bruhlhart. Another outsider like Bertone, he had successfully cleaned up the shady finances of the secretive Principality of Liechtenstein: for instance, he returned the assets sequestered by Saddam Hussein to the new Iraqi government. Keen to have IOR placed on the OECD 'white list' of clean banks, in 2010 he became head of the Egmont national financial intelligence agencies, which monitored significant money flows across the world.

Upon becoming Pope, Francis selected eight cardinals, all but one being outsiders to the Vatican, as well as lay advisers, to undertake reform of the Curia (central administration) which he described as a 'leprosy'. In an effort to place

IOR on a better financial footing to avoid past hiccups, and much to the satisfaction of the reformist Anglo-German clerics, in 2014 Pope Francis set up the Secretariat for the Economy and appointed the Australian Cardinal Pell to administer it. Pell proposed two sweeping changes, much to the discomfiture of diehard Vatican officials. APSA Administration of the Patrimony of the Holy See had hitherto managed papal property and finance, together with the monies granted by Mussolini in compensation for the loss of papal territories after 1870. Henceforth, APSA would be split into a finance ministry for administering the securities holdings; whilst Mussolini's monies would be hived off into IOR.

A new IOR Board was set up with a full-time president, the first being a German banker Ernst von Freyberg; and succeeded by a Frenchman, Jean Baptiste Franssu, who had previously worked for Invesco Europe asset management group. The Board painstakingly sifted through all 33,000 accounts held by 18,000 customers, of which 3,350 were closed and 750 deemed undesirable. On the debit side, Pell blotted his copybook, being accused of excessive spending on business travel and a lavish apartment. 23 accounts were frowned upon by the FIA, of which two went to court and six were shelved. Shortly before the Vatican introduced its new laws on money laundering, two million euros were spirited off into Switzerland.

The second part of Pell's reform concerned the transfer of IOR's investment portfolio to VAM Vatican Asset Management, leaving IOR to concentrate on financing salaries, dioceses, religious institutions and missionaries. Another source of income for the Vatican was its sale of petrol and cigarettes at discounted prices, along with other items, bringing in some 60mE per annum. Jubilee celebrations held every 25 years are ostensibly a religious celebration, but the arrival of millions of pilgrims helps to replenish the Vatican coffers; along with extraordinary jubilees, the last being held in 2015. High fees were charged for sainthoods. A recent innovation for IOR is impact investing, which nicely combines good works with making money, currently involving one billion euros.

Intent on presenting a robust attitude towards illicit finance, Pope Francis appointed Monsignor Ricca to oversee the IOR and keep him closely informed, assisted by a special commission to override the bank's secrecy rules. Yet again the project was grounded, since Ricca not only clashed with Pell but also became embroiled in a fog of homosexual activities based on the presence of a gay group within the Vatican. Francis condemned the gay lobby but seemed sympathetic towards homosexuality.

Hopes of a cleaner IOR were dashed in 2013, when IOR's director P. Cipriani and his deputy M. Tulli resigned following the arrest of a Vatican cleric, Monsignor N. Scarano, a former banker. Accused of money laundering in an earlier case, Scarano was now charged with having bribed a Carabiniere police officer with 400,000 euros in order to smuggle 20mE in cash into Italy from Switzerland; but the financial broker failed to deliver the money into that country. Cipriani and Tulli were also linked to Tedeschi's money laundering affair.

'Suffer the little children to come unto me'

A disturbing element of the Vatican's affairs concerns the widespread incidence of child abuse. The first cases came to light in Ireland during the 1990s, where two million Irish Catholics are served by some 4,500 priests. In 2001 Pope Wojtyla ordered all reasonable allegations to be reported to the Confederation of Doctrine of the Faith CDF, formerly the Holy Inquisition. It emerged that since the 1950s, there had been over 3,000 cases. Since 2004, 848 priests have been defrocked for molestation and rape of both boys and girls; and with lesser punishment meted out to 2,572 clerics, mostly elderly so that they could retain their pension, or transferral to another diocese. Many bishops are loth to report such incidents, there being no judicial duty to inform the secular authorities as per a 1922 decree, or indeed in many other countries. Solely the Pope can investigate allegations against bishops under canonical law, reinforced by the upper echelons of the Vatican who advised bishops not to report cases to the police.

In 2014 Francis set up a commission but it proved ineffective. He initiated the Red Hat enquiry into the private lives of his 224 advisers. He appointed Marie Collins, an early Irish victim, to head it but she later resigned since the CDF refused to reply to victims' letters. A British victim appointed to the CDF was suspended without explanation. The commission recommended the setting up of a tribunal to deal with the bishops not taking action on charges of paedophilia; as well as offer guidelines on how to deal with the offence: they were not taken up. Francis, being too indulgent towards his own, dismissed allegations concerning seven bishops who subsequently resigned.

The Vatican claimed diplomatic immunity on behalf of a Polish archbishop to avoid legal investigation by the Warsaw prosecution. Other culprits were Archbishop Pell; and Cardinal K. O'Brien, Scotland's most senior cleric. The American Cardinal McCarrick from Newark state, a former archbishop of Washington DC and who had supported Benedict's bid for the papacy, was defrocked. A Buenos Aires priest was imprisoned for 15 years. In 2018 an American jury accused 300 priests out of some 1000 cases, whilst 62% of American Catholics objected to Pope Francis' management of the affair. For many Catholics the paedophilia revelations were the last straw: they deserted the Church in droves, especially in the emerging world, disgusted by the Vatican's refusal to protect innocent minors. Whatever happened to the simple lifestyle and teachings of Jesus Christ?

Chapter Twenty-Two

A New Dawn?

The general election in March 2018 resulted in a hung Parliament, with no outright winner. It was conducted on the new two round electoral system for both local and national elections, voted through by Renzi's government, based on 40% FPTP and 60% PR as before, but whereby voters can now switch allegiance on the second round. The result ushered in a new order: the up and coming M5S Five Star Movement which secured 222 seats in the Chamber of Deputies, securing 33% of the vote; and the more seasoned Lega Nord with 263 seats, led by Matteo Salvini, thereby making it the largest party with 36% of the vote. Renzi's centre left PD party took third place, having lost over half of its seats, now reduced to 117, being just 23% of the votes cast. Seats in the Senate were respectively 112, 135 and 57. Renzi had also fared badly in the Euroelections, dropping from his peak in 2014 of 41% to just 19%. As he had vowed, he resigned, to be replaced by Pier Luigi Bersani. Significantly M5S performed poorly in Milan, the financial powerhouse of Italy, where 36% of its businessmen and financiers, highly dubious of the new wave groups, voted for PD, as against under 20% for M5S.

The core of the LN/M5S vote consisted of 18-34-year olds, who resented the old party system. Youth unemployment stands at 30%: graduates suffer from a mix of no work experience combined with a difficult entry into a restricted job market still highly protected by trade unions. One third of youngsters continue to live in the family home since they have no work. Both M5S and LN favour a return to retirement at age 62 to free up the jobs market but which adds to the pressure on the national finances, already critically top heavy with pension payouts. In the South there are a million jobless and so many still migrate north, as after the war, in the hope of better prospects, but which only aggravates the employment problem.

Lega Nord did remarkably well in Salvini's native South, known there simply as the League, in order to attract voters. Roberto Fico, previously an environmental activist and now Speaker in the Deputies, was the lead candidate in Naples. LN secured all the FPTP seats in Sicily, in part because it had promised a flat rate income tax of 20%, to be offset by the sale of state property. LN thus increased its vote there to 17%, taking ground from Berlusconi's FI which now dwindled to 13%. Locals had had enough of *Il Cavaliere's* autocratic wheeling and dealing, rejecting his crooked political cronies in favour of new faces with, hopefully, a straighter approach towards the business of government and public administration. Berlusconi had expected to broker a deal with LN, however, in March 2018 he was summoned for trial on the grounds of having paid witnesses to claim he had not paid for underage sex in the Ruby case. Besides, he was barred from Parliament until 2019 over his conviction for tax fraud, for which he had the effrontery to appeal to the European Court of Human Rights in Strasbourg.

The success of M5S and Lega mirrored new parties elsewhere, for instance in Spain with the populist left-wing *Podemos* We Can, the right-wing *Ciudadanos* Citizens and the Vox party which was strong in Andalucia: all equally weary of the old political set-up. Their popularity suggests a retreat away from the rigours of all-inclusive globalisation towards the calmer environs of national insularity. Such a trend mirrors the demand for autonomy in 27 European regions.

Another vote winner for M5S and LN was their stance on excessive and illegal immigration (currently high in Brescia, east of Milan) mirrored by Marine Le Pen of *Front National* in France and AfD *Alternativ fur Deutschland* in Germany (in 2018 AfD took 16% of the national vote) both of which are aligned with M5S and LN: the latter sit with AfD and UKIP in the European Parliament. Other countries have recently joined in the criticism of the EU's immigration policy: Sweden, Hungary, Poland, Netherlands, Austria and Britain (some 600,000 Italians dwell in the latter). M5S and LN both oppose the EU since the northern countries, especially France and Germany, together with the hardliner J-C Juncker, former President of Luxembourg and a controversial choice as President of the EU Commission, have been reluctant to offer assistance to Italy either on absorbing immigrants or contributing to their costs. Berlin sees immigration as a Mediterranean problem, yet Chancellor Merkel has welcomed a million Syrians.

A major factor in the election campaign was the negative effect of the rigid Euro on the Italian economy, with devaluation no longer possible to make Italian exports more competitive and so improve GDP. Both M5S and LN want to reduce taxes yet increase expenditure, and have muttered about leaving the Euro: Italexit, endorsed by Paolo Savona, an economist and industry minister in the 1990s, and prospective finance minister, who described the Euro as a 'German cage'. Italians resent the restraint on growth imposed by the robust Germanic maxima of 3% and 60% on the budget deficit and national debt, which inhibits the increase of public expenditure to promote employment and improve public services. Yet leaving the Euro would mean dealing with the choppy waters of international finance. President Mattarella, who succeeded the aged Napolitano, opposed Savona's appointment for his stance: he was replaced by Giovanni Tria.

M5S and LN have since toned down their attitude hoping that the EU will cancel some of the national debt (as happened with Greece) which currently stands at around 130% of GDP. With the highest level of borrowing after Greece, Italy is considering the issuance of mini BOTs (short dated Treasury bills) to repay her arrears of 33bn euros owed to government suppliers, and with possibly the first ever issuance of 50-year BTP bonds. In fact, for years Italian citizens have funded much of the government debt through their traditional purchase of BOTs.

Having failed to ally with PD, M5S resolved the two-month hiatus by agreeing to join forces with Lega under the premiership of Giuseppe Conte, a law professor and former judge but with no political experience; and with the blessing of President Mattarella. A Sicilian by birth, Mattarella went into politics following the murder of his brother, who was president of Sicily, by the Mafia. Luigi di Maio, M5S leader, and Matteo Salvini, Lega leader, were appointed joint deputy PMs. Interestingly both Salvini and Di Maio hail from the South, along with Marco Minniti (see below): a welcome break from northern dominance, and perhaps at long last a hint of better times for Southerners.

M5S was founded in 2009 as a protest group by the comedian Beppe Grillo and G. Casalegio, an internet businessman but who has since died. Grillo was barred from standing in the election since he had been convicted of manslaughter in a car accident. The radical playwright, Dario Fo, was a member, but sadly he too died in 2016. M5S view themselves as a movement, with spokespersons rather than traditional party deputies, in an effort to shake off the usual left right contest. Internet based, M5S uses online ballots, reminiscent of Berlusconi's television referenda, to promote direct democracy such as the choice of candidates. M5S wish to reduce the national debt, yet at the same time increase public expenditure for jobs and reduce taxes. M5S was already in the ascendant in 2013, when Grillo took 11% of the vote in his first election from eight million voters, especially amongst the young, and which secured him 47 seats in the Deputies and 19 in the Senate. A number of PD members have drifted towards M5S. On the debit side, Grillo has become increasingly autocratic, like Renzi and Berlusconi. Some things do not change.

M5S is gaining in popularity as a new wave, the second largest group nationally, and now supported by some former PD members. They are pacifist, being friendly towards Russia but cool towards America; whilst comfortable middle-class voters support M5S on environmental matters such as the fight against a rail link through Val di Susa between Turin and France (part has been completed but protests continue) though it is supported by Lega & Prodi. They have muttered about holding a referendum on EU membership, as in Spain. They support honesty in politics and are anti global. M5S wish to reduce the national debt, yet at the same time increase public expenditure for jobs and reduce taxes.

The initial breakthrough for M5S occurred in 2012, with its election of Federico Pizzarotti as mayor of Parma, though he has since left the movement. In 2016, Virginia Raggi, a lawyer by profession, became M5S mayor of Rome, taking 67% of the vote. She cancelled the capital's bid to hold the 2024 Olympics, given the capital's huge debt crisis (and endorsed by Pope Francis). There were also protests in Milan over the cost of the 2015 Expo exhibition, though its revenues helped to revive some run-down areas. Unfortunately, Raggi, somewhat naïve, soon blotted her copybook, coming up against the realities of Roman politics through her embroilment in a corruption scandal. Against the advice of M5S leaders she had chosen as her cabinet deputy one Raffaele Marra, who was well versed in the byzantine art of Roman politics. Appointed director of the Heritage department for the region of Lazio, he became involved in shady deals with one Scarpelloni, a property dealer, who is alleged to have given 368,000 Euros to Marra's wife in order to buy an apartment in Rome. Apparently Marra also took out three insurance policies on Raggi, who claimed to know nothing of the matter. She was placed under investigation concerning irregularities over the falsification of public documents; whilst Marra was arrested on charges of corruption. So much for a clean start.

Raggi's predecessor Ignazio Marino, a Genoese and so an 'outsider' to Romans, had served as PD mayor of Rome for two years. A rare breed of honesty and faction free management in a web of cronyism and corruption, he was well acquainted with the uphill task of improving the historic capital's fabric, with its erratic transport system plagued with bus strikes because of plans to privatise them. The capital, heavily in debt, is bestrewn with neglected parks and mountains of rotting rubbish awaiting collection, as in Naples, having exhausted the supply of disposal sites, partly due to the round-up of mafia groups in cahoots with local officials. Turin, Italy's fourth largest city and now a popular tourist venue, also came under M5S control with the election of Chiara Appendino, company executive and former student at the Bocconi, and replacing P.Fassino PD as mayor of Turin. She has faced much criticism from backing down over nationalising water supplies, a cornerstone of M5S policy.

Lega Nord, now known simply as *Lega* to give the League a national patina, was founded by Umberto Bossi. He became embroiled in a corruption scandal and was replaced by Roberto Maroni, a pal of Berlusconi and later Minister of the Interior and President of Lombardy, and where LN has traditionally been strong. With a population of 30 million, the region is seeking greater autonomy. Since 2013 it has been managed by Matteo Salvini. A former Communist, at the age of 17 he joined LN, and now sits in the Senate as a member for his native Calabria. Akin to M5S, Lega shuns the traditional class division of left and right, describing itself as a movement, and has always resented the transfer of hard-earnt northern funds to '*Roma ladrona*' thieving Rome. Salvini is close to Marine Le Pen over immigration policy.

As ever splinter parties continue to appear, underpinning the inherently individualistic nature of Italian politics, and inhibiting unity. R Fitto, former governor of Puglia, runs a small party *Noi con l'Italia* which enjoys strong support in the South, which is keen to reduce immigration and have a flat rate of income tax. P.Bersani, former PD leader, now runs LEU *Liberi ed Uguali*, with roots in Modena since 1946 and which includes disaffected PD members. Another small group is the neo-Fascist FFI Brothers of Italy based in Rome; also a small pacifist DC rump.

The Veneto is also pressing for greater regional independence, especially in regard to taxation and immigration levels. Both it and Lombardy account for 30% of Italian GDP. With its proud history and vibrant medieval economy, the city of Venice was an independent republic for a thousand years until it joined the Italian state in 1866. The Venetian dialect is considered a language in its own right. Historically, the Veneto region, with a population of some four million souls, is the site of many military conflicts, previously with the Hapsburgs; then during the Great War when a million Italians died, with Italy's bitter defeat at Caporetto vindicated by her decisive victory over the Germans at Vittorio Veneto in 1918. Previously a Catholic/DC stronghold, it has shifted centre left.

The 1970s witnessed the decline of the vast industrial complex at Porto Marghera in the Venetian lagoon, which once provided work for some 18,000 people in steel, chemicals and shipping, but which brought about serious pollution, and with the labour force further shrunk by automation and expansion of the services sector. Fincantieri is still a major employer in Trieste for European shipbuilding. During the 1980s, the Veneto region experienced an economic renaissance, drawing upon centuries of highly skilled craftsmanship. A myriad of SMEs family firms have been involved in contributing strongly to the economy, establishing specialist areas centred on provincial capitals and exporting high quality niche products, especially to discerning Germany. Top firms include Luxottica sunglasses; also Benetton near Treviso, which started up after the war and is now an international exporter of clothing. Treviso also produces furniture, specialist sports and dance shoes. Vicenza, a major industrial area, specializes in textiles, jewellery and fur coats; whilst Verona concentrates on cakes and confectionery.

Harking back to a pre1860s regionalism, in 1980 the Liga Veneta appeared to promote the region's autonomy, supported by LN and a communist-socialist alliance. In 1985 Venetian separatists were arrested. In December 2016, 89% of its population supported a Venexit to remove the unfair burden of national debt, calling to mind the fight for autonomy by Catalonia, Spain's richest region. In October 2017, two referenda were held in Lombardy and Veneto over autonomy. In the former there was a 38% turnout of which 95% voted yes, whilst the latter saw a 57% turnout with 98% in favour. Lombardy used electronic voting tablets which it afterwards donated to local schools.

Immigration: The cost of colonialism?

Immigration has been a thorny problem for many years. Italy's extensive and easily accessible coastline, together with its proximity to Africa, has drawn Italy towards colonisation in the Horn of Africa since the 19th century: Somalia, Eritrea and Ethiopia (formerly Abyssinia). During the 1960s, many Italians worked in the Libyan oilfields, until Gadafy refused them permission to return after their holidays. Libya has been a major supplier of oil and gas to Italy; and later Algeria.

The 1990s witnessed the arrival of 'vu compra' (you buy) Africans, along with refugees from the Bosnian war begging on the Milan metro. In 1990 the first law was passed on controlling immigration. In 2002 Berlusconi lifted visa restrictions on Romania before that country officially joined the EU in 2007. Most Romanians have integrated quite well, of which there are about 100,000, mostly Roma gypsies. However, following an attack in Rome on a female in 2000 by a Roma gypsy, expulsion orders were issued, endorsed by an EU directive.

In 2006 illegal migrants reached the small island of Lampedusa from the Canaries and Africa. Berlusconi brokered a deal with Gadafy, whereby funds would be granted to Libya in return for a more rigorous control of migrants. The Arab Spring, which began in 2010 as a protest against repressive regimes, led to the fall of Gadafy and spread to Tunisia, Egypt and Syria, which brought about a surge in migration. An increasing number of Italians, led by the Lega and M5S, resent the high level of immigration on grounds of security, employment and housing issues. After a century of emigration, Italy has now become a place of immigration.

There are currently some half a million illegal immigrants in Italy, many of which cannot be expelled since their countries of origin refuse to take them back. The Dublin Accord stipulates that the first port of entry receiving migrants must offer them asylum. The EU 1997 Directive ordains that illegal migrants be fingerprinted and registered in the first host country of arrival. Many are not registered and proceed to France, Austria and Switzerland, but by late 2015 these countries had tightened their borders, and so causing a build-up of migrants in Italy, where there are currently some 160,000 registered in reception centres. Hungary has classified aid to migrants as a crime. Sweden, Poland and Slovakia also object to illegal immigration. Describing human trafficking as the new slave trade, Renzi mooted a migration compact to help refugees by increasing aid to Africa through the issue of joint EU bonds. Chancellor Merkel was sceptical over Italy's financial ability to honour the commitment.

In 2014 some 170,000 migrants arrived by sea into Italy, thrice the number in the previous year; and of which 142,000 came from Libya. The second largest group hail from Tunisia. Renzi set up the Triton operation to deal with the immigration crisis, however several northern EU governments refused to offer funds, considering the problem to be the concern of southern countries. In 2015 over 700 drowned in a shipwreck in the Mediterranean; whilst some 1,600 migrants have lost their lives travelling from Libya to Lampedusa, considered one of the worst routes in the world. An EU deal with Turkey has stemmed the flow of migrants into Greece, where 10,000 currently live in camps, and with slow processing. Rejected applicants remain on the islands rather than be returned. In 2017 some 112,000 migrants arrived in Italy, mostly from Libya.

The prime mover over immigration has been Marco Minniti. As Interior Minister, he has overseen the repatriation of some 22,000 Libyans, reducing their migration by some 70%. A Calabrian by birth, he was an admirer of the Communist D'Alema, then later gravitated centre left. Well educated and technically competent, he was in charge of the Intelligence services for two decades, during which time he travelled extensively in Libya, where he developed a deep knowledge of the rival tribal militias who run the human smuggling networks. His understanding of such affairs is perhaps facilitated by his upbringing and knowledge of Byzantine politics in Calabria.

In 2017 Minniti brokered a deal between Italy and the tribal warlords in the remote south of Libya, to prevent migrants passing from Niger across the Sahara to the Mediterranean coast. Moreover, he arranged an agreement in Tripoli with 14 Libyan mayors in an effort to stop human trafficking. A United Nations agency is now working in Libya, whilst Italy has begun to train Libyan coastguards in the interception and return of migrants, and so with fewer losses at sea. As a result of these measures the rate of immigration has dropped significantly, and with the repatriation of 1,200 Libyans.

Salvini of the Lega has taken a robust stance. In August 2018 he closed Italian ports, refusing to allow 177 refugees off an Italian rescue ship, unless the EU guaranteed to place them in other EU countries. Maroni has decreed that migrants must leave if they have no work after three months. In 2018, 14,000 souls arrived by sea, far less than the previous year, in part thanks to Renzi and the UN recognising the revolutionary government in Tripoli, which has supported the search and rescue operations.

Manovra: The Budget

In October 2018, Giovanni Tria, the seventy-year-old Finance Minister, presented his *Manovra* Budget to Parliament. He replaced P.Savona who